*University of London Historical Studies*

XXXI

HENRY LABOUCHERE
AND THE EMPIRE
1880–1905

This volume is published with the help of
a grant from the late Miss Isobel Thornley's
Bequest to the University of London

# HENRY LABOUCHERE AND THE EMPIRE 1880-1905

by
R. J. HIND

UNIVERSITY OF LONDON
THE ATHLONE PRESS
1972

*Published by*
THE ATHLONE PRESS
UNIVERSITY OF LONDON
*at 2 Gower Street London* WC1
*Distributed by Tiptree Book Services Ltd*
*Tiptree, Essex*
U.S.A.
*Oxford University Press Inc*
*New York*

© *R. J. Hind* 1972

ISBN 0 485 13131 5

*Printed in Great Britain by*
WESTERN PRINTING SERVICES LTD
*Bristol*

# ACKNOWLEDGEMENTS

I am deeply indebted to Professor W. H. G. Armytage, Professor J. O. Baylen, Mr H. E. Bell, Miss M. V. Bryce, Lord Buckton, Sir W. L. S. Churchill and the Hon. R. F. E. S. Churchill, the earl of Derby and Mr H. E. Jones, the duke of Devonshire and Mr T. S. Wragg, Sir C. A. Gladstone, Bt, and Sir E. W. Gladstone, Bt, Viscount Harcourt, Dr K. W. Humphreys on behalf of the Trustees of the J. Chamberlain Papers, Lord Primrose and Mr A. S. Bell, Princess Francesca Ruspoli, the marquess of Salisbury and Dr J. F. A. Mason, and Earl Spencer for access to, or for information about, or for permission to use the papers listed in the bibliography. In this respect, as well as for other courtesies, I have also to thank the staffs of the Bodleian Library, the British Library of Political and Economic Science, the British Museum, the India Office Library, the Library of Christ Church College, Oxford, the Library of New College, Oxford, the Library of Rhodes House, Oxford, the National Library of Ireland and the Council of Trustees, the National Library of Scotland, Newcastle upon Tyne Central Library, the Public Record Office, Trinity College Library, Cambridge, the University Library, Birmingham, the University Library, Cambridge, and the University of London Library. The South African Public Library, Cape Town, kindly supplied copies of H. Labouchere's letters to J. F. X. Merriman and permission to use them.

My grateful thanks are also due to Miss W. D. Coates and Mr Baillie of the National Register of Archives and to officials of the following libraries and archives: Archives of the Cabinet Office; Central Library, Manchester; Central Public Library, Northampton; Chetham's Library, Manchester; City of Liverpool Public Libraries; Companics Registration Office; Cornwall Record Office; Department of the Taoiseach, Dublin; Estate Office, Elvaston Castle, Derby; Gladstone Library, National Liberal Club; Guildhall Library; Joint Archives Committee,

The Castle, Carlisle; the *Daily Telegraph* Library; Library of the Durham Colleges in the University of Durham; Library of the House of Commons; Library, University College, Cork; National Library of Wales; Northamptonshire Record Office; Northumberland Record Office; Public Library, Carlisle; Public Libraries, Rochdale; Public Libraries, Sunderland; Public Record Office of Northern Ireland; Reference Library, Central Library, Leeds; John Rylands Library, Manchester; Scottish Record Office; University Library, Manchester; University Library, Sheffield; Dr William's Library, London; City Library, Durban; Government Archives, Pretoria; Cape, Free State and Transvaal Archives; Public Library, Johannesburg; South African Public Library, Cape Town; Archives of the Public Library of South Australia; Fisher Library, University of Sydney; Mitchell Library, Sydney; Parliamentary Library, Brisbane; State Library of Victoria.

I wish to express my appreciation to Sir G. P. Labouchere, K.C.M.G., Colonel P. H. Labouchere, O.B.E., Count Michael de la Bedoyère, Messrs Lewis & Lewis, members of the Thorold family and particularly the Reverend H. Thorold, for assistance in my unsuccessful search for the papers of H. Labouchere.

Constable & Co. Ltd, the General Council of the Press, Staples Press, the Council of Foreign Bondholders, the Financial Information Co. Ltd, the Offices of the Council, the Stock Exchange, London, the *Financial Times*, the *Observer*, and Williams, Deacon's Bank Ltd, kindly supplied relevant information.

Amongst others whom I must thank individually are Professor P. Aranguren, Dr J. E. Butler, Professor M. R. D. Foot, Mr V. A. Hatley, Professor M. Jacorossi, Mr A. A. H. Knightbridge, Professor C. Cruise O'Brien, R. T. Paget, Q.C., M.P., Mr H. Pearson, Mr G. E. Scott and Mrs E. Servadio-Cortesi.

The generosity of the Central Research Fund, University of London, and the Institute of Education, University of Newcastle upon Tyne, made it possible for me to submit the latter portions of this study in 1966 to the University of London in fulfilment of the requirements for a Ph.D. degree. It has been substantially improved as a result of positive and constructive criticism from Professor I. R. Christie, Dr I. M. Cumpston, Mr

C. H. D. Howard and Professor P. N. S. Mansergh. To Dr Cumpston my debt is so great that it can be acknowledged rather than expressed adequately. A research grant from the University of Sydney facilitated the preparation of the final typescript. The staff of the Athlone Press gave me indispensable guidance and assistance.     R.J.H.

## CONTENTS

| | |
|---|---|
| Abbreviations | ix |
| I. Henry Labouchere and Aspects of his Social and Political Environment | 1 |
| II. Attitudes towards the Empire: The Great Debate | 39 |
| III. Irish Issues, 1880–1884 | 52 |

Introduction, 52; Home Rule, 58; Coercion, 65; Land, 80; Other Issues, 86

| | |
|---|---|
| IV. Irish Issues, 1885 and 1886 | 96 |
| V. Egypt, 1880–1886 | 144 |
| VI. South Africa, 1880–1886 | 182 |
| VII. India and Cyprus, 1880–1886 | 196 |

India, 196; Cyprus, 210

| | |
|---|---|
| VIII. Closer Union of the Empire, 1880–1886 | 213 |
| IX. Conclusion | 228 |
| Select Bibliography | 253 |
| Index | 265 |

## ABBREVIATIONS

|  | The papers of |
|---|---|
| B.P. | A. J. Balfour |
| Bt.P. | John Bright |
| C.B.P. | Sir H. Campbell-Bannerman |
| C.D.P. | Sir C. W. Dilke |
| Cs.P. | Sir R. A. Cross |
| Cy.P. | L. and K. Courtney |
| De.P. | eighth duke of Devonshire |
| Dy.P. | fifteenth earl of Derby |
| G.P. | W. E. Gladstone |
| Ge.P. | second Earl Granville |
| H.G.P. | H. J. Gladstone |
| H.P. | Sir E. W. Hamilton |
| Hn.P. | T. Harrington |
| I.P. | Sir Stafford H. Northcote |
| J.B.P. | J. Bryce |
| J.C. | J. Chamberlain |
| M.G.P. | M. Gladstone (Mrs H. Drew) |
| M.P. | A. Milner |
| R.C.P. | Lord Randolph Churchill |
| R.P. | first marquess of Ripon |
| S.P. | fifth Earl Spencer |
| Sd.P. | W. T. Stead |
| Sm.P. | Sir G. S. Clarke |
| Sy.P. | third marquess of Salisbury |
| S.S.P. | S. Storey |
| W.V.H.P. | Sir W. V. Harcourt |

References to the papers of Sir C. W. Dilke and Sir E. W. Hamilton, which do not specify correspondents, relate to their journals.

## ABBREVIATIONS

| | |
|---|---|
| B.M. Add. MSS. | Additional Manuscripts in the British Museum |
| C.H.B.E. | *Cambridge History of the British Empire* |
| C.R.O. | Companies Registration Office, London |
| Hansard | Hansard's *Parliamentary Debates* |
| N.L.I. | National Library of Ireland |
| N.L.S. | National Library of Scotland |
| P.R.O. | Public Record Office, London |
| T.C.L. | Trinity College Library, Cambridge |
| T.R.H.S. | *Transactions of the Royal Historical Society* |

CHAPTER I

# Henry Labouchere and Aspects of his Social and Political Environment

HENRY DU PRÉ LABOUCHERE was born in London in 1831 and received his education at Eton and Trinity College, Cambridge. His grandfather, Pierre César Labouchère, became a partner in the financial house of Hope of Amsterdam, married into the Baring family, and laid the foundations of the family fortune. His uncle, Henry Labouchere, was Sir F. Baring's cousin and brother-in-law: he was accepted as a whig, had a distinguished political career, and became Lord Taunton. His father, John Labouchere, 'almost a professional Puritan',[1] was a pillar of Exeter Hall. One of his sisters married the bishop of Rochester, perhaps the primmest member of the Anglican episcopate.

Labouchere rebelled against many aspects of this environment. He was an agnostic, a heavy gambler, and he spent much of his time in Bohemian company. He had a difference of opinion with his examiners at Cambridge and left the university without a degree. His personal code of morality was not puritanical. In 1861 W. S. Blunt found him 'entirely in the society of whores and croupiers',[2] and, according to T. H. S. Escott, Labouchere was the original of George Eliot's Grandcourt in *Daniel Deronda*.[3]

For a decade after 1854 Labouchere was a member of the diplomatic service and served in Washington, Munich, Stockholm, Frankfurt, St Petersburg, Dresden and Constantinople. He settled in England in 1864, the year after his father's death, and quickly entered politics. He represented Windsor in the

[1] T. P. O'Connor, *Memoirs of an Old Parliamentarian*, ii, 75.
[2] W. S. Blunt, *My Diaries* (1932), 17 Jan. 1912, p. 791.
[3] T. H. S. Escott, *Personal Forces of the Period*, p. 189.

house of commons from July 1865 until April 1866 when he was unseated on petition for various acts of bribery committed by his agents although it was not proved that he consented to, or approved of, such acts. He then represented Middlesex between April 1867 and December 1868. During this phase of his career Labouchere impressed J. S. Mill.[4] He also secured a parliamentary victory of considerable importance for, as a result of his successful motion of 26 May 1868,[5] the government itemized estimates for the diplomatic and consular services separately, and thus gave members the opportunity to cross-examine spokesmen of the foreign office. Labouchere failed to secure re-election for Middlesex and was unable to secure nomination for another constituency until 1880, when his twenty-five-year association with Northampton began.

While Labouchere was in the parliamentary wilderness he was active in the theatre, on the stock exchange where he established his reputation as a financial authority, and in journalism. He joined a syndicate which purchased the *Daily News* in 1868, and bought one-quarter of the shares for £14,000. The proprietors, of whom A. Morley, H. Oppenheim and Labouchere were the most important, reduced the price of the newspaper to one penny. It became profitable during the Franco-Prussian war when its daily circulation trebled.[6] During this war, Labouchere remained in Paris throughout the siege, and the articles he sent to the *Daily News* played a considerable part in the transformation of its fortunes. The correspondence of P. Rylands indicates that Labouchere anonymously used the *Daily News* for his own political purposes in the 1870s,[7] but no evidence of this nature has come to light for a later period. In connection with the *Daily News* there is an example of the difficulty Labouchere presents the student. In a letter to Sir H. Campbell-Bannerman in 1901, Labouchere alleged that he sold his shares in the *Daily News* when it 'drifted into Imperialism'.[8]

---

[4] B. and P. Russell (eds.), *The Amberley Papers*, i, 476–7.
[5] Hansard, 3rd ser., 192, 927–39, 26 May 1868.
[6] H. R. F. Bourne, *English Newspapers*, ii, 283.
[7] L. G. Rylands, *The Correspondence and Speeches of Peter Rylands, M.P.*, pp. 142, 189, 191, 193.
[8] C.B.P., B.M. Add. MSS., 41222, fo. 70, Labouchere to Campbell-Bannerman. 5 Nov. 1901.

According to Sir J. R. Robinson, the manager of the newspaper, Labouchere sold his interest shortly after the formation of Gladstone's fourth administration in 1892. Labouchere, contrary to his expectations, was not included in this administration. He wished to attack Gladstone through the *Daily News* but the other proprietors were not amenable, so he sold his shares between July 1892 and July 1893.[9]

On 4 January 1877 the first issue of *Truth* appeared. Labouchere owned and edited this weekly society journal, which was an immediate financial success. In 1885 its annual profits were reputed to be £14,000.[10] Circulation figures for *Truth* do not appear to be available, but in the 1880s they may be estimated as 30,000 per week. The rate for advertisements was fifty per cent more for *Truth* than for any comparable journal[11] and the weekly circulation of the *World*, its nearest equivalent, was 20,000. Contributions to *Truth* were anonymous, but internal and external evidence indicates that Labouchere wrote its political comments and several of its financial articles. J. H. McCarthy affirmed that *Truth* was 'read wherever the English language is spoken', and that it provided a 'chivalrous defence of the oppressed, the unpopular, the unjustly judged'.[12] Lord Carnarvon described it as a 'vile paper'.[13]

Labouchere's election as the 'Christian' member for Northampton forged the link between his political and journalistic activities. In 1881 he described himself as a 'Journalist and Member of Parliament'.[14] He was the 'most pugnacious of publicists'[15] in both spheres, and thus broke openly the Victorian convention whereby the journalist commented upon the actions of the politician and neither trespassed upon the fields of the other.[16] Gladstone, in 1892, criticized Labouchere for 'fighting first in the open and then behind the curtain of the Press',[17]

---

[9] Sir J. R. Robinson, *Fifty Years of Fleet Street*, p. 377; C.R.O., 338 N, *Daily News*.
[10] *Northampton Mercury*, 18 July 1885.
[11] R. Mosse, *General Newspaper Catalogue and Advertisers' Guide, 1882/3*, pp. 34, 65.
[12] J. H. McCarthy, *England under Gladstone, 1880–1884*, p. 42.
[13] Sy.P., Carnarvon to Salisbury, 28 Nov. 1882.
[14] C.R.O., 1275 N, *Truth*.
[15] G. R. Isaacs, *Rufus Isaacs, First Marquess of Reading*, p. 94.
[16] J. A. Spender, *The Public Life*, ii, 116.
[17] F. E. Hamer (ed.), *The Personal Papers of Lord Rendel*, pp. 99–100.

and considered that he outwitted himself 'in handling his own case through *Truth*'.[18]

Labouchere's connection with *Truth* probably gave him a privileged position in parliament. He was essentially an aggressive attacking politician who often left his defensive position vulnerable. In 1886 Lord R. Churchill arranged for Sir M. Hicks Beach 'to follow Labouchere who would be sure to make a fool of himself & give a good opening for an effective reply'.[19] Often, however, opportunities of this nature were neglected. As Sir R. Temple noted, few politicians were prepared to enter the lists with Labouchere because they did 'not care to be branded and vilified in a Society paper'.[20]

Labouchere used *Truth* for a variety of purposes. It was a self-erected pulpit from which he attempted to influence opinion about political developments. It gave him scope to oblige his political associates, and, by request, he would 'puff' a book by Healy,[21] or 'look after' Churchill's father-in-law.[22] It was a medium through which he wrote favourably or unfavourably about shares: and if he were criticized for doing this because he had a personal interest, he blandly retorted, 'what greater proof can I give of my belief in the shares I write up than buying them? Or ... of my disbelief in a share than my selling it?'[23] The facility with which Labouchere could make his views known may have made him inclined to talk down to an imaginary audience. It may also account for the fact that he rarely joined associations, such as the Indian Reform Association or the British Home Rule Association, which hoped to mould public opinion.

When Labouchere re-entered parliament in 1880 he was one of the 347 liberals who provided Gladstone's second administration with an absolute majority of 42 in the Commons. The party, however, was disunited. Radicals had seized the initiative in the country and in the party, but Gladstone thrust aside the radical ladder by which he had climbed and secured for the whigs pre-

---

[18] G.P., B.M. Add. MSS., 44332, fo. 234, Gladstone to Marjoribanks, 8 Sept. 1892.
[19] Sy.P., Churchill to Salisbury, 22 Aug. 1886.
[20] Sir R. Temple, *Letters and Character Sketches from the House of Commons*, p. 27.
[21] H.G.P., B.M. Add. MSS., 46016, fo. 105, Healy to Labouchere, 22 July 1886.
[22] R.C.P., 1158, Labouchere to Churchill, undated [?Dec. 1885].
[23] P. H. Emden, *Randlords*, p. 166.

dominance in the cabinet. A struggle, in which Labouchere was a vigorous combatant, raged between the radicals and whigs. He argued that whigs' sympathies lay with the conservatives whom they ought to join, that they emasculated liberal legislation, and that they were traitors within the liberal camp.[24] In May 1883 W. Rathbone indicated in a letter to Gladstone the effects of internal strife and lack of positive leadership upon the party as discontent and increasing incoherence and ineffectiveness.[25] By 1883 Harcourt feared that liberals would be remembered as 'the grossest blunderers who ever mismanaged & destroyed great opportunities'.[26] Gladstone failed to educate and guide his supporters, and this failure was particularly disastrous in the cabinet where his inability to resolve divisions resulted in procrastination, 'Disunion adjourned',[27] and compromise. In September 1885, Hartington abhorred 'the prospect of returning . . . to office, especially . . . with colleagues among whom so much difference of opinion will exist on almost every conceivable subject'.[28] Gladstone was master of the country but he could not control the Commons.[29] 'Men, not measures' caused him great difficulty but, apart from his ineptitude in dealing with politicians, he had begun to practise popular politics since 1876. The process had begun whereby the electorate came to matter more to him than the parliamentary party or cabinet unity. Parallel with his neglect of cabinet meetings during parliamentary recesses to formulate policy and prepare legislation was his tendency to appeal directly to public opinion. Thus in speeches at Leeds and the Guildhall in October 1881 he outlined proposals to devolve some authority upon new local institutions to be set up in Ireland before he had attempted to persuade his colleagues in the cabinet to accept such a policy.

Many characteristics of Gladstone's leadership and of internal strife within the liberal party became more pronounced after 1885. Between 1886 and 1892 the party was in opposition and

[24] *Fortnightly Review*, xxxiii (1 March 1883), 373; *Daily News*, 14 Dec. 1883.
[25] A. Ramm (ed.), *The political correspondence of Mr Gladstone and Lord Granville, 1876–1886*, vol. i, p. xxxi.
[26] Ge.P., P.R.O., 30/29/29, Harcourt to Granville, 16 Oct. 1883.
[27] C.D.P., B.M. Add. MSS., 43926, fo. 27, 5 Aug. 1884.
[28] De.P., 340.1805, Hartington to Gladstone, 10 Sept. 1885.
[29] B.P., B.M. Add. MSS., 49688, fo. 37, Salisbury to A. Balfour, 15 Jan. 1881.

acted in close association with the Irish parliamentary party until November 1890 and then with the anti-Parnellites. During this period the National Liberal Federation approved a comprehensive programme for the party at Newcastle in October 1891: it included home rule, disestablishment in Wales and Scotland, employers' liability, extension of small holdings, district and parish councils, triennial parliaments and abolition of entail. Gladstone appeared to adopt the programme and thus conveyed the impression that the party was committed to it. The programme failed to act as a centripetal force. Many liberal politicians resented the attempt by the caucus to impose policy upon them; individual items in it alienated liberals who might otherwise have remained loyal; and it did not represent a dominant policy or a constructive approach to social or economic problems that might have secured the party additional support to counteract defections. These defections had increased when the party adopted home rule. Gladstone's dominant political interest in the latter part of his career was the home rule issue but immediate causes of his resignation in March 1894 included opposition to an increase in naval estimates and his inability to enlist support in the cabinet for an attack upon the upper chamber which had rejected home rule and mutilated fatally measures dealing with employers' liability and local government.[30]

No generally acceptable successor to Gladstone emerged before or for some years after his final retirement. Lord Rosebery succeeded him as prime minister and leader of the party but he depended upon Harcourt in the Commons. Their relationship was not harmonious initially and it deteriorated steadily. Even at its inception Rosebery's government was deeply divided internally and it lost the will to exist in June 1895. Its Irish, Welsh, Scottish and radical supporters tended to put sectional interests before those of the party and its opponents could destroy or modify any non-financial measure in the Lords. The achievements of the liberal government were considerable: they included Harcourt's budget, the Local Government act of 1894, and important administrative reforms which brought the eight-hour day to many employees of the state, enforced free education more extensively and reformed the

[30] P. Stansky, *Ambitions and Strategies*, pp. 38–9, 78–9.

administration of the Poor Law. Nevertheless, the party was in disarray. During the general election of 1895 unionists attacked liberals' commitment to home rule. A movement of $4\frac{1}{2}$ per cent among the electorate transformed a unionist parliamentary minority of 43 seats into a majority of 152. Even this defeat, the greatest suffered by either party since 1832, failed to induce leading liberals to seek alternative political arrangements to provide united leadership and more constructive and relevant policies. Rosebery remained leader of the party until 6 October 1896. Harcourt unofficially acted in this capacity until December 1898, and on 6 February 1899 Campbell-Bannerman accepted the leadership of a party still deeply divided on external policy and issues such as home rule, disestablishment, temperance, old age pensions and the eight-hours issue. Liberals lost the general election of 1900 almost as conclusively as that of 1895.

The liberal party's heterogeneous character and its relationships with Irish nationalists after 1886 provided opportunities for Labouchere to become more prominent in politics. One section of the party that was anxious for a strong liberal government 'radical in Home Affairs'[31] became discernible after 1887. It had support from younger politicians such as Asquith, Sir E. Grey, Haldane and Buxton, and it was influenced and often led by Rosebery. Its supporters, who were suspicious of home rule and inclined to favour forward imperial policies, came to be known as liberal imperialists. Labouchere led another group which was the most industrious and outspoken of the party in the late 1880s. It gave positive support to home rule, concentrated primarily upon political objectives and between 1889 and mid-1891 was 'equipped with "whips" and other emblems of a distinct organization'.[32] Its activities in May 1889 indicate aspects of its domestic programme: it attempted to secure leasehold enfranchisement, to abolish university representation and the hereditary principle in connection with parliamentary representation, and to disestablish the Welsh Church.[33]

Such actions were the application of a policy Labouchere

[31] G. M. Trevelyan, *Grey of Fallodon*, p. 34.
[32] *Annual Register*, 1889, p. 79.
[33] Hansard, 3rd ser., 335, 889–959, 1 May 1889; 335, 1760–1808, 10 May 1889; 336, 70–120, 14 May 1889; 336, 430–84, 17 May 1889.

commended to Herbert Gladstone when liberals lost the general election of 1886. Labouchere was convinced that Chamberlain would 'never aid in turning out'[34] the conservatives while Gladstone remained in public life. He acted upon this assumption by attacking Chamberlain personally and attempting to embarrass him politically by demonstrating that radical fervour was more militant in the liberal party than among unionists. Labouchere doubted whether liberals would secure a majority on home rule alone and argued that while there should be no equivocation on this issue the party should abandon land purchase schemes, produce a 'good all round radical programme', be 'very militant' and organize. This would give liberals a good chance of victory provided that the Irish 'be kept straight, and that the country should not come to the conclusion that the Tories are working smoothly in office'.[35] To secure the former objective Labouchere kept himself informed of developments within the Irish parliamentary party and helped co-ordinate activity between its members and radicals. Thus he adopted some of T. P. O'Connor's suggestions about land purchase when he spoke in parliament on 23 August 1886.[36] Labouchere raised the question of a speech made by Churchill at Belfast in February 1886 allegedly at Parnell's request for the Irish leader considered it 'better for an English than an Irish member' to raise the issue.[37] Apparently Labouchere was so successful in keeping the Irish straight that he was credited with having them 'at his back' by 1890.[38]

O'Shea's divorce on 17 November 1890, subsequent actions of liberal leaders and Parnell, and struggles amongst Irish parliamentarians[39] put at hazard the fruits of Labouchere's

[34] H.G.P., B.M. Add. MSS., 46016, fo. 117, Labouchere to H. Gladstone, 21 Aug. [1886].
[35] H.G.P., B.M. Add. MSS., 46016, fo. 111, Labouchere to H. Gladstone, 31 July [1886].
[36] H.G.P., B.M. Add. MSS., 46016, fos. 121-2, T. P. O'Connor to Labouchere, 21 Aug. 1886; Hansard, 3rd ser., 308, 287-90, 23 Aug. 1886.
[37] W.V.H.P., Labouchere to Harcourt, 3 Sept. 1886; Hansard, 3rd ser., 308, 1228-33, 3 Sept. 1886.
[38] C.B.P., B.M. Add. MSS., 41233, fo. 82, W. M. Ewan to Campbell-Bannerman, 31 Aug. 1892.
[39] C. Cruise O'Brien, *Parnell and his Party, 1880-1890*, pp. 279-313; F. S. L. Lyons, *The Fall of Parnell, 1890-1891*; F. S. L. Lyons, *The Irish Parliamentary Party, 1890-1910*; J. L. Hammond, *Gladstone and the Irish Nation*, pp. 602ff.; M. Davitt, *The Fall of Feudalism in Ireland*, pp. 638ff.

## SOCIAL AND POLITICAL ENVIRONMENT

efforts to concert the actions of radicals and Irish nationalists. By 1892 he was reputed to have lost caste with both groups of Irish nationalists and to be 'regarded with considerable resentment'[40] by them. Labouchere's correspondence with Herbert Gladstone and Harcourt is tantalizingly ambiguous about the part he played during the crisis which became more acute as Parnell's intention to ignore the political consequences of his domestic arrangements by remaining leader of the Irish party became more apparent. Labouchere told Harcourt, whose influence upon Gladstone during this period was calamitous, of McCarthy's views of the situation on 23 November 1890. McCarthy considered that Gladstone should write to Parnell and that the Irish leader should be informed immediately that he would probably receive such a letter. McCarthy could not find Parnell, and Labouchere, allegedly at his suggestion, tried to deliver the warning. He too failed to contact Parnell or his secretary, Campbell, despite visits to the International Club and the National Liberal Club but he left a letter for Molloy to forward.[41] Labouchere wrote again on 25 November 1890, the day when Morley failed to read to Parnell Gladstone's private warning before the meeting of the Irish party which, in ignorance of Gladstone's opinion that Parnell's 'continuance at the present moment in the leadership would be productive of consequences disastrous in the highest degree to the cause of Ireland',[42] re-elected him, and when Gladstone, Harcourt and Morley precipitately decided to publish the letter. Labouchere told Harcourt that 'All that was possible has been done to get up an Irish rebellion' and that Sexton and McCarthy had seen Parnell who had refused either to resign or to call another meeting of the party. Twenty-eight members had requested the party's secretary to summon a meeting on 26 November and Barry had promised to rush a resolution. In Labouchere's opinion this could not be guaranteed as the Irish were 'horrid cowards' and he suggested that if this plan failed 'we must try to get the Irish Bishops to lead a revolt in Ireland'.[43] Labouchere

---

[40] C.B.P., B.M. Add. MSS., 41233, fo. 82, W. M. Ewan to Campbell-Bannerman, 31 Aug. 1892.
[41] W.V.H.P., Labouchere to Harcourt, 23 Nov. [?1890].
[42] J. L. Hammond, p. 647.
[43] W.V.H.P., Labouchere to Harcourt (copy), 25 Nov. 1890.

wrote to Herbert Gladstone on 17 December 1890, eleven days after the division of the Irish party into forty-five anti-Parnellites and twenty-six Parnellites. He referred to a letter which the author has not been able to trace: 'That little matter about which I wrote to you is I think satisfactorily arranged. Meetings will be held all over Ireland.' He also sent information about Irish party funds. He stated that anti-Parnellites hoped to receive money from America when the problem of the leadership was resolved but that meanwhile they would appreciate 'a good [? subscription] here' for evicted tenants. According to Labouchere, Archbishop Walsh had concluded that his attempts to keep the *Freeman* neutral through his influence over Mrs Gray were inadequate and so he approved publication of another newspaper to put forward the views of the anti-Parnellites. This letter also contained the anti-Parnellites' opinion that they would crush Parnell in three months, their remarkably accurate estimate of the majority their candidate, Sir J. Pope Hennessy, would secure at the Kilkenny by-election, and the allegation that conservatives paid for Parnell's election in 1880 through Healy.[44] Political developments in the latter part of 1890 modified Labouchere's attitude towards home rule, for in December 1890 he suggested to Harcourt that the next liberal government should give electoral reform precedence over home rule.[45]

Labouchere's attempts to secure for liberals effective support from the Irish members continued although he thought they were acting like emancipated helots. He considered Dillon's vanity prodigious, O'Brien 'one of the most self-seeking of scoundrels', and the only 'reliable' men Barry, Sexton, Lane and Healy 'who with all his faults can be absolutely trusted to keep his word'. Labouchere was cognizant of assistance to thirty-four anti-Parnellites who were unable to support themselves financially before April 1891, and were unable to meet outstanding debts of £700 incurred during the election of Sir J. Pope Hennessy. 'These funds were procured without its being possible to say that they came from the Liberal Party and given to Barry the Treasurer.' Labouchere 'never came across a lot of

---

[44] H.G.P., B.M. Add. MSS., 46016, fos. 146–7, Labouchere to H. Gladstone, 17 Dec. [1890].
[45] W.V.H.P., Labouchere to Harcourt, 31 Dec. 1890.

men for whom I have a greater contempt. If they were only corrupt it would be more easy to deal with them, but amongst the leaders there is a perpetual struggle between their corruption & their vanity, and they are often ready to sacrifice the former to the latter.'[46] However, he considered sentiment and chivalry out of place in politics and 'with the greatest difficulty'[47] initiated negotiations between the Parnellites and anti-Parnellites in May 1892 on the eve of the general election. Discussions that followed were fruitless but were the closest the party came to reunion before 1898. At the polls Irish electors of 1892 gave a verdict in favour of the anti-Parnellites and of 'the liberal alliance, and against the policy of independent opposition so consistently advocated by the Parnellites'.[48] One of Labouchere's objectives, a parliamentary majority that would allow Gladstone to proceed with home rule, was partially attained by the election of seventy-one anti-Parnellites.

After his exclusion from the liberal government of 1892 to 1895 Labouchere was a 'leper, whom the Queen would always have sitting at the gate ... scratching his sores'[49] and his political significance declined. In parliament he was described by Bartley as the leader of the 'Discontented Brigade' 'said to number 40'.[50] Nevertheless, he persisted in his attempts to produce greater cohesion among Irish representatives and to link them with radicals. Within a month of Rosebery's speech of 12 March 1894 that was interpreted as adjourning home rule *sine die* and which brought into greater question the value to the Irish of the liberal alliance, Labouchere carried suggestions from Healy to Redmond. According to Redmond's memorandum, dated 9 April 1894, Healy admitted that he was beaten and invited Redmond to lead a reunited party in order to forestall Dillon.[51] Redmond dismissed the proposals as 'impossible' and divisions within the Irish party persisted. Labouchere

---

[46] W.V.H.P., Labouchere to Harcourt, 2 Jan. 1891; 6 Nov. 1891.
[47] F. S. L. Lyons, *The Irish Parliamentary Party, 1890–1910*, pp. 35–6; N.L.I., MS. 8577(1), J. J. Clancy to J. E. Redmond, 24 May 1892.
[48] F. S. L. Lyons, *The Irish Parliamentary Party*, p. 37.
[49] W.V.H.P., Labouchere to Harcourt (copy), 23 Nov. 1892; cf. E. Longford, *Victoria, R.I.*, pp. 519–20.
[50] Hansard, 4th ser., 8, 455, 3 Feb. 1893.
[51] N.L.I., J. E. Redmond Papers, 9 April 1894.

also knew of other ways in which some of the Irish representatives could be influenced. In July 1892 he suggested to Harcourt that a liberal administration should introduce payment for members of parliament: £200 per annum 'will go far to quiet the Irish' and 'indispose them to risk... another General Election'.[52] When the government neglected his advice, he introduced a bill to secure payment of members on 23 February 1893.[53] In January 1895 he confided in Dilke: £10,000 would enable Healy to submit candidates to the local conventions who would have their expenses paid and would agree to act with radicals.[54] The day after the liberal government's defeat Labouchere informed Campbell-Bannerman that the 'Parnellites are quite ready to be here on permanence, it is a mere question of money, and just as we paid last year the "Antis" to be here, the Parnellites will be paid to be here after the Cork election'.[55]

From his correspondence it is impossible to ascertain whether Labouchere was personally involved in these alleged financial transactions between liberals and Irish nationalists. He was however in the confidence of some leading Irish politicians and admirably placed to act as paymaster if in fact such payments were made. Whatever his position in this respect he maintained close contacts with some Irish representatives. As early as January 1891, he offered one of *'our* Irish' to speak in the constituency of S. Storey, a fellow radical.[56] The papers of J. E. Redmond and Campbell-Bannerman indicate that between 1899 and 1905 Labouchere intermittently helped establish a common policy for liberals and Irish nationalists on issues such as Campbell-Bannerman's criticism of the government's policy in South Africa, and the possibility of the Irish moving a home rule amendment in 1902. He also helped concert tactics but found the liberal party's organization inept.

---

[52] W.V.H.P., Labouchere to Harcourt, 14 July 1892.

[53] Hansard, 4th ser., 9, 156, 23 Feb. 1893.

[54] C.D.P., B.M. Add. MSS., 43892, fo. 198, Labouchere to Dilke, 25 Jan. [1895]. This proposal, from which nothing apparently materialized, was presumably for a private transaction between Healy and a group of English radicals.

[55] C.B.P., B.M. Add. MSS., 41222, fo. 6, Labouchere to Campbell-Bannerman, 22 June [1895].

[56] S.S.P., Labouchere to Storey, 6 Jan. 1891.

'Redmond tells me that if he has 36 hours' notice he will have all his Irish ready to come into the House at a given hour for a snap vote. But our whips—including H. Gladstone—are utterly worthless for this sort of warfare.'[57]

Before the defeat of Gladstone's second home rule bill in 1893 Labouchere recognized that home rule alone was not a practical proposition. He considered that it should be a portion of liberalism and associated with radical domestic reforms. In the years after 1893 he helped to keep liberals committed to the home rule cause, but, as in his electoral manifesto of 1895, he argued more strongly that 'Home Rule should be granted, not only to Ireland, but to all the component parts of the United Kingdom'.[58] At the end of his political career, the intransigence of the house of lords induced him to revert to proposals he advanced in 1881: concede to the Irish 'rights of self-government in their own affairs'; once they obtained a Council radicals 'would leave them to get the rest'.[59]

Labouchere's antipathy to the Lords was as constant as his advocacy of substantial devolution of authority. In 1884 he argued that its members acted as Janissaries of the conservative party and that radicals should abolish the house of lords.[60] In parliament he attacked its hereditary character in 1883, 1885, 1888 and 1889, and gained increasing support. In 1896 he and Dilke directed the campaign of some twenty members against 'the irresponsible and privileged members of the non-elective branch of the legislature'. Their objective was to 'compel' the liberal party to 'secure the sympathy of the working classes by the active promotion of . . . land, labour and social reforms' but they offered no specific programme and concentrated their attacks against the institution which offered the 'strongest and most obstinate resistance' to reform.[61] Labouchere, unlike John Morley, was not inhibited from supporting social or economic reforms by strict adherence to doctrines of the Manchester School. In 1894 he claimed that modern radicalism favoured

[57] C.B.P., B.M. Add. MSS., 41222, fo. 109, Labouchere to Campbell-Bannerman, 25 Feb. 1904.
[58] *Northampton Daily Reporter*, 3 July 1895.
[59] *Northampton Daily Reporter*, 25 March 1905.
[60] *Fortnightly Review*, xxxvi (1 Sept. 1884), 326–9.
[61] *Annual Register*, 1896, p. 84.

'Collectivism and Individualism'[62] and in the nineties he favoured the eight-hour day and public ownership of railways and mines. Nevertheless his attitude towards the Lords indicates a basic weakness in his and other radicals' position. In order to curtail its powers it was first necessary to mobilize opinion against the upper chamber on an issue, preferably social or economic, of major importance and this in view of the composition of the liberal party was difficult if not impossible. Only Gladstone might have used successfully the home rule issue to mobilize opinion against the Lords for this purpose but he was prevented from doing so in 1894 by the attitude of his colleagues, his age and the condition of his eyes. To attack the Lords as radicals did and promise 'fundamentally important' reforms later was a somewhat sterile exercise and appears to indicate inverted priorities. On the other hand, different groups within the liberal party were much more likely to combine to attack the Lords than to agree upon a relevant programme of domestic reform. Party leaders had concluded that the Newcastle programme, 1891, had been a mistake and the electorate came to be invited to support a party with a creed but no specific policy. Liberalism represented 'one thing in one constituency and another thing in another' and thus could not, in the opinion of Keir Hardie and Ramsay MacDonald, 'retain the support of intelligent and serious reformers'.[63]

Similarities exist between Labouchere's attitudes towards forward imperial policies and the house of lords. He was strongly inclined to emphasize criticism of imperial expansion and exposure of what he considered the fallacious arguments of those who supported it. His promises of vague or varied domestic reform as alternative uses for the expenditure involved, statements such as 'We have want and misery here; we have great labour questions, and if we have money to spend—it is money taken from the mass of the people—let it be spent on the wellbeing of the people' were subsidiary to his attacks. Nevertheless, in his opinion every radical had the duty 'to see . . . that we do not drift into responsibilities abroad which may come in advance of . . . reforms at home'. He kept the pledge, made on

[62] H. Labouchere and H. M. Hyndman, *Debate on Socialism, 1894*, p. 12.
[63] *Nineteenth Century*, lxviii (Jan. 1900), 21.

3 February 1893, that he would 'always' object to 'all' protectorates and annexations.⁶⁴

Labouchere protested strongly when the liberal government, in which Rosebery often hauled reluctant colleagues after him, or the two subsequent unionist administrations permitted imperial expansion to occur. One consequence of leading this campaign was that Labouchere made fissures within the liberal party wider and deeper. He and other radicals repeatedly raised issues connected with Uganda, Egypt and South Africa. Their protests were frequently ignored and their questions were often only partially answered. Agitation about imperial issues increased within the liberal party and made bitter opponents of groups within it that otherwise had much in common. Labouchere, for instance, stated that 'in domestic politics' Rosebery was a 'very sensible man'.⁶⁵ By 1899 the situation existed in which 'No two people who spoke' at the National Liberal Club in January 1899 agreed 'about future imperial policy'.⁶⁶ This disunity was clearly shown in parliament.

After 1882 Labouchere's attitude towards British imperial policy was consistent, independent and courageous and by the nineties he was a leading representative of the extreme wing of the Little Englanders. The position from which he did not move significantly was that the government should initiate policies that would prepare the way for the evacuation of Egypt: the 'Khedive and the people of Egypt . . . have a laudable desire for national independence; they want Home Rule, precisely as the Irish want Home Rule, and . . . they ought to have it, just as the Irish ought to have it'.⁶⁷ Such policies were not viable during the latter part of his career and he concentrated upon attacking aspects of administration, publicizing the use of British financial resources, exposing instances of injustice and curtailment of liberty in order to argue that British policy dissipated imperial resources and militated against imperial interests and those of the peoples governed. As in the earlier part of his career Labouchere devoted little attention to Indian affairs but his

⁶⁴ Hansard, 4th ser., 8, 478, 456, 477, 3 Feb. 1893.
⁶⁵ H. Labouchere and H. M. Hyndman, p. 13; Hansard, 4th ser., 10, 545, 20 March 1893
⁶⁶ *Annual Register*, 1899, p. 7.
⁶⁷ Hansard, 4th ser., 8, 457, 3 Feb. 1893.

position was unequivocal. *Truth* argued in September 1897 that British difficulties there must multiply with the 'increase of Western enlightenment', and that by taxing 'absolute necessaries of existence' Indian revenue was raised in 'direct contradiction to all the principles on which our own budget is framed'. *Truth* believed that the famine of 1896 revealed serious deficiencies in British rule:

if one country takes upon itself to rule another country, it is bound to see to the well being of its inhabitants. . . . [These] evils are the outcome of our tenure of India as we practise that tenure. We ought long ago to have endeavoured to gradually teach the natives how to govern themselves. But this we have not been prepared to do, because we know that self-government would mean that India is no longer to be drained of her resources for our benefit. . . . The entire basis of all self-government is trust in the people. So long as we do not trust the natives of India, we must . . . maintain the autocratic rule of force . . . with India on our hands, and with its countless millions ruled by the sword, it is little less than lunacy to add to our Empire millions of Africans who are a curse and a burden. Surely it would be more in accordance with not only the dictates of policy but of humanity for us rather to see that the subject races now under our sway should not die of starvation, and to make an effort to convert them from slaves into citizens, our equals and our friends.[68]

Labouchere opposed British policy towards Africa particularly vehemently. When liberals came to power in 1892 they had to formulate policy for Uganda. Rosebery, virtually unaided, evaded opposition from Gladstone, Harcourt, J. Morley and a majority in the cabinet between September and December 1892 and made retention of Uganda virtually inevitable. Important steps in this process were the decision by the cabinet on 30 September 1892 to support the ailing Imperial British East Africa Company during the first three months of 1893, confirmation of Sir G. Portal's appointment on 23 November 1892 as imperial commissioner with instructions to inquire and report, and the secret instructions of 1 and 7 December 1892 in which Rosebery, independently of his colleagues, urged Portal to conclude treaties with tribal rulers in Uganda.[69] Labouchere

[68] *Truth*, 23 Sept. 1897, p. 762.
[69] R. Oliver and G. Mathew (eds.), *History of East Africa*, vol. i, chs. x, xi; P. Stansky, p. 13.

realized the likelihood that existed of an additional imperial commitment. Herbert Gladstone sent a letter he received from Labouchere to be read to his father on 19 December 1892 but Gladstone's secretary, Sir A. West, refused: 'it was an Uganda attack on Rosebery. It would open up old wounds, and Mr Gladstone would have to defend his policy and his colleagues if he read it, and this he could not do.'[70] This letter appears to have disappeared but Labouchere wrote to Herbert Gladstone again later in December. He pointed out ways in which Rosebery had dissociated himself from the cabinet, argued that it was a mistake to prolong the existence of the I.B.E.A. Company after 31 December 1892, and proposed the dispatch of a second commissioner to effect withdrawal from 'this absurd retention'.[71]

On 3 February 1893 Labouchere spoke in the Commons in favour of evacuation from Uganda and launched a clear, perceptive and well-documented attack. He warned that Portal might only be in Uganda a short time before the Company withdrew, that if he took over the country even provisionally 'then our responsibility would be actual', that 'it would be exceedingly difficult to withdraw afterwards', and that unless he were told to evacuate 'the necessary result of his mission will be that Uganda will be annexed'. To counter the argument that Christians would be massacred if the British withdrew, he proposed, amidst laughter, that Portal should be instructed to pay for their evacuation on the grounds that this policy was more rational than to appropriate a country with two million inhabitants in order to protect a thousand Christians. Labouchere explained that fifteen missionaries had died of illness in transit to or in Uganda and three others had been involved in incidents unconnected with their spiritual duties, to put their deaths in perspective. He referred to American missionaries in Africa who did not request their government to annex territory, and considered it 'extraordinary' 'that people should advocate sending armed forces to foreign countries in order to aid missionary labour'. He dismissed economic arguments in

---

[70] H. G. Hutchinson (ed.), *The Private Diaries of Sir Algernon West*, 19 Dec. 1892, p. 95.
[71] H.G.P., B.M. Add. MSS., 46016, fos. 162–3, Labouchere to H. Gladstone, 30 Dec. [1892].

favour of retention by using Lugard's testimony to claim that the only suitable export was ivory, that freight charges from the coast would be £300 per ton, and that a railway would cost £3,000,000 and need an annual subsidy of £300,000. The government would be 'unwise and ridiculous' to interfere in Uganda if it did not intend to build a railway and if it had this intention its members would 'have to eat their own words'.[72]

Gladstone had some difficulty in dealing with these shrewd thrusts. He claimed that if the government had instructed Portal to effect evacuation it would have added to British responsibilities, that Portal had no instructions to act as an administrator and no commission of administration for a later date.[73] Labouchere remained sceptical and returned to the attack in March. He refuted arguments in favour of retention more comprehensively and surprised Gladstone by asserting that Portal had the right to interfere with tribal governments. Uganda, so Labouchere argued, had virtually no products, no medium of exchange to purchase British goods, was unhealthy and unsuitable for colonization. In addition, Christianity had recently lost ground there owing to its association with 'Maxim guns and the loss of... independence'. Its inhabitants, among whom domestic slavery was widespread, were divided into warring factions, were surrounded by persistent enemies and they only embarked on slave raids 'to carry up the trade that was done with Uganda'. He claimed that Portal had the power to establish a temporary protectorate and predicted that the matter would be settled before parliament was consulted. Moreover, if Britain took Uganda, pressures for the appropriation of the Sudan would increase: 'our being in Egypt was used as an argument in favour of taking Uganda—just as, when they had taken Uganda, that would be used as an argument... to remain in Egypt for ever'. Labouchere considered that the people of Uganda were 'as strong Home Rulers as the Irish themselves' and regretted that the government was willing to 'squander all the resources of the Empire' annexing territory such as theirs while it was unwilling to give 'anything' if it was a 'question of

[72] Hansard, 4th ser., 8, 455–78, 3 Feb. 1893.
[73] Ibid., 478–88.

SOCIAL AND POLITICAL ENVIRONMENT 19

improving the slums, relieving misery, or giving employment to people at home'.[74]

In the House a majority of 322 rejected Labouchere's arguments.[75] He made no further move until 1 June 1893 when he harried Sir E. Grey, spokesman of the foreign office in the Commons, with a series of questions about Uganda. The last of these, 'Are we to understand that under certain circumstances Sir Gerald Portal has a right to hoist the British flag in Uganda, and to assume a Protectorate?', caused Grey to seek refuge in silence.[76] Portal raised the British flag at Kampala on 1 April 1893 and parliament had to wait until 1 June 1894 before the government eventually announced its policy for Uganda:[77] a commissioner for Buganda, a sub-commissioner for communications, the purchase of the Company, and no railway.

Labouchere opposed the conservative government's request for a grant-in-aid for the preliminary survey for the Uganda railway in 1892 and was the 'most whole-hearted and continuous opponent of British dealings with Uganda, and the most unrestrained of critics'.[78] In 1893 he sounded the alarms against the liberal government's policy on the grounds that it would result in annexation. When this occurred he proved the 'most uncompromising and consistent opponent of retaining Uganda'.[79] He particularly relished exposing such details of inefficiency in the Uganda railway as the existence of 90 locomotives and 202 passenger carriages for one daily train[80] and arguing that the railway had not reduced the slave trade.[81] Labouchere protested strongly about the continued existence of domestic slavery and scorned the idea of a 'country being well administered when its inhabitants number millions, and its administrators under a hundred'.[82] He also gave prominence to the problem of forced labour in Uganda and other parts of Africa where there was imperial activity, partly on

[74] Hansard, 4th ser., 10, 539–49, 20 March 1893.
[75] Division Lists, 1893, No. 33, 20 March 1893.
[76] Hansard, 4th ser., 12, 1731–4, 1 June 1893.
[77] Hansard, 4th ser., 25, 181–94, 1 June 1894.
[78] M. F. Perham, *Lord Lugard*, i, 330.
[79] Ibid., i, 399.
[80] Hansard, 4th ser., 83, 138, 14 May 1900.
[81] Hansard, 4th ser., 82, 298, 30 April 1900.
[82] Hansard, 4th ser., 79, 894, 22 Feb. 1900.

humanitarian grounds and partly because 'Working men in England have votes, and working men in Africa have not.'[83]

Labouchere was even more vigilant and active in connection with developments in Southern Africa than with those in East Africa. In March 1892 Baron H. de Worms informed him that the British South Africa Company derived power to 'legislate for the preservation of peace and order' in regions such as Mashonaland from clause ten of its charter. Labouchere pressed further and asked, unavailingly, the source from which the crown derived the power to 'claim sovereignty over all natives within the area of British influence'.[84] He criticized the indirect exercise of British power through the B.S.A. Company, argued that ultimate responsibility for its actions rested with the British government, and predicted that the company would eventually burden the government with additional liabilities. In parliament he raised issues such as its concession of 600,000 acres to the Mashonaland Development Company. Buxton informed him that directors of the B.S.A. Company assured the colonial office that there was 'no intention of interfering with native occupation in this sparsely-populated country'. Labouchere was not impressed and asked whether a representative of the colonial office in the vicinity could ensure that the directors kept this engagement. Buxton restated that the government had 'no administration in Mashonaland, and no right to exercise jurisdiction'.[85]

Labouchere ferreted to unearth information about a wide range of issues connected with Lobengula, the Matabele, Bechuanaland and the B.S.A. Company. Buxton conceded that some of his questions were 'rather difficult to answer' and disparaged others by referring to them as conundrums.[86] While Labouchere's persistence did much to make information available and to induce the government to state its position, the liberal administration conveyed the impression that it might be withholding some relevant facts. On 9 November 1893, for instance, Buxton declined 'to give any specific answer' about the

[83] Hansard, 4th ser., 82, 304, 30 April 1900.
[84] Hansard, 4th ser., 2, 539–40, 10 March 1892.
[85] Hansard, 4th ser., 12, 70–2, 4 May 1893.
[86] Hansard, 4th ser., 15, 203–5, 21 July 1893.

possible exclusion of correspondence from printed parliamentary papers dealing with relations between Lobengula and the B.S.A. Company before the latter's invasion[87] of Matabeleland in October 1893, 'or to state whether such portion of the correspondence, if any, which may have been omitted'[88] strengthened or weakened Labouchere's case.

Labouchere promptly moved the adjournment of the House on the 'impolicy of permitting' the B.S.A. Company 'to establish any claim' 'with regard to the territory or government of Matabeleland'. He interpreted information he had obtained in parliament, from Blue Books and from reports in the press to argue that Lobengula had acted justly, had not precipitated hostilities with the Company, and had little responsibility for the war. Labouchere considered that the British government had been overborne by 'Rhodes and his pernicious Company'. He claimed that Sir H. Loch's 'exceedingly difficult position' as high commissioner responsible for Mashonaland, Matabeleland and Bechuanaland, and governor of Cape Colony in which Rhodes was prime minister and head of the B.S.A. Company, had helped to create the situation in which Dr Jameson became convinced that Loch would permit him to invade Matabeleland. Labouchere detected financial jobbery behind 'this so-called march of progress' in which two thousand Matabele were killed or wounded 'against the loss of two white men'. In his detailed explanation of the financial background of the establishment of the B.S.A. Company he asserted that the value of the royal charter to the interested capitalists was over £3,900,000, and that it led investors to believe that the 'Company was respectable, that the amount of capital was legitimate, and that the whole of the proceedings would be honestly conducted'. Labouchere assured the House that this was not the case. He made public the shareholdings of Beit, Rhodes, Rudd and N. de Rothschild and found that 'Among these patriots and pillars of the Empire there were two aliens.' He regretted that it was difficult to ascertain facts about the B.S.A. Company because its charter exempted it from the liability of sending returns to Somerset House, but he expressed the opinion that its promoters initially made

[87] See E. A. Walker, *History of Southern Africa*, pp. 426–9.
[88] Hansard, 4th ser., 18, 540, 9 Nov. 1893.

substantial profits and that the Company was in difficulties by 1893, dependent upon a 'loan of some £3,000 per month from De Beers. It could not get more money from the public, and bankruptcy seemed inevitable.' One part of the process to regain public support consisted of 'puffs' which 'appeared in most of the newspapers' thanks to Rhodes' 'wonderful' influence: another was the invasion of Matabeleland.[89]

In the short debate that followed Labouchere's allegations were dismissed rather than answered. The prime minister, Gladstone, to whom Labouchere allocated the duty of securing that 'henceforward everything should be conducted with justice, mercy, and humanity' retorted that nothing had occurred to justify a censure of Rhodes 'who enjoys the almost unbounded confidence of the free community in which he lives'.[90] Buxton, who trembled on the brink of an oration about the 'terrible dangers' facing a 'handful of men' until Labouchere interpolated 'Maxim guns', reiterated that the 'Company alone, were responsible' for events in Matabeleland: the policy of the government was to preserve peace if possible and to ensure that if hostilities did occur they 'should have every justification' and 'every moral certainty of success'. He totally disagreed with Labouchere's argument that if a 'Company has absolutely no money, has spent all its capital, and can only borrow by seizing the property of its neighbours, it may be wise to do so'.[91]

Despite his failure to stop such 'filibustering and massacring expeditions' Labouchere kept South African issues firmly before the House. He compelled Buxton to admit that neither the high commissioner nor the B.S.A. Company exercised authority in Matabeleland before Jameson's incursion and that they subsequently did so by 'right of conquest'.[92] Buxton also conceded that as a result of the Company's actions British taxpayers would have to meet expenditure 'on behalf of the Bechuanaland Police', and that the government would allow no arrangement in Matabeleland to prejudice 'safeguards for the protection and rights of the natives'.[93] Labouchere thus demonstrated that

[89] Hansard, 4th ser., 18, 543–64, 9 Nov. 1893.
[90] Ibid., 597.
[91] Ibid., 579–90.
[92] Hansard, 4th ser., 19, 373–4, 4 Dec. 1893.
[93] Ibid., 634, 7 Dec. 1893.

although the Company had sole responsibility it had incurred additional responsibilities towards natives and more financial obligations for the British government. His case that the Company had gained land by slaughtering its inhabitants was strengthened when he could draw attention to reports that it had selected sites for townships 'on the largest visible gold belt yet seen in the country'.[94] To counter arguments about the sparse native population in Matabeleland Labouchere asked if the government contemplated 'carrying out this scheme of taking away from all persons all land beyond the absolute requirements of individuals in England as well as in Africa'.[95] Labouchere was convinced of the necessity of a searching inquiry into the scope of concessions granted by Lobengula, the pledges given him by the crown, the causes and origins of the war in Matabeleland and the way in which it was conducted, before any final settlement was made but Buxton refused to entertain the idea.[96]

Thus in 1893 a liberal government established the precedents whereby the B.S.A. Company embarked upon policies which added to British responsibilities but which the government was not prepared to take to parliament. Labouchere, the Company's main critic, was rebuffed and Gladstone showed that the government resented his hostility. Nevertheless, Labouchere's attacks upon the Company, its methods and leaders, continued remorselessly and increased significantly after Jameson's incursion into the Transvaal in December 1895, by which time Chamberlain was secretary of state for the colonies.

Labouchere immediately suspected that there was 'no paying gold, except in very small quantities in Matabeleland, and that some *coup* was needed to keep' the Company solvent.[97] He considered it more reasonable to suppose that Beit and Rhodes wished to make money by relieving the Rand mineowners of grievances about taxation and to permit Rhodesia to remain viable by annexing to it the Johannesburg district, than that they were unduly concerned about such Uitlander

[94] Ibid., 1044, 11 Dec. 1893.
[95] Ibid., 1169, 12 Dec. 1893.
[96] Ibid., 826–7, 8 Dec. 1893.
[97] C.D.P., B.M. Add. MSS., 43892, fo. 211, Labouchere to Dilke, 11 Jan. [1896].

grievances as the right of children in Johannesburg to learn English in school. From January 1896 *Truth* put forward Labouchere's views, pungently and at length, about the 'shameful and abominable' actions of the filibusters behind whose raid was a 'great financial conspiracy' and a Company 'every farthing' of whose profits came from 'the pockets of British investors... stained with the blood of African natives'.[98] On 11 February 1896 Labouchere moved for a 'much wider inquiry into the Company's financial and political history than that for which the Government was prepared'[99] then or later. *The Times* argued unsuccessfully against his inclusion as a member of the committee that inquired into the Jameson Raid between 5 February and 13 July 1897 on the grounds that he was too biased to give an impartial verdict.[100] Ultimately his assessment of the committee's discoveries differed from that of his associates and he submitted his own draft report which, however, was defeated by ten votes to one, and discredited in advance for he failed to establish that the raid was organized for special personal speculations and stock-jobbing purposes. Thus the charges he emphasized so strongly rebounded upon him. On the other hand radicals, on Chamberlain's authority, understood that the committee of inquiry would examine the way the B.S.A. Company raised capital and distributed and manipulated shares [101] but the committee prevented this.

From January 1896 Labouchere had been in a cleft stick on this matter. One of the characteristics of *Truth* was the way in which it exposed individuals that Labouchere suspected of fraud, speculation or misrepresentation. Victims of persistent attacks frequently initiated legal proceedings against him for libel or defamation of character. It is therefore probable that he hoped the attacks in *Truth* upon leading shareholders of the B.S.A. Company would result in legal proceedings in the course of which he might secure evidence not otherwise obtainable. The financiers, however, ignored his allegations except in the committee where, as Labouchere complained to Harcourt,

[98] *Truth*, 9 Jan. 1896, pp. 79–81; 16 Jan. 1896, pp. 142–6, 155–6.
[99] S. Maccoby, *English Radicalism, 1886–1914*, p. 215.
[100] *History of 'The Times'*, iii, 219.
[101] Hansard, 4th ser., 51, 1095, 26 July 1897.

Beit challenges me to prove this & that stated in *Truth*. The chairman allows him to do this, & to read extracts from *Truth* as though the business of the Committee was to consider if what I have said in a newspaper be true. Beit has his remedy at law & he does not take it. . . . Why does the Committee allow the [? challenge] and the quotations to be read, & then not allow me to show my case?[102]

Labouchere was not convinced by emphatic denials of his charges given on oath in the committee and his draft report repeated the allegations though in the case of Rhodes he conceded that in addition to being 'strongly influenced by financial considerations of a personal character', 'he may have been' to some 'extent influenced by a vague, hazy idea of a vast African federation under the British flag, extending from the Nile to Cape Town, in which he would play a leading part'.[103] It was perhaps coincidental that stock exchange lists show that the price of B.S.A. Company stock fell 'very considerably' in the latter part of 1895: presumably 'men in the know' disposed of substantial quantities of their holdings.[104] The committee restricted Labouchere's attempts to explore the Company's financial background. For instance, he wished to know how the duke of Abercorn initially obtained his shares. He was overruled by the committee and could not ask the duke, who was neither a substantial shareholder nor a substantial seller, any question relating to his shares other than whether he had bought or sold any shares in the Company in the last six months of 1895. According to Labouchere's account, published later in *Truth*, he 'declined to put it, for it did not cover what I wished to elicit, not only from the directors, but from other witnesses'. Labouchere

was determined not to be beaten, and after the enquiry was over . . . managed to get from the books of the Company the amounts held by the chief shareholders in April 1896 (after the Raid) and also some particulars of shares owned by them as original shareholders and as a result of an allocation of shares in July 1895.

He considered the information 'instructive' but it was not sufficiently detailed or precise to prove his case either in

[102] W.V.H.P., Labouchere to Harcourt, 28 May 1897.
[103] Parl. Pap., 1897, ix (311), p. lix, 12.
[104] P. H. Emden, *Randlords*, p. 199.

connection with Matabeleland in 1893 or the Transvaal two years later. Even so his attitude towards the Company appears to have more justification if the facts he published were correct, and Rhodes by March 1896 had disposed of 136,594 shares and Beit 114,880 shares from individual holdings of 166,057 and 122,376 respectively: of shares held jointly they sold 220,891 from a holding of 221,400. Moreover, they 'did not register transfers' when they occurred.[105]

Only two members of the committee of inquiry, E. Blake, an Irish nationalist, and Labouchere, attempted to investigate thoroughly the Raid and its ramifications. The decision to confine inquiries to the Raid itself owing to alleged lack of time seriously hindered them. So did obstruction, which Labouchere claimed was 'rampant',[106] and the ineptitude and circumspection of their colleagues. Unionists did not wish to embarrass their colonial secretary; and liberals, of whom Harcourt, Campbell-Bannerman and Buxton were the most important, were strangely credulous and tolerant of witnesses' vagaries. The principal objective of Harcourt, who actually wanted Chamberlain as the committee's chairman and consistently assumed that he was not involved in the Raid, was the condemnation of Rhodes.[107] This he gained in the report but lost in the subsequent debate by what he described as Chamberlain's 'most culpable error'[108] in defending the personal honour of Rhodes in the House.[109] Labouchere's effectiveness in the committee was reduced initially because he shared Harcourt's belief in Chamberlain's innocence until April 1897[110] and in 1896 had been eager to support Chamberlain to help him crush the B.S.A. Company.[111] In the committee Labouchere received little support and frequently found himself in a minority of one or two. Blake withdrew from the committee on 2 July 1897 owing to the 'incompleteness' of the inquiry.[112] Labouchere attended its

[105] *Truth*, 8 March 1900, pp. 571ff.; Sd.P., Labouchere to Stead, 21 Oct. 1899.
[106] Hansard, 4th ser., 79, 681, 20 Feb. 1900.
[107] P. Stansky, pp. 240–2.
[108] Hansard, 4th ser., 79, 650, 20 Feb. 1900.
[109] Hansard, 4th ser., 51, 1169, 26 July 1897.
[110] W.V.H.P., Labouchere to Harcourt, 5 April 1897.
[111] C.D.P., B.M. Add. MSS., 43892, fo. 211, Labouchere to Dilke, 11 Jan. [1896].
[112] P. Stansky, p. 243.

next meeting, had his draft report rejected overwhelmingly, and followed Blake's example. His report complained of the omission of the Boers' views of the Uitlanders' grievances, the 'singular reticence of Mr Rhodes in his evidence' and the defective memory of Flora Shaw. In his opinion the 'Committee cannot pretend to have become possessed of a perfect and full knowledge of everything' connected with the Raid and the 'alleged complicity of the Colonial Office has not been probed to the bottom'.[113]

Labouchere's labours were not as completely wasted as rejection of his report might indicate. As a result of his tenacity Flora Shaw admitted significant deficiencies in her earlier evidence and failed to remove uneasiness about her connections with the colonial office and the conspirators.[114] The committee not only permitted Hawksley to defy it and thus withhold important telegrams but it prevented Labouchere from resuming his examination and this, as he explained to the Commons after the failure of his attempt to bring Rhodes' solicitor to the Bar of the House, violated his right as a member of a parliamentary committee and 'created the suspicion that it was prompted by fear lest' Hawksley 'be too communicative'.[115] Some of the uneasiness that existed and exists about the committee can be traced to the persistence of Labouchere, the obstacles he encountered, the information he obtained and his willingness to keep issues connected with the inquiry alive subsequently. During the Boer war he supported in parliament and in *Truth*[116] the proposed reopening of the inquiry, and in August 1901 claimed that the Raid 'was the primary cause of the war, but what was worse... was the manner in which we had treated it'.[117] He argued that 'peace and prosperity can only be restored to South Africa when all suspicion is removed, that the Secretary of State for the Colonies was actuated by his previous relations with the Rhodes–Jameson conspiracy in forcing on a war'.[118]

---

[113] Parl. Pap., 1897, ix (311), pp. xlviii, 16; lii, 42; liii, 46; xlvii, 3; lxii.
[114] *History of 'The Times'*, iii, 234, 240.
[115] Hansard, 4th ser., 51, 311–12, 16 July 1897; 1109, 26 July 1897.
[116] Hansard, 4th ser., 79, 674, 20 Feb. 1900; *Truth*, 1 March 1900, pp. 502ff.
[117] Hansard, 4th ser., 98, 1175, 2 Aug. 1901.
[118] *Northampton Mercury*, 24 Aug. 1900.

After 1895 Labouchere warned of the increasing danger of war in South Africa. He conceded that Uitlanders' grievances existed, was convinced that they were 'a mere pretext' and had grave doubts about the genuineness of petitions and counter-petitions. He protested about the increase of British garrisons 'as a menace to President Kruger ... to bring home to him the guilt of resisting a raid on his country',[119] asked why this was occurring, and what distinction existed between the Cape and Natal and other self-governing colonies in this respect.[120] He argued that there was opposition to Rhodes and his policies together with anger at his nominal punishment for the Raid amongst sections of the English community in South Africa such as that which supported the Afrikander Bond. The Dutch in the Cape, he argued, were 'as loyal as any of our colonists'. He claimed that reports to the contrary published by English newspapers represented 'falsehood upon falsehood and mis-statement upon mis-statement' derived from suspect sources influenced by Rhodes in South Africa, the South African League whose officers' statements, on General Butler's testimony, produced 'a large measure of suspicion', and the selection of dispatches published.[121] Rhodes, he continued, sought turmoil in South Africa to upset Schreiner, prime minister of the Cape, and have the balance of power redressed with British bayonets. Labouchere also regretted that Milner accepted unquestioningly many allegations about Schreiner and that the British government did not approach Kruger through him rather than Milner. Labouchere's comments, however, were by his standards comparatively restrained, partly one suspects because he did not wish to aggravate a delicate situation, partly because he wished to keep Campbell-Bannerman, the new leader of the party, from too close an association with liberal imperialists, and partly because he wished to commit liberals to oppose the war.

According to J. F. X. Merriman, British policy persuaded the Boers that

concession will secure them nothing and that England wants their country and a bloody revenge. . . . They will accept their fate with

---

[119] *Truth*, 18 Aug. 1898, p. 407.
[120] Hansard, 4th ser., 70, 256–8, 21 April 1899.
[121] Hansard, 4th ser., 75, 771–9, 28 July 1899.

determination and die fighting, saying that rather than have a republic dominated by Rhodes and his creatures they will have after the war a British colony and fight the Empire constitutionally.[122]

As the war clouds darkened Labouchere made a final attempt to prevent hostilities. In August 1899 he suggested to Montagu White, a representative of the Transvaal government in London, ways in which war might be avoided. During the war some of his letters and others of a similar nature from Dr Clark, J. Ellis, Merriman and de Villiers were captured and their publication by the British government covered a large section of the opposition 'consistently hostile to the war, with dangerous odium'.[123] Labouchere defended his actions vigorously and attacked Chamberlain in parliament[124] and in *Truth* where he published the correspondence between himself and Montagu White on 23 August 1900.

On 17 October 1899, the first opportunity after the outbreak of hostilities, he supported John Dillon's attempt to secure arbitration between the British government and the Boers for 'some scheme which will protect the honour and interest of the Empire, of South Africa, and of the Transvaal'. The war, he argued, was 'so impolitic, that the animosity between the two races will then be so aggravated, that our victory will do more harm than if we made some reasonable arrangement at the present time'. Labouchere could not 'accept the responsibility' of washing his hands 'of an injustice like this' but other liberals acted differently.[125] Campbell-Bannerman abstained; Asquith, Buxton and Haldane voted against the motion Labouchere seconded.[126] He opposed the conduct of negotiations that preceded the war and on 20 October 1899 promised, 'I shall vote on every occasion on which I get an opportunity against this iniquitous ... impolitic ... vile war.'[127]

However he did not probe as deeply or divide the House as frequently as he did after the general election of 1900 for he did

[122] J.B.P. (Bodleian), Merriman to Bryce, 15 Aug. 1899.
[123] S. Maccoby, *English Radicalism, 1886–1914*, p. 300. See *Annual Register*, 1900, pp. 177, 185–91.
[124] Hansard, 4th ser., 88, 221–32, 7 Dec. 1900.
[125] Hansard, 4th ser., 77, 101–12, 17 Oct. 1899.
[126] Division Lists, 1899, No. 2, 17 Oct. 1899.
[127] Hansard, 4th ser., 77, 436, 20 Oct. 1899.

not wish to weaken the morale of troops fighting to repel the Boer incursion into the Cape[128] or to press an untimely confrontation between Little Englanders and liberal imperialists. Yet during this period when, as he later regretted, he was 'too flabby',[129] his position was unequivocal. Once the Boers were 'practically driven . . . out of our territory', he protested against the iniquitous continuation of a war to destroy the independence of the republics on the grounds that this policy would accentuate racial feuds in South Africa where the 'majority in our own colonies are of Dutch extraction'.[130]

Labouchere's attacks on the war, Chamberlain and Milner and their policies became increasingly effective from the latter part of 1900. Labouchere conceded that annexation of the republics, which he had previously opposed, could not be rescinded[131] but from 13 December 1900 he reiterated that they should be made self-governing colonies as soon as possible, with as much independence as existed *mutatis mutandis* in the Native States of India, Australia and Canada. In January 1902 he suggested that annexation would lose its odium if explained to Boer leaders as an attempt to 'effect a union between independent countries for their mutual advantage'. He added that a republic was amongst the sovereign states within the German empire.[132] Such proposals rested upon firm foundations. Labouchere was convinced that 'conquest and surrender would be the most injurious . . . thing that could happen to the Empire'. Conquest would 'sow the seeds of disaffection' among an increasing population of a nationality which could only be crushed by depopulation. British immigrants afforded no solution to this problem owing to their inability to compete with an 'abundant mass of cheap labour'. 'A federation based upon conquest and the predominance of the race representing the minority over the majority . . . would not be a Commonwealth but . . . a garrisoned dependency consisting of new citizens forced into citizenship without the sympathies of citizens' who 'would

---

[128] Hansard, 4th ser., 83, 1571, 17 May 1900.
[129] Hansard, 4th ser., 88, 234, 7 Dec. 1900.
[130] Hansard, 4th ser., 80, 761, 13 March 1900.
[131] Hansard, 4th ser., 88, 778, 13 Dec. 1900.
[132] Hansard, 4th ser., 101, 390, 20 Jan. 1902.

SOCIAL AND POLITICAL ENVIRONMENT 31

think that they were being treated as an inferior race'.[133] He used the annexation itself to support his argument: 'Self-government is not a privilege. It is a right, and I assert that every man as soon as he becomes a citizen of this Empire has that absolute right.'[134]

Labouchere advanced such arguments to counter the policy of the government which he thought would create 'a new Ireland'[135] in South Africa and a 'festering sore' within the empire[136] at a time when no common policy existed within the liberal party. The *Annual Register* estimated in 1900 that sixty-two liberal members were imperialists, thirty were 'on the fence' with Campbell-Bannerman, sixty-eight were pro-Boers and twenty-seven were undecided.[137] Bitterness between the extreme wings of the party increased during the general election of 1900 and some liberal imperialists, through the Imperial Liberal Council, recommended certain candidates to 'patriotic' voters and proposed a purge of pro-Boers after the election. By June 1901 a series of incidents brought long-standing divisions within the party to a head. Campbell-Bannerman's condemnation at the National Reform Union on 14 June 1901 of the 'methods of barbarism' employed by British forces in the war indicated his more positive attitude towards South African affairs.[138]

The following three weeks were the most critical of his career for he was convinced that some liberal imperialists, sheltering behind Asquith, intended to deprive him of the leadership.[139] Labouchere, who made serious efforts to 'eschew wild cat politics'[140] in order not to weaken Campbell-Bannerman's position, leapt into the fray. He had earlier failed to arrange an Irish seat for J. F. X. Merriman, who with J. W. Sauer represented the Afrikander Bond in England. These delegates reluctantly concluded that liberals 'as a party have no . . . intention

[133] Hansard, 4th ser., 89, 247–57, 15 Feb. 1901.
[134] Hansard, 4th ser., 92, 147, 28 March 1901.
[135] *Truth*, 11 Jan. 1900, p. 71.
[136] Hansard, 4th ser., 101, 395, 20 Jan. 1902.
[137] *Annual Register*, 1900, p. 165.
[138] *Annual Register*, 1901, p. 153.
[139] J. A. Spender, *Life of the Right Hon. Sir Henry Campbell-Bannerman*, i, 338ff.
[140] C.B.P., B.M. Add. MSS., 41222, fo. 34, Labouchere to Campbell-Bannerman, 7 Nov. [1900].

of making South Africa a parliamentary question, or of endeavouring to give any lead to that body of opinion which regards the war as a mistake . . . we can get no reply from the leaders'.[141] Labouchere, however, enabled them to speak at Northampton on 12 June 1901.[142] A week later, he presided over a 'packed', well-organized pro-Boer meeting at the Queen's Hall at which Sauer was the principal speaker. He did this, although he had 'some doubt' as to the wisdom of such a meeting, for he 'did not wish to . . . shirk'.[143] A resolution was passed by acclamation at this meeting demanding the immediate offer of 'complete independence' to the Boer republics.[144] This was more extreme than a motion which came from the platform. Campbell-Bannerman partially resolved the crisis at a meeting of the party on 9 July 1901.[145] Divisions of opinion remained, but the views of an increasing proportion of the party came closer to those of the pro-Boers.

Labouchere played an important part in keeping the views of those who opposed the war influential within the liberal party and before the public. His attacks ranged widely and he attempted to counter the 'widespread credulity' which, in his opinion, was the 'most serious factor' in the political situation.[146] He criticized the financial arrangements for war expenditure on the grounds that each generation should pay for its own follies.[147] He continued to allege that sectional interests profited from the war and was a driving force behind the radicals' campaign against the way in which the government granted contracts.[148] He charged mine-owners in South Africa with some responsibility for the war by seeking a reduction in taxation upon mines and by desiring harsher laws against natives such as fiscal policies that would compel them to work in the mines.[149]

[141] J.B.P. (Bodleian), Merriman to Bryce, 11 March 1901.
[142] *Northampton Daily Reporter*, 13 June 1901.
[143] Merriman Papers, South African Library, Cape Town, Nos. 200, 204, Labouchere to Merriman, [?12], 18 June 1901.
[144] *Times*, 20 June 1901.
[145] *Annual Register*, 1901, pp. 159ff. See R. H. Jenkins, *Asquith*, pp. 131–46.
[146] *Truth*, 11 Jan. 1900, p. 73.
[147] Hansard, 4th ser., 77, 536, 23 Oct. 1899; 94, 663, 20 May 1901; *Northampton Daily Reporter*, 7 March 1901.
[148] Hansard, 4th ser., 94, 1317, 7 June 1901; 103, 172, 893, 1270, 17, 24, 27 Feb. 1902.
[149] Hansard, 4th ser., 98, 1520, 6 Aug. 1901.

Thus he reconciled protection of native interests with pleas for 'free trade in labour'[150] in a South African context. It was Labouchere who gave early warning of the political hazards of importing Chinese labour for the Transvaal mines. As on so many occasions during the preceding two decades he failed on 27 May 1903 to obtain an opportunity for members to discuss the question before the government took a final decision. The success of the subsequent campaign against 'Chinese Slavery' presumably made Chamberlain rue that he made what had become a conventional response to requests of this nature from Labouchere: 'discussions at the present time would be entirely premature'.[151]

Labouchere considered himself as a 'pro-Englander' rather than a pro-Boer.[152] He stated that opponents of the war had as much solicitude for the interests of the empire as those who disagreed with them, and added that it took more courage while war fever raged for a member to oppose it and risk his seat, his popularity and his position in the country than to glide with the stream.[153] He also helped to keep alive the argument that the 'progress of democracy at home is to be arrested by adventure and grab abroad'.[154] Even before he defended the Boers' 'noble determination'[155] to preserve their independence he claimed for a sovereign in Africa 'the same consideration as the head of a state in Europe',[156] and for communities there rights of self-determination and self-government. Thus in 1887 he considered that the views of Zulus should be known before Britain annexed Zululand[157] and in 1893 that those of Egyptians should be tested to discover whether they wished the British to remain.[158] In 1894 he supported 'Home Rule in Africa as well as in Ireland'[159] and regretted that by 'international law, in the making of which Africans have no voice,

---

[150] Hansard, 4th ser., 126, 363, 27 July 1903.
[151] Hansard, 4th ser., 123, 14, 27 May 1903.
[152] Hansard, 4th ser., 96, 918, 4 July 1901.
[153] Hansard, 4th ser., 92, 154, 28 March 1901.
[154] *Truth*, 22 Feb. 1900, p. 445.
[155] Hansard, 4th ser., 89, 250, 15 Feb. 1901.
[156] *Truth*, 30 Jan. 1896, p. 262.
[157] Hansard, 3rd ser., 315, 68, 16 May 1887.
[158] Hansard, 4th ser., 11, 1657, 1 May 1893.
[159] Hansard, 4th ser., 25, 212, 1 June 1894.

the natives of Africa have no absolute right of ownership in their own land'.[160] Thus he claimed that annexation of parts of Africa, which was 'based upon the idea of making the black owners of the territory work for the white men',[161] was facilitated. The process ended the slave trade but 'replaced it by making the Africans slaves at home'. Britain did not benefit, for profits from these 'new markets for our goods' never equalled the cost of 'securing and retaining them'.[162] The 'huge expanses' of West Africa added to the empire were 'not of the slightest use'.[163]

Labouchere asserted that the British were 'without exception, the greatest robbers and marauders in regard to... annexations that ever existed', were 'worse than other countries' because they plundered hypocritically and 'always pretended' that it was 'for other people's good'.[164] Their 'arrogance', 'injustice' and 'greed' were 'leading all foreign nations to increase their navies'.[165] Although Labouchere argued that the £500,000,000 'squandered' on the aggrandizement of the empire would have secured 'excellent and very necessary things at home' such as old age pensions at 60, improvements in the educational system and 'more comforts' for labourers,[166] he did not stress the domestic implications of active imperial policies regularly and systematically.

No-one who witnessed Labouchere's zeal in 1905 would have imagined that he had decided to retire from politics and had disposed of his London house and of Pope's Villa, Twickenham, in 1903. He was still endeavouring to increase the party's effectiveness and worked with W. S. Churchill and Lloyd George to make liberal members more conscientious by threatening to publish lists of attendance.[167] He told Herbert Gladstone that he did not 'believe in Members of 74'[168] but a stronger

[160] *Truth*, 3 March 1898, p. 522.  [161] *Truth*, 17 Feb. 1898, p. 390.
[162] *Truth*, 30 Dec. 1897, p. 1710.  [163] *Truth*, 18 Aug. 1898, p. 407.
[164] Hansard, 3rd ser., 315, 529, 19 May 1887.
[165] *Truth*, 1 Feb. 1900, p. 254.
[166] *Northampton Daily Reporter*, 6 Aug. 1903; Hansard, 4th ser., 75, 552, 27 July 1899; *Truth*, 25 Aug. 1898, p. 467; *Northampton Mercury*, 11 May 1900.
[167] S. L. Hughes, *Press, Platform and Parliament*, pp. 76–82.
[168] H.G.P., B.M. Add. MSS., 46016, fo. 178, Labouchere to H. Gladstone, 19 Dec. [?1905].

reason for his retirement resulted from his exposure of H. Hess in 1898.[169] Hess secured his revenge by obtaining letters sent by Labouchere, before he represented Northampton, to G. A. Sala, the journalist who was Labouchere's witness to R. Pigott's confession in 1889. The first letter advised Sala to buy shares in a cable company because the *World*, of which Labouchere was financial editor, was going to announce that the government intended to buy it: the second letter advised Sala to dispose of his shares because a later issue of *World* would announce that the rumour had no foundation. Hess published these letters and sent a copy of his pamphlet to each member of parliament. Healy commented tersely, 'After their publication... Labouchere did not again stand for Parliament.'[170]

In the light of such activities and his actions in connection with Egyptian finance during the early 1880s Labouchere's attitude towards the B.S.A. Company cannot be taken at face value. He may have regretted that he had not profited from its activities, and his attacks may have been designed to depress the value of its shares so that he could speculate in them at an appropriate time. On the other hand it is significant that he made no similar charges against the I.B.E.A. Company or the Royal Niger Company although he objected to all chartered companies. Beneath all his comments about the B.S.A. Company there is an undercurrent of sustained, probably honest, anxiety about the Company and its practices which appears to indicate that the poacher had turned gamekeeper. Although he made serious charges against the Company without evidence and thus discredited his case, he was a financial expert who had personal experience of manipulating the stock exchange with the help of the press, and so his arguments and allegations were perhaps worthy of more consideration than they were given. Above all he wanted the facts to be known so that the public could draw its own conclusions. When thwarted he was ruthless. He paid £100 to secure information about ownership of shares in the B.S.A. Company[171] and published it in *Truth*.

[169] *Truth*, 10 March 1898, pp. 586–9.
[170] T. M. Healy, *Letters and Leaders of My Day*, i, 308–9.
[171] Sd.P., Labouchere to Stead, 21 Oct. [1899].

Labouchere was strongly inclined to colour his criticisms of policies by making personal attacks upon politicians such as Rosebery or Chamberlain who supported them. In some ways these were particularly effective because they were often amusing, founded upon personal knowledge of the individuals concerned and shrewd understanding of their strengths and weaknesses. But if it was his intention to cut these politicians down to size so that their policies would be examined more critically, his plan backfired for he was treated as irresponsible. This attitude towards him was reinforced by the fact that he was no respecter of persons. He christened Gladstone the Grand Old Man and initiated the story about his habit of playing cards with an ace up his sleeve and claiming that the Almighty placed it there. He even had the temerity to suggest that Queen Victoria should economize and travel by a Cook's tour rather than in the royal yacht. Equally he was no respecter of the occasion and after the death of Lord Beaconsfield his voice struck a discordant note in the harmony of the eulogies.

Labouchere claimed with some justice, 'I say openly what I think'[172] and he delighted in exposing political cant and humbug, particularly that associated with arguments advanced to support active imperial policies. He painted everyone, including himself, in the darkest colours. Yet his iconoclasm did not extend to communities that resisted what were, in his opinion, unjust or unwise policies of the British government. His cynicism disguised his conviction that the policies in which he believed would ultimately prevail; and his remarkable openness illuminated slightly events in the twilight regions of politics and of finance where it is difficult to corroborate evidence.

His dislike of hypocrisy may perhaps explain in part his actions in 1892 when Gladstone 'with his usual loyalty to the Queen, took the whole responsibility of Labouchere's exclusion' upon himself.[173] Labouchere spurned opportunities to enhance his reputation as an independent, politically disinterested member who wished to remain unmuzzled. He was bitterly disappointed for it was generally accepted that he had strong claims

---

[172] *Truth*, 6 June 1895, p. 1391.
[173] H. G. Hutchinson (ed.), *The Private Diaries of Sir Algernon West*, 12 Aug. 1892, p. 47. I was unable to consult the Royal Archives.

upon the party.¹⁷⁴ He did not disguise his feelings and he published relevant correspondence between himself and Gladstone in *Truth*. Shortly afterwards he failed to secure appointment as ambassador to the U.S.A., not least because he did not temper his attacks upon the policies of Rosebery, the foreign secretary.¹⁷⁵ Even so, he pressed this request with singular ineptitude. Labouchere's subsequent criticisms of the liberal government's policies towards East and Southern Africa were partially discounted on the grounds that they were prompted by malevolence sired by frustrated ambition.

Labouchere was a paradoxical figure. To a certain extent he was regarded as a renegade by the upper class to which he belonged by birth. Yet he remained sufficiently well established to be able to ask Rosebery and the prince of Wales to dine with him. At his exquisite dinner parties, where guests were resplendent and the best of everything was provided, he wore a seedy dinner jacket, of which his wife had tried to dispose, ate a little cold ham and munched dry bread. He was a delightful companion, gentle and modest, a kind and true friend but he could be an implacable enemy. It is difficult to reconcile his pose as a detached observer of human folly with his political audacity and his defence of the oppressed and exploited in *Truth* for these activities brought him threats, some of which were carried out, of physical punishment. He did not waver before such threats: he simply became more pugnacious and more inclined to ridicule his opponents. Despite the fact that he was 'constitutionally averse to everything venerable, traditional and imperial', his ability impressed political opponents such as Sir R. Temple.¹⁷⁶ Flora Shaw was so captivated by 'the intelligence of his conversation' that she expressed to him in 1905 'the faith that was in me with regard to the real value of the empire ... making of us a finer race than history has seen before'.¹⁷⁷ When granted his privy councillorship, an honour to which he had aspired for two decades, he behaved with characteristic effrontery when he was sworn in. He attacked the upper

---

[174] Sir R. Temple, p. 30; W.V.H.P., Harcourt to Labouchere, 25 Nov. 1892; N.L.I., MS. 11010, J.B.P., T. Wemyss Reid to J. Bryce, 15 Nov. 1892.
[175] The correspondence between Labouchere and Rosebery on this issue is available at the National Library of Scotland.
[176] Sir R. Temple, pp. 28–9. [177] M. F. Perham, *Lord Lugard*, ii, 232.

chamber and the established church but after 1890 lived in Old Palace Yard from which he virtually overlooked the house of lords and Westminster Abbey. Labouchere supported a wide range of political reforms but totally opposed the enfranchisement of women.[178] Even the situation in his constituency was paradoxical. Northampton, one of the most radical constituencies in the country, was for this wealthy radical a pocket borough in which he came to owe much to socialists while the manufacturers, although liberals, worked for his destruction.[179]

[178] Hansard, 4th ser., 131, 1339-44, 16 March 1904.
[179] Sd.P., Labouchere to Stead, 29 Sept. 1900.

CHAPTER II

# Attitudes towards the Empire: The Great Debate

IN THE 1870s and 1880s a great debate took place about the nature of the empire and about British imperial policy. Bodelsen suggested that the fate of the thirteen American colonies, the dominance of the Manchester School, acceptance of the argument that benefits would be greater from free trade, the concession of internal self-government to colonies in British North America and Australasia after 1840 and their encroachment upon powers (with the exception of control over foreign policy) reserved to the imperial parliament, produced a 'belief in separation as an ultimate certainty', and a reluctance to 'countenance sacrifices on the part of the mother country on behalf of the colonies' among 'the majority of mid-Victorian statesmen of both parties'.[1] Then, at the end of the 1860s, the influence of the anti-colonial school culminated and in 'the course of one decade' an 'astounding change' took place.[2] Bodelsen attributed the transformation to particular causes such as the gradual withdrawal of troops from self-governing colonies after 1862 and the reduction of British expenditure for colonial military purposes, the rapid growth of the chief colonies of settlement, improvements in communication which facilitated continuation of the imperial connection, and perhaps even made closer union possible, and the revival of interest in emigration at the end of the 1860s. He suggested that more general causes for the change included reaction against so extreme a movement as the Manchester School, the growing belief that colonists were 'largely animated by a romantic attachment to the mother country',[3] the willingness of other powers to acquire colonies

---

[1] C. A. Bodelsen, *Studies in Mid-Victorian Imperialism*, p. 43.
[2] Ibid., p. 79.    [3] Ibid., p. 80.

together with the possibility that they might annex such of Britain's colonies as might choose to cut the cable, and the general tendency in Europe and America against particularism and towards amalgamation. Bodelsen considered that perhaps the most important of the forces transforming public opinion towards the empire was the gradual change of outlook on commercial and foreign policy.[4]

Bodelsen, however, ignored India to which over half the questions asked in parliament between 1859 and 1865 on imperial affairs referred and to which *The Times* in the same period devoted over two hundred leading articles. He also presented evidence to support his argument that needs qualification. He omitted the phrase 'The day may come when' from a quotation from the *Quarterly Review* of 1863 when he selected, 'rich ... colonies ... will claim a dissolution of partnership', and he did not mention that the long article was a plea for imperial unity.[5] He correctly stated that Cornewall Lewis favoured separation in 1862 but ignored the way subsequent speakers such as Viscount Bury and Disraeli dissociated themselves from his views.[6] His claims that widespread indifference to the empire existed in political circles need to be balanced by the fact that the proportion of questions asked in parliament on imperial (including Indian) affairs averaged slightly over $14\frac{1}{2}$ per cent of the total between 1859 and 1865, that *The Times*, which favoured the imperial connection, gave substantial coverage to imperial affairs, and that there were speeches in parliament and articles in journals which advocated the possession, retention and development of the empire as an opportunity for, or a duty of, the Anglo-Saxon race.[7]

By his neglect of India and Ireland, two of the most important fields of imperial experience since the sixteenth century, and his failure to give sufficient weight to those who favoured the imperial connection Bodelsen made the 'astounding change'[8]

[4] Ibid., p. 81.
[5] *Quarterly Review*, cxiv (July 1863), 151; C. A. Bodelsen, p. 37.
[6] Hansard, 3rd ser., 168, 860–73, 25 July 1862; C. A. Bodelsen, p. 39, n.2.
[7] Hansard, 3rd ser., 176, 1674–5, 18 July 1864; 179, 905–9, 26 May 1865; *Times*, 20 Aug. 1860; 14 Oct. 1864; 7 Jan. 1865; *North British Review*, xxxiii (Nov. 1860), 86–7; xxxvi (May 1862), 535–60. I am exceptionally indebted to P. Amey for information, references and advice about Bodelsen's *Studies*.
[8] C. A. Bodelsen, p. 79.

of opinion seem more abrupt than was the case. Attitudes towards imperial issues, which were often shaped by earlier traditions, were more complex and diverse. Although there were humanitarian influences upon British colonial policy, humanitarians advocated widely differing policies after 1834 and they and their detractors shared the conviction that British society had a higher destiny than expansion.[9] Precedents existed for the Colonial Reformers' views on emigration in R. F. Gourlay's *Statistical Account of Upper Canada* ... (1822), and in the efforts of Sir R. Wilmot Horton, under-secretary of state for the colonies in Lord Liverpool's tory administration, to mobilize opinion on this issue. In the press the argument that responsible government would strengthen the empire by removing the oppression of imperial administration and bind colonies to the mother country with ties of reciprocal goodwill was voiced[10] before 1840. The *Annual Review* of 1803 anticipated some of the arguments of the Manchester School when it proposed that colonies should be founded independent or autonomous on the grounds that they would be neutral during the wars of the mother country whose territories would consequently be less vulnerable.[11] The views of the Colonial Reformers and Little Englanders were closer than might appear. Both considered that colonists should have financial as well as political responsibility. The former asserted that the concession of self-government to the colonies would bind them to Britain with ties of interest and affection, and of the latter Cobden affirmed in 1850 that the severance of colonies from the 'country of their origin would be an evil' and suggested imperial federation as a possible way of reconciling freedom and unity.[12]

Robinson and Gallagher have shown that public opinion and British policy were basically imperial in character between 1845 and 1860, have argued that this was discernible in overseas trade, investment, emigration and culture rather than in political or constitutional changes, and have claimed that the objective of British policy was trade with informal control wherever

[9] J. S. Galbraith, 'Myths of the "Little England" Era', *American Historical Review*, lxvii (1961–2), 43.
[10] *Critical Review*, 3rd ser., xvi (March 1809), 328; *Morning Chronicle*, 31 May 1827.
[11] *Annual Review*, ii (1803), 324.
[12] Quoted by J. S. Galbraith, p. 36.

possible but trade with the responsibilities of administration where necessary.[13] This, however, did not preclude vigorous protests from doctrinaire free-traders who, though 'quick to discover and denounce' all forms of imperial expansion, were ineffective politically for some years after the success of Palmerston and the policies he represented in the Don Pacifico debate of 8 to 9 July 1850.[14] To Galbraith's salutary reminder that the 'spectrum of opinion on colonial policy was much narrower than the language of partisan politics would seem to indicate'[15] could be added the warning that opinion did not necessarily divide along party lines. Thus in the administration of 1868–1874 liberals such as Gladstone and Cardwell planned to separate the defence systems of Britain and the colonies 'to take the withdrawal of the troops to its logical and undeniably dismembering conclusion',[16] while others such as Forster championed one 'great' imperial 'confederation'.[17] Disraeli, in 1872, in his retrospective criticism of the 'attempts of Liberalism to effect the disintegration of the Empire' could not 'conceive how our distant colonies can have their affairs administered except by self-government'.[18] Koebner and Schmidt hold the view that a 'distinctive conservative attitude' towards imperial questions 'was scarcely in evidence before the second Salisbury administration'.[19]

General acceptance of the act of union by English politicians also narrowed the area of controversy until the latter part of the nineteenth century. The relationships between Irish, British and imperial affairs warrant closer examination than they have received. Harlow discerned a tendency to accept the 'illusion of political union'[20] between England and Ireland, and with it an

[13] R. Robinson and J. Gallagher, 'The Imperialism of Free Trade', *Economic History Review*, 2nd ser., vi (1953), 1–15.
[14] O. Macdonagh, 'The Anti-Imperialism of Free Trade', *Economic History Review*, 2nd ser., xiv (1961–2), 489–501.
[15] J. S. Galbraith, p. 42.
[16] C. F. Goodfellow, *Great Britain and South African Confederation, 1870–1881*, pp. 31–2.
[17] Quoted by C. A. Bodelsen, p. 105.
[18] Crystal Palace Speech, 24 June 1872: C. A. Bodelsen, p. 121; R. Koebner and H. D. Schmidt, *Imperialism*, pp. 103, 104, 107, 108, 109–12.
[19] R. Koebner and H. D. Schmidt, p. 111.
[20] V. T. Harlow, *The Founding of the Second British Empire, 1763–1793*. i, 501.

evasion of the implications of Ireland upon the empire. The issues which arose as a result of the renunciation of British jurisdiction in 1782 'were "imperial" issues, because they involved the structure of the Empire as a whole and called in question the traditional concepts upon which it had been founded'.[21] The failure of attempts to stabilize Irish political autonomy by a treaty providing for an agreed contribution by Ireland for imperial defence in return for the removal of restraints upon Irish commerce resulted in the 'arid alternative of political absorption'.[22] England in an age of war and revolution demanded greater assurances than the 'only chain' the Irish, represented by a narrow protestant electorate, would consent to wear, 'the dear ties of mutual love and mutual freedom'.[23]

Significant changes occurred in Ireland after the union. D. O'Connell, the first prominent politician in Britain to keep in touch continuously with the general public, secured catholic emancipation in 1829. Religious differences in Ireland intensified and this with the reviving social vigour of catholicism helped to alter the attitude of protestants to the union. Possibly a majority of them opposed it in 1800 but they increasingly came to identify it with the preservation of their own interests. Thus when O'Connell began to campaign for repeal of the union after 1829 and in a more sustained and well-organized way after 1840, protestant opinion as a whole opposed him.[24] With the campaign for repeal once again the structure of the empire and the principles upon which it had been founded were questioned. In general, repeal was equated with a return to the constitutional relationship of 1782. While currents of opinion existed that demanded that 'Ireland should have nothing to do with an empire which cumbered the earth and whose ruin would be a blessing to humanity',[25] hostility to the empire was not automatically a corollary of support for repeal: 'who', asked O'Connell, 'is the man who does not desire to be a member of the great and glorious British empire?'[26]

[21] Ibid., i, 550.
[22] Ibid., i, 538.
[23] Quoted by V. T. Harlow, i, 528, Charlemont to Rockingham, 17 April 1782.
[24] R. B. McDowell, *Public Opinion and Government Policy in Ireland, 1801–1846*, p. 35.
[25] Quoted by R. B. McDowell, p. 239; *Nation*, 9 Dec. 1843.
[26] Quoted by R. B. McDowell, p. 170; *Pilot*, 1 Nov. 1837.

There were various suggestions for some measure of devolution within the United Kingdom in 1844, the year when O'Connell opted for a federal solution. In 'addition to local parliaments for Great Britain and Ireland'[27] federalists required 'more for Ireland than the simple repealers do ... that there should be for questions of imperial concern, colonial, military, naval and of foreign alliance and policy, a congressional or federative parliament in which Ireland should have her fair share and proportion of representation and power'.[28] The concern of leaders of both English parties towards federal proposals was indicative of the significance they attached to them as a 'more modest and more dangerous substitute for repeal'.[29] The repeal movement, however, disintegrated and from the late 1840s agrarian issues secured greater attention than political claims.

Ireland came to occupy a prominent place in discussions about the empire in the 1870s and 1880s and developments in other parts of the empire were related to it. When Irish members of parliament put the case for home rule in 1874 Hartington argued that the question could only be considered from an imperial point of view. In 1886 the choice between Irish self-government and imperial security appeared stark and from Gladstone's opponents two themes were constantly advanced: the Irish would use the proposed political concessions to secure complete separation; the home rule bill was synonymous with the 'disintegration' or 'dismemberment' of the empire. Yet Gladstone wished to apply classical solutions derived from Colonial Reformers to the Irish problem. He drew extensively upon the best constitutional precedents such as the British North America act; and he was determined to maintain the 'unity of the empire' and strengthen it with ties of mutual affection. Irish representatives had stressed that there was 'incalculable mutual advantage' in a policy of home rule and 'no question of dismemberment of the Empire'[30] in 1882. Nevertheless almost one-third of liberal members were unconvinced and opposed home

---

[27] Quoted by R. B. McDowell, p. 238; *Nation*, 12 Oct. 1844.
[28] Quoted by K. B. Nowlan, *The Politics of Repeal*, pp. 74–5; *Nation*, 19 Oct. 1844.
[29] K. B. Nowlan, p. 74.
[30] Hansard, 3rd ser., 266, 193ff., 209–11, 8 Feb. 1882.

rule in 1886. This division, a recent study argues, heralded a 'sea-change in British imperial attitudes' for in debates on home rule between 1886 and 1893, in which the origin of new attitudes to the empire can be traced, the issues at stake were the ' "integrity" of the whole British empire' as well as the government of Ireland.[31] Rosebery, however, contended that divisions in Gladstone's second administration and the schism of 1886 had 'far more to do with foreign and Imperial questions'[32] than with Ireland. There is little doubt that there was an intimate association between liberals' treatment of these issues, which did much to stimulate drastic reappraisals of attitudes towards imperial issues, the vigour of the home rule debate, and its relevance to other parts of the empire. Goschen, for instance, argued that if concessions were made to Irish 'evil doers' the 'result would be that every subject race, that India, that Europe would know that we were no longer able to cope with resistance'.[33]

In 1868, if Koebner and Schmidt are to be believed, there was 'little evidence' that the 'unity or integrity of the British Empire was a cause which could count on many supporters';[34] this, more probably, was the consequence of a consensus of opinion in its favour rather than the reverse. But even if greater weight is given to Ireland, India and the crown colonies and the latter view is accepted, it does not follow that there was any discernible uniformity of method to secure agreed objectives such as the integrity of the empire or general acceptance of principles and relationships upon which the unity of the empire was to be based. Initially discussions about the nature of the empire tended to concentrate primarily upon relations between Britain and those parts of the empire over which it had progressively less control, the self-governing colonies. The question at issue was whether these colonies were to develop into a decentralized, autonomous, free and co-operative association in which British influence operated through the minds and hearts of men in local communities, through enlightened self-interest and mutual

[31] D. G. Hoskin, 'The genesis and significance of the 1886 'Home Rule' split in the liberal party' (Cantab., Ph.D. No. 4787, 1964), p. 1.
[32] *Annual Register*, 1901, p. 165.
[33] Hansard, 3rd ser., 304, 1477, 1481, 13 April 1886.
[34] R. Koebner and H. D. Schmidt, p. 90.

affection, or whether alternative policies might lead to a more coherent, centralized form of imperial organization through institutions. In certain respects the aims of those who advocated either course were not necessarily far apart. Goldwin Smith affirmed that the 'connexion of blood, sympathies and ideas' would be unaffected by political separation. 'And when our colonies are nations, something like a great Anglo-Saxon federation may ... arise out of affinity and mutual affection.'[35] For Dilke the strongest argument in favour of separation was 'that it would bring us a step nearer to the virtual confederation of the English race'.[36] From the other camp came proposals to strengthen imperial bonds before the colonies gained further control over their own affairs. These proposals often advocated the establishment of some form of assembly in which representatives from Britain and the self-governing colonies would have responsibilities for imperial defence and its financial implications.

When imperial and foreign policy became increasingly interconnected as a result of the purchase of the Suez Canal shares in 1876 and developments in connection with the Eastern Question in 1877-8, the place of India in the empire became a complicating theme in this debate. It brought racial relationships and responsibilities within the empire into greater prominence and helped to polarize opinion about the character of the empire. Controversy turned on issues such as the moral and constitutional problems raised by the transfer of Indian troops to Malta, the alleged pervasion of the empire with militaristic and expansionist tendencies, the possibility of maintaining and the merit of a scattered, maritime, multi-racial empire in which power was centralized in the hands of the British prime minister and in which the justification for authority over subject races rested on superiority of power and race. Disraeli claimed that his administration, 1874-1880, shrank 'from the responsibility of handing to our successors a weakened or diminished Empire'. The use of Indian troops had apparently shown an ability to 'wield the Forces of an united Empire'.[37] His opponents claimed that conservatives' expansionist policies

[35] Quoted by C. A. Bodelsen, p. 56.
[36] Quoted by R. Koebner and H. D. Schmidt, p. 89.
[37] Quoted by R. Koebner and H. D. Schmidt, pp. 140-1.

in Southern Africa, the eastern Mediterranean, the north-west frontier of India, and in Fiji weakened the empire by adding additional burdens and a 'multitude of needless and mischievous engagements'[38] to it, subverted parliamentary government, diverted attention and resources from domestic requirements and supplied false imperial ideals. 'Empire is greatness; leagues of land are empire; your safety is measured by the fear you strike into other nations; trade follows the flag: he that doubts is an enemy of the country.'[39] The profound differences had widespread ramifications. In 1877, for instance, E. Dicey equated Britain's right to acquire Egypt with its right to hold India, crown colonies such as Gibraltar and Singapore, and even Ireland.[40] Gladstone, on the other hand, warned that Egypt would be 'the almost certain egg of a North African Empire', questioned the value of the canal 'for our military communications with India, under the varied... contingencies of war', claimed that Britain had 'a great duty towards India' but 'no interest... except the well being of India itself': the 'material greatness of our nation lies within the compass of these islands'.[41] He later stated that the one limit to the extension of local government in the British Isles was that 'Nothing can be done... to weaken or compromise the authority of the Imperial Parliament.'[42]

In his Midlothian campaign Gladstone stated that Britain should foster the strength of the empire by just legislation and economy at home, preserve to other nations the blessings of peace, strive to cultivate the concert of Europe, avoid needless engagements, acknowledge the equal rights of all nations and, subject to these limitations, follow policies animated by love of freedom.[43] In office he failed to implement these policies partly because liberals were deeply divided on imperial issues towards which the attitude of radicals and whigs was often, but not invariably, diametrically opposed.

---

[38] W. E. Gladstone, *Political Speeches in Scotland, November and December, 1879, and March and April, 1880*, i, 64, 26 Nov. 1879.
[39] Quoted by R. Koebner and H. D. Schmidt, p. 145.
[40] *Nineteenth Century*, ii (1877), 301.
[41] Ibid., pp. 153, 156, 158.
[42] W. E. Gladstone, i, 87, 26 Nov. 1879.
[43] Ibid., i, 115–16, 27 Nov. 1879.

Moreover, it was difficult to apply the principles Gladstone enunciated during his Midlothian campaign in an Irish, South African, Afghan, Indian, Egyptian and Cypriot context without encountering serious domestic, imperial or international repercussions. Imperial problems and internal dissensions drove the liberal government to resort to coercive legislation in Ireland, and to military operations in South Africa, in Egypt and the Sudan, and in Afghanistan. By direct and indirect means the liberal government added extensively to imperial responsibilities. It was as difficult to reconcile these decisions with such articles of the liberal creed as 'force is no remedy' or 'peace, retrenchment, and reform' as with Gladstone's Midlothian principles.

Gladstone's second administration often secured direct or tacit conservative support for its imperial policy. This in conjunction with the pronounced contrast which existed between liberals' pre-election statements and their actions in office created a situation which Labouchere was quick to exploit. His position was unassailable, for, as Lord Acton pointed out, there was 'no answer to Labouchere'[44] when he contrasted liberal precepts with liberal practice. The parliamentary situation allowed Labouchere to oppose the imperial policy of the government which he otherwise supported, and yet he could truthfully tell his constituents that throughout a session he had not voted with the conservatives. It also gave him the opportunity to attack the whigs by preaching the rectitude of radicals' views towards the empire, and by asserting that radicals were custodians of the true policy of, and for, the liberal party. He claimed that whig influence was warping the policy of the liberal government, and that by protesting against it he strengthened the position of radicals in the cabinet. He argued that an acquisitive policy was unjust and that it militated against Britain's interests by postponing reform and by dissipating her resources.

It would be misleading to attribute the vagaries or the expansionist nature of British imperial policy between 1880 and 1886 to liberal dissensions alone. Many preceding administrations had internal difficulties, but no comparable expansion of the

[44] H. Paul (ed.), *Letters of Lord Acton to Mary Gladstone*, 7 May 1881, p. 99.

empire took place. The pressures and problems which helped form liberal policy in the 1880s combined unusual and recurrent features in imperial history at a time when events of the preceding two decades had revolutionized European and international relations. The successful use of force to preserve the American union, and to unite Italy and Germany, allied to foreign nations' increasing reliance upon protectionist policies, mocked the Manchester School's predictions of a prosperous pacific era founded upon free trade. Even Britain's self-governing colonies rejected free trade. In Britain a severe agricultural and industrial depression coincided with indications that the sharp edge of the nation's economic efficiency was becoming blunter: a minority movement agitated for 'fair trade'. Confidence that the 'excellency of the manufactures of Great Britain aided by the credit at which they can be sold, will force a vent through every obstacle, which can be opposed to them',[45] which the Committee for Trade voiced in 1784, had evaporated a century later. Yet the constancy of British governments' solicitude for mercantile and industrial interests remained, and the desire to safeguard existing, or to capture new fields of economic exploitation, and to protect the arteries through which trade flowed, played an important part in determining imperial policy.[46] The same concern, married to a desire to minimize expenditure and responsibility, induced the government to turn to earlier precedents and sanction the Borneo and the Royal Niger chartered companies.

From the 1850s the discoveries of Livingstone and other explorers drew attention to the possibility of economic opportunity in vast regions which European enterprise had neglected. At the same time their revelations about the widespread nature of the slave trade and of barbaric practices in Africa revitalized humanitarian activity. Interest in the extension of 'commerce', 'Christianity' and 'civilization' often fused. The power and resources of voluntary enterprise were slender. Nevertheless, in the 1880s and 1890s they were strong enough to create or use situations beyond imperial frontiers and to 'work' them through

[45] V. T. Harlow and A. F. Madden (eds.), *British Colonial Developments, 1774–1834*, p. 264.
[46] See D. C. M. Platt, *Finance, Trade and Politics in British Foreign Policy, 1815–1914*.

influential parliamentary and extra-parliamentary lobbies in order to justify a forward imperial policy.

International rivalry brought problems of imperial defence and imperial communications into strong relief. It also provided the most important single stimulus to British expansion in the 1880s. The appetite of European powers for extra-European possessions, which was closely associated with the tension and the complexity of their relations on the continent after the Congress of Berlin, 1878, was as unprecedented as the speed with which they began to satisfy it. The German empire took South West Africa in April 1884, Togoland and Kamerun in October 1884, part of New Guinea in December 1884, and part of East Africa in March 1885. Leopold of Belgium obtained some 900,000 square miles of the Congo hinterland in July 1885. Obstacles to Russian expansion in the Balkans increased her pressure upon Afghanistan and India. In itself this competitive atmosphere added weight to commercial and humanitarian arguments in Britain: annexations by foreign powers decreased the area in which free trade could operate and British civilization enlighten; they could also threaten imperial possessions. The intrusion of foreign colonization into regions which had been a British preserve created new, and aggravated old problems. Britain was satisfied with previously existing conditions but it joined, or perhaps one should say initiated, the vast enclosure movement. In Britain, according to H. Merivale, regret that the age had passed when 'the world seemed all open' to British enterprise mingled with feelings that imperial ties were 'weakening and loosening' and that ' "something ought to be done" ' to 'arrest further disintegration'.[47]

Developments inside the British empire during the nineteenth century complicated the problems facing British statesmen, for they had to face internal imperial difficulties as well as external pressures. The concession of internal self-government obliged them to consider or consult colonial opinion over issues as far apart as the dispatch of Irish informers to Australia, or policy towards South West Africa and New Guinea. Furthermore, British policy was reaping fresh harvests and had to meet challenges presented by national agitation in Ireland, the

[47] *Fortnightly Review*, vii (1870), 155, 153.

Transvaal,[48] and, after 1883, in India where it was embryonic. Internal imperial crises often coincided and reacted upon each other. These internal tensions weakened the effectiveness of British policy. Ireland made heavy demands upon Britain's military resources and its parliamentary time. Moreover, although Egypt was not part of the empire, the British occupation, and the hybrid nature of British authority there, inhibited Britain's actions. The Egyptian question received the 'highest priority'[49] and it became the 'pivot of imperial policy'.[50]

[48] F. A. van Jaarsveld, *The Awakening of Afrikaner Nationalism*, p. 214: 'Afrikaner nationalism ... is not found in South Africa before 1877.'
[49] R. Robinson and J. Gallagher, 'The Imperialism of Free Trade', *Economic History Review*, 2nd ser., vi (1953), 14.
[50] A. J. P. Taylor, *The Troublemakers*, p. 87.

# CHAPTER III

# Irish Issues, 1880–1884

### INTRODUCTION

THE imperial government had never resolved the political relations between England and Ireland to the satisfaction of both countries. Ireland endured colonial status until 1782, though its proximity to England, married to its natural poverty, rendered this subjection particularly onerous. Changes in the political and military situation during the American struggle for independence and the stimulus of American example enabled a restricted protestant Irish electorate to win 'complete legislative independence'[1] though it was 'constitutionally almost impotent'.[2] Pitt terminated this attempt to accommodate an autonomous Ireland in the empire,[3] but the act of union of 1800 did nothing to satisfy Irish aspirations. Pressures from Ireland created endemic crises in the imperial parliament, which was intrinsically English in character,[4] and in the relations between England and Ireland. In 1829 and 1846 they contributed to the disintegration of the conservative party: in 1886 they helped to split the liberal party.

A fatal concatenation of events had made Ireland's position in the empire as anomalous as her problems were intractable. Her geographical position raised exceptional considerations of defence. Most British colonies in which European settlement

---

[1] J. S. Watson, *The Reign of George III, 1760–1815*, p. 389.
[2] Sir D. L. Keir, *Constitutional History of Modern Britain, 1485–1951*, p. 434.
[3] 'I have been reading Union speeches & debates, & I am surprised at the narrowness of the case, upon which that Parliament was condemned. I think the unavowed motives must have been the main ones.' G.P., B.M. Add. MSS., 44157, fo. 187, Gladstone to Forster, 25 Oct. 1880.
[4] J.B.P., N.L.I., MS. 11010, J. Bryce to R. J. Bryce, 27 June 1882: 'what is and must be *the English* parliament—for the vast English majority gives it its character'.

INTRODUCTION 53

existed had acquired considerable, if restricted, practices of internal self-government, along a conventional, evolutionary path, by 1880. The Irish, though a 'mother' nation, had virtually none for a constitutional fetter chained them to England. Considerable Irish communities lived in different parts of the empire and in the United States of America[5] and they provided invaluable assistance[6] for the 'active' elements in the Irish population and organizations that arose to assist them. An important Irish community settled in England. Those enfranchised constituted a significant element in some elections.[7] English working men viewed many Irishmen as potential or actual economic competitors[8] and considerable antipathy existed between them.[9] Amongst the upper classes this dichotomy of interest did not exist. Some powerful English landowners, such as Lord Londonderry, Lord Lansdowne and Lord Hartington, possessed considerable estates in Ireland. Irish landowners often resided permanently in England and exerted considerable influence upon the English landed classes. The latter suspected that reforms in Irish land law might form a precedent for legislation in the rest of the United Kingdom and that agitation in Ireland would spread to other parts of the British Isles. In fact, the Irish Land League tentatively endeavoured to stir up crofter agitation in the Scottish highlands, and Davitt intended to exploit agrarian unrest in Wales and establish the Welsh Land League.[10] Moderating influences operated less strongly in Ireland than elsewhere in the empire: 'men of property and

[5] Parl. Pap., 1881, xciv (38), 708. Emigrants from Ireland 1880: 78.1 per cent to U.S.A.; 2.7 per cent to Australia; 1.6 per cent to New Zealand; 3.2 per cent to Canada; 0.2 per cent to other countries; 14.2 per cent to England, Scotland and Wales. The number of emigrants rose from 37,587 in 1876 to 95,517 in 1880.

[6] N.L.I., MS. 9229, J. F. X. O'Brien Account Books show that money from communities in New Zealand, Canada and Australia assisted Irish nationalists. Most financial assistance came from the United States of America.

[7] L. G. Rylands (ed.), *The Correspondence and Speeches of Peter Rylands, M.P.*, p. 245, indicates that Irish politicians swung the Irish vote in Burnley and in Manchester to support Rylands and Bright.

[8] Mrs J. Bright (ed.), *Speeches of Jacob Bright, M.P., 1869–1884*, 11 Dec. 1880, p. 77: 'we have the greatest ... interest in doing justice to Ireland ... The people of this country do not want too many Irishmen to come over here to compete with their labour.'

[9] E. Welbourne, *The Miners' Unions of Northumberland and Durham*, pp. 199ff.

[10] M. Davitt, *The Fall of Feudalism in Ireland*, p. 228; *Freeman's Journal*, 18 Jan. 1886.

creditors', Gladstone complained, 'are so powerless ... that they can do nothing except call for extra national, which will be represented as anti national, help'.[11] The Irish representatives at Westminster were at the mercy of one or both English parties. The exigencies of English politics, and the influence of Irish landowners in the house of lords, reacted adversely upon Irish legislation. The executive and judiciary, backed by the Royal Irish Constabulary,[12] operated in Ireland in a way which had no imperial counterpart. The frequency with which these instruments of government were used to apply exceptional law to Ireland was as unusual in the empire as the use of the armed forces of the crown to enforce it.[13] The lord lieutenant and his chief secretary governed Ireland from Dublin castle but were responsible solely to the imperial parliament.[14] The landowners dominated local administration.[15]

Ireland under the Union was enabled, through her representation in the parliament of the United Kingdom, to play her part in the making of economic policies for the United Kingdom as a whole but, unlike the overseas colonies of settlement after the concession of responsible self-government, she lacked the power to promote her own economic interests, for example by way of protective duties, as distinct from those of the rest of the United Kingdom.[16] In view of the wide disparity in economic and social conditions between Great Britain and Ireland this was felt by Irish nationalists and some independent observers to place Ireland at a grave disadvantage. The population of Ireland was decreasing[17] yet certain areas remained chronically

[11] G.P., B.M. Add. MSS., 44158, fo. 76, Gladstone to Forster, 18 Dec. 1880; cf. T. W. Reid, *The Life of the Right Hon. W. E. Forster*, ii, 330, Forster to Ripon, 17 July 1881.
[12] Henry George provided details of the exceptional character of this body in the *Fortnightly Review*, xxxi (1 June 1882), 783–4.
[13] British garrisons had been withdrawn from most self-governing colonies.
[14] J. Cowen on 22 December 1883 described the government of Ireland as 'the least national and the most centralised Government in Europe'. E. R. Jones, *Life and Speeches of J. Cowen, M.P.*, p. 249.
[15] D. C. Savage, 'General Election of 1886 in Great Britain and Ireland' (Lond. Ph.D., 1958), p. 390.
[16] See Parl. Pap., 1880, lxvii (28), 425. The rates levied by Canada (20 to 30 per cent *ad valorum*) were the highest.
[17] 1841: 8,175,124. 1851: 6,552,385. 1870: 5,418,512. 1880: 5,327,099. C. Woodham-Smith, *The Great Hunger*, p. 411; Parl. Pap., 1881, xciv (38), 725.

over-populated. Religious differences exacerbated political, agrarian and economic difficulties. The Orange party became more organized[18] as Gladstone's agrarian legislation of 1870 and 1881, with its subsequent amendments, removed injustices that had tended to unite protestant and catholic tenant farmers, and as the pressure for home rule became more effective in Ireland and at Westminster. Nevertheless, as 'early as 1843 a petition was organized in Belfast for the maintenance of the Union, or, if Home Rule came, for giving Ulster a legislature of its own'.[19] Two minorities, the protestants and the landowners, agitated for the retention of the union between the two islands as democratic advances made possible by the electoral reforms of 1872, 1884 and 1885, and indicated by the growth of Parnell's parliamentary following and the upsurge of English radicalism jeopardized their position.[20] During the 1880s conflicts in Ireland and in parliament which reacted directly and indirectly upon each other, and upon other imperial and international matters, brought home rule within the area of practical politics. In May 1882, for instance, the Canadian parliament submitted to the imperial authorities an address that supported home rule for Ireland.[21] W. E. Forster, in 1880, did not wish any grant of autonomy to the Boers to form a precedent for Ireland,[22] while G. O. Trevelyan feared that an Irish parliament would form a dangerous precedent for India.[23] Davitt, on the other hand, suggested to Parnell in 1883 that the Irish should provide a seat in parliament for Dadabhai Naoroji and so give 'a direct voice in the House of Commons to countless millions of British subjects who were ruled despotically'.[24] The 'heavy Irish demand' weakened Britain's military position to such an extent that there were insufficient regular troops for routine garrison

[18] D. C. Savage, 'The origins of the Ulster unionist party, 1885–6', *Irish Historical Studies*, xxii (1960–1), 185ff.
[19] D. P. Barritt and C. F. Carter, *The Northern Ireland Problem*, p. 15.
[20] Conservatives estimated that the 1880 election produced '113 extreme or unclassed Radicals' in the house of commons. A. Lang, *The Life, Letters and Diaries of Sir Stafford Northcote, First Earl of Iddesleigh*, ii, 149.
[21] A. B. Keith (ed.), *Speeches and Documents on British Colonial Policy, 1763–1917*, pp. 193–5.
[22] G.P., B.M. Add. MSS., 44157, fo. 134, Forster to Gladstone, 6 June 1880.
[23] T. Macknight, *Ulster as it is*, ii, 140.
[24] M. Davitt, p. 447.

duties in other parts of the British Isles.[25] At the same time, the demands of legislation for Ireland prevented Gladstone from paying 'any attention to Egypt' during the period when Egyptian affairs were reaching a climax.[26] However, it was not the wider aspects of the Irish struggle but the constancy of Irish agitation, and political changes in Britain, such as the tacit alliance between the conservatives and Parnellites in the second part of 1885, which brought the home rule issue to the fore in 1886.

Irish discontent and misery, which expressed themselves in extreme forms of social disorder that bordered on revolution[27] in 1880, reflected the social and political consequences of a severe agricultural depression upon a disaffected society with land laws which were defective so far as they concerned tenants. Evictions and lawlessness increased; emigration from Ireland was twice as heavy in 1880 as in 1879; more people were in workhouses and many more received outdoor relief; bank deposits declined steadily between 1876 and 1880; and the tonnage cleared from Belfast, Cork and Dublin declined between 1878 and 1884, particularly in the case of Dublin.[28] Bad weather, foreign competition, excessive competition for land, and an undue inflation of credit, produced partly by a series of prosperous seasons and partly by the security of the 1870 land act, caused the depression. Few alternative means of subsistence existed in Ireland apart from agriculture and landowners operated from a favoured legal, and a strong economic position. Consequently serious abuses such as localized overcrowding and minute subdivision of farms, arbitrary increases of rents and unreasonable payments for tenant right, flourished.[29] Many small farmers owed to shopkeepers and others at usurious rates between four and ten times the amount of their annual rent.[30] Landowners

---

[25] S. Childers, *The Life and Correspondence of the Right Hon. Hugh C. E. Childers*, ii, 104, Childers to Sir G. Wolseley, 18 Aug. 1882.

[26] B. H. Holland, *The Life of Spencer Compton, Eighth Duke of Devonshire*, i, 365, Hartington to Granville, 11 July 1882.

[27] F. S. L. Lyons, *The Fall of Parnell, 1890–1891*, p. 9.

[28] Parl. Pap., 1880, lx (21); Parl. Pap., 1881, xciv (38), 705; Parl. Pap., 1881, xlvii (33), 274; *Bankers Magazine*, xli (1881), 306; xlv (1885), 1032.

[29] Parl. Pap., 1881, xv (1), 7.

[30] Parl. Pap., 1881, xvi (2), 841.

maintained their control with evictions; tenants retaliated with outrages.[31]

The emergence of Parnell as the dominant Irish leader was of the utmost importance in making it possible for the 'new departure'[32] in Irish politics to materialize. Between 1875 and 1879 the agrarian crisis created the worst situation in Ireland since the famine. Initially, two Fenians, M. Davitt and J. Devoy, led the agrarian revolt without assistance from Irish parliamentarians. From June 1879, however, Parnell came to assume control of the land agitation. In October 1879 he became the first president of the Irish National Land League.[33] Parnell combined in one concerted national movement agrarian agitation in Ireland, with political agitation at Westminster and in Ireland, and he was able to secure support from the Irish-Americans, and the opportunist elements in Fenianism.[34] After his success at the general election of 1880,[35] he ensured that Irish issues convulsed parliament for he was then directing a movement 'of revolutionary inspiration, from within a relatively conservative and constitutional party'.[36]

Land reform dominated the 1880 election in Ireland[37] but in England the primary issues were those of foreign and colonial policy raised by Gladstone's Midlothian speeches.[38] The liberal government met parliament without an Irish land policy[39] and Gladstone lacked a definite policy for Ireland in

[31] John Dillon before the Queen's Bench, on 14 Dec. 1886, quoted John Bright's views in 1849, 'It is only *by these acts of vengeance* periodically committed that they can *hold in suspense* the *arm* of the proprietor.' (The italicized words are underlined on the document.) N.L.I., MS. 9226, J. F. X. O'Brien Papers.

[32] T. W. Moody, 'The New Departure in Irish Politics, 1878–1879', H. A. Crone, T. W. Moody, D. B. Quinn (eds.), *Essays in British and Irish History in Honour of J. E. Todd*; M. Davitt, pp. 116ff.

[33] Four of the League's leading officials were Fenians: Biggar and Egan (treasurers), Davitt and Brennan (secretaries).

[34] C. Cruise O'Brien, *Parnell and his Party, 1880–1890*, p. 5.

[35] C. Cruise O'Brien (p. 26) calculated that 24 Parnellites, 21 whigs, and 14 non-aligned home rule members secured election; M. Davitt (p. 238) gave the figures as 36 Parnellites and 28 additional home rule members; and J. L. Hammond (p. 175) considered that the election secured the return of 32 Parnellites and 26 additional home rule members.

[36] C. Cruise O'Brien, pp. 9–10.

[37] Lord Eversley, *Gladstone and Ireland*, p. 108; Davitt (p. 233) disagreed with this opinion.       [38] J. Chamberlain, *A Political Memoir, 1880–1892*, p. xi.

[39] Lord Eversley, p. 113.

1880.[40] Irish unrest, however, provoked the imperial parliament into legislative activity. The government had to decide whether to give priority to coercive or remedial legislation but against the background of Irish turbulence reforms justifiable in their own right often appeared as concessions to violence. Most liberal members lacked clear views about policy for Ireland. Thus in 1882 the editor of the *Contemporary Review* could not secure the opinions of any English liberal on the Irish question for they feared to commit themselves 'against the Government view—whatever that may turn out to be'.[41] Some liberals such as J. Bryce supported coercion in 1881 but opposed it the following year; others such as P. Rylands and John Bright who had appeared sympathetic towards home rule opposed Gladstone's first home rule bill.[42] The majority followed Gladstone's lead.

### HOME RULE

Labouchere, however, had positive views about policy towards Ireland and acted independently. Although he became an early English advocate of home rule this was not necessarily the corollary of his statements in the early part of 1880. At this time 'no important Liberal, not even John Morley, was specifically on record as favouring Home Rule',[43] so it is not surprising that Labouchere's electoral manifesto omitted reference to it. Nevertheless his pre-election speeches at Northampton gave some indication of his views. He claimed that Lord Beaconsfield, who by means of a letter to the lord lieutenant 'endeavoured to focus the attention of the electorate on the question of Ireland',[44] had attempted to strengthen the conservatives' position unfairly by fostering dissension between England and Ireland.

---

[40] J. L. Hammond, *Gladstone and the Irish Nation*, p. 167.

[41] H.P., B.M. Add. MSS., 48616(5), Godley to Hamilton, 5 April 1882.

[42] F. E. Hamer (ed.), *The Personal Papers of Lord Rendel*, p. 83. In 1892 Gladstone contended that Bright objected to placing the Irish nation under the leaders of the home rule cause: in his speeches against home rule Bright never argued about the disintegration of the empire.

[43] B. D. Rubinstein, 'The Decline of the Liberal Party, 1880–1900' (Lond., Ph.D., 1956), p. 70.

[44] W. F. Monypenny and G. E. Buckle, *The Life of Benjamin Disraeli, Earl of Beaconsfield* (1929), ii, 1386; *Times*, 9 March 1880, Beaconsfield to Marlborough, 8 March 1880.

Labouchere was convinced that the union was 'absolutely necessary' for the well-being of both countries, and argued that the 'only way to consolidate and strengthen' it was 'to do everything ... that will conduce to a good feeling between both countries'.[45] He favoured a considerable extension of local government in England and Ireland and on 25 March 1880 admitted that he was 'not ... entirely'[46] opposed to home rule.

He did not give prominence to Irish issues at any stage of his electoral campaign. His statements about local government and home rule were equivocal but they pointed to his sympathetic attitude towards devolution of political authority. He gave no further indication of his views on this topic during the second parliamentary session of 1880 but when he spoke at Northampton in October 1880 he was more explicit. Part of the policy he recommended 'to make Ireland an integral part of England, and ... the Irish people satisfied' entailed devolution of authority from Westminster to allow the Irish to 'regulate their own affairs, and make Irish laws for the Irish nation'.[47]

It is, however, difficult to ascertain with any degree of precision the scope of the political devolution Labouchere entertained for considerable elasticity of expression existed, and persisted at least until 1886,[48] about 'what is styled (*in bonam partem*) "Local Government" and (*in malam*) "Home Rule"'.[49] *Truth* stated on 18 November 1880:

> Home Rule must be conceded so far as to allow the Irish to manage their own local matters. To a Parliament in Dublin England never will consent. Even though its functions were strictly limited, it would be far too much of an *Imperium in Imperio*. But I cannot understand why there should not be a Provincial Assembly in each Irish Province, with powers akin to those of a State Legislature in America.[50]

In private Labouchere used different phraseology. He claimed, in a letter to Chamberlain on 17 December 1880, which the latter forwarded to Gladstone, that the establishment of four

---

[45] *Northampton Mercury*, 27 March 1880.
[46] *Northampton Evening Herald*, 27 March 1880.
[47] *Northampton Mercury Daily Reporter*, 28 Oct. 1880.
[48] See M. Hurst, *Joseph Chamberlain and Liberal Reunion*, p. 27, n.2.
[49] J. L. Hammond, p. 183.
[50] *Truth*, 18 Nov. 1880, p. 633.

elected county boards exercising 'qualified home rule within the limits of the County' would secure substantial Irish support.[51]

From 27 January 1881 Labouchere advocated the concession of 'some sort ... of Home Rule to enable ... [the Irish] to manage their own affairs'[52] in parliament, as well as in his constituency and *Truth*. He advocated this policy despite the inclement political climate caused by the interaction of Irish agrarian unrest, coercive policies of the liberal government, Gladstone's monumental agrarian legislation of 1881, and the reactions of members of parliament to these and subsequent developments.

However, it was particularly through *Truth* that he tried to influence public opinion. Earlier in January 1881, before Labouchere first mentioned the desirability of devolution of authority to Ireland in the House, *Truth* contended that each locality had the 'right ... to settle its local affairs'. It prophesied that the 'cry for Home Rule ... now confined to Ireland, will be raised in England, Scotland, and Wales'.[53] It questioned England's 'moral right' to impose its views on Ireland, considered the 'independence of the locality' a primary cause of the prosperity of the United States, and implied that Ireland would become prosperous if it secured home rule.[54] It favoured extensive concessions for Ireland:

leave her to govern herself... only stipulating that, as we are convinced that Imperial Union between England and Ireland is a geographical and political necessity, we shall decline to argue this point, but take advantage of our being the stronger to enforce it.[55]

In the opinion of *Truth* the only solution of the Irish problem lay in the recognition 'that the Irish have a right to legislate in everything that locally affects Ireland and does not endanger the unity of the Empire'. It did not favour 'an Irish Parliament co-equal with the Imperial Parliament', but proposed separate assemblies for England, Scotland and Ireland, modelled upon the United States' constitution, with a superior imperial parliament.[56] That many people considered 'legislative indepen-

[51] G.P., B.M. Add. MSS., 44125, fos. 53-6, Labouchere to Chamberlain, 17 Dec. 1880. There is no copy in the Chamberlain papers.
[52] Hansard, 3rd ser., 257, 1525, 27 Jan. 1881.
[53] *Truth*, 6 Jan. 1881, p. 6.   [54] *Truth*, 13 Jan. 1881, p. 41.
[55] *Truth*, 20 Jan. 1881, p. 77.   [56] *Truth*, 27 Oct. 1881, p. 540.

dence in local matters'[57] impracticable puzzled *Truth*, for it considered decisions by England on local Irish issues most unsatisfactory. It affirmed that 'the right to govern depends on the assent of the governed'[58] and argued that if the English were to govern by law, then the laws had to conform to the views of the majority of Irishmen. Moreover, 'Self-government can only be learnt by experience' and the 'first step to educate a nation is to trust its people'.[59] *Truth* exhorted its readers to

> discuss the question of a federal union between Great Britain and Ireland without foregone prejudice, and without cursing everyone as a traitor, who believes that such a union would strengthen, rather than weaken, that political connection between the two islands, which is rendered necessary owing to their geographical position.[60]

It asked whether laws were 'to be enacted in every part of the British Empire by the assent of the governed, with the . . . single exception of Ireland'.[61]

On 3 November 1881 *Truth* published a digest of several alleged conversations between Labouchere and Parnell. The latter stated that as England would never assent to separation between the two islands, and as the Irish could not otherwise obtain it, he considered it beyond the realm of practical politics. Labouchere advised Parnell to support Gladstone's proposed bill for county boards, which if established would 'constitute the true representation of the country'. Delegates from these boards would form a 'self-acting Parliament' which the English could not disregard. In this way, Labouchere suggested that the Irish could 'arrive progressively at their legislative independence in Irish matters'.[62] He gave an example of his advanced views on specific issues in these conversations with Parnell. Labouchere favoured the transfer of the police to Irish control on the grounds that English taxpayers would otherwise subsidize taxpayers in Ireland.[63] This question prompted Gladstone, in February 1883, to ascertain whether the executive or the local authority controlled the police in six European capitals.[64] In 1886 Sir J. MacDonald, the Canadian prime minister,

---

[57] *Truth*, 1 Dec. 1881, p. 701.
[58] *Truth*, 3 Nov. 1881, p. 576.
[59] *Truth*, 2 June 1881, p. 743.
[60] *Truth*, 3 Nov. 1881, p. 576.
[61] *Truth*, 8 Dec. 1881, p. 739.
[62] *Truth*, 3 Nov. 1881, p. 576.
[63] Ibid.
[64] H.P., B.M. Add. MSS., 48607(8), Gladstone to Hamilton, 21 Feb. 1883.

considered the question of the control of the police the main obstacle to home rule.[65]

Labouchere's arguments about Irish affairs appeared to satisfy his constituents when he addressed them on 13 December 1881 but they convinced only one of the local newspapers, the radical *Northamptonshire Guardian*. The *Northampton Herald* argued that it was too late to settle the Irish problem by the concession of local self-government for, in its view, Irish leaders desired to have the 'government of Ireland turned over to them'.[66] The *Northampton Mercury* criticized his federal proposals on the grounds that their implementation would necessitate a revolution that would weaken the empire and leave England with the maximum of responsibility and the minimum of power. It also stated that home rule proposals aggravated the difficulty of persuading Englishmen and Irishmen to treat each other with the respect due to fellow citizens.[67] Both of these newspapers attacked Labouchere's statement that only 'Silly, foolish, ignorant people' thought that a devolution of legislative authority to Ireland would lead to the 'disintegration of the empire'.[68] The *Northampton Herald*, for instance, asserted that this would occur 'by a very short and direct course'.[69] Neither newspaper reported the sentence which followed Labouchere's remarks about the 'ignorant people'. 'An empire', he said, 'is not strong by its institutions, but by the love and affection of its peoples.'[70]

Labouchere informed his constituents on 1 February 1882 that he would continue to act in parliament to 'unite England in the bonds of good feeling by mutual concession'.[71] In the House on 16 February 1882 he reaffirmed his belief in the efficacy of home rule and claimed that Gladstone had made it a practical political issue in his Guildhall speech on 13 October 1881, which, in addition to announcing Parnell's arrest, treated home rule as 'conceivably reasonable'.[72] The extract of Glad-

[65] *St Stephen's Review*, 2 Jan. 1886.
[66] *Northampton Herald*, 17 Dec. 1881 (leader).
[67] *Northampton Mercury*, 17 Dec. 1881 (leader).
[68] *Morning Post*, 14 Dec. 1881. Report of Labouchere's speech of 13 December 1881.
[69] *Northampton Herald*, 17 Dec. 1881 (leader).
[70] *Morning Post*, 14 Dec. 1881.
[71] *Daily News*, 2 Feb. 1882.
[72] J. N. Figgis and R. V. Laurence (eds.), *Lord Acton's Correspondence*, i, 176.

stone's speech that Labouchere cited contained the following statements:

> Home Rule may be understood in any one of 100 senses, some of them perfectly acceptable and even desirable, others of them mischievous and revolutionary . . . I . . . will hail with satisfaction and delight any measure of local government for Ireland, or for any portion of the country, provided only that it conforms to this one condition—that it shall not break down and impair the supremacy of the Imperial Parliament.[73]

In parliament Labouchere recognized that it would be 'exceedingly difficult to reconcile Imperial control and local independence' but asserted that this would not be an insurmountable obstacle to Gladstone.[74] However, in comments outside the House Labouchere minimized this problem. For instance, in the *Fortnightly Review* of 1 February 1884 he suggested that the problem of finding an arbiter between the imperial and Irish legislatures could be resolved by a 'cursory glance' at the American constitution.[75]

*Truth* stated on 23 February 1882 that Gladstone's statements, which in addition to the Guildhall speech included two striking speeches in favour of home rule in the Commons,[76] had brought home rule within 'measurable distance'.[77] In March it advised the Irish to act upon Gladstone's suggestion and draft a home rule scheme that would secure 'full local self-government'[78] without weakening the imperial connection. This, in its view, would demonstrate the possibility of constitutional change and show that Irish agitation was not orientated towards separation. On 1 November, Healy, in the *Fortnightly Review*, stated that Irish members declined to frame such a scheme because they had no power to implement it and because it would be extensively criticized.[79] Three years later, however, Labouchere induced Healy to draft a home rule scheme.

[73] Hansard, 3rd ser., 266, 839, 16 Feb. 1882.
[74] Ibid., 840.
[75] *Fortnightly Review*, xxxv (1 Feb. 1884), 224.
[76] Hansard, 3rd ser., 266, 263–6, 9 Feb. 1882; 864–7, 16 Feb. 1882.
[77] *Truth*, 23 Feb. 1882, p. 265. On 25 May 1882, *Truth* (p. 712) observed that action generally followed Gladstone's declarations.
[78] *Truth*, 9 March 1882, p. 334.
[79] *Fortnightly Review*, xxxii (1 Nov. 1882), 630–1.

*Truth* continued to draw upon dissimilar manifestations of Irish discontent to insist that disaffection would only cease when Ireland obtained home rule.[80] It considered that if the English attempted to govern any one of their colonies as they governed Ireland there would be disaffection in it immediately.[81] The concession to Ireland of powers similar to those enjoyed by states in the American union would not, in its view, affect the integrity of the empire.[82] It would show that union with England was not synonymous with injustice to Ireland and thus remove Irish objections to it.[83] However, if the Irish attempted to disrupt the union after they had received home rule, *Truth* considered that 'public opinion'[84] would support the use of force to maintain it.

Labouchere rarely made detailed proposals about devolution of power but he gave specific indications of political changes he envisaged when he defended the views he had expressed on 27 October 1884 during the Maamtrasna debate. In a letter to his constituents, on 4 November 1884, he proposed 'a local Assembly, with full local powers, established in each of the four provinces of Ireland, and the Executive in the hands of some sort of Council, of which Irish M.P.'s would form part'.[85] Two days later *Truth* referred those of its readers who wished to understand the Parnellites' attitude to an article by Healy in the *Fortnightly Review* of 1 November 1884,[86] and it expanded proposals Labouchere made to his constituents.

Each Irish Province should have a local assembly with the same power—*mutatis mutandis*—as is possessed by a State Legislature in America, and the Executive power should be in the hands of an Irish Privy Council, of which the principal Irish Members would form a part. A Secretary of State for Ireland should be appointed, who should be *persona grata* to the Irish and who would act in conformity with the Council.[87]

Throughout this period, Labouchere's attitude towards Irish

---

[80] *Truth*, 1 Feb. 1883, p. 153; 24 May 1883, p. 721; 5 July 1883, p. 10; 22 Nov. 1883, p. 719.     [81] *Truth*, 25 Oct. 1883, p. 577.
[82] *Truth*, 22 Dec. 1883, p. 867.     [83] *Truth*, 25 Oct. 1883, p. 577.
[84] *Truth*, 24 May 1883, p. 721. The expression is unqualified.
[85] *Northampton Mercury*, 8 Nov. 1884.
[86] *Fortnightly Review*, xxxvi (1 Nov. 1884), 649ff.
[87] *Truth*, 6 Nov. 1884, p. 711.

political aspirations lacked the authoritarian tendency discernible in Chamberlain, who wrote to Gladstone on 23 December 1880 recommending concessions which the Irish could be compelled to accept.[88] Equally it contained none of Chamberlain's suspicion of home rule which was apparent even when he fought to make the coercion bill of 1882 less rigorous. Chamberlain then argued that unless some provisions were relaxed 'Home Rule, with all its possible dangers and consequences, will be within measurable distance'.[89] Labouchere's position was close to that of J. E. Redmond who stated in Brisbane on 13 April 1883 that Parnellites intended 'to restore to Ireland representative government . . . [as] a middle course between separation . . . and over-centralisation . . . [so] that the Empire which Ireland had a share in building up should not be dismembered'.[90] Moreover, responsible ministers supported reforms, some parts of which though much less advanced were not too dissimilar from those commended by Labouchere. On 19 January 1885, the policy Spencer outlined to Harcourt consisted of 'two big measures', 'the complete reform of Local Government in Ireland' and substitution of a 'Secretary of State for the Lord Lieutenant'.[91] The negative side of Spencer's policy was further coercive legislation: Labouchere invariably opposed coercion because it preceded redress of Irish grievances. Labouchere did not explain his assertion that separation would be as disadvantageous to Ireland as to England but the arguments he used on 29 April 1886 were: 'where were the Irish to separate to? . . . How could they maintain a great army and navy? . . . we were the greatest buyers of Irish produce . . . where . . . would the Irish be if we shut our ports?'[92]

COERCION

Labouchere consistently opposed the application of coercive policies to Ireland. In 1880 the liberal government administered

[88] G.P., B.M. Add. MSS., 44125, fos. 57–8, Chamberlain to Gladstone, 23 Dec. 1880.
[89] S.P., Chamberlain to Spencer, 20 May 1882.
[90] *Queensland Times*, 17 April 1883.
[91] S.P., Spencer to Harcourt (copy), 19 Jan. 1885.
[92] *Ipswich Free Press*, 1 May 1886.

Ireland without resort to exceptional legislation for it allowed the coercive law of 1875 to lapse but Irish unrest, aggravated by the Lords' rejection of the Compensation for Disturbance bill, induced it to consider repression. In November 1880 rumours circulated 'curiously & mysteriously rife... as to dissensions in the Cabinet'[93] about coercion. Chamberlain dated Forster's final decision to adopt stringent measures as 21 November 1880.[94] On that day Labouchere wrote to J. Graham,[95] secretary of a committee of English radicals formed to support the government's efforts to frame just and equitable legislation for Ireland. This committee probably represented the Anti-Coercion Association which met on 24 November 1880 and decided to produce the *Radical*, a newspaper opposed to coercion.[96] Labouchere considered that the London radical clubs should make the administration aware that it could only expect radical support for coercion if outrages continued after redress of Irish grievances. He advised radicals to frame resolutions carefully, so that the government could draw no encouragement to seek exceptional powers from them, while the Irish could deduce that radicals would support repression under certain circumstances.

*Truth* in 1880 favoured therapeutic policies for Ireland and argued that the only logical alternative to concessions such as devolution of authority was coercion. The suspension of habeas corpus and military control of Ireland with passive resistance by the Irish would lead to an impasse: as the English could not prosecute an entire nation they would have to govern Ireland as the Russians governed Poland.[97]

In 1881 political developments Labouchere feared materialized. The government's major legislative enactments were the Protection of Person and Property (Ireland) act[98] and the land act. It gave priority to the first measure notwithstanding Glad-

---

[93] H.P., B.M. Add. MSS., 48630, fo. 91, 18 Nov. 1880.
[94] J. Chamberlain, *A Political Memoir, 1880–1892*, p. 9; cf. G.P., B.M. Add. MSS., 44157, 44158 for the correspondence between Gladstone and Forster in 1880.
[95] *Northampton Mercury Daily Reporter*, 23 Nov. 1880, Labouchere to J. Graham, 21 Nov. 1880.
[96] F. W. Soutter, *Recollections of a Labour Pioneer*, pp. 99ff.
[97] *Truth*, 30 Dec. 1880, p. 840.
[98] Hereafter referred to as the coercion bill or act of 1881.

stone's consistent reluctance to adopt coercion. Both bills convulsed parliament and misunderstandings between liberals and Parnellites proliferated. Even the magnitude of Gladstone's agrarian reform did not offset the adverse effects either of the preceding struggle over the coercion bill, or of this act's operation. Parnellites were aggrieved because the coercion act deprived Irishmen of fundamental guarantees of liberty possessed by Englishmen and also because the government had not consulted them about its agrarian legislation.[99] Coercion followed by agrarian reform failed to restore tranquillity to Ireland. Lawlessness persisted and on 13 October 1881 the government arrested Parnell.[100]

The independence of Labouchere's attitude towards the government's Irish policy became much more pronounced in 1881. He justified his actions by claiming that opposition by radicals to the government's coercive policy helped Gladstone, whom he described as the 'John ... paving the way for the coming Radical millennium',[101] to strengthen his position in the cabinet *vis-à-vis* the whigs. When the government introduced the 1881 coercion bill a small group of radicals including Labouchere[102] joined some Irish members[103] to oppose it: others such as Chamberlain and John Bright accepted coercion reluctantly in order to secure substantial agrarian reform.

Labouchere opposed the coercion bill in the Commons on 18 January 1881, primarily because it preceded remedial legislation. He prophesied that landowners, supported by coercive legislation, would evict more vigorously and that this would envenom the feelings of Irishmen.[104] A week later he unsuccessfully suggested an adjournment and an arrangement on procedure between the government and the Irish members who

[99] J. L. Hammond, pp. 240–1.   [100] *Times*, 14 Oct. 1881.
[101] *Morning Post*, 14 Dec. 1881. This had been the opinion of Salisbury in 1880. B.P., B.M. Add. MSS., 49688, fo. 22, Salisbury to Balfour, 10 April 1880. Granville, however, was of the opinion that while Gladstone 'remains a political leader, he is a *conservative* power'. Ge.P., P.R.O., 30/29/28, Granville to Argyll, 11 July 1885.
[102] Cowen, Thompson, Labouchere, Bradlaugh, Lawson in order of votes recorded against coercion in 1881. Full table in T. M. Healy, *English votes and Irish votes* (G.L., 6221).
[103] J. L. Hammond, p. 209. Fifty-one Irish members opposed coercion, 29 abstained, and 22 supported it.
[104] Hansard, 3rd ser., 257, 954–6, 18 Jan. 1881.

opposed the coercion bill. When some members interpolated their dissent he retorted that the Irish members were not 'lepers' but the representatives of an important part of the United Kingdom entitled to the same treatment as other members.[105] On 27 January 1881 he supported his unsuccessful amendment to the coercion bill with a 'clever, rascally, mischievous speech'[106] which included the observation that his 'private convictions' would not endanger the government as conservatives supported its coercive policy. He argued that the condition of Ireland did not justify suspension of habeas corpus and he analysed critically Forster's return of outrages to strengthen his case. He indicated several glaring anomalies in the return and defied members to find any community of similar size as law abiding as the Irish had been during the early part of 1881. The purpose of the act, he affirmed, was to enable landowners to collect rents.[107]

According to the *Radical*,[108] Labouchere feared that his constituents might not support him if he opposed coercion. In order to strengthen his position he may have prompted the Anti-Coercion Association, through R. A. Bennett who was connected with *Truth*, to pass a resolution which congratulated Northampton upon the actions of its representatives in opposing coercion.[109] Nevertheless some of his constituents reacted vigorously to his opposition. On 9 February 1881 the Northampton Liberal and Radical Union met to consider the actions of Northampton's members of parliament who were supporting the Irish nationalists on this issue. The 'long and excited'[110] discussion indicated the division of opinion that existed about the conduct of Labouchere, and of Bradlaugh who offered to resign. J. Gurney, the association's president, was denounced as a tyrant for refusing to put to the vote a resolution which criticized the conduct of the members of parliament for Northamp-

---

[105] Ibid., 1419, 25–26 Jan. 1881.
[106] L. Masterman (ed.), *Mary Gladstone—Mrs Drew, her diaries and letters*, 28 Jan. 1881, p. 216.
[107] Hansard, 3rd ser., 257, 1511–27, 27 Jan. 1881; cf. T. P. O'Connor, *The Parnell Movement*, p. 421; J. H. McCarthy, *England under Gladstone, 1880–1884*, p. 118.
[108] *Radical*, 15 Jan. 1881.
[109] *Radical*, 22 Jan. 1881. The association met on 18 January 1881.
[110] *Northampton Mercury*, 12 Feb. 1881.

ton. Two days after this meeting, Labouchere sent Gurney a letter which included many of the arguments he had used earlier and which provided a detailed justification of his actions.[111] In this letter, which the Northampton newspapers published on 19 February, Labouchere did not compromise his principles and he defiantly stated that 'nothing would induce me to remain silent when I believe that speech may be useful in the cause of liberty'.[112] On 23 February the association resumed its 'stormy' proceedings over the conduct of Labouchere and Bradlaugh but after three hours' debate the members secured the support of a 'clear majority'.[113] While Labouchere did not move from the position he had taken, he owed much to the firmness of J. Gurney who prevented a vote being taken at the end of the meeting on 9 February, for there were clear indications that a resolution which criticized Labouchere and Bradlaugh would have been carried. Labouchere had no further difficulties with his local association despite the fact that he continued to act independently. He may have secured his base by greater vigilance, by the strength of his arguments, and by the harmony between his principles and liberal traditions.[114]

The delicacy of Labouchere's relationship with his constituents did not cause him to weaken the vigour of his support for Irish nationalists. In the Commons he spoke six times in February 1881[115] in vain attempts to induce the government to temper coercion with concession. With Bradlaugh and J. Cowen, who represented Newcastle upon Tyne as a radical, he brought into strong relief the arbitrary nature of the coercion bill and the extent to which Irish liberties lay at the mercy of the chief secretary.[116] F. H. O'Donnell went so far as to claim that this assistance from English radicals deepened the feeling in

---

[111] *Northampton Mercury*, 19 Feb. 1881; *Northamptonshire Guardian*, 19 Feb. 1881; *Daily News*, 14 Feb. 1881.
[112] The *Northampton Herald*, on 19 February 1881, considered that Labouchere exhibited 'bad logic and worse spirit' and 'scandalously' disregarded the solemnity of the question.
[113] *Northampton Mercury*, 26 Feb. 1881.
[114] He may have used other methods of persuasion too, for in 1898 he told Sir W. V. Harcourt that the local association was 'sound . . . in the sense that I pay everything, & it does whatever is wanted'. W.V.H.P., Labouchere to Harcourt, 25 May 1898.
[115] 7, 11, 15, 18, 21, 25 February.      [116] Lord Eversley, p. 143.

America that Ireland was being harshly treated.[117] Labouchere strove to minimize the retrospective operation of the measure[118] and to reduce the period during which habeas corpus would be suspended.[119] He argued, somewhat inconsistently with his attribution of the measure to Irish landlords, that the coercion bill threatened the 'whole people of Ireland' and would alienate all classes in Ireland from the English connection. He had previously stated that Irish members had every justification to oppose the coercion bill vigorously but he showed an awareness of the prejudice generated in England by the obstruction of parliamentary business. Although not blameless himself in this respect, he advised Irish members to avoid it and allow their case to stand on its merits.[120]

The Commons, with new rules of procedure, passed the coercion bill on 28 February 1881. The government promptly introduced a complementary measure, the Peace Preservation (Ireland) bill,[121] which passed through the lower house by 11 March. Labouchere criticized it on 2 March on the grounds that it was being passed against the wishes of Irish members who considered it unwarranted, and that the House perpetuated Irish alienation from the English connection by legislating specifically for Ireland. He contended that the government abetted 'disunion and separation' when they made distinctions between English and Irish law. As he lacked confidence in Irish magistrates he desired some form of appeal to a higher tribunal. He suspected that conservatives supported the government's coercive legislation in the hope that they would obtain additional electoral support at the next general election by widening the breach between liberals and Irish members.[122]

Labouchere drew attention to some of the consequences of coercion. He commented favourably about Davitt before and after his reimprisonment.[123] In May his sympathy for another

---

[117] F. H. O'Donnell, *A History of the Irish Parliamentary Party*, ii, 15; cf. D. Anderson, '*Scenes*' *in the Commons*, p. 261.
[118] Hansard, 3rd ser., 258, 694, 11 Feb. 1881.
[119] Ibid., 1420–2, 21 Feb. 1881.
[120] Ibid., 1774, 1783, 1784, 25 Feb. 1881.
[121] It is usually referred to as the Arms bill.
[122] Hansard, 3rd ser., 259, 26–30, 2 March 1881.
[123] Hansard, 3rd ser., 257, 1523, 27 Jan. 1881; 258, 1775, 25 Feb. 1881.

Irish leader caused him to ask Forster about the condition of Dillon, who was ill in Kilmainham prison.[124] In June 1881 he tried to ascertain whether landlords were taking advantage of the coercive legislation to compel the government to support them in evictions, 'the exercise of injustice'.[125] He also drew attention to specific instances of proposed evictions as when he asked whether current information about particularly harsh eviction decrees granted against tenants of Mrs Blake was correct, and if so whether the chief secretary would refuse police aid to enforce the evictions.[126] This question closely resembled one of a more general nature by Parnell[127] when the Lords rejected the Compensation for Disturbance bill in 1880 and received a similar answer from Forster: 'the Government would do wrong to refuse her the protection of the law'.[128] *Truth* consistently opposed the application of coercive legislation to Ireland and repeatedly stated that the government had to choose between a policy of coercion or concession: in its opinion no *via media* existed. It argued that Irish tenants when organized by the Land League possessed greater power than landlords, and would have prevented rackrenting if the government had not applied coercive legislation which allowed landlords to evict. Thus it claimed that the 'strength of the Empire' supported injustice in Ireland.[129] It deplored the 'no-rent' proclamation issued by Parnell and other League leaders on 18 October 1881, five days after their imprisonment, because it was a blunder that had given the government the technical right to suppress the Land League.[130]

Application of the coercion act of 1881, imprisonment of League leaders, and suppression of the Land League on 20 October 1881, brought little tranquillity to Ireland. Agitators entered secret societies and impunity from punishment spread like a plague.[131] Some agrarian discontent remained for poorer tenants and leaseholders did not benefit from the land

---

[124] Hansard, 3rd ser., 261, 23, 9 May 1881.
[125] Hansard, 3rd ser., 262, 344, 13 June 1881.
[126] Ibid., 849, 20 June 1881.    [127] Hansard, 3rd ser., 255, 314, 5 Aug. 1880.
[128] Hansard, 3rd ser., 262, 851, 20 June 1881.    [129] *Truth*, 15 Dec. 1881, p. 774.
[130] *Truth*, 27 Oct. 1881, p. 540. See C. Cruise O'Brien, pp. 73–4; M. Davitt, pp. 330–9.
[131] G.P., B.M. Add. MSS., 44160, fo. 99, Forster to Gladstone, 12 April 1882.

act of 1881 and arrears of rent meant that many tenants, otherwise eligible, could not benefit from its provisions. In 1882 the administration tried to work in conjunction with Parnellites, rather than in opposition to them, and despite O'Shea's mismanagement of the Kilmainham negotiations, which brought parliamentary opprobrium to the liberal government,[132] and the Phoenix Park murders on 6 May 1882, which led to more stringent coercive legislation for Ireland, the Kilmainham settlement endured,[133] though not in a way that benefited radicals.

On 1 February 1882 Labouchere informed his constituents that he would continue to act in parliament as he had done in the previous year to end 'ill-feeling ... on both sides of the Channel'.[134] Thus he provided the government with a 'little friendly criticism' of its Irish policy on 16 February. He argued that liberals had been unable to maintain laws to protect both property and liberty and had sacrificed the latter to preserve the former. He attacked Forster's administration of the 1881 coercive legislation and asserted that arbitrary power invariably caused injustice. He condemned the imprisonment of Parnell, indicated the weaknesses in the chief secretary's reasons for this action, and was particularly bitter about Forster's contention that Parnell did not mean what he said.[135]

The government released Parnell, Dillon and O'Kelly from Kilmainham on 2 May 1882 following negotiations[136] between Chamberlain and Parnell with O'Shea and McCarthy as intermediaries and hoped to administer Ireland without resort to coercive legislation. Chamberlain, according to McCarthy, expected to be appointed chief secretary when Forster resigned, and the Parnellites took him 'fully into their confidence' at this time.[137] However, Lord F. Cavendish secured the position and he and Burke the under-secretary were assassinated on 6 May 1882. Four days later Harcourt introduced the Prevention of Crime (Ireland) bill.[138] In the cabinet a bitter struggle raged between Chamberlain, and Harcourt and Spencer, the lord

[132] J. L. Hammond, p. 286.  [133] C. Cruise O'Brien, pp. 83–4.
[134] *Daily News*, 2 Feb. 1882.
[135] Hansard, 3rd ser., 266, 835–40, 16 Feb. 1882.
[136] J. Chamberlain, pp. 27–62.  [137] *Review of Reviews*, xii (July 1895), 26.
[138] Hereafter referred to as the coercion bill, or act, of 1882.

lieutenant.¹³⁹ Chamberlain wanted a moderate bill, specifically directed against intimidation and outrages,¹⁴⁰ or at least such modifications in the bill as the government, in his opinion, would have conceded if it had been a 'Scotch Bill opposed by Scotch members'.¹⁴¹ Spencer thought Chamberlain relied excessively on Irish members' statements in view of the fact that many of them were 'sore and exasperated' by the government's victory over the Land League.¹⁴² Harcourt 'declined to make any concessions to Parnell's wishes'.¹⁴³ Gladstone, though sympathetic to Irish requests, intended to pass the bill 'unimpaired in essence' after a speech by Dillon which he considered 'lifted the banner ... of illegality and ... revolt from Parnell'.¹⁴⁴ While a fierce outburst of anti-Irish feeling, certain scenes of which were compared with the Gordon riots,¹⁴⁵ and popular outcry for stringent measures supported the cabinet's determination to coerce Ireland, Labouchere courageously endeavoured to influence the cabinet, parliament, and public opinion at an inopportune time.

Labouchere sent Chamberlain, who was a particularly close associate at this time,¹⁴⁶ eight letters about the 1882 coercion bill. On 16 May he enclosed a draft of the bill with Healy's amendments upon it, which Parnell had later scrutinized.¹⁴⁷ In a covering letter he explained that their main objections were to constructive treason and the length of the bill's operation. Parnell, he asserted, would oppose the bill without obstruction if the government met his party 'in the conciliatory spirit of the amendments'.¹⁴⁸ Labouchere's letter the next day asserted that, in Healy's opinion, the newspaper clause ought to be restricted,

¹³⁹ S.P., Granville to Spencer, 11 June 1882.
¹⁴⁰ S.P., Chamberlain to Spencer, 24 May 1882.
¹⁴¹ J. Chamberlain, p. 66. Memorandum circulated by Chamberlain on 20 May 1882.   ¹⁴² S.P., Spencer to Chamberlain (copy), 25 May 1882.
¹⁴³ S.P., Granville to Spencer, 11 June 1882.
¹⁴⁴ S.P., Gladstone to Spencer, 24 May 1882.
¹⁴⁵ J. Denvir, *The Irish in Britain to the Death of Parnell*, p. 296.
¹⁴⁶ If Sir W. H. Lucy's memory was correct, Labouchere and Chamberlain were inseparable until the end of the 1885 session, and their relationship was closer than that between Chamberlain and Morley. *Cornhill*, n.s., xxxii (1912), 388.
¹⁴⁷ The draft of this bill has not been located.
¹⁴⁸ J.C., 5/50/8, Labouchere to Chamberlain, [?16 May 1882]; A. L. Thorold, *The Life of Henry Labouchere*, p. 161. The original reads 'obstruction', not 'abstention' as in Thorold, and 'disquieted' instead of 'disgusted'.

the search clause ought to contain provision for nominative warrants and provision for compensation if searchers damaged property, and that the right of appeal ought to exist from a county court judge to the queen's bench.[149] On 22 May Labouchere informed Chamberlain that Parnell approved of the arrears bill, which the government introduced on 15 May 1882, and thought it would soothe Ireland provided concessions were made in the coercion bill.[150]

Early in June, during Chamberlain's absence from parliament, Labouchere wrote to Grosvenor,[151] allegedly at Parnell's request, in an attempt to persuade the government to exclude treason, unless it were defined, and treason felony from the coercion bill.[152] Labouchere stated that if Parnell could not secure these concessions he might lose control of the Irish national movement to extremists such as Egan. Later in the letter, however, Labouchere affirmed that Parnell had stated that nationalists such as Dillon were isolated and without influence, while the Fenians were powerless, because they received no money from Americans who disapproved of the 'no-rent manifesto'.[153] Parnell, Labouchere continued, stated that if the government passed a provisional measure to protect poorer tenants until the land courts decided their cases, expanded the purchase clauses of the land act, and appointed a royal commission to inquire into the condition of agricultural labourers,[154] the Irish leaders would consider the land agitation closed and would strive to obtain some measure of local self-government: not 'any extreme Home Rule measure, but only such a one as he [Parnell] conceived Mr Gladstone could grant'.[155]

[149] J.C., 5/50/3, Labouchere to Chamberlain, 17 May 1882; A. L. Thorold, p. 162.

[150] J.C., 5/50/4, Labouchere to Chamberlain, 22 May 1882; A. L. Thorold, pp. 162-3.

[151] G.P., B.M. Add. MSS., 44315, fos. 76-9, Labouchere to Grosvenor, [?2 June 1882].

[152] On 8 June 1882, *Truth* (p. 783) still considered that the government might make concessions to the Parnellites.

[153] This may have caused liberal leaders to underestimate the difficulty of Parnell's position.

[154] *Truth*, on 1 June 1882 (p. 751), published these 'moderate proposals of accommodation'.

[155] G.P., B.M. Add. MSS., 44315, fo. 78, Labouchere to Grosvenor, [?2 June 1882].

Grosvenor, who replied the same day, would not commit the government but he requested Labouchere to advise Parnell to raise the question of treason and treason felony at the report stage as this would enable the government to consult its Irish officials.[156]

Labouchere resumed his correspondence with Chamberlain on 3 June 1882 when he gave him an account of his exchange with Grosvenor, and details of the three remedial measures desired by Parnell. He also stated that although 'Harcourt was the difficulty' reasonable grounds existed for anticipating concessions from the government on treason and treason felony at the report stage.[157] On 8[158] and 9 June[159] he sent Chamberlain further details about the importance to Parnell of modifications to the intimidation clause. Labouchere mentioned that Russell, Bryce and Davey were attempting to draft an amendment to restrict the application of this clause. In his next letter on 10 June,[160] Labouchere supplied details of the need for closer definition of certain parts of the coercion bill and of the need for a barrister to sit with the residential magistrates.[161]

Later in the bill's progress through the Commons, on 24 June, Labouchere reported to Chamberlain that he had spoken to Parnell, as Chamberlain had requested, and gave his

---

[156] G.P., B.M. Add. MSS., 44315, fos. 80–2, Grosvenor to Labouchere, 2 June 1882.

[157] J.C., 5/50/5, Labouchere to Chamberlain, 3 June 1882; A. L. Thorold, pp. 164–5. This may be the letter referred to when Gladstone wrote to Chamberlain on 8 June 1882. His attitude was that 'It is not for me to take any notice of what some would call the threat that things may revert to what they were.' J. Chamberlain, p. 68. It may well be an undated letter, from Labouchere to Chamberlain (G.P., B.M. Add. MSS., 44125, fo. 150) which Gladstone sent to Granville with the following comment: 'Please consider with care what should be said in the Cabinet ... on the subject of the enclosed letter. I take it upon me to let you know the case as it stands between Parnell and Egan but I beg of you to be kind enough not to let it go further. The question is what can and what should be said in the Cabinet ... My opinion is that if Parnell goes, no restraining influence will remain; the scale of outrage will soon be enlarged and no repression can avail to put it down.' J. L. Hammond, p. 361.

[158] J.C., 5/50/6, Labouchere to Chamberlain, 8 June 1882; A. L. Thorold, p. 165. The original reads 'Davey' not 'Davy'.

[159] J.C., 5/50/9, Labouchere to Chamberlain, 9 June 1882; A. L. Thorold, pp. 166–7.

[160] J.C., 5/50/10, Labouchere to Chamberlain, 10 June 1882; A. L. Thorold, pp. 168–9.

[161] Under the 1882 coercion act trained assessors assisted residential magistrates.

answer. Parnell, according to this account, stated that as his party had not obtained the concessions it expected, it would confine its activity to parliament and would allow the government and extremists 'to fight it out in Ireland'. He expressed his desire to implement the Kilmainham policy 'and to work with the Government in bringing the active phase of Irish agitation to a close', but said that he was unable to do this if he were suspected of ulterior motives and could show no gains for his party.[162]

Labouchere's attempts to influence the cabinet via Chamberlain failed. He was not the most important intermediary between the government and the Parnellites. Chamberlain used Captain O'Shea in this capacity[163] and after 2 June 1882 Mrs O'Shea was an intermediary between Gladstone and Parnell.[164] It is impossible to ascertain whether Labouchere 'unfortunately' was 'made by Parnell ... his spokesman', or whether he took 'upon himself to act as ... ambassador between the Parnellites & the Govt.'[165] However, Labouchere supported his attempts to obtain concessions outside parliament with such vigorous opposition to the coercion bill of 1882 in the Commons that O'Shea convinced Harcourt, perhaps too easily, that 'the main author of the obstruction is Labouchere, who organizes, instigates, and provokes it far beyond the desire of the Irish themselves out of sheer love of mischief'.[166] On 18 May when the government carried the second reading of the coercion bill, Labouchere predicted that the measure would fail because it attacked the people of Ireland in addition to ruffians with the result that most Irishmen would not co-operate with the government to prevent outrages.[167]

He attacked clauses of the bill when he joined the Irish in

---

[162] J.C., 5/50/11, Labouchere to Chamberlain, 24 June 1882; A. L. Thorold, pp. 169–70.
[163] J. Chamberlain, p. 64.
[164] K. Parnell, *Charles Stewart Parnell*, i, 269–71.
[165] H.P., B.M. Add. MSS., 48632, fos. 65, 70, 9 and 20 June 1882. One suspects that E. W. Hamilton's second opinion was correct.
[166] A. G. Gardiner, *The Life of Sir William Harcourt*, i, 448, Harcourt to Gladstone, 18 June 1882. On 23 June 1882 O'Shea advised Chamberlain to speak to Labouchere if he wished to reduce obstruction. J.C., 8/8. O'Shea appears to exaggerate Labouchere's influence with Irish members and to attribute false motives for his actions. [167] Hansard, 3rd ser., 269, 985–90, 18 May 1882.

their 'spirited but constitutional'[168] opposition to the bill. He helped to have clause four of the bill amended so that the intimidation clause did not deprive the Irish of liberties secured to Englishmen by the trade union legislation of 1875.[169] He offered advice on procedure to Parnell[170] and in the latter's absence 'took upon himself the duty of amending',[171] with qualified success, the bill's provisions in connection with treason and treason felony. The government had not made the concessions on these issues for which he had hoped on 3 June. After the suspension of twenty-five Irish members for obstruction during an all-night session, 30 June to 1 July, and the voluntary withdrawal of Parnellites from participation in debates on the coercion bill, Labouchere tried to move amendments for Healy and Redmond. The chairman prevented this, so he moved Redmond's amendment in his own name and announced his intention to bring up Healy's later.[172] On 7 July, the day of the coercion bill's third reading, Labouchere moved an amendment that aimed to secure aliens favourable treatment which he thought accorded with the wishes of Irish members.[173] He moved several other amendments and in his concluding speech on this bill expressed the view that the 'friends of Ireland and the friends of sound Liberalism' had been outvoted.[174] Even at this late stage he advised the government to introduce a short bill directed against outrages and boycotting and assured it that Irish members would not oppose such a measure.

On 11 May 1882 *Truth* argued that the extremists who murdered Cavendish and Burke intended to end the government's policy of conciliation and hinder the removal of causes of discontent between Ireland and England. It claimed, however, that arguments used the previous week to justify the change from

---

[168] C. Cruise O'Brien, p. 83.
[169] Hansard, 3rd ser., 270, 403, 7 June 1882; 270, 877, 12 June 1882.
[170] Hansard, 3rd ser., 269, 2024, 2 June 1882; 270, 1100, 13 June 1882.
[171] Hansard, 3rd ser., 271, 1488, 4 July 1882.
[172] Ibid., 1207-8, 30 June-1 July 1882.
[173] Ibid., 1835, 7 July 1882.
[174] Ibid., 1838, 1839, 1843, 1844, 1849, 7 July 1882. During the committee stage of the bill, Labouchere spoke on 22 different days, often more than once. The Division Lists of 1882 reflect his nice balance between abstention and opposition to the coercion bill. In 124 divisions, he abstained 62 times, voted with the minority 60 times, and was twice a teller for defeated amendments.

coercive policies were equally valid.[175] Its next issue criticized the coercion bill of 1882 because its provisions were designed to control the press, public meetings and open political agitation, as well as criminals; it prophesied that the government would receive no help from Irishmen in its struggle against crime; and it regretted the passing of a propitious 'opportunity to unite the Irish and English in a common policy for the maintenance of law, order, and liberty'.[176]

Labouchere continued to express similar opinions. In part of an article in the *Fortnightly Review* of March 1883, he touched upon Irish affairs. He asserted that the 'Kilmainham treaty' was a figment of conservatives' brains and that the release of the Irish leaders would have produced 'a new departure in the relations of the Parliamentary Irish with the Liberal Party'[177] if the government had omitted some clauses from the coercion act of 1882. He took a similar line when he spoke at Huddersfield on 17 March 1883.[178] He deplored outrages and assassinations but he also reminded his audience of the centuries of misgovernment borne by Ireland, and informed it that while a 'single injustice' remained there he would try to remove it. He claimed for Ireland the same liberty for public meetings and the expression of political opinion as existed in England. *Truth* continued to oppose coercive legislation for Ireland partly on the grounds that 'repression only intensifies a popular movement'.[179]

During the Maamtrasna debate, on 27 October 1884, Labouchere demonstrated unequivocally his opposition to coercion in an Irish context and his sympathy for the Parnellites' case.[180] A savage multiple murder was committed during August 1882 in a part of Connemara where destitution and non-political agrarian strife were endemic. These murders set in motion a sequence of events that brought the judicial decision upon the culprits into question and with it the English administration of justice in Ireland. Labouchere considered much of the debate irrelevant to the basic problem which, in his opinion, was

[175] *Truth*, 11 May 1882, pp. 639–40.
[176] *Truth*, 18 May 1882, pp. 677–8. The murders appalled the Parnellites who vigorously denounced their perpetrators.
[177] *Fortnightly Review*, xxxiii (1 March 1883), p. 374.
[178] *Huddersfield Chronicle*, 19 March 1883.  [179] *Truth*, 23 Aug. 1883, p. 269.
[180] Hansard, 3rd ser., 293, 296–8, 27 Oct. 1884.

whether there ought to be an inquiry into the trial. He favoured an inquiry on the grounds that if similar circumstances had arisen in England and a demand for an inquiry had won widespread support amongst English political and ecclesiastical leaders the government would have granted one. Moreover, he believed Irish disaffection arose because of the application in Ireland of a system of justice which differed from that in England. He concluded his short speech by advising Harrington that the amendment he had moved, and which had given rise to the debate, might gain more support if he omitted the part of it which criticized the general administration of law in Ireland. Harrington revised his amendment to 'satisfy the modest scruples'[181] of Labouchere, but the amendment remained, in effect, a vote of censure on Lord Spencer's administration and was defeated.[182]

Lord Spencer's country seat was near Northampton and his administration of Ireland earned him much respect in the borough. Labouchere explained to his constituents, in a letter dated 4 November 1884,[183] his reasons for supporting an inquiry into the Maamtrasna sentences. He argued that the coercion act of 1882 had turned the Commons into a court of appeal for Irish judicial decisions and that as a juror he had to decide impartially. He regretted that the intemperate language of Irish members and their reckless attacks upon individuals made it difficult for most English liberals to support them but this, he urged, did not affect the issue. He praised the statesmanship of Spencer and Trevelyan and suggested that their failure to achieve a *modus vivendi* between the English and their 'Irish fellow countrymen' indicated the need for a fundamental change in the system of governing Ireland. *Truth*, on 30 October 1884, suggested that the disparity between the 25,000 troops garrisoned in Ireland and the 3,320 in Scotland was an instructive comment on English policy and recommended a suspension of the coercion act of 1882 in order to ascertain whether it was still necessary.[184]

---

[181] *Times*, 28 Oct. 1884 (3rd leader).
[182] Division Lists, 1884–5, No. 1, 28 Oct. 1884.
[183] *Northampton Mercury*, 8 Nov. 1884; *Northamptonshire Guardian*, 8 Nov. 1884.
[184] *Truth*, 30 Oct. 1884, pp. 670–1.

## LAND

Labouchere's views on Irish agrarian problems, coercion and home rule were interdependent. In parliament on 27 January 1881 he doubted whether the establishment of fixity of tenure in Ireland would weaken the imperial bond between England and Ireland and he was 'not prepared to admit that English Members had the right to legislate regarding the tenure of land in Ireland except to register the opinions of the majority of the Irish nation'.[185] *Truth* developed the latter of these views. In February 1882 it claimed for the Irish power to legislate 'in regard to property or anything else of local application',[186] and stated that alternative schemes 'ought to break down'[187] if the British tried to impose their policies upon the Irish. It also placed the problem in an imperial context. There was

> no more reason why we English should claim the right to make land laws for Ireland than for Canada or New Zealand ... The laws of Canada or of New Zealand may be, in our opinion, bad; but our opinion in regard to them is not asked, nor can we pretend to set ourselves up as judges of them.[188]

Labouchere did not refer to Irish agrarian issues during his electoral campaign of 1880, but his attitude towards aspects of them began to emerge in the parliamentary session that followed. On 22 June 1880 he elicited from Forster, the chief secretary, the information that the government hoped that the schedule for the Compensation for Disturbance bill was final.[189] This measure, which the Lords later rejected, would have enabled some tenants in certain parts of Ireland to claim compensation for the disturbance of evictions if they could prove that they were unable to pay their rent because of the two preceding bad harvests and were prepared to continue the tenancy on equitable terms but that the landlord had refused such terms. A month later Labouchere regretted that the bill did not apply to the whole of Ireland and voted with the minority in an attempt to

---

[185] Hansard, 3rd ser., 257, 1513, 27 Jan. 1881.
[186] *Truth*, 23 Feb. 1882, p. 265.
[187] *Truth*, 20 April 1882, p. 535.
[188] *Truth*, 6 April 1882, p. 471.
[189] Hansard, 3rd ser., 253, 540, 22 June 1880.

prevent its regional application.[190] He also supported in the division lobbies O'Connor Power's amendment which aimed to attract the government's attention to the gravity of the Irish tenants' position,[191] a bill designed to secure fixity of tenure in Ireland,[192] and McCarthy's attempt to secure adequate representation for Irish tenants upon a commission inquiring into the operation of the 1870 land act.[193]

When Labouchere addressed his constituents in October 1880 he stated that English radicals meant to act in a just and generous spirit towards Ireland but were not prepared to make good deficiencies of rent to Irish landlords. He advocated fixity of tenure for Irish tenants, recognized that the Land League had certain legitimate aims, and considered that its confederation of Irish tenants to force landlords to reduce extortionate rents 'by moral means' justifiable. At the same time, he deplored outrages and the failure of Irish leaders to condemn them.[194] Labouchere never mentioned in public more detailed information he possessed about the League. Davitt later admitted that some of its local branches were 'used as a shield for the ulterior ends of the more advanced movement'.[195] Labouchere told Chamberlain in December 1880 that they were composed of men 'entirely without character' who ignored the central committee: 'The mass of the people are getting weary of the domination which these Local Branches exercise, and only hold to them, because they believe that the League itself is likely to secure to them the redress of all reasonable grievances.'[196]

*Truth* echoed the views Labouchere expressed to his constituents but its comments were more detailed and its proposals more advanced. It emphasized the wide support for the Land League,[197] prophesied that imprisonment of its leaders would not prevent the spread of boycotting,[198] and, presumably to

---

[190] Hansard, 3rd ser., 254, 848, 19 July 1880; Division Lists, 1880, (2), No. 67, 19 July 1880.
[191] Division Lists, 1880, (2), No. 2, 20 May 1880.
[192] Ibid., No. 33, 30 June 1880.      [193] Ibid., No. 94, 5 Aug. 1880.
[194] *Northampton Evening Herald*, 28 Oct. 1880; *Northampton Mercury Daily Reporter*, 28 Oct. 1880.
[195] M. Davitt, p. 311.
[196] G.P., B.M. Add. MSS., 44125, fos. 53-6, Labouchere to Chamberlain, 17 Dec. 1880.
[197] *Truth*, 30 Dec. 1880, p. 839.      [198] *Truth*, 9 Dec. 1880, p. 747.

secure the League greater working-class support in England, claimed that it applied trade union principles in an Irish context.[199] The duke of Argyll, whose sympathies lay with the landlords, saw the situation in similar terms for he complained of the 'great agrarian strike' in Ireland.[200] In 1881 H. Broadhurst, an English trade union leader, 'resented the comparison made by some Irishmen between the Land League and the English trade unions'.[201] *Truth* also expressed an approval of Irish nationalist leaders that was absent initially in Labouchere's speeches. It praised Parnell's leadership of his party, congratulated him for making land reform imperative,[202] and referred to Davitt as the 'noble minded founder of the Land League'.[203] It explained the harsh realities of Irish land tenure, gave figures to show that Irish landowners levied £712,000 annually in excess of the land's value and argued that this caused the disturbances.[204] It also placed Irish terrorism in perspective: 'never has what may be termed almost a revolution of an entire country proved successful with so little bloodshed'.[205]

*Truth* advocated redress of all land grievances,[206] and, in particular, the conversion of the occupier of the land into its owner[207] by a system of compulsory land purchase which, in turn, depended upon strong organs of local government which did not exist in 1880 in the United Kingdom:

> allow every county in Ireland to force all proprietors to sell their land, and to take payment in land bonds of the county. Rent would then become a land tax, and, as if any individual did not pay the tax, it would have to be borne by his neighbours, all would have a direct interest in seeing that no-one shirked his liabilities.[208]

In parliament Labouchere's views were more circumspect. On 18 January 1881 he first emphasized the restraining influence of the Land League and argued that its suppression would

---

[199] *Truth*, 16 Dec. 1880, p. 770; 30 Dec. 1880, p. 840.
[200] R.P., B.M. Add. MSS., 43628, fo. 30, Argyll to Ripon, 1 Dec. 1880.
[201] J. L. Hammond, p. 208, n.1. By 1886 the papal newspaper *Moniteur de Rome* used a trade union analogy to describe the situation in Ireland. *Freeman's Journal*, 17 Dec. 1886.
[202] *Truth*, 23 Dec. 1880, p. 805.
[203] *Truth*, 16 Dec. 1880, p. 771.
[204] *Truth*, 28 Oct. 1880, p. 538.
[205] *Truth*, 30 Dec. 1880, p. 840.
[206] *Truth*, 18 Nov. 1880, p. 633.
[207] *Truth*, 30 Dec. 1880, p. 840.
[208] *Truth*, 26 Aug. 1880, p. 273.

canalize Irish opposition into secret societies. In this speech he temporarily abandoned his opposition to compensation for landlords and suggested that 'the people of England would willingly vote' an indemnity to cover landowners' losses if the government introduced legislation to establish a truce in Ireland before it applied coercive policies.[209] He continued to act intermittently on behalf of Irish tenants and twice[210] failed to secure them greater protection before Gladstone introduced his land bill on 7 April 1881. On 25 February 1881, the second of these occasions, he concentrated upon tenants who held less than ten acres, whose position was parlous, and who were to be exempted from the provisions of the agrarian legislation of 1881. However, he paid little attention to Gladstone's land bill of 1881 which was perhaps 'the most revolutionary measure that passed through Parliament in the nineteenth century'.[211]

Labouchere expressed his views on agrarian issues more clearly outside the House. *Truth*, on 24 February 1881, drew attention to the 200,000 tenants who farmed less than ten acres and the gravity of their position, the day before Labouchere raised the matter in parliament.[212] He did not mention in parliament the six improvements to the land bill, which British governments subsequently made to the land laws, that *Truth* recommended in April 1881.[213] The Local Registration of Title act, 1891, established local registries and a central land registry;[214] the land act of 1887 admitted leaseholders to the benefits of the act of 1881;[215] the land purchase act of 1885 enabled some tenants to borrow the entire purchase price while subsequent acts in 1888, 1896, 1903 and 1909 increased the

---

[209] Hansard, 3rd ser., 257, 954–6, 18 Jan. 1881.
[210] Ibid., 1511–27, 27 Jan. 1881; 258, 1780, 25 Feb. 1881.
[211] J. L. Hammond, p. 167. Labouchere did not speak on the bill. In 124 divisions he supported the government 37 times and opposed it on 16 occasions in attempts to afford tenants greater legal protection, and to oppose the Lords' amendments.
[212] *Truth*, 24 Feb. 1881, p. 245. Parl. Pap., 1881, xvi (2), 843 analysed Irish landholdings as follows: not exceeding 1 acre, 48,448; between 1 and 5 acres, 74,809; between 5 and 15 acres, 171,383.
[213] *Truth*, 21 April 1881, pp. 541–2.
[214] R. B. McDowell, *The Irish Administration, 1801–1914*, p. 132.
[215] M. Davitt, p. 326.

capital available for this purpose and modified the terms on which it was borrowed;[216] the act of 1909 first included qualified provision for compulsory purchase;[217] the land act of 1881 itself substituted a different tribunal of first instance for county court judges, for the lord lieutenant under its provisions appointed assistant commissioners, two or more of whom acted as a court of first instance in fair rent cases;[218] legislation in 1886 for crofters in Scotland first contained provisions to reduce individual litigation[219] but in Ireland the problem tended to persist.[220]

Labouchere did not combine such prescience with any campaign in the press, in parliament, or in the constituencies. Relief for tenants burdened with arrears of rent, for instance, could well have been added to the six improvements to the land bill advocated by *Truth*. Labouchere considered the lack of provisions for such tenants a major defect of the act of 1881 but he virtually ignored this problem until the government introduced the arrears bill[221] in 1882. Then, in July 1882, he concentrated upon protesting against the possibility of English taxpayers having to pay debts owed to Irish landlords.[222] He also failed to carry an amendment designed to prevent a harsh landlord from profiting from his previous 'injustice'.[223] He had previously stated at Northampton on 13 December 1881 that radicals could not compensate Irish landowners for losses incurred through the operation of the land act for if this were done, landowners whom the land courts had 'found guilty of felony against humanity', would be paid in proportion to their iniquity.[224]

[216] J. E. Pomfret, *The Struggle for Land in Ireland, 1800–1923*, pp. 228–31, 260–9, 271–5, 291–308.
[217] Ibid., pp. 308–11.
[218] R. B. McDowell, *The Irish Administration*, p. 219.
[219] J. L. Hammond, p. 226.
[220] L. P. Curtis, Jr, *Coercion and Conciliation in Ireland, 1880–1892*, pp. 342–3, 354–5.
[221] By its provisions tenants on holdings valued on Griffith's valuation at £30 or less, paid one year's arrears, and if they satisfied Land Commissioners that they could not pay earlier arrears, the state made a gift to the landlord of half the outstanding debt while the remainder was cancelled. J. L. Hammond, p. 302.
[222] Hansard, 3rd ser., 272, 155, 11 July 1882.
[223] Ibid., 472, 476, 14 July 1882; Division Lists, 1882, No. 262, 14 July 1882.
[224] *Northampton Mercury*, 17 Dec. 1881.

Some of Labouchere's arguments and proposals were similar to some of those advanced by conservatives who supported voluntary schemes of land purchase after 1881. They were also open, in part, to the objection of 'making the purchasers guarantee one another'[225] that Forster levelled against Childers' scheme in 1880. In April 1882 Longfield, chief judge of the Irish landed estates court, produced a plan that included provision for recovery of losses from county rates and the opinion that 'It is not likely, that a man's neighbours will assist or encourage him to resist the payment of a just debt when the consequence of a successful resistance will be that they must pay it themselves.'[226] Lord G. Hamilton's scheme in 1883 provided for local authorities to issue debentures secured on local rates. Such proposals by conservatives depended upon guarantees from the central government.

*Truth* opposed the use of the resources of the United Kingdom to compensate sectional class interests in Ireland and the use of such resources for land purchase there. It also argued against the issue of bonds to finance land purchase on the grounds that these would be held mainly in England: wealth would drain annually from Ireland and England would become Ireland's landlord. Its prophecy that the Irish would eventually 'repudiate their liability to an alien absentee'[227] was fulfilled in the 1930s. *Truth*'s remedy rested upon the concession to Ireland of local self-government. Then, if they chose, the Irish could follow the policy *Truth* attributed to Parnell in November 1881 and buy out landowners with bonds based on the security of Ireland, held by Irishmen and American sympathizers.[228] Alternatively the Irish could convert rent into the payment of interest on a loan and pay off Irish landowners in bonds secured upon Irish taxes. *Truth* considered that the United Kingdom should bear the financial responsibility for a scheme of land purchase only if it applied to the whole of the United Kingdom: if it were limited to one kingdom the liability should be limited to that one alone.[229]

[225] G.P., B.M. Add. MSS., 44158, fos. 39–46, W. E. Forster to Gladstone, 8 Dec. 1880.
[226] J. E. Pomfret, p. 223.
[227] *Truth*, 20 April 1882, p. 534.   [228] *Truth*, 3 Nov. 1881, p. 576.
[229] *Truth*, 20 April 1882, pp. 534–5; *Truth*, 28 June 1883, p. 903.

## OTHER ISSUES

Labouchere's diagnosis of Ireland's maladies and his prescriptions for them were associated with his desire to secure Parnellite support for the liberal party and more particularly for its radical wing. As early as March 1880 he may have appealed to Parnellites outside his electorate, in which an Irish element was insignificant, for he recorded his support for an inquiry into Irish grievances.[230] Imprecision of reported speech precludes a definite conclusion but this may have been synonymous with a pledge candidates for English constituencies had to give if they wished to secure Irish electors.[231] Labouchere considered Parnellites sound on most radical issues and was more sympathetic towards them from 1880 than most English radicals.[232] In 1881 he affirmed his belief that upon issues such as the land question and devolution of authority to the counties 'the Democracy of England and Ireland ought to unite'[233] and in 1882 he equated Parnellites with the 'Leaders of the Irish nation'.[234] *Truth* considered that Parnell would hold the balance of power at Westminster after the subsequent election for it concurred with Parnell's prediction that his party would then secure approximately seventy-five seats.[235]

Labouchere reinforced his public activities with private attempts to influence political developments. In 1880 he made contacts with some Parnellites, perhaps when he supported them in parliament, perhaps in his advocacy of Bradlaugh's case, or perhaps through his journalistic activities, and earned some confidences from them. On 17 December 1880 he sent Chamberlain details of developments in Parnellite circles and pleaded for agrarian reform together with the establishment of elected county boards. Labouchere wrote approximately six weeks after the government prosecuted Parnell, Biggar, Dillon, T. D. Sullivan and Sexton for their Land League activities but

---

[230] *Northampton Mercury*, 27 March 1880; 3 April 1880; *Northampton Evening Herald*, 31 March 1880.
[231] *Fortnightly Review*, xxvii (1 Feb. 1880), 216.
[232] J. L. Hammond, p. 359; S. Maccoby, *English Radicalism, 1853–1886*, p. 268.
[233] Hansard, 3rd ser., 258, 1785, 25 Feb. 1881.
[234] Hansard, 3rd ser., 269, 987, 18 May 1882.
[235] *Truth*, 1 Feb. 1883, p. 153.

before the trials had begun, and ten days before the meeting which led to the defection of twelve whiggish home-rulers headed by Shaw from Parnell's leadership in January 1881. At a time when Davitt feared that the right wing of the Irish national movement might coalesce with the priests and wrest control from the active section,[236] Labouchere stated that there was a

*pronunciamento* simmering amongst Parnell's following in the House ... He is now entirely in the hands of Davitt, and practically only the figure head of the ultra Fenians. Davitt's later uttrances [*sic*] are very distasteful to all the M.P.'s who are not actually returned with the money of the League,[237] and who consequently are not entirely dependent on it. The first fruits of this feeling showed itself in the proclamation that the League issued a few days ago denouncing outrages. The hard and fast slaves of the League in Parliament are not above six or seven in number.

Labouchere claimed that a Parnellite member, whom he did not name, considered that he could secure a majority of Parnellites at their meeting on 4 January 1881 to support a government measure that embodied fair rent, fixity of tenure and free sale. 'In confirmation of these divided counsels, T. P. O'Connor, who is a sort of Secretary of Parnell, told me' that such a measure 'would be accepted by the majority of the Parnellites after a few general protests'. Labouchere also included O'Connor Power's complaint that the chief secretary 'never consulted them about his contemplated course of action'. He warned Chamberlain that 'if a coercion Bill be brought in before the effect of concession has been tried, moderate and ultra Leaguers will be brought together'. The crux of his argument was that Parnell's apparent subservience to the 'far abler' Davitt, the objections of many of his followers to Davitt's 'wild theories', and the possibility of some consultation between the chief secretary and Parnellites provided the government with a 'golden opportunity to win over many of the Leaguers themselves'.[238] In his

---

[236] J. Devoy, *Devoy's Postbag*, ii, 23, Davitt to Devoy, 16 Dec. 1880.
[237] There was 'no party machine ... to pay candidates' expenses, ... although a certain amount of Land League money ... found its way into the war-chests of candidates favoured by the League'. C. Cruise O'Brien, p. 41.
[238] G.P., B.M. Add. MSS., 44125, fos. 53–6, Labouchere to Chamberlain, 17 Dec. 1880. Chamberlain sent the letter to Gladstone.

subsequent correspondence with Chamberlain, Labouchere emphasized the need to temper the severity of the coercion bill of 1882 to secure Parnellite support for liberals and on 9 February 1884 he tried to persuade Chamberlain to angle for Irish nationalist support: in his opinion the government would benefit if more radicals supported Parnellites because 'it would tend to an alliance'.[239]

Labouchere's advocacy of an alliance between English radicals and Irish nationalists and his prediction that this, if it materialized, would facilitate the passage of reforms for both countries, rested upon his calculation that such an alliance would drive whigs from the liberal party, tilt its internal balance to the left and yet permit liberals to retain, perhaps with Parnellite assistance, a parliamentary majority. Between 1880 and 1885 the prospect of such a political combination met strong resistance in some liberal circles. On 28 December 1883, for instance, Harcourt informed Gladstone that he and Hartington desired an 'open... conspicuous... incurable' breach between liberals and Parnellites. They dreaded 'the tendencies of Chamberlain who seems... to be always hankering after a policy which would secure the Parnellite vote'.[240]

However, some Parnellites favoured an alliance with English radicals on the grounds that it would divide English political forces, extend the Parnellites' conflict to England by attacking the British landed classes in the interests of the working classes, and weaken English supporters of Irish landlords.[241] Dillon originated this plan and McCarthy was one of the first to whom he suggested the possibilities of co-operation with English radicals in Parnellite circles.[242] So far as one can determine, Labouchere shared these views. He also considered that such an alliance would realign political forces by driving conservative influences from the party of progress. Moreover, if precedents for agrarian reform and devolution of power were established in Ireland they would be applied in England and would overthrow the landed classes with 'their arrogant pretensions, their absurd notions of social supremacy, their love of interference, their

[239] J.C., 5/50/19, Labouchere to Chamberlain, 9 Feb. 1884.
[240] A. G. Gardiner, i, 489.
[241] M. Davitt, p. 308.　　　　[242] J. McCarthy, *Reminiscences*, ii, 375.

encumbered estates, and their foolish ideas respecting their political *status*'.²⁴³ He proposed co-ordination of the activity of metropolitan radical clubs in November 1880²⁴⁴ but apparently he was not associated with McCarthy, Hyndman and Cowen when they attempted to federate them in 1881. The foundation of the Democratic Federation by Hyndman with Cowen's assistance between March and June 1881 stemmed from an unsuccessful attempt to co-ordinate radical clubs' activities. Its programme included adult suffrage, land nationalization, and legislative independence for Ireland.²⁴⁵ A manifesto issued by Parnell on 13 February 1881 advocated a

> junction between English democracy and Irish nationalism upon a basis of Ireland's right to make her own laws, the overthrow of territorialism in both countries, and enfranchisement of labor [*sic*] from crushing taxes ... [to] secure lasting friendship, based on mutual interest and confidence, between the two countries.²⁴⁶

In 1881 Irish leaders addressed English working-class audiences about Irish agrarian problems and Irish coercion acts,²⁴⁷ and won some extra-parliamentary support.²⁴⁸ They put their case to readers of some English journals.²⁴⁹

Parnell, in C. Cruise O'Brien's view,²⁵⁰ was probably sceptical of support from English radicals in 1881, but had cultivated it to secure his leadership of the Irish national movement when he turned away from revolutionary activity. During the debate on the coercion bill of 1882 hostility between English radicals and Parnellites became apparent.²⁵¹ The Irish party moved

---

[243] *Truth*, 21 April 1881, p. 542.
[244] *Northampton Mercury Daily Reporter*, 23 Nov. 1880, Labouchere to J. Graham, 21 Nov. 1880.
[245] C. Tsuzuki, *H. M. Hyndman and British Socialism*, pp. 36ff.; E. Belfort Bax, *Reminiscences and Reflexions of a mid and late Victorian*, p. 74; W. K. Lamb, 'British Labour and Parliament, 1867–1893' (Lond., Ph.D., 1933), p. 422.
[246] M. Davitt, pp. 307–8.
[247] *Daily News*, 17 Feb. 1881, McCarthy at Hackney; 18 April 1881, Parnell and T. P. O'Connor at Newcastle upon Tyne; 6 June 1881, Parnell at Hyde Park.
[248] *Radical*, 15 Jan. 1881.
[249] *Contemporary Review*, xxxviii (1880), 981, T. P. O'Connor; xliii (1883), 747, F. H. O'Donnell; *Nineteenth Century*, viii (1880), 861, J. McCarthy; xi (1882), 841, J. McCarthy; xiv (1883), 131, A. M. Sullivan; *Fortnightly Review*, xxxii (1882), 625, T. M. Healy.
[250] C. Cruise O'Brien, p. 63.    [251] *Hansard*, 3rd ser., 271, 1852, 7 July 1882.

decisively to the right and during 1883 the left wing of the Irish national movement lost its influence. According to Hyndman the Irish parliamentary party hated the Democratic Federation and tried to injure Davitt by connecting him with it.[252] In 1884 Parnell attacked Davitt for his land nationalization schemes and for his association with English radicals. Irish 'nationalist organs and speakers went out of their way to sneer at the radicals'.[253] This hostility sprang partly from disappointment at radicals' failure to oppose effectively coercion for Ireland, but primarily because previous dalliance with radicals had alarmed the Irish clergy who now staunchly supported the parliamentary party and the National League, established in October 1882. The National League differed from the Land League in that it was not an autonomous agrarian organization. The Irish parliamentary party dominated it and its programme was essentially orientated towards attainment of national self-government although it also included reform of the land laws, local self-government, extension of the franchise and economic development.[254] The National League supplied the national electioneering machinery which the parliamentary party had previously lacked. These developments affected the support Parnellites gave English radicals. For instance, in 1880 almost half the Parnellite party voted in favour of Bradlaugh's admission to parliament: in 1884 the entire party opposed it. This opposition provoked the Liberal and Radical Union at Northampton to express its 'indignation and disgust at the ungrateful conduct of Irish members' who, in opposing the affirmation bill, had ignored the steady support Labouchere and Bradlaugh had given them 'at the risk of much ill-odour among their constituents'.[255]

As Parnellite coolness towards English radicals became more apparent after July 1882, political developments reduced the opportunities for Labouchere to demonstrate his solidarity with them. Irish problems, particularly those connected with land, local self-government and coercion, continued to exercise and

[252] M.P. (5), Hyndman to Stead, 10 Nov. [?1884].
[253] C. Cruise O'Brien, p. 88.
[254] M. Davitt, p. 375.
[255] *Northamptonshire Guardian*, 12 May 1884. The executive passed this resolution on 7 May.

divide opinion within the cabinet but they did not lead to additional legislation. Agrarian legislation of 1881 arrested the development of large-scale capitalistic farming in Ireland which had previously been the basis of liberal economic policy. This legislation stimulated demands from Irish landlords and tenants for schemes of land purchase, and debates in parliament in 1883 demonstrated conservative support for Parnellite demands for this policy and for governmental development of Ireland's economy. The need to implement land purchase was one argument in favour of local self-government in Ireland: others were that devolution of power would bring co-operation, breed mutual affection and obviate the need for coercion. Gladstone, as he admitted to Granville in September 1881, was 'rather advanced as to Home or local rule'[256] and he considered 'Sound and strong local institutions for Ireland' the 'proper precondition'[257] for land purchase or state-sponsored economic development there. Chamberlain from 1883 increasingly supported state-aided economic reconstruction in Ireland. Harcourt and Hartington favoured the firm maintenance of law and order which in an Irish context meant coercion. Hartington opposed devolution of power to provincial councils in 1882 as a 'long step towards Home Rule and a representative body for all Ireland'.[258] Moreover, Irish affairs received less attention in the two years after 1882 than in the two preceding years for other reasons than division of opinion within the cabinet. Egyptian troubles and agitation for the extension of the franchise dominated politics. The intensity of Irish discontent declined as Gladstone's agrarian legislation had its effect; and the coercion act of 1882, which did not expire until August 1885,[259] enabled the lord lieutenant to suppress its manifestation in conventional political agitation. Gladstone showed marked reluctance to legislate for Ireland, even upon Spencer's recommendation.[260] Parnell, for personal and political reasons, tended to withdraw from the political scene and in 1883 and 1884 Healy and

---

[256] A. Ramm (ed.), *The Political Correspondence of Mr Gladstone and Lord Granville, 1876–1886*, i, 291, Gladstone to Granville, 13 Sept. 1881.
[257] G.P., B.M. Add. MSS., 44546, fo. 116, Gladstone to Spencer (copy), 21 May 1883.
[258] B. H. Holland, i, 345–6, Hartington to Granville, 15 April 1882.
[259] J. E. Pomfret, pp. 227–8. [260] J. L. Hammond, p. 341.

Sexton became caretakers of the party in parliament. The Parnellites prepared for the next general election.

Labouchere first stated that he wished to rally Parnellite members to the liberal party on 15 February 1881, although *Truth* hinted at this policy three months earlier.[261] He continued to pursue this objective despite changing responses from Parnellites to English radicals. Between 1880 and 1882 he actively opposed coercive policies, advocated devolution of political authority, and commented sympathetically, so far as tenants were concerned, on agrarian problems in Ireland. He sought to remove what was, in his opinion, the 'most regrettable hostility'[262] that developed during debates on coercive legislation in 1882 partly by reiterating these views in subsequent years. However, in doing so he paid less attention to agrarian problems and more to his advocacy of home rule. In parliament and in communications to his constituents, in speeches such as that at Huddersfield in March 1883,[263] in articles in the *Fortnightly Review*[264] and in *Truth*, his attitude remained sympathetic towards Parnellites and their political programme and in favour of an alliance amongst radicals in different parts of the United Kingdom.[265] This support for Parnellites was the more striking because *Truth* complained that they were making it difficult for radicals to support them by opposing the affirmation bill.[266] Labouchere, who alleged that the English press fanned Anglo-Irish animosity by its 'persistent abuse and misrepresentation',[267] slightly redressed this balance through *Truth*. He also embarked upon a certain amount of misrepresentation for his own purposes. A letter Labouchere sent Chamberlain in February 1884[268] suggests that *Truth*'s iconoclastic criticisms of Orangemen in 1884, which showed no awareness of, or sympathy for, the difficulties of their position, and which seriously underesti-

---

[261] *Northampton Herald*, 26 Feb. 1881, Labouchere to S. P. Blaxley, 15 Feb. 1881; *Truth*, 18 Nov. 1880, p. 634.
[262] Hansard, 3rd ser., 271, 1852, 7 July 1882.
[263] *Huddersfield Chronicle*, 19 March 1883; *Northampton Mercury*, 24 March 1883.
[264] *Fortnightly Review*, xxxiii (1 March 1883), 369ff.; xxxv (1 Feb. 1884), 223ff.
[265] *Truth*, 1 Feb. 1883, p. 153; 5 July 1883, p. 10; 22 Nov. 1883, p. 719; *Fortnightly Review*, xxxv (1 Feb. 1884), 224.
[266] *Truth*, 24 May 1883, p. 721.
[267] *Fortnightly Review*, xxxv (1 Feb. 1884), 224.
[268] J.C., 5/50/19, Labouchere to Chamberlain, 9 Feb. 1884.

mated their political influence,[269] were designed to help rally Parnellites to English radicals.

He also attempted to secure this objective in other ways. Some of the policies he advocated in an Irish context had a wider relevance and provided opportunities for radicals and Parnellites to work together. In October 1881 *Truth*[270] proposed what was later called home rule all round but Labouchere appears to have made no attempt to mobilize opinion in other parts of the United Kingdom for this policy. He did, however, participate in attempts to extend the land agitation to England. In speeches at Daventry[271] and Kettering[272] in 1883 he regretted that the Irish land act did not apply to other parts of Britain and on 9 January 1884 he took the chair at a meeting of the Land Reform Union: H. George and M. Davitt were the principal speakers and H. Broadhurst, T. Barclay, and Sir G. Campbell attended.[273]

Labouchere's support for Parnellites in parliament continued but in the absence of major legislation for Ireland it was comparatively restrained and sporadic. At the end of the parliamentary session of 1882, Gladstone, taunted by Churchill, offered to hold an inquiry into the release of Parnell and other prisoners from Kilmainham. Neither the government nor the Parnellites welcomed this prospect: Labouchere blocked a motion by Yorke for a select committee of inquiry,[274] and he prevented a similar attempt to reopen the question in 1883. He protested about issues such as the high cost of criminal proceedings[275] and inflammatory Orangist speeches made by Johnson, an Irish official.[276] He also transmitted information privately to the government. Thus in January 1884 he informed Grosvenor, the chief whip, that Parnellites would support the reform bill provided that it included extension of the franchise and that the government undertook to pass the measure in its entirety or resign.[277] In 1883 and 1884 he voted intermittently with

---

[269] *Truth*, 3 Jan. 1884, p. 12; 28 Feb. 1884, p. 301; 12 June 1884, p. 880.
[270] *Truth*, 27 Oct. 1881, p. 540.   [271] *Northampton Mercury*, 6 Jan. 1883.
[272] *Daily News*, 14 Dec. 1883.   [273] *Morning Post*, 10 Jan. 1884.
[274] *Northampton Mercury*, 25 Nov. 1882; *Northampton Daily Chronicle*, 21 Nov. 1882.
[275] Hansard, 3rd ser., 276, 1874, 8 March 1883; 276, 1984, 9 March 1883.
[276] Hansard, 3rd ser., 282, 136, 23 July 1883; 282, 1136, 31 July 1883.
[277] H.P., B.M. Add. MSS., 48635, fo. 66, 16 Jan. 1884.

Parnellites on Irish issues: he demonstrated his support most conspicuously during the Maamtrasna debate in October 1884.[278]

By 1884 Labouchere had established himself as a prominent English supporter of the Parnellites and as a minor channel of communication between them and some members of the administration. He tended to put his proposals for Ireland initially to his constituents, to develop them in *Truth*, and to express them more temperately in the Commons than in his journal. The absence of documentary evidence precludes identification of his sources of information but one might suggest that they included McCarthy, who was employed by the *Daily News* of which Labouchere was part proprietor, and Healy with whom Labouchere corresponded in 1885. Labouchere's reports of alleged conversations with Parnell in *Truth* and in a speech at Huddersfield need to be treated with caution for he may have used this form of expression for journalistic and rhetorical effect.

Labouchere's views harmonized with those of the Parnellites but in some respects they had a different emphasis. On 16 August 1879 the National Land League demanded the creation of a 'small proprietary, which alone can fully satisfy the Irish people'.[279] Parnell on 2 October 1881 linked the land question closely with attainment of 'legislative independence'.[280] Parnellites first moved an amendment in favour of home rule to the address in answer to the queen's speech on 8 February 1882.[281] The Irish National League, on 17 October 1882, gave priority to the 'restitution to the Irish people of . . . a parliament elected by the people of Ireland'[282] over the establishment of a peasant proprietary. From 27 October 1880 Labouchere gave precedence to devolution of authority so that the Irish could 'regulate their own affairs, and make Irish laws for the Irish nation'[283] and be empowered to implement and underwrite schemes of

---

[278] Division Lists, 1884, No. 27, 5 March 1884; No. 55, 4 April 1884; No. 178, 23 July 1884; Division Lists, 1884–5, No. 1, 28 Oct. 1884; No. 18, 19 Nov. 1884.
[279] M. Davitt, p. 162.
[280] C. Cruise O'Brien, p. 71.
[281] Hansard, 3rd ser., 266, 193ff., 8 Feb. 1882.
[282] M. Davitt, p. 375.
[283] *Northampton Mercury Daily Reporter*, 28 Oct. 1880.

compulsory purchase. His support of the compulsory principle remained so pronounced that W. H. Smith wrote to A. J. Balfour in 1889, 'It is clear that no compulsory system of purchase can be applied by us, but what will be the position of the landlords when Harcourt, Labby and Parnell are in office?'[284]

[284] B.P., B.M. Add. MSS., 49696, fo. 110, W. H. Smith to A. J. Balfour, 29 Oct. 1889.

## CHAPTER IV

## Irish Issues, 1885 and 1886

FOUR administrations faced the problem of Irish nationalism between 1885 and 1886. In this period only Gladstone's third administration attempted to solve the problem of the government of Ireland by conceding home rule. Nevertheless, in conservative circles currents of opinion favoured Irish aspirations. Pope Hennessy believed England would 'be kept weak' until Ireland was 'as independent & as loyal as Canada or Australia'.[1] Carnarvon argued that the 'only hope' in the 'general interests of the Country & of the Irish loyalists' was 'some fair and reasonable arrangement for home rule'.[2] Hicks Beach spoke 'strongly' to the queen 'in the direction of large concessions to Irish sentiment'.[3] When Lord Salisbury spoke at Newport on 7 October 1885 he stated that 'at present' he had seen no proposals that caused him to anticipate a settlement of the Irish question by means of imperial federation. He held out no promises to the Irish but he did not bar the way for some measure of local government for Ireland provided that it proceeded *pari passu* with similar developments in other parts of Britain. He said that the cabinet was 'strongly of the opinion that large reforms ... in the direction of increasing powers to local government' were 'absolutely necessary'; 'that people in the localities should govern themselves'; and that it was a first principle of the conservatives 'to extend to Ireland as far as we can all the institutions in this country'. His emphatic repudiation of any policy which would affect the 'integrity of the Empire'[4] was as common in speeches of English liberals who supported home rule, as in those of politicians who opposed it.

---

[1] N.L.I., MS., 8005, 1881. Sir C. G. Duffy Papers, Pope Hennessy to Duffy, 5 Feb. 1881.
[2] Sy.P. Carnarvon to Salisbury, 5 Feb. 1885.
[3] Ibid., 25 Nov. 1885.   [4] *Times*, 8 Oct. 1885.

However, on 14 December 1885 a propitious opportunity to tackle the problem of Irish government passed when the conservatives decided that 'it was not possible for the Conservative Party to tamper with the question of Home Rule'.[5] Their dalliance with Irish nationalists in the second part of 1885 inflamed the question, strengthened Parnell's position in Ireland,[6] and made it more difficult for Gladstone to implement his therapeutic policy.

As a result of their decision to oppose home rule the conservative party remained united. The liberal party adopted home rule and the party split in 1886, though many of the fissures were apparent earlier. In 1885 dissensions riddled the party. Wide differences of opinion were apparent between various political speeches particularly between those which advocated whig or radical policies. Prominent liberals jostled for political advantage for the time when Gladstone took his 'early hermitic retreat from this wicked world'.[7] Personal antipathies such as those which existed between Chamberlain and Gladstone[8] appear to have had political significance. Gladstone's position was unique. He alone could hold the party together, and both whigs[9] and radicals[10] wished to secure his support if the party disintegrated. Nevertheless, the cleavage of opinion about Irish policy created a situation where secessions from Gladstone's second administration were 'inevitable' in Lord Derby's opinion: only defeat on the budget in June 1885 prevented liberal disunity becoming 'a public scandal'.[11] The adoption of home rule removed the veneer of party cohesion and part of the right wing headed by Hartington, and part of the left wing, manœuvred by Chamberlain, defected.

[5] G. E. Buckle (ed.), *Letters of Queen Victoria*, 2nd ser., iii, 711, Salisbury to Queen Victoria, 14 Dec. 1885.
[6] Unless 'Parnell soon receives a staggering blow, all Ireland will go over to him not even excepting the landlords'. Cy.P., R(S.R.) 1003, 4, fo. 87, E. W. O'Brien to Courtney, 14 Oct. 1885.
[7] B.P., B.M. Add. MSS., 49688, fo. 28, Salisbury to Balfour, 16 June 1880.
[8] Chamberlain hated Gladstone; Chamberlain's 'socialism' repelled Gladstone. C.D.P., B.M. Add. MSS., 43926, fo. 37, 28 Oct. 1884; Ge.P., P.R.O., 30/29/29, Gladstone to Granville, 9 Sept. 1885.
[9] B. H. Holland, *The Life of Spencer Compton, Eighth Duke of Devonshire*, i, 404, Hartington to Duke of Devonshire, 14 Jan. 1884.
[10] J. L. Hammond, *Gladstone and the Irish Nation*, p. 392.
[11] Dy.P., X24, Derby to Lansdowne, 15 June 1885.

Labouchere's influence on political affairs was greater than might be expected of a member of parliament who had not held office. Perhaps the closeness of his relationship with Irish nationalists such as Healy was unique. His relations with Chamberlain and Lord Randolph Churchill were also close and he corresponded frequently with Herbert Gladstone. He appears to have been used by Gladstone as a sounding board[12] to ascertain the minimum demands of the Irish nationalists, for, particularly in the latter part of 1885, Herbert Gladstone's letters to Labouchere were drafted by his father or seen by him before they were sent.[13] Labouchere's overriding aim was to 'capture the G.O.M. for Home Rule . . . & the Liberal party'[14] and he was indefatigable in his attempts to do this.

Until the liberal government's defeat on 8 June 1885, there were few indications that he would, perhaps, do 'more for the Home Rule Bill than any member but . . . Gladstone'.[15] On 2 March 1885 he sent to Herbert Gladstone and Sir F. Knollys a warning, allegedly from J. McCarthy, that the proposed visit of the prince of Wales to Ireland was 'undesirable' and that loyal demonstrations in the north would produce counter-demonstrations in the south. He also urged upon Herbert Gladstone the desirability of a temporary suspension of the 1882 coercion act with an understanding that if Ireland remained tranquil it would not be renewed. He alleged that Parnell had intimated to him his intention to propose to the conservatives that his party would vote with them for three years and 'let Home Rule sleep for a time' provided that they voted money for land purchase and public works.[16] In parliament he referred twice to Irish affairs. In May 1885 he failed to obtain from Campbell-Bannerman a return of agrarian outrages for the preceding year.[17] Later in the month, Lord Randolph Churchill

[12] H.P., B.M. Add. MSS., 48642, fo. 50, 13 Dec. 1885.
[13] I am indebted to Professor M. R. D. Foot for his explanation of the working of Gladstone's secretariat, which made this conclusion possible. On 21 December 1885 W. E. Gladstone drafted the reply which H. Gladstone sent to Labouchere, H.G.P., B.M. Add. MSS., 46015, fo. 98, W. E. Gladstone to H. Gladstone, 21 Dec. 1885.
[14] R.C.P., 1199, Labouchere to Churchill, 23 Dec. 1885.
[15] *Leicester Daily Post*, 8 June 1886.
[16] H.G.P., B.M. Add. MSS., 46015, fos. 24–6, Labouchere to H. Gladstone, 2 March 1885. [17] Hansard, 3rd ser., 298, 487, 14 May 1885.

'intimated that a conservative government would not' renew[18] the 1882 coercion act when he claimed, at the St Stephen's Club, on 20 May 1885, that 'at the present moment' no justification existed for exceptional legislation in Ireland, and that it would be impolitic to renew such legislation during the 'last days of this unlucky Parliament'.[19] The following day, Labouchere begged Gladstone to act in a 'most generous spirit' and not perpetuate ill-feeling between Ireland and England by endeavouring to renew certain clauses of the 1882 coercion act which would expire in August 1885.[20] He made no speeches in the constituencies, but in June 1885 he wrote to the *Northampton Mercury*[21] to argue that Lord Spencer's intention to renew some clauses of the 1882 coercion act[22] was the strongest evidence that some change in Anglo-Irish relations was necessary. Labouchere could not envisage the end of coercive legislation if it were justified initially on the ground that crime made it necessary, and subsequently because crime would reappear if it were not renewed. He considered the liberal government's simultaneous consideration of devolution of authority to Ireland and the withdrawal of some guarantees of freedom illogical. He reaffirmed his belief that in comparison with coercion 'concession to Ireland's legitimate demands is the greater and wiser policy'.[23]

*Truth* had published similar arguments in January 1885.[24] It defended Parnell's right to urge his fellow-countrymen to vote for home rule[25] and insisted that he had no connection with dynamite outrages.[26] It thought Spencer's administration of the 1882 coercion act was like a spur on the heel of a child, 'an instrument of irritation and not of coercion'. To illustrate the point it stressed the paradoxical position which arose when

---

[18] W. L. S. Churchill, *Lord Randolph Churchill*, i, 391.
[19] *Times*, 21 May 1885.
[20] Hansard, 3rd ser., 298, 1086–7, 21 May 1885.
[21] *Northampton Mercury*, 13 June 1885.
[22] G.P., B.M. Add. MSS., 44312, fo. 38, [?28 March 1885]. Spencer's cabinet memorandum expressed the desire to have the clauses 'applied to the United Kingdom and made part of the permanent law of the country... it would remove the reproach... which exceptional legislation brings'.
[23] *Northampton Mercury*, 13 June 1885.
[24] *Truth*, 8 Jan. 1885, p. 54.     [25] *Truth*, 29 Jan. 1885, p. 167.
[26] *Truth*, 5 Feb. 1885, p. 209; 26 Feb. 1885, p. 331.

journalists such as O'Brien and Sullivan could express themselves freely in the press while 'half-articulate' members of parliament were forbidden to address public meetings.[27] In March 1885 *Truth* thought Parnell reasonable in turning to conservatives, for, in its opinion, not only would they vote large sums for public works and land purchase, but liberals would be more likely to support home rule and object to the 'perpetual state of siege' in Ireland if conservatives were in power.[28] In May 1885 it cynically described the operation of coercion in Ireland, and attacked Gladstone's decision to renew certain clauses of the 1882 coercion act.[29]

On 8 June 1885 conservative and Irish members joined forces to defeat the liberal government which was weakened by radical abstentions.[30] A minority conservative government held office with Irish support until the completion of electoral reforms. The general election took place between 23 November and 19 December 1885.

During the remaining weeks of the existing parliament Labouchere concentrated upon extra-parliamentary activity. His speeches before the election[31] invariably harmonized with the programme outlined in his electoral manifesto of 1885: 'I would give to Ireland the fullest measure of Home Rule, consistent with the integrity of the Empire.'[32] He made only one speech after Parnell's manifesto of 20 November 1885 had directed Irish electors in England to vote against the liberals. Labouchere was one of four named exceptions[33] to this directive, but as there was no significant Irish element among the Northampton electorate,[34] this probably had little bearing upon his re-election with an increased majority.

[27] *Truth*, 12 Feb. 1885, p. 249.
[28] *Truth*, 12 March 1885, p. 407.   [29] *Truth*, 21 May 1885, p. 805.
[30] J. L. Hammond, pp. 373–4. The Division Lists of 1885 (No. 201, 8 June) show that Labouchere voted.
[31] He spoke at Walworth, 13 July; East Finsbury, 13 October; Camberwell, 14 October; Marylebone, 20 October; Portsmouth, 23 October; London Central Club, 26 October; Northampton, 29 October; Camberwell, 5 November; Westminster, 6 November; Chelsea, 11 November; Southwark, 16 November; Northampton, 13, 18, 20 and 24 November.
[32] *Northampton Mercury*, 14 Nov. 1885.
[33] The others were T. C. Thompson, J. Cowen, S. Storey: W. H. O'Shea was in a different category.
[34] I am indebted to Mr R. T. Paget, Q.C., M.P., for this information.

Healy recognized that *Truth* gave the Parnellites 'great help' in their struggle for home rule.[35] Its criticism of Chamberlain was particularly interesting in view of Labouchere's long correspondence with him. It is possible that Chamberlain's hostility to the Irish had become fixed during July 1885[36] when Parnell and the Irish clergy spurned his Irish local government proposals, and the Irish press attacked the visit he and Dilke proposed to make to study in Ireland 'the plan of devolution by Parliament to Wales and Scotland and Ireland of much business that at the present time Parliament is incompetent to discharge'.[37] On 2 July 1885 *Truth* considered this visit would do little good as the Irish were neither 'cordially disposed' to Chamberlain and Dilke nor sure of their sincerity. It advised them to remember that 'the gentleman to whom a horse is offered for sale does not usually burst out into wild laudation over the proffered animal'.[38] A week later it criticized the Irish local government proposals Chamberlain had inspired in the July issue of the *Fortnightly Review*, on the grounds that he committed the mistake he was attempting to remedy.

That fault is 'alien' legislation for Ireland. Yet here ... the 'alien' Mr Chamberlain [is] legislating with the minutest particularity upon every detail of a proposed Irish Local Government scheme... It is not for 'alien' statesmen, or an 'alien' Parliament to meddle in these matters. The duty of the Imperial Parliament is simply to call into existence a local authority, *viz.*, an Irish legislature, and to leave ... [it] to settle all things Irish, and among others, the relation of 'County Boards' to the 'National Council'.[39]

In September *Truth* thought Chamberlain unwise to act 'in the character of the Prophet Isaiah, crossed with the late Lord Macaulay, and "cocksure" as to every detail of the future Irish constitution'. It believed Gladstone's views on Ireland accorded

---

[35] H.G.P., B.M. Add. MSS., 46015, fo. 32, Healy to Labouchere (copy), 7 Oct. 1885.
[36] C. Cruise O'Brien, *Parnell and his Party 1880–1890*, pp. 99–102.
[37] *Northampton Herald*, 27 June 1885, Dilke speaking at Chelsea on 22 June. W. Morris, in the *Commonweal* of July 1885, suggested that they wished to acclimatize themselves 'to the atmosphere of Nationalism—or to try and outflank Mr Parnell'.
[38] *Truth*, 2 July 1885, pp. 10–11.     [39] *Truth*, 9 July 1885, p. 53.

with those of radicals.[40] In the October issue of the *Fortnightly Review* Labouchere repeated some of *Truth*'s arguments and pleaded for home rule as a just, expedient, safe and practical policy.[41]

*Truth* deprecated the hostility between radicals and Parnellites[42] and recommended an alliance between them,[43] yet it offered radical support for any conservative attempt to 'hatch the ... Disraeli egg ... and "do for Ireland by law all that a revolution would do for her"'.[44] It warned liberals that the terms 'home rule' and 'local government' were not synonymous and advised candidates to express themselves vaguely 'to leave room for any new convictions which may be forced upon you at the last moment'.[45] In October, five weeks before Parnell's directive, it prophesied that the Irish in England would vote conservative not because of conservative promises but in order to reduce an anticipated liberal majority so that the Parnellites would be too influential to be disregarded in parliament.[46] On 26 November, however, it condemned the manifesto as a 'palpable ... mistake'[47] for it argued that while a conservative government would not concede a large measure of home rule, a liberal ministry would have defections on this issue. *Truth* criticized the manifesto a week later because it might result in a liberal government dependent upon Irish support: it believed that in these circumstances Gladstone would have difficulty in persuading his party to follow him. The solution it offered for this contingency was for a committee of English and Irish members to draft a home rule scheme based upon the integrity of the empire and the full supremacy of Ireland in local affairs, and with an understanding that its rejection by either house of parliament would precipitate a dissolution.[48]

*Truth* considered Ireland the one difficulty ahead of democracy,[49] and thought the settlement of this problem would per-

---

[40] *Truth*, 24 Sept. 1885, pp. 474, 476. Chamberlain, on 8 September at Warrington, though prepared to concede 'the greatest measure of local government', declared his opposition to home rule.
[41] *Fortnightly Review*, xxxviii (1 Oct. 1885), 484–5.
[42] *Truth*, 23 July 1885, p. 131.
[43] *Truth*, 25 June 1885, p. 1004.
[44] *Truth*, 18 June 1885, p. 967.
[45] *Truth*, 2 July 1885, p. 11.
[46] *Truth*, 15 Oct. 1885, p. 590.
[47] *Truth*, 26 Nov. 1885, p. 834.
[48] *Truth*, 3 Dec. 1885, p. 871.
[49] *Truth*, 1 Oct. 1885, p .515.

mit the English to concentrate upon internal reforms.[50] It minimized the Orange problem by giving examples of co-operation between nationalists and protestants[51] and by arguing that the new franchise virtually eliminated Orangemen as a political factor.[52] To a large extent it evaded this intransigent problem. Cynicism occasionally flavoured its arguments on Irish affairs: 'The Irish Question . . . is not . . . a question of principle, but merely a question of votes. The Irish go for self-government; neither of the English parties really wants to grant it; but either . . . will grant it to "dish" the other.'[53]

The views of *Truth* on the Irish agrarian question may have alienated some supporters of the home rule principle and hardened some people's opposition, for not only were its views extreme, but they had an English relevance. To enlist its readers' sympathy for Irish and Scottish tenants it gave an inimitable description of a Connaught mountain farm. It contended that rent from such farms came not from the land but the 'sweat of the unfortunate tenants, when they . . . slave in the harvest fields or mines of England'.[54] *Truth* warned its readers that the agricultural depression in Ireland was worsening, that tenants could not sell their produce, and that these factors disturbed the 1881 land act settlement, for declining returns transformed rents which had been equitable into rack-rents.[55] It thought Ireland's condition resembled that of a country emerging from a disastrous war;[56] and it stressed that, although the country was tranquil, it was not the executive's duty to collect landlords' outstanding rents, their 'bad debts'.[57] At the end of 1885 it published a table giving seventy-eight examples of reductions of rent, ranging from 41.4 per cent in the case of Lord Ashbrook to 10 per cent for the earl of Enniskillen, imposed upon the estates of peers holding land in Ireland by the Irish land courts, with comments about the landlords' insistence, before the 1881 land act, that they charged fair rents.[58]

---

[50] *Truth*, 17 Dec. 1885, p. 953; 31 Dec. 1885, p. 1034.   [51] *Truth*, 29 Oct. 1885, p. 673.
[52] *Truth*, 3 Sept. 1885, p. 366.   [53] *Truth*, 9 July 1885, p. 53.
[54] *Truth*, 1 Oct. 1885, pp. 515–16.   [55] *Truth*, 3 Sept. 1885, p. 366.
[56] *Truth*, 13 Aug. 1885, p. 254.   [57] *Truth*, 8 Oct. 1885, p. 555.
[58] *Truth*, 31 Dec. 1885, p. 1031. E.g. 40.4 per cent Lord Mountmorres, 30.0 per cent Earl Russell, 27.2 per cent earl of Dufferin, 26.5 per cent duke of Manchester, 17.0 per cent marquess of Lansdowne, 15.0 per cent duke of Devonshire.

In July 1885 *Truth* emphasized that until the policy of Ireland's prospective local legislature was known, land purchase schemes would gain little support, for the 'man who buys land on the eve of a revolution is more speculative than prudent'.[59] In November it argued that

> Parliament could deprive every landowner of his property ... [as] title to all property is dependent upon Parliament maintaining it. Title to Irish property must, consequently, be dependent upon the Irish Representative Council maintaining it, if Home Rule in local matters, not affecting the integrity of the Empire, is to be anything beyond a sham.[60]

In its view, land belonged to the community and, as the landlord was the tenant in perpetuity of the state, the state could insist upon its tenant subletting so that the community would not suffer. It considered this doctrine 'equally applicable in England, Scotland, Wales and Ireland',[61] and continued to object to land purchase because of the financial obligations that would fall upon English taxpayers.

*Truth* described home rule as 'union upon the broad principle of justice', the policy to end disunion in the British Isles. It countered suggestions that the demand for home rule was ephemeral, and that the Irish parliamentary party would soon disintegrate, by stating that history proved that when once nationalist feeling sprang up it never died.[62] It predicted that if the English opposed Irish demands with a *non possumus* England would have to adopt a repressive policy for a long time and that even the Irish landlords would not gain. It saw no possibility of separation if the Irish gained home rule, but argued that if they did the English would 'be in a better position to quell overt disaffection, than ... to deal with an entire nation banded together to render our rule impossible'. However, it asked Englishmen to realize that devolution of authority to Ireland entailed a local Irish parliament 'if concessions are not to be used against us'.[63]

The tone of *Truth* indicates that Labouchere doubted the wisdom of Chamberlain's inflexible attitude to Irish affairs.

[59] *Truth*, 23 July 1885, p. 132.
[60] *Truth*, 12 Nov. 1885, p. 755.
[61] Ibid.
[62] *Truth*, 24 Dec. 1885, p. 994.
[63] *Truth*, 31 Dec. 1885, pp. 1033-4.

Consequently, his correspondence with Chamberlain, which lasted until the eve of the defeat of Gladstone's first home rule bill in June 1886, was probably an attempt to persuade him to accept home rule rather than an expression of 'frank admiration of and political devotion to Mr Chamberlain'.[64] Labouchere's views were more advanced and much more responsive to Irish pressures than Chamberlain's. In December 1885 the latter suggested, as if he were the first to advocate the idea, that 'the only way of giving *bona fide* Home Rule . . . is the adoption of the American Constitution'.[65] Labouchere had proposed a similar solution as early as October 1881.

Hammond may be correct in asserting that Labouchere had a bad effect[66] on Chamberlain by informing him of his correspondence with Herbert Gladstone and certain Irish leaders, for there are indications that Chamberlain felt that he ought to have been informed of developments by Gladstone.[67] This, however, is not Hammond's contention. His view is that Labouchere made Chamberlain feel that Gladstone's interest in the Irish question was 'chiefly inspired by the desire to get rid of Chamberlain's troublesome enthusiasms for social reform',[68] and in this writer's view the correspondence barely justifies this interpretation.[69] The emphasis Labouchere laid upon Gladstone's eagerness for office may have had more influence upon Chamberlain.[70] Another criticism Hammond levels is that Labouchere confirmed Chamberlain in his dislike of Parnell. This may have some weight, but after the events of July 1885 Labouchere's influence must have been marginal in this respect, and in any case, by dealing with Healy, Labouchere hoped to turn to account the 'difficulties in the character of Parnell by getting up a sort of revolt amongst his lieutenants'.[71]

[64] A. L. Thorold, *The Life of Henry Labouchere*, p. 235.
[65] J.C., 5/50/38a, Chamberlain to Labouchere (copy), 26 Dec. 1885; A. L. Thorold, p. 272.
[66] J. L. Hammond, p. 417; cf. H. Harrison, *Parnell, Joseph Chamberlain and Mr Garvin*, pp. 131, 140.
[67] J. Chamberlain, *A Political Memoir*, p. 167.   [68] J. L. Hammond, p. 417.
[69] It appears to have sprung from Chamberlain who wrote to Labouchere in this vein on 20 October.
[70] J.C., 5/50/23, Labouchere to Chamberlain, 20 Oct. 1885.
[71] H.G.P., B.M. Add. MSS., 46015, fo. 91, Labouchere to H. Gladstone, 19 Dec. 1885.

Labouchere may have misled Herbert Gladstone about his correspondence with Chamberlain. He asserted, for instance, that he did not know why Chamberlain wrote to him at length,[72] and when he forwarded two of Chamberlain's letters to Herbert Gladstone, he urged him to preserve secrecy as he was 'by way of being one of his adherents'.[73] Moreover, he informed Herbert Gladstone that he had not alluded to his letters when he visited Chamberlain on 16 December 1885.[74] If this statement was true, its validity did not extend to the period before or after the visit. It is, however, quite possible that these deceptions failed to convince Gladstone who had previously encountered a vivid example of Labouchere's double-dealing in connection with Egypt.[75] Thus Gladstone, or his son, may have played upon this characteristic and used Labouchere to keep Chamberlain in touch with his attitude to the Irish demand for home rule. Gladstone's mistaken belief, expressed immediately after a visit by Chamberlain to Hawarden, that he and Chamberlain were 'pretty well agreed'[76] on the Irish question strengthens this hypothesis, at least temporarily. Gladstone's position, even after the *ballon d'essai* of 16 December 1885, which Derby believed 'announced his adhesion to H.R.',[77] remained august: 'all ideas ascribed to me are in truth other people's opinions of my opinions: as the colours of the rainbow are in us, not in it'.[78] Paradoxically, Herbert Gladstone's use of Labouchere may have preserved secrecy, for if Chamberlain had made information public he would have embarrassed only Labouchere. Moreover, Labouchere was probably more circumspect in the press than Herbert Gladstone had anticipated, and his restraint might have been a factor in Herbert Gladstone's decision to fly the Hawarden kite. Gladstone's reluctance to consult his senior colleagues about the Irish question in the latter part of 1885 stemmed partly from endemic leakages of information by

---

[72] Ibid., fo. 61, Labouchere to H. Gladstone, 8 Dec. 1885.
[73] Ibid., fo. 125, Labouchere to H. Gladstone, 28 Dec. 1885.
[74] Ibid., fo. 83, Labouchere to H. Gladstone, 17 Dec. 1885.
[75] Ge.P., P.R.O., 30/29/27, 22 June 1883. See p. 167. below
[76] Ge.P., P.R.O., 30/29/29, Gladstone to Granville, 8 Oct. 1885.
[77] Dy.P., X12, 21 Dec. 1885, Derby's writing on a letter to him from Granville.
[78] G.P., B.M. Add. MSS., 44303, fo. 364, Gladstone to Stead, 18 Dec. 1885.

members of his second administration.[79] By using his son and Labouchere, Gladstone kept Chamberlain advised informally about his attitude towards Ireland and about developments that were taking place: at the same time Gladstone retained his freedom to manœuvre.

Labouchere communicated with Lord Randolph Churchill as well as with some liberals and some Parnellites. Churchill in turn sent some of the information he received from Labouchere to Salisbury.[80] Salisbury welcomed this information[81] but presumably was unaware of the information leaked to Labouchere by Churchill or of the press arrangements made between them. Early in 1886 Labouchere established relations between Lucy, the editor of the *Daily News*, and Churchill 'on the understanding that he is to reveal to us everything & we are personally to puff him'.[82] It is difficult to assess how far Labouchere was merely transmitting political 'gossip', how far he deliberately attempted to precipitate a crisis inside the conservative party, and perhaps inside the liberal party too, and how far he was congenitally unable to keep a secret. The 'most rare thing in the world', he assured Herbert Gladstone, 'is to be able to keep a secret. People tell them in the strictest confidence to others, in order to increase their own importance.'[83] He vowed that he 'would not confide a secret to Churchill'.[84]

When the liberal government resigned on 13 June 1885, Labouchere immediately wrote to Herbert Gladstone about F. H. Hill, editor of the *Daily News*, the chief metropolitan liberal newspaper. He stated that Hill, who had been editor since 1868, was unable 'to present political matters in a popular manner', and that the liberal party suffered as a result. He added that two-

---

[79] B. H. Holland, ii, 108, Gladstone to Hartington, 2 Jan. 1886.
[80] The Salisbury Papers show that Churchill sent Salisbury five letters which he had received from Labouchere. Churchill sent them to Salisbury on 25 July 1885, 27 September 1885, 1 October 1885, 26 December 1885, and 7 January 1886.
[81] Sy.P., Churchill to Salisbury, 25 Dec. 1885.
[82] H.G.P., B.M. Add. MSS., 46015, fo. 148, Labouchere to H. Gladstone, 12 Jan. 1886.
[83] Ibid., fo. 112, Labouchere to H. Gladstone, [Sat.? Dec. 1885].
[84] Ibid., fo. 137, Labouchere to H. Gladstone, 30 Dec. 1885.

thirds of the cabinet had complained to him about Hill.[85] In 1885 Labouchere appears to have persuaded his fellow proprietors, of whom H. Oppenheim and A. Morley were the most important,[86] that an editorial change was necessary. He had failed to displace Hill (in favour of Escott) three years previously,[87] but on this occasion he was more successful. He took the initiative in finding a replacement for Hill who was 'summarily dismissed'[88] in December 1885. Labouchere had offered H. W. Lucy his position in July and November. Lucy accepted at the third time of asking and assumed control in January 1886. The change was opportune so far as the home rule issue was concerned, for Hill became a unionist while the *Daily News* was the only London morning paper to support Gladstone's home rule policy though the proprietors, according to Lucy, gave him no instructions on this matter.[89] Lucy did not prove a satisfactory editor for he too could not present political developments in popular terms, but Labouchere 'could find no-one else'.[90] Labouchere twice intervened to make the *Daily News* more positive in its approach to Irish affairs. He had J. Macdonald appointed as the paper's special correspondent in Ireland, to try to 'counteract the trash of the *Times* & other such papers',[91] and arranged for him to meet Healy and organize a 'plan of operations'.[92] He also arranged for J. Morley to write the Irish leaders in the *Daily News*.[93]

[85] Ibid., fo. 29, Labouchere to H. Gladstone, 13 June [1885]. Granville, for instance, found Hill 'loyal but clumsy'. H.P., B.M. Add. MSS., 48618(4), Granville to Hamilton, 5 Jan. 1884.

[86] F. M. Thomas, *Fifty years of Fleet Street*, p. 375. On 9 January 1886 Harcourt informed Hartington that the dismissal of Hill was 'Labby's doing'. De.P., 340. 1887.

[87] J.C., 5/50/12, Labouchere to Chamberlain, 9 Jan. 1883.

[88] H. R. F. Bourne, *English Newspapers*, ii, 385; cf. H.G.P., B.M. Add. MSS., 46015, fo. 137, Labouchere to H. Gladstone, 30 Dec. 1885.

[89] H. W. Lucy, *Sixty Years in the Wilderness*, i, 112, 129ff.

[90] J.C., 5/50/30, Labouchere to Chamberlain, 1 Dec. 1885. There may be significance in the fact that this is the first mention of the editorial change to Chamberlain. Labouchere offered R. B. Brett the editorship on 5 February 1886. M. V. Brett (ed.), *Journals and Letters of Reginald (Baliol Brett) Viscount Esher*, i, 123.

[91] H.G.P., B.M. Add. MSS., 46015, fo. 142, Labouchere to H. Gladstone, 6 Jan. 1886.

[92] Ibid., fo. 143, Macdonald to Labouchere, 5 Jan. 1886.

[93] Ibid., fo. 148, Labouchere to H. Gladstone, 12 Jan. 1886; cf. J. Saxon Mills, *The Life of Sir E. Cook*, pp. 49–50.

On 17 July 1885 Labouchere begged Chamberlain to be 'revolutionary' and obtain the support of the Irish.[94] Chamberlain's reply the next day reflected his disenchantment with the Parnellites, implied that he no longer desired their support and expressed the opinion that English radicals would not favour 'further concessions to Irish opinion'. He predicted that liberals would secure a majority at the general election over conservatives and Parnellites combined, and, more accurately, that eventually conservatives would reject a policy of concessions on home rule.[95]

Later in the month Labouchere informed Chamberlain about a long discussion he had held with Healy. Labouchere pressed the advisability of an alliance between Parnellites and radicals, and elicited from Healy the nationalists' intention to direct the Irish in England to vote conservative. Healy disparaged Parnell and Davitt, but emphasized the Irish party's insistence upon cohesion. He stated that if liberals committed themselves to a 'big scheme' of home rule, he would propose that Parnellites should not compromise themselves with the conservatives, and that no voting manifesto should be issued.[96]

Shortly before the dissolution of parliament in August 1885, Herbert Gladstone asked Labouchere, if the latter's report to Chamberlain was true, to arrange some form of *modus vivendi* with the Irish, in order to gain time for Gladstone to prepare the whigs for the possibility of joint action with the Parnellites. Labouchere also alleged that in correspondence with him Herbert Gladstone cloaked his father's views with ' "I" or "I think my father" as had been arranged'.[97] Gladstone, however, repeatedly denied that he was negotiating with the Parnellites.[98] Nevertheless, it seems certain that he was cognizant of the Irish members' views which Labouchere transmitted, and of his son's replies. Rosebery advised Gladstone of his fear that 'Labouchere may consider Herbert's letters to him as an authoritative

---

[94] J.C., 5/50/20, Labouchere to Chamberlain, 17 July 1885.
[95] J.C., 5/50/20a, Chamberlain to Labouchere (copy), 18 July 1885; A. L. Thorold, pp. 229–30.
[96] J.C., 5/50/21, Labouchere to Chamberlain, 22 July 1885; A. L. Thorold, pp. 230–2; J. Chamberlain, p. 311.
[97] J.C., 5/50/22, Labouchere to Chamberlain, 18 Oct. 1885; A. L. Thorold, pp. 237–9.   [98] B. H. Holland, ii, 100, Gladstone to Hartington, 17 Dec. 1885.

indication of your plan. I ... admit that there is a certain guarded wording as regards the source, but the veil is too thin to disguise the inspiration.'[99] Herbert Gladstone asserted in his memoirs published in 1928 that he had expressed his own views about his father's position in his letters to Labouchere.[100]

In October 1885 Labouchere informed Chamberlain and Herbert Gladstone about the views of Davitt and Healy. On 7 October Healy, in a letter to Labouchere, praised Gladstone and deplored Parnell's action in raising the issue of protection, but warned that the Parnellites would oppose the liberals at the elections unless they learnt Gladstone's intentions on home rule and arranged a compromise with him.[101] Davitt, who wrote to Labouchere two days later, echoed Healy's praise of Gladstone and his condemnation of protection. Davitt was convinced that Parnell would be unable to carry protection if the Irish had a national assembly.[102] When he communicated with Herbert Gladstone on 10 October, Labouchere mentioned the Parnellites' dislike of Chamberlain, and the probability that they would make more concessions for Gladstone than for Chamberlain.[103] Herbert Gladstone replied on 12 October and stated that he believed his father would abide by the Irish section of his electoral address,[104] and that, provided the unity of the empire was maintained, there was no limit to the powers he would give Ireland for the management of her own affairs. He believed that Gladstone approved of the nationalists' attempt to induce the conservatives to 'take up' home rule, but felt that 'unless

[99] G.P., B.M. Add. MSS., 44288, fo. 286, Rosebery to Gladstone, 20 Dec. 1885. Rosebery and Gladstone apparently discussed the trustworthiness of Labouchere without arriving at any conclusion. Gladstone continued to make use of him. G.P., B.M. Add. MSS. 44288, fo. 276, Rosebery to Gladstone, 11 Dec. 1885.

[100] H. J. Gladstone, *After Thirty Years*, p. 310.

[101] H.G.P., B.M. Add. MSS., 46015, fos. 31-2, Healy to Labouchere (copy), 7 Oct. 1885.

[102] Ibid., fos. 38-9, Davitt to Labouchere (copy), 9 Oct. 1885; A. L. Thorold, p. 234.

[103] Ibid., fo. 30, Labouchere to H. Gladstone, 10 Oct. 1885.

[104] 'To maintain the supremacy of the Crown, the unity of the Empire, and all the authority of Parliament necessary for the conservation of that unity, is the first duty of every representative of the people. Subject to this governing principle every grant to portions of the country of enlarged powers for the management of their own affairs is, in my view, not a source of danger, but a means of averting it, and is in the nature of a new guarantee for increased cohesion, happiness, and strength.' *Times*, 19 Sept. 1885.

they wish permanently & unconditionally to sink or swim with
the Tories, they had better bring the matter to a very speedy
upshot'. Gladstone thought it inexpedient to make specific proposals at this stage. In fact he expected the Irish to 'speak
plainly & publicly' through their representatives. Nevertheless,
he drew attention to 'the protection of the minority in a
country so long torn by dissensions' as a particularly difficult
problem. Herbert Gladstone offered to meet Labouchere, and
to 'throw light on points of difficulty' in further correspondence.[105]

Labouchere enclosed a letter, dated 15 October, from Healy
when he next contacted Herbert Gladstone. Healy stated that
Parnell had confidence in obtaining home rule from whichever
English party won the election, and that he had asked Sexton
and himself to draft a home rule scheme. Parnell, he suggested,
thought in terms of abolishing the lord lieutenancy, of assessing
Ireland's imperial obligation by taking the average of Ireland's
contributions to the imperial exchequer, less the cost of governing the country, and of retaining Irish representation at Westminster for imperial affairs. Healy equated the 'minority' with
the protestants.[106] Herbert Gladstone replied on 18 October.
He strongly urged the Irish to come to terms with the conservatives on the home rule issue before the election, for otherwise the
latter might jib at the fence and be kept in office by exasperated
liberals. Dealing with certain points raised by Healy, Herbert
Gladstone cleared up the misunderstanding about the 'minority'.
He said that the 'greatest difficulty' in his father's view was 'the
protection not of the Protestant minority but of the landlords'.
He thought that Gladstone would only act if he had a strong
parliamentary majority. He tried to reassure Healy by arguing
that if the house of lords rejected a home rule measure passed by
a strong liberal government, the latter 'must resign', but he
believed it was 'infallibly certain' that an incoming conservative government 'must make the concession'. He sought information about Irish intentions from Labouchere and stated that

[105] H.G.P., B.M. Add. MSS., 46015, fos. 33-6, H. Gladstone to Labouchere (copy), 12 Oct. 1885.
[106] Ibid., fos. 41-2, Healy to Labouchere (copy), 15 Oct. 1885; A. L. Thorold, pp. 235-7.

if liberals attempted to settle the problem of the government of Ireland, 'it must be with the frank co-operation of the Irish members'.[107] Labouchere promised to press these views upon the Irish members, and stated that Parnell, 'a natural trickster', was the obstacle to a compromise.[108] Nothing materialized from this initial overture which was perhaps a logical sequel to Gladstone's manifesto of 17 September.

Labouchere kept Chamberlain informed of Gladstone's 'endeavour to square the Irish', with injunctions to tell no-one other than J. Morley. On 18 October he reported that he had advised Herbert Gladstone that Parnell 'did not want an arrangement... but that it might be possible to influence him through Healy and others'. He deduced that Gladstone hoped to unite liberals on Irish legislation and make that his *cheval de bataille*, but that he would do nothing without Irish support, and this Labouchere thought he would not obtain. Labouchere suggested 'one grand Bill for local government in both islands, ... settling the difference between local and imperial Sessions' as a way to provoke conservative opposition and win Irish support.[109]

On 20 October Chamberlain thanked Labouchere for confirming his suspicions about Gladstone's intentions. In Chamberlain's view, liberals and Irish nationalists would not establish a *modus vivendi* but his reasons for this belief differed completely from those of Labouchere who had merely stated that he did not think the Irish would give Gladstone an assurance of general support on home rule. Chamberlain thought there would be no agreement partly because of Parnell's untrustworthiness, and partly because 'all liberals are getting weary of making concessions to Parnell'. He rejected Labouchere's suggestion that local government proposals for the whole of Britain could be incorporated in one bill because he felt that conditions were 'absolutely dissimilar' in Ireland. Like Labouchere, he believed

---

[107] H.G.P.,B.M. Add. MSS., 46015 fos. 43–7, H. Gladstone to Labouchere (drafts and copy which Gladstone had seen), 18 Oct. 1885. Many phrases in this letter are identical with those used by Gladstone when he wrote to H. Gladstone on 18 October 1885. Cf. J. L. Hammond, pp. 446–7.

[108] Ibid., fo. 48, Labouchere to H. Gladstone, 20 Oct. 1885.

[109] J.C., 5/50/22, Labouchere to Chamberlain, 18 Oct. 1885; A. L. Thorold, pp. 237–9, omits a reference to Gladstone's 'endeavour to square the Irish'.

that Gladstone thought he could unite liberals on Irish policy. In this letter, Chamberlain appeared to be more concerned that this would delay the secession of the whigs than that attention to Irish affairs would delay social legislation in England.[110]

On 20 October Labouchere again wrote to Chamberlain and enclosed Herbert Gladstone's letter of 18 October, a copy of which he also sent to Healy. Labouchere stressed the difficulty of the land question so long as Gladstone declined to admit that its regulation in Ireland was involved in local government, and that ownership of land did not affect the unity of the empire. He again commended a composite bill to give local self-government in Britain and 'substantial home rule' in Ireland, coupled with Chamberlain's plan for compulsory purchase of land by local authorities in both islands.[111] Chamberlain's reply of 23 October ignored Labouchere's suggestions, intimated that Gladstone would be 'ill-advised' to propose a separate parliament for Ireland, and declared that his own proposals were the most that radicals would accept.[112]

Mrs O'Shea had approached Gladstone during 1885, but he repulsed her overtures, which culminated with a 'Proposed Constitution for Ireland'[113] sent on 30 October.[114] From Parnell and from Healy he was becoming familiar with Irish requirements. He was also becoming impressed by the *'enormous advantage'* derived from the nationalist request for a derivative chamber acting under imperial authority, instead of a repeal of the act of union which would have reinstated a parliament having *'original* authority'.[115] Gladstone spoke at Edinburgh on

---

[110] J.C., 5/50/22a, Chamberlain to Labouchere (copy), 20 Oct. 1885; A. L. Thorold, pp. 239–40. H. Gladstone claimed that if home rule were shelved Gladstone intended to retire, and Chamberlain would have led the liberal party. H. J. Gladstone, pp. 287, 310.

[111] J.C., 5/50/23, Labouchere to Chamberlain, 20 Oct. 1885; A. L. Thorold, pp. 240–1.

[112] J.C., 5/50/23a, Chamberlain to Labouchere (copy), 23 Oct. 1885; A. L. Thorold, p. 241. The proposals were for extensive local government, but not self-government. Chamberlain expressed irritation at the way in which Parnell dropped them in July 1885. See *Irish Historical Studies*, viii (1952–3), 237ff., 324ff., for the documents and C. H. D. Howard's analysis of the Irish 'central board' scheme, 1884–5.

[113] K. Parnell, *Charles Stewart Parnell*, ii, 18–20.

[114] J. L. Hammond, p. 419.

[115] B. H. Holland, ii, 94, Gladstone to Hartington, 18 Nov. 1885.

9 November, and the next day Parnell publicly invited him to speak explicitly on home rule and to frame a constitution for Ireland. He indicated that the English party which offered most to Ireland would win the Irish vote. A week later, at West Calder, Gladstone announced that there could be no authoritative representation of Irish opinion until after the election, and that he could not usurp the functions of a minister. Parnell thus failed to extract any public promise from Gladstone, and on 21 November he directed the Irish in England to vote against the liberals.[116] The directive was highly inflammatory; it showed scant respect for English public opinion, and it did much to antagonize many liberals. The Parnellites had considered this course of action since July, but, if Labouchere's report to Harcourt was correct, the manifesto 'was written by T. P. O'Connor, and Parnell had calmly added the [other] signatures on his own authority'.[117] In addition, Labouchere was 'certain that T. P. O'Connor has been bought' by the conservatives.[118]

Private communications had continued. Healy pleaded for an understanding between the leaders of the liberals and Parnellites. He suspected that requests for a draft home rule scheme from the Irish aimed to discomfort the nationalists but he prophesied that if liberals tackled the problem after the election the Irish would be reasonable.[119] On 16 November, Herbert Gladstone replied and gave a greater commitment than he had done previously. He enumerated six aspects of the Irish government which a conference between liberals and Parnellites could discuss if the Irish declared for home rule at the election, and if the liberals secured a majority.[120] Parnell was unaware of this letter when he directed the Irish to vote against the liberals.[121]

The information which passed between Healy and Herbert

---

[116] C. Cruise O'Brien, p. 105.

[117] W.V.H.P., Labouchere to Harcourt, 4 March 1886.

[118] H.G.P., B.M. Add. MSS., 46015, fos. 64, 71, Labouchere to H. Gladstone, 9 and 10 Dec. 1885.

[119] The only evidence of this letter which has so far come to light is in part of a letter written by Labouchere to Chamberlain on 12 November 1885. J.C., 5/50/25; A. L. Thorold, pp. 241–2.

[120] H.G.P., B.M. Add. MSS., 46015, fos. 49–52, H. Gladstone to Labouchere (copies), 16 Nov. 1885.

[121] J.C., 5/50/27, Healy to Labouchere, 22 Nov. 1885.

Gladstone, with Labouchere as the intermediary, has several interesting features. In the first place, secretarial markings indicate that Gladstone saw each of the three letters which his son sent to Labouchere. Herbert Gladstone confirmed that his father intended to stand by the Irish section of his electoral address and that if he implemented home rule it would be with the 'frank co-operation' of the Irish representatives. Herbert Gladstone failed to secure the Irish minimum from Healy, just as Healy failed to obtain similar information from Gladstone. Yet both Herbert Gladstone and Healy showed some of their cards. Herbert Gladstone warned Healy about the danger of an unresolved flirtation between Parnellites and conservatives, indicated that his father was particularly concerned about the 'protection of the minority', and then explained that this referred to the landlords, not the protestants. Herbert Gladstone's letter of 16 November, which was presumably a final bid for an agreement with the Parnellites before the election, offered 'a splendid departure ... from the old practice of ascertaining through Dublin Castle the wishes of the minority in order to coerce the majority'. He proposed a conference between the Irish representatives and liberals to discuss six aspects of the problem of the government of Ireland after the election:

1. the maintenance of the unity & integrity of the Empire. 2. An Irish Chamber for Irish affairs. 3. Irish representatives to sit at Westminster for Imperial Affairs. 4. The equitable division of Imperial charges by fixed proportions. 5. Protection of the Minority in Ireland. 6. Suspension of the Imperial authority for all civil purposes in Ireland.[122]

The third and fourth points were identical with Parnell's views as Healy had described them on 18 October: the second and sixth points conceded the abolition of the lord lieutenancy.

The flow of information between Healy, Labouchere and Herbert Gladstone recommenced before the election results were finally known. To Herbert Gladstone, Labouchere portrayed Parnell as a 'dreamy figurehead'[123] whose lieutenants could

[122] H.G.P., B.M. Add. MSS., 46015, fos. 49–52, H. Gladstone to Labouchere (copies), 16 Nov. 1885.
[123] Ibid., fo. 91, Labouchere to H. Gladstone, 19 Dec. 1885.

'coerce'[124] him into an agreement with the liberals to settle the home rule question provided that he was unaware of the steps taken by them to corner him. Labouchere thought Parnell did not want the home rule question to be settled in case he lost his commanding position.[125] This assessment appears unrealistic. However, Parnell had difficulties in his party about 'a domestic detail' and the electoral support he was giving W. H. O'Shea. It was only in February 1886, by which time the liberals and Parnellites were political allies, that Parnell demonstrated his authority during the Galway election.[126] On the other hand, Labouchere sent Herbert Gladstone J. McCarthy's views about Parnell's attitude towards a home rule settlement which conflicted with his own.[127] Labouchere saw himself as the intermediary between Gladstone and the Parnellites.[128] Gladstone denied this unequivocally. On 16 December, for instance, he told Mrs O'Shea that he was not in communication with Labouchere.[129] Five days later Gladstone asked his son to thank Labouchere for a letter that contained 'much that is interesting [and] may become important'.[130]

In the resumed correspondence Herbert Gladstone dealt primarily with the principles that would guide his father's policy on home rule if he formed an administration, but occasionally he desired specific information from the Parnellites. Doubts that Gladstone might translate his home rule declarations into a narrow scheme plagued Healy. Herbert Gladstone, via Labouchere, reassured Healy on 10 December. He stated

---

[124] H.G.P., B.M. Add. MSS. 46015 fo. 134, Labouchere to H. Gladstone, 30 Dec. 1885. On 19 December Healy told Labouchere that he could 'arrange everything' himself. Healy alleged that he had seen McCarthy, Harrington, O'Brien and Dillon, and, by the 20th, T. P. O'Connor. H.G.P., B.M. Add. MSS., 46015, fo. 85, Labouchere to H. Gladstone, 19 Dec. 1885; fo. 95, 20 Dec. 1885.

[125] H.G.P., B.M. Add. MSS., 46015, fos. 60, 71, 134, Labouchere to H. Gladstone, 8, 10 and 30 December 1885.

[126] C. Cruise O'Brien, pp. 166–84; T. W. Moody, 'Parnell and the Galway Election of 1886', *Irish Historical Studies*, ix (1954–5), 319ff.

[127] H.G.P., B.M. Add. MSS., 46015, fo. 74, Labouchere to H. Gladstone, 14 Dec. 1885.

[128] Sy.P., Churchill to Salisbury, 22 Dec. 1885.

[129] G.P., B.M. Add. MSS., 44269, fo. 249, Gladstone to K. O'Shea (copy), 16 Dec. 1885.

[130] H.G.P., B.M. Add. MSS., 46015, fo. 98, Gladstone to H. Gladstone, 21 Dec. 1885.

that his father was 'anxious to proceed on the first opportunity' on the basis of the six conditions listed in his letter of 16 November and to frame a 'broad and generous scheme'.[131] Two weeks later he gave another assurance: his father would 'go forward or fall'[132] even if the liberal party disintegrated.[133] This perhaps reassured Healy, for he revealed the type of restrictions which he thought the Irish could accept. On 19 December, Labouchere sent Herbert Gladstone Healy's views on the veto, the protection of the minority, the judiciary, taxation and a governor.[134] Early in January 1886 Healy, through Labouchere, offered Gladstone security for the permanence of a home rule settlement if it were made by him:

I undertake to say, though Parnell may have said that he would offer no guarantees, that we would call a national Convention to ratify it, and thenceforth treat as a traitor everyone who afterwards opposed it, or did not loyally abide by it.[135]

The correspondence pinpointed the fact that the Irish '*could* not agree to any veto by the Imperial Parliament. This is the crucial test with the masses.'[136] According to Labouchere, the Irish argued that if the queen had the veto, she acted upon the advice of her English ministers: its exercise by the house of commons would place the Irish at the mercy of English party exigencies, and would compel them to subordinate their views on taxation to those of the English electorate.[137] He suggested to Herbert Gladstone that they might accept the veto if it were exercised by a royal governor and a reconstituted Irish privy council.[138]

Herbert Gladstone tested Irish reaction by suggesting that the veto might be exercised by the crown, normally on the advice of an Irish ministry but on specific questions such as religion, commerce and perhaps taxation, on the advice of the

[131] Ibid., fo. 69, H. Gladstone to Labouchere (copy), 10 Dec. 1885.
[132] Ibid., fo. 116, H. Gladstone to Labouchere (copy), 25 Dec. 1885.
[133] Ibid., fo. 132, H. Gladstone to Labouchere (copy), 29 Dec. 1885.
[134] Ibid., fos. 86–9, Labouchere to H. Gladstone, 19 Dec. 1885.
[135] Ibid., fo. 146, Healy to Labouchere (copy), 7 Jan. 1886.
[136] Ibid., fo. 93, Labouchere to H. Gladstone, 19 Dec. 1885. The emphasis is Labouchere's.
[137] Ibid., fo. 120, Labouchere to H. Gladstone, 26 Dec. 1885.
[138] Ibid., fo. 113, Labouchere to H. Gladstone, undated [?19 Dec. 1885].

imperial ministry. He recognized that this was a 'most delicate subject as it would be difficult to distinguish between the questions belonging to one or the other ministry'. Despite the fact that Labouchere had previously told him that the Irish would not accept the proposal, Herbert Gladstone asked if the Irish could accept the Irish privy council, as then constituted, as the holder of the veto.[139] Labouchere repeated that they would 'naturally insist' upon reconstitution.[140]

Other strands of the home rule skein reached Hawarden in this correspondence. For instance, on 10 December Herbert Gladstone suggested that certain provisions in the American constitution might be adapted to give the Irish landlords adequate security.[141] Labouchere, the same day, anticipated this proposal by advising him that Parnell had criticized Chamberlain's local government scheme, on the grounds that it left questions about conflicting jurisdiction to courts composed of Englishmen. Moreover, he alleged that Parnell 'strongly insisted upon the Irish Assembly being called a Parliament'.[142] Shortly before the liberals and Parnellites joined forces to overthrow the conservatives in January 1886 Labouchere wrote to Herbert Gladstone:

Parnell ... asked me to suggest, that a Bill for Home Rule and for the settlement of the land question by some scheme of land purchase would, in his opinion be a good course. He would rather that the latter were settled by the Imperial Parliament, because he says that, in this case, he ... can hold his own in Ireland ... and answer for the tranquillity of the Island.[143]

Labouchere also kept Herbert Gladstone in touch with general political developments. He mentioned J. McCarthy's appointment with Lord Carnarvon on 13 December 1885,[144] and sent information about the conservatives' views which he culled from Lord Randolph Churchill. On 3 December

[139] H.G.P, B.M. Add. MSS., 46015, fos. 116–17, H. Gladstone to Labouchere, 25 Dec. 1885.
[140] Ibid., fo. 119, Labouchere to H. Gladstone, 26 Dec. 1885.
[141] Ibid., fo. 69, H. Gladstone to Labouchere (copy), 10 Dec. 1885.
[142] Ibid., fo. 72, Labouchere to H. Gladstone, 10 Dec. 1885.
[143] Ibid., fos. 170–1, Labouchere to H. Gladstone, 26 Jan. 1886.
[144] Ibid., fo. 74, Labouchere to H. Gladstone, 14 Dec. 1885. Carnarvon asked McCarthy 'whether ... Parnell would accept an "Inquiry", during which the Conservatives might be educated'. McCarthy rejected the offer.

IRISH ISSUES, 1885 AND 1886 119

Labouchere stated that the conservatives intended to oppose home rule,[145] and in view of this Herbert Gladstone wondered whether the Parnellites intended to 'press on the main question'.[146] On 14 December, immediately after a cabinet meeting, Labouchere telegraphed the news to Herbert Gladstone that the conservatives would meet the new parliament, ask for a vote of confidence, and, if it were refused, 'bundle out with joy'.[147]

A week later he forwarded to Herbert Gladstone an account of conversations he had had with Lord Randolph Churchill. It was rich in details about prospective conservative tactics and contained the information that the conservatives would not offer a central assembly to Ireland and that if Gladstone did propose home rule, Lord Randolph intended to 'have the 800,000 Orangemen in arms within a few weeks'.[148] Herbert Gladstone thought this threat was 95 per cent 'bunkum'.[149]

Churchill, on the other hand, thought Labouchere provided him with 'most useful information'.[150] Their views about Gladstone's methods probably tallied: in Labouchere's view, Gladstone 'could give lessons to Machiavelli'.[151] Labouchere alleged that Gladstone was 'mad to come in', and that he would 'give anything to the Irish' but for the need to conciliate the whigs.[152] He doubted Gladstone's sincerity in offering to assist the conservatives if they tackled the home rule question, and asked Churchill if he had considered the possibility that Gladstone might take office with Irish help and then, following the precedent of the franchise bill of 1884, propose conferences with Salisbury.[153] Labouchere, in the same period that he

[145] H.G.P., B.M. Add. MSS., 46015, fo. 55, Labouchere to H. Gladstone, 3 Dec. 1885. [146] Ibid., fo. 59, H. Gladstone to Labouchere (copy), 7 Dec. 1885.
[147] Ibid., fo. 76, Labouchere to H. Gladstone, 14 Dec. 1885. On 17 December he stated that the cabinet had decided to angle for the moderate liberals (fo. 78). In October conservatives made overtures to Hartington. B.P., B.M. Add. MSS., 49696, fo. 8, W. H. Smith to A. Balfour, 24 Oct. 1885.
[148] H.G.P., B.M. Add. MSS., 46015, fos. 103-8, Labouchere to H. Gladstone (2nd letter), 22 Dec. 1885.
[149] Ibid., fo. 116, H. Gladstone to Labouchere (copy), 25 Dec. 1885.
[150] Sy.P., Churchill to Salisbury, 27 Sept. 1885.
[151] R.C.P., 1238, Labouchere to Churchill, [?2 Jan. 1886].
[152] R.C.P., 1158, Labouchere to Churchill, [?10 Dec. 1885]. The evidence does not support these opinions.
[153] R.C.P., 1243, Labouchere to Churchill, 4 Jan. 1886.

reassured Herbert Gladstone that there was nothing to fear from Chamberlain, intimated to Churchill that Gladstone might suffer defections from the radical, as well as the whig, section of the liberal party. He commented on Chamberlain's recalcitrance towards home rule,[154] and his desire to 'let the question slide'. Chamberlain, he said, was in a 'condition of fury against Gladstone who had not consulted him in any way'.[155] Labouchere later advised Churchill that Chamberlain was wavering, and that 'party hacks' were manœuvring to thwart Gladstone.[156]

In his letters to Churchill, Labouchere did not give details of the limitations to the sovereignty of an Irish assembly which Healy thought the Irish could accept. He stated that no arrangement existed between Parnell and Gladstone,[157] and on 1 January 1886 he told Churchill: 'Nothing will be settled until your Queen's Speech is known.'[158] However, during a meeting with Churchill on 22 December 1885, he mentioned J. McCarthy's meeting with Carnarvon, and he appears to have been more specific. He advised Churchill that Gladstone and Parnell's lieutenants had agreed about 'every difficulty' except the veto.[159] Three days later he informed Churchill about his letter which would appear in *The Times* in which the 'scheme to which the Irish would assent with groans and protests is put in black and white'.[160] He made no mention of the genesis of this letter which *The Times* published on 28 December.

A significant feature of Labouchere's correspondence with Churchill was his repeated assertion that radicals would move an amendment to the address, pledging parliament to implement home rule.[161] In the new parliament of 1886 they did not move a home rule amendment, but if radicals had done so they would have given conservatives considerable parliamentary advantage. Labouchere thought Gladstone would be obliged

[154] R.C.P., 1521, Labouchere to Churchill, 1 Jan. 1886; cf. Nos. 1158, 1170; these undated letters were written in December 1885.
[155] Sy.P., Churchill to Salisbury, 22 Dec. 1885.
[156] R.C.P., 1255, Labouchere to Churchill, 6 Jan. 1886.
[157] R.C.P., 1170, 1158, Labouchere to Churchill, [?2 Dec. 1885, ?10 Dec. 1885].
[158] R.C.P., 1521, Labouchere to Churchill, 1 Jan. 1886.
[159] Sy.P., Churchill to Salisbury, 22 Dec. 1885.
[160] R.C.P., 1206, Labouchere to Churchill, 25 Dec. 1885.
[161] R.C.P., 1199, 1206, Labouchere to Churchill, 23 and 25 Dec. 1885.

to support a home rule amendment but he was 'by no means certain' of its success if it met conservative opposition.[162] On 7 January 1886 Labouchere admitted to Churchill that he would be 'quite satisfied' if Gladstone voted for a home rule resolution.[163]

Labouchere told Chamberlain about the information he gleaned from Churchill. He also kept him *au fait* with the information he sent to, and received from Herbert Gladstone.[164] In his letters, Labouchere did not tell Chamberlain about McCarthy's meeting with Carnarvon but he probably discussed this when he visited Highbury from 16 to 17 December. The only significant development in the political situation which Labouchere kept from Chamberlain was that Labouchere's letter which *The Times* published on 28 December contained the Irish minimum on home rule. When he communicated with Chamberlain, Labouchere appears to have calculated that the more Chamberlain knew about political developments, apart from the Irish minimum, the easier it would be to induce him to support home rule. If this was the case, he failed. However, he may have sent detailed accounts of Herbert Gladstone's views of his father's attitude, and of Healy's willingness to come to terms, in order to prevent Chamberlain pledging himself against the concession. In this he succeeded though neither his arguments, nor his analysis of, and revelations about political developments moved Chamberlain significantly closer to Gladstone's views. Nevertheless, the information Labouchere sent Chamberlain and the discussions they had on 16 and 17 December appear to have had a restraining effect upon Chamberlain. The *Annual Register* noted that when Chamberlain spoke at Birmingham on 17 December he 'displayed more than ordinary caution in dealing with the home rule question'.[165]

Labouchere tried to show Chamberlain that his own and radicals' interest made Chamberlain's acceptance of home rule essential. He was certain that it was an issue which would drive the whigs from the liberal party and strengthen Chamberlain's

---

[162] R.C.P., 1158, Labouchere to Churchill, [?10 Dec. 1885].
[163] R.C.P., 1261, Labouchere to Churchill, 7 Jan. 1886.
[164] J.C., 5/50/26ff.; A. L. Thorold, pp. 243ff.
[165] *Annual Register*, 1885, p. 190.

claim to Gladstone's mantle.[166] Moreover, he believed that, if radical hostility frustrated Irish aspirations, radicals would not benefit as the English electorate would prefer conservatives to 'fight with the Irish'.[167] Chamberlain wished to avoid 'positive committal', to 'lie low',[168] and 'wait and see'.[169] Labouchere criticized this attitude on the grounds that Chamberlain based it on the false assumption that the Parnellites and the conservatives would act as he desired.[170]

Labouchere sent Herbert Gladstone the information which he received from Chamberlain. He gave Herbert Gladstone a detailed account of Chamberlain's position on 17 December, and this included Chamberlain's declaration that he would oppose any home rule scheme similar to that outlined by the *Standard*. A week later he commented about Chamberlain's recalcitrance on the home rule question. Labouchere transcribed parts of Chamberlain's letters, and sent others complete to Herbert Gladstone. He indubitably tried to convince Herbert Gladstone that there was nothing to fear 'beyond talk' from Chamberlain, and that Chamberlain would 'knock under' to Gladstone,[171] but he also sent Herbert Gladstone sufficient evidence to allow him to judge for himself. In particular, two of Chamberlain's proposals, which were radical and contradictory, and in marked contrast to his attitude later, lent weight to Labouchere's assessment. On 26 December, Chamberlain proposed to Labouchere separate legislatures for England, Scotland, Wales, possibly Ulster, and the other Irish provinces, with an imperial legislature at Westminster for foreign affairs, the army, the navy, the post office and customs, and with a supreme court. Chamberlain believed that in this scheme

[166] J.C., 5/50/32, 34, 37, Labouchere to Chamberlain, 8, 19, 23 Dec. 1885; A. L. Thorold, pp. 248, 252, 255.

[167] J.C., 5/50/38, Labouchere to Chamberlain, 24 Dec. 1885; A. L. Thorold, p. 261.

[168] J.C., 5/50/37a, Chamberlain to Labouchere (copy), 24 Dec., 1885; A. L. Thorold, p. 262.

[169] J.C., 5/50/40a, Chamberlain to Labouchere (copy), 27 Dec. 1885; A. L. Thorold, p. 273.

[170] J.C., 5/50/41, Labouchere to Chamberlain, 28 Dec. 1885; A. L. Thorold, p. 273; H.G.P., B.M. Add. MSS., 46015, fo. 126, Labouchere to H. Gladstone, 28 Dec. 1885.

[171] H.G.P., B.M. Add. MSS., 46015, fos. 111, 125–6, Labouchere to H. Gladstone, 22 (2nd letter) and 28 Dec. 1885.

the Lords would go. I do not suppose that the 5 Legislatures would desire a 2nd Chamber apiece. Each would have its own ministry, responsible to itself. The authority of the Crown would not survive for very long. One of the Legislatures would refuse to pay the Prince of Battenberg's annuity or some such matter, & I do not think that the others would fight for it.[172]

On 3 January 1886, Chamberlain temporarily abandoned his federal proposals and suggested that 'England's authority . . . be confined exclusively to the measures necessary to secure that Ireland shall not be a *point d'appui* for a Foreign Country'. In view of Chamberlain's later insistence upon Irish representation, it is remarkable that he should have stated, 'the worst of all plans would be one which kept the Irishmen at Westminster while they had their own Parliament in Dublin'.[173]

Labouchere failed to win Chamberlain's support for home rule at this time, and he also failed to arrange terms between Gladstone and Healy. A primary reason for Gladstone's refusal to particularize was the fact that the conservative government had not declared its policy with the result that 'in the face of the world' the alliance between conservatives and Parnellites still existed.[174] On 17 January 1886 Healy told Labouchere that the Irish 'had nothing but a repudiation of the principles attributed to him [Gladstone] by the "Revelations", and this *plus* good intentions is not sufficient ground for us to decide on'.[175] In the period of political deadlock which existed in December 1885 and in part of January 1886, Gladstone had offered his support to conservatives if they tackled the question of the government of Ireland. Labouchere tried to break the deadlock. He sounded Herbert Gladstone[176] and Churchill[177] to see if Gladstone or Salisbury would answer a letter from him. Had

---

[172] J.C., 5/50/38a, Chamberlain to Labouchere (copy), 26 Dec. 1885.
[173] J.C., 5/50/43a, Chamberlain to Labouchere (copy), 3 Jan. 1886; A. L. Thorold, p. 279.
[174] H.G.P., B.M. Add. MSS., 46015, fo. 99, H. Gladstone to Labouchere (copy), 21 Dec. 1885.
[175] Ibid., fo. 155, Healy to Labouchere (copy), 17 Jan. 1886.
[176] Ibid., fo. 119, Labouchere to H. Gladstone, 26 Dec. 1885; fos. 131–2, H. Gladstone to Labouchere (copy), 28 Dec. 1885.
[177] R.C.P., 1202, 1206, Labouchere to Churchill, [?24 Dec. 1885], 25 Dec. 1885; Sy.P., Churchill to Salisbury, 26 Dec. 1885; A. L. Thorold, p. 271, Churchill to Labouchere, 26 Dec. 1885.

either statesman done so he would have committed himself to implement home rule or to oppose it. Both Salisbury and Gladstone rejected this naïve overture.

Labouchere made a more positive contribution in helping to crystallize opinion about home rule. He was aware of 'the undoubted hostility' that existed in 'England to Ireland & Home Rule',[178] and since the end of 1880 *Truth* had attempted to reduce this feeling. By the end of 1885 the home rule question was urgent: liberals and Parnellites wished to know the other's minimum demands, yet, on tactical grounds alone, neither could be precipitate. On 28 December 1885 *The Times* published a letter from Labouchere which indicated the Irish minimum on home rule. An important feature of this letter was the fact that Healy had written a considerable part of it.[179] Labouchere wished to show that the Parnellites were practical and 'very yieldy in details'.[180] He privately advised Herbert Gladstone that the letter was designed 'not to define an entire arrangement, but to set forth guarantees, as specimens of the sort which the Irish would accept'.[181] *The Times*, in a leading article, argued that Labouchere's proposals embraced 'powers hardly distinguishable from complete independence' for it believed the 'checks ... limitations, and guarantees' were 'manifestly illusory'.[182] The letter provoked a vigorous debate in *The Times* to which Labouchere made three further contributions.[183] In one letter he described the Irish leaders as 'inoffensive but intelligent creatures, uniting the innocence of sheep, the gentleness of doves, and the intelligence of Statesmen!'[184]

The defeat of the conservatives on 27 January 1886 over J. Collings' 'three acres and a cow' amendment, partially resolved the delicate political situation which had existed since parlia-

[178] H.G.P., B.M. Add. MSS., 46015, fo. 119, Labouchere to H. Gladstone, 26 Dec. 1885.
[179] Ibid., fo. 122, Labouchere to H. Gladstone, 27 Dec. 1885.
[180] Ibid., fo. 118, Labouchere to H. Gladstone, 25 Dec. 1885.
[181] Ibid., fo. 122, Labouchere to H. Gladstone, 27 Dec. 1885.
[182] *Times*, 28 Dec. 1885.
[183] *Times*, 30 Dec. 1885, 4, 5 Jan. 1886.
[184] N.L.S., Rosebery Papers, 32, Labouchere to Rosebery, 2 Jan. 1886.

ment met on 21 January. Liberals were 'hopelessly at sea'[185] on the home rule issue: a whig amendment pledging parliament to maintain the legislative union, or a Parnellite home rule amendment would have shattered them. Labouchere, whom Kate Courtney described in her journal as the 'recognized... go-between of the Irish',[186] helped to co-ordinate liberal and Parnellite activity. He discussed the situation with Herbert Gladstone and sent him information from Healy and Parnell. He told him of Chamberlain's failure to persuade Parnell to shelve home rule for a 'large operation of land purchase'. He also prevented a collapse of the opening debate in parliament by provoking an 'Orangeman... grinding his teeth' at him to speak.[187]

On 22 January Labouchere criticized in parliament that section of the queen's speech which related to Ireland but he did not divide the House on it. He challenged the view that the legislative union was a fundamental constitutional law by arguing that the disestablishment of the Irish Church in 1869 had already modified it, and that, in any case, it was unconstitutional to argue that certain laws were immutable. He taunted conservatives about their policy towards Ireland, and about their desire to turn parliament into an Irish faction fight. He quoted from a speech made by Chamberlain at Islington, on 17 June 1885 before the 'central board' scheme collapsed, in which he claimed that the 'Irish government was founded on the bayonets of 30,000 soldiers, encamped permanently in a hostile country', to argue against such a system of government.

He attacked the conservative government for confusing the issues of local government and home rule, and for insisting that the latter was synonymous with separation. He asked its supporters whether they knew that in Hungary, Sweden, Norway, Switzerland and Germany, local governments existed 'absolutely independent in all local matters of the Imperial Government' and whether they considered Canada and other colonies

---

[185] H.G.P., B.M. Add. MSS., 46015, fo. 157, H. Gladstone to Labouchere (copy), 18 Jan. 1886.    [186] Cy.P., Journal, R.(S.R.) 1003, 22, fo. 79, [?23 Jan. 1886].
[187] Chamberlain, p. 178. Chamberlain asserted that he gave the memorandum to W. H. O'Shea. Labouchere asserted that he made the communication to Parnell for Chamberlain. He sent it to H. Gladstone on 24 January. H.G.P., B.M. Add. MSS., 46015, fos. 161, 168, Labouchere to H. Gladstone, 22, 24 Jan. 1886.

'an integral part of our Empire'. He asserted that as 'the British Empire was composed not only of these Islands, but also of our Colonies', its integrity 'would be unimpaired, if there were a dozen Parliaments in Scotland, Wales and Ireland'. Liberals, he alleged, desired 'to unite the local independence of Ireland, with the maintenance of Imperial authority'.

He believed the act of union of 1800 was 'one of the most conspicuous failures in political history'. He admitted that the Irish land question complicated the home rule issue, but he challenged conservatives to substantiate their contention that the Irish would confiscate the land if they were granted home rule. So far as religious problems were concerned, he asserted that sectarianism was stronger in England than in Ireland but that Orangemen used religious differences in Ireland to perpetuate ill feeling. He rejoiced that many Orange candidates had been defeated in Ulster.

Labouchere requested members of parliament to believe Parnellites' statements that they did not desire separation. He stated that they would give 'every species of guarantee that could be desired', but he believed this was unnecessary. 'England was far stronger than Ireland, and would hold the forts and command the troops . . . and could destroy the country in a fortnight. . . . Our real guarantee was the Army, and the fact that we were the stronger power.'

He thought home rule would be opposed 'by those who wished to stave off democratic changes in this country; for if they could engage this country in perpetual disputes about Ireland, they knew that they would arrest democratic progress'. He predicted that if conservatives provoked a 'war between the two countries' they 'would remain in power, with some short intervals, for the next 20 years'.[188]

In January 1886 *Truth* advocated a substantial home rule scheme on the grounds that the 'fewer points of contact' between England and Ireland 'the less probability is there of friction'. It warned its readers that the Irish would require a parliament and would not accept a veto of the imperial parliament. It suggested that English opinion would not favour an imperial veto as a 'disturbing influence' to party government

[188] Hansard, 3rd ser., 302, 225–35, 22 Jan. 1886.

would remain. *Truth* believed that if the English granted home rule, the Irish would neither confiscate land nor legislate unjustly towards minorities. It thought they would soon be 'as proud of forming an integral part of the Empire as is Canada or Australia'.[189] However, if it were refused, *Truth* prophesied that English law would be inoperative as it would lack an Irish social sanction.[190] It criticized minor concessions such as county self-government, as it considered this would not satisfy the Irish and would merely provide them with 'leverage for ... more organized agitation'.[191]

*Truth* considered that Irish landlords would receive better terms from an Irish parliament than from the imperial parliament for the 'first care of an Irish Government' would be to 'consolidate the nation by conciliating and winning over to Nationalism every anti-national interest'. However, it felt that if Irish landlords' strength prevented the English dealing with Ireland 'justly' then 'terms must be made'.[192]

During Gladstone's third administration Labouchere strove to ease the passage of the first home rule bill through parliament. He tried to prevent Chamberlain from opposing home rule, and he attempted to persuade Gladstone to make concessions to Chamberlain's point of view. He continued to act as a link between the Parnellites and the liberals, but his importance in this respect declined appreciably for Parnell and Morley were in frequent communication. He played upon public opinion through *Truth* and the *Daily News*. In addition, he organized a 'packed' radical home rule demonstration in London on 22 April, which, in Herbert Gladstone's opinion, was of 'great importance'.[193]

---

[189] *Truth*, 7 Jan. 1886, pp. 10–11. This was Labouchere's first public expression of opinion about the imperial veto.   [190] *Truth*, 14 Jan. 1886, p. 53.
[191] *Truth*, 21 Jan. 1886, p. 92.   [192] *Truth*, 28 Jan. 1886, pp. 133–4.
[193] H.G.P., B.M. Add. MSS., 46016, fo. 30, H. Gladstone to Labouchere (copy), 10 April 1886. Labouchere paid £50 towards the cost of the meeting and H. Gladstone contributed £100 which he could not obtain from official party funds. For their correspondence about this meeting see H.G.P., B.M. Add. MSS., 46016, fos. 26–7, 30–1, 33, 40, 85, of 10, 13, 26 April, 8 June 1886. Labouchere admitted to Chamberlain the justice of *The Times*' charge, on 23 April, that he had indulged in cheap rhetoric: Labouchere stated that he had merely wished to 'distinguish between the principle of the Bill and its details'. J.C., 5/50/57, Labouchere to Chamberlain, 23 April 1886; cf. *Times*, 23 April 1886; J. M. Robertson, *Charles Bradlaugh*, ii, 369.

Chamberlain left the cabinet on 16 March 1886. At the end of the month Labouchere wrote to him and repeated many of his earlier arguments. He entreated Chamberlain to come to some arrangement on 'this damned Irish question' and not wreck radical prospects 'for the sake of minor details about Irish Government'. He told Chamberlain about radicals' hostility to 'any employment of English credit for ... Irish landlords or ... tenants' and he predicted the defeat of Gladstone's scheme for the purchase of Irish land.[194] Chamberlain's cool response[195] failed to deter Labouchere from continuing efforts to weaken his resolution. He pointed out that in connection with customs and excise, and the exclusion of Irish members, Gladstone was making concessions to Chamberlain's point of view.[196]

On 17 April Chamberlain stated that he wanted an arrangement with Gladstone. Chamberlain asserted that he considered it essential that Irish representatives should remain at Westminster, and that imperial control over imperial taxation in Ireland continue. Moreover, in this letter Chamberlain required Gladstone to 'abandon all the so-called safeguards in connection with the Constitution of the new legislative body in Dublin'. Chamberlain thrust the responsibility upon Labouchere of bringing pressure upon the whips, and of obtaining these assurances from Gladstone.[197] Labouchere, in reply, tried to induce Chamberlain to support the second reading of the home rule bill by suggesting that radicals would be masters of the bill in committee and could then see 'Gladstone ... bleed to death instead of being murdered'.[198]

Labouchere explored another approach when he attempted to win Chamberlain's support for a resolution which a radical

[194] J.C., 5/50/50, Labouchere to Chamberlain, 31 March 1886; A. L. Thorold, pp. 289-90.
[195] H.G.P., B.M. Add. MSS., 46016, fos. 21-2, Chamberlain to Labouchere, 31 March 1886.
[196] J.C., 5/50/52, Labouchere to Chamberlain, 15 April 1886; A. L. Thorold, p. 291.
[197] J.C., 5/50/52a, Chamberlain to Labouchere (copy), 17 April 1886 (1st letter); A. L. Thorold, p. 292. The original reads 'whips' and 'assurances', not 'Whigs' and 'assurance' as in Thorold.
[198] J.C., 5/50/54, Labouchere to Chamberlain, 19 April 1886; A. L. Thorold, p. 294.

demonstration in London would adopt on 22 April.[199] This would have pledged Chamberlain not to oppose the bill's second reading, but he was not drawn. For although Chamberlain alleged that he supported the home rule principle his attitude appears to have hardened and changed since 17 April. He wished to 'bind' the three kingdoms together and he feared Gladstone's scheme would result in the 'absolute separation' of Ireland.[200]

Gladstone bore Chamberlain's resignation with singular fortitude. He was not inclined to make concessions to him,[201] and may have shared J. Morley's view that Chamberlain only intended conciliation if the government surrendered 'at every point'.[202] Moreover Gladstone's position strengthened when, on 6 May, the National Liberal Federation inflicted a 'great facer'[203] upon Chamberlain, its creator, and accepted the prime minister's policy. On the other hand, Gladstone told Granville that his views were 'perfectly elastic' and that he would 'accept almost any means'[204] to pass the bill's second reading, provided its principles were retained. However, he would not compromise the government's dignity, for on this depended its authority.[205]

Chamberlain focused his criticism upon clause twenty-four, the bill's 'most unpopular feature',[206] which terminated Irish representation at Westminster. Many liberals believed this was 'the bribe . . . however illogical',[207] and many who opposed the bill would have supported in committee Irish withdrawal from Westminster.[208] Originally Gladstone intended to grant the Irish control over customs and excise, but, because of English opposition, he withdrew this power. This alteration affected the

[199] J.C., 5/50/54, 55, 56, Labouchere to Chamberlain, 19 and 20 April 1886; A. L. Thorold, pp. 294–5.
[200] J.C., 5/50/56a, b, Chamberlain to Labouchere (copy), 21 April 1886; A. L. Thorold, p. 296. The original reads 'bind', not 'join' as in Thorold.
[201] H.P., B.M. Add. MSS., 48643, fo. 98, 22 April 1886; 48644, fo. 27, 6 June 1886.
[202] G.P., B.M. Add. MSS., 44255, fo. 75, J. Morley to Gladstone, 19 April 1886.
[203] H.P., B.M. Add. MSS., 48643, fo. 112, 6 May 1886.
[204] Ge.P., P.R.O., 30/29/29, Gladstone to Granville, 30 April 1886.
[205] H.P., B.M. Add. MSS., 48608(8), Gladstone to E. Hamilton, 16 May 1886.
[206] H.P., B.M. Add. MSS., 48643, fo. 78, 10 April 1886.
[207] S.P., Granville to Spencer, 28 Dec. 1885.
[208] G.P., B.M. Add. MSS., 44179, fo. 118, Granville to Gladstone, 16 May 1886.

allied question of Irish representation for the severance of the principles of representation and taxation had serious constitutional implications. In addition, the withdrawal of the Irish right to participate in imperial affairs was perhaps the strongest factor in giving the complexion of separation to the scheme. Chamberlain's criticism of clause twenty-four was largely destructive and he refused to send Labouchere a draft to show his proposals were viable.[209] As Herbert Gladstone pointed out, no working draft for retention existed, and unconditional retention would give the Irish 'absolute predominance' in imperial, English, Scottish and Welsh affairs.[210]

The most important of Labouchere's attempts to mediate between Gladstone and Chamberlain collapsed on 10 May 1886.[211] He had communicated with Chamberlain,[212] Herbert Gladstone,[213] and, less frequently, with A. Morley, the chief liberal whip,[214] and J. Morley,[215] the chief secretary of Ireland. He appeared to have brought Gladstone and Chamberlain closer together. On 8 May, Chamberlain received from Labouchere an assurance that the cabinet had just agreed to the concessions he desired. The precise details of the agreement were to remain secret if negotiations collapsed,[216] and appear to have disappeared. They presumably consisted of full Irish representation by right on all matters of taxation, and by address on any question of imperial policy, together with the development of some procedure by which Irish views on matters excluded from their legislature could reach the imperial par-

[209] J.C., 5/50/59, 60, Labouchere to Chamberlain, 1 May 1886; A. L. Thorold, pp. 300–2.

[210] H.G.P., B.M. Add. MSS., 46016, fos. 62–3, H. Gladstone to Labouchere (copy), 2 May 1886; J. L. Hammond, p. 528.

[211] D. C. Savage, 'The General Election of 1886 in Great Britain and Ireland' (Lond., Ph.D., 1958) (pp. 66ff., 267ff.), provides a detailed account of these transactions.

[212] J.C., 5/50/51–77; A. L. Thorold, pp. 390ff.

[213] H.G.P., B.M. Add. MSS., 46016, fos. 26–62.

[214] A. L. Thorold, p. 307; G.P., B.M. Add. MSS., 44253, fos. 5, 7, A. Morley to Gladstone, 19 April, 3 May 1886.

[215] G.P., B.M. Add. MSS., 44255, fo. 74, J. Morley to Gladstone, 19 April 1886. Chamberlain's letters to Labouchere circulated among liberal leaders via H. Gladstone and J. Morley.

[216] J.C., 5/50/71, Labouchere to Chamberlain (telegram), 8 May 1886; A. L. Thorold, p. 307; H. W. Lucy, Labouchere to Lucy, 5 April 1898, p. 121; *Truth*, 14 Oct. 1908, pp. 877–80.

liament.²¹⁷ Gladstone, the cabinet and Parnell had no intention of conceding full representation on all matters without reserve.²¹⁸ Many liberals considered that the exclusion of Irish representatives from Westminster was 'one of the pillars'²¹⁹ of home rule. Chamberlain telegraphed the 'absolute surrender' of Gladstone to his political associates. One of them, W. H. O'Shea, showed the telegram to Parnell. He informed Gladstone, who then told a reporter that he had yielded nothing to Chamberlain.²²⁰

On the evening of 8 May, Labouchere spoke at Hastings. He returned to London the next day unaware of the latest tensions which had arisen between Gladstone and Chamberlain. He wrote to Chamberlain, 'You went for "full representation", and, as I understand it you get it.'²²¹ Chamberlain's reply indicated recent developments.²²² Labouchere and A. Morley sent a messenger to Gladstone and discovered that the premier stood by his agreement to make the concessions, though he had reservations about one aspect of it.²²³ Labouchere visited Chamberlain and told him this. Later, on 9 May, J. Morley called on Labouchere, and, according to the latter's account to Chamberlain, warned that as the cabinet faced problems connected with 'the right of the Irish to come here by requisition of the Dublin Parliament on all Imperial matters',²²⁴ Gladstone might be vague when announcing this part of the changes arising from the concessions to Chamberlain. If this were the case, then Herschell, the lord chancellor, would consult Chamberlain later.

On 10 May, before the debate, Labouchere told Chamberlain that he had perhaps over-emphasized the problems associated with a definition of 'imperial affairs' in his previous

---

[217] J. L. Hammond, p. 526; D. C. Savage, p. 273; J. K. Lindsay, 'The Liberal Unionist Party' (Edin., Ph.D., 1955), p. 139.
[218] G.P., B.M. Add. MSS., 44647, fo. 93, cabinet memorandum by Gladstone, 4 May 1886.
[219] J.B.P. (Bodleian), 7 fo. 216, E. A. Freeman to Bryce, 2 May 1886.
[220] Gladstone's irritation may have been increased by Chamberlain's aggressive insistence upon full Irish representation; see *Times*, 8 May 1886.
[221] J.C., 5/50/72, Labouchere to Chamberlain, 9 May 1886; A. L. Thorold, p. 308.
[222] J.C., 5/50/71a, Chamberlain to Labouchere (copy), 9 May 1886; A. L. Thorold, p. 309.     [223] H. W. Lucy, p. 120.
[224] J.C., 5/50/73, Labouchere to Chamberlain (2nd letter), 9 May 1886; A. L. Thorold, pp. 308-9.

letter. 'I had been fighting [with J. Morley] for the exact words, and was cross about their not being precisely as I understood they would be.' He reported that J. Morley had repeatedly disavowed any 'intention to dodge', and asked Chamberlain to give him any scheme for demarcation between imperial and Irish affairs that he had, so that he could give it to Gladstone before he spoke.[225]

On 10 May, Chamberlain and his supporters came to parliament 'believing that they were squared... with speeches ready' to accept Gladstone's 'announcement that he would give way about the Irish members remaining in the Imperial Parliament as a symbol of the Irish... being under its supremacy'.[226] Gladstone's ambiguity disillusioned them: 'the manner of his speech as much as its matter... offended Chamberlain'.[227]

Herbert Gladstone held Labouchere responsible for the misunderstanding, and alleged that he had thought the concessions agreed on 8 May would not satisfy Chamberlain. Nevertheless he conceded that his father was not 'as clear and forcible as usual in expounding what he proposed to concede'.[228] However, on 11 May he told Labouchere that any deficiency in Gladstone's speech sprang from his not having 'sufficiently mastered the difficulties'. He continued, 'I think now he [Gladstone] has arrrived at what may distinctly be a basis of conciliation... founded on the three points.... When Herschell sees C[hamberlain] tomorrow he may be able to give substantive proposals.'[229]

On the same day Labouchere had advised Herbert Gladstone that any concessions to Chamberlain had to be 'absolutely definite' and that Irish representation on 'all matters of Imperial

---

[225] J.C., 5/50/74, 75, Labouchere to Chamberlain, 10 May 1886; A. L. Thorold, pp. 309–10.
[226] Cy.P., Journal, R.(S.R.) 1003, 22, fo. 122, 10 May 1886.
[227] J. L. Hammond, p. 527.
[228] Ibid., p. 530, H. Gladstone to Henry Gladstone, 14 May 1886.
[229] J.C., 5/50/76, H. Gladstone to Labouchere, 11 May 1886. 'The objects which I have been striving to influence my Father... are (1) Full representation on taxation (2) Power to Irish Par$^{mt.}$ to have direct share in imperial & excluded subjects (3) Effective supremacy of Crown & Par$^{mt.}$ over Irish Par$^{mt.}$' There does not appear to be a copy of this letter in the papers of H. Gladstone.

interests including ... taxation'[230] might save the bill. He contended that Chamberlain had arrived at the 'very lowest point consistent with his uttrances [*sic*]'.[231] Their discussions neglected one point: on 11 May, Chamberlain declined to meet Herschell as 'no good could come of any private interview'.[232]

Labouchere's next move, prompted by Herbert Gladstone, was to sound Chamberlain[233] about the possibility of the party voting 'unitedly for the Bill, as a resolution (the Bill being subsequently withdrawn)'.[234] Although Chamberlain had made a similar proposal to Labouchere on 4 May, he stated on 17 May that he was pledged to oppose the second reading of the home rule bill.[235] The next day, Labouchere launched a vigorous personal attack upon Chamberlain in parliament.[236] He did this as a 'matter of tactics' in the hope that Chamberlain would reply in a similar vein and thus demonstrate that he was actuated by personal motives.[237]

Gladstone's meeting with liberal members of parliament at the foreign office on 27 May tilted the balance of political advantage inside the liberal party decisively in his favour for he appeared to have drawn supporters from Chamberlain. The following day Labouchere asked Herbert Gladstone if he could ask the prime minister a series of questions in parliament. Labouchere hoped that Gladstone would answer his questions simply and in the affirmative on 28 May: and had Gladstone done so, he would have given an 'official *imprimatur*' in the House to the concessions agreed at the meeting the previous day.[238] Herbert Gladstone may not have told his father about this offer

---

[230] H.G.P., B.M. Add. MSS., 46016, fo. 66, Labouchere to H. Gladstone (1st letter), 11 May 1886.

[231] Ibid., fo. 70 (2nd letter, the foliation of which is fos. 68–71, fos. 54–5).

[232] J.C., 5/50/75a, b, Chamberlain to Labouchere (copies), 11 May 1886; A. L. Thorold, p. 311.

[233] J.C., 5/50/78, Labouchere to Chamberlain, 17 May 1886; A. L. Thorold, pp. 312–14.

[234] H.G.P., B.M. Add. MSS., 46016, fo. 77, Labouchere to H. Gladstone, 18 May 1886.

[235] J.C., 5/50/78a, Chamberlain to Labouchere (copy), 17 May 1886; A. L. Thorold, pp. 314–15.

[236] Hansard, 3rd ser., 305, 1330–45, 18 May 1886.

[237] H.G.P., B.M. Add. MSS., 46016, fo. 78, Labouchere to H. Gladstone, 18 May 1886.

[238] Ibid., fos. 81–2, Labouchere to H. Gladstone, 28 May 1886.

which was neglected. Then, on 29 May, Hicks Beach provoked Gladstone in parliament, and the prime minister seemed to withdraw much that he had offered on 27 May. Chamberlain seized this opportunity and met his supporters on 31 May. They startled political circles by deciding 'not to abstain, but to vote against the Bill, thus ensuring its defeat'.[239]

Labouchere had directed his speeches[240] and his journalistic activities towards saving the home rule bill. *Truth* commented regularly but circumspectly about developments in connection with the home rule crisis. On 18 and 24 March, and on 24 May, the *Daily News* published letters from Labouchere which were detailed and which suggested ways of securing the passage of the home rule bill. Much that he knew he did not reveal in the two newspapers in which he had a proprietary interest. As he said to W. T. Stead: 'I cannot utter in *Truth* or in the *Daily News* for I know *privately* ... too much ... to be able to speak ... publicly about it.'[241]

Labouchere's views on the Irish question appear to have changed in the first half of 1886. Between 1880 and 1885 he had opposed schemes of land purchase in Ireland which carried an imperial guarantee. In the early part of 1886 he was prepared to accept proposals of this type in order to ease the passage of the home rule bill. On 24 March, however, Churchill told Salisbury that Labouchere was making Herculean efforts to persuade Gladstone to abandon his land purchase bill,[242] and, by the end of April 1886, Labouchere's attitude had hardened into open opposition. On 18 March, *Truth* reluctantly accepted land purchase as 'ransom to a band of brigands',[243] but the following week it raised four objections and thenceforth opposed it. *Truth* argued that if Irishmen could be trusted with home rule, they were competent to deal with the land question; that it was a 'questionable financial transaction' to buy out landlords on a

---

[239] Cy.P., Journal, R.(S.R.) 1003, 22, fo. 135, 31 May 1886.
[240] *Times*, 23 April 1886; *Northampton Daily Reporter*, 24 April 1886; *Suffolk Times and Mercury*, 30 April 1886; *Ipswich Free Press*, 1 May 1886; *Northampton Daily Reporter*, 13 May 1886.
[241] Sd.P., Labouchere to Stead, 4 June 1886. Professor J. O. Baylen kindly supplied copies of Labouchere's letters to Stead.
[242] Sy.P., Churchill to Salisbury, 24 March 1886.
[243] *Truth*, 18 March 1886, p. 408; cf. *Daily News*, 24 March 1886.

falling market; that guarantors, who in this case were British taxpayers, usually had to pay what they guaranteed; and that even if the British retained money from Irish revenues to meet the guarantee, they might have to choose between returning it or bringing the Irish government to a standstill.[244] Similarly, Labouchere wished to end Irish representation at Westminster, but, by 27 May, he publicly advised Gladstone to yield the principle in order to pass the home rule bill.[245] Such changes of attitude were neither wholly inconsistent nor merely tactical. Labouchere's primary objective was to secure the implementation of the home rule policy in Ireland. Moreover, he believed that if home rule were conceded, the way in which it was painted was immaterial, for 'in ten years' time it will have taken the colour of the country'.

*Truth* criticized Chamberlain and tried to reduce the amount of support he received from radicals. It stated that his 'somersaults in the mud of explanation' reduced his influence.[246] It also suggested that Chamberlain and Caine manipulated the meeting of their supporters on 31 May, by planting twenty-two of Hartington's supporters, and by being less than honest in the use they made of John Bright's letter to Chamberlain.[247]

Labouchere's correspondence with Stead illustrates his attitude towards the home rule bill, and his approach to Chamberlain. For two weeks after Chamberlain's resignation, Labouchere did not communicate with him. He made little reference to him in *Truth*, and on 17 March he urged Stead to ignore him too.[248] In this way Labouchere hoped to emphasize Chamberlain's isolation. After the collapse on 10 May of Labouchere's attempt to bring Gladstone and Chamberlain together, he asked Stead to publish an account of the latter's refusal to discuss the situation with Herschell, the lord chancellor.[249]

On 2 June, Labouchere tried to persuade Stead that Chamberlain knew that the Irish could not have an independent parliament if they had full representation at Westminster and that he demanded the latter to stultify the former. He continued,

[244] *Truth*, 25 March 1886, pp. 444–5.
[245] *Truth*, 27 May 1886, p. 806.     [246] *Truth*, 22 April 1886, p. 603.
[247] *Truth*, 3 June 1886, p. 849. On 2 June Labouchere asked Stead to publish his account of this meeting. See *Pall Mall Gazette*, 4, 5 June 1886.
[248] Sd.P., Labouchere to Stead, 17 March 1886.     [249] Ibid., [?16 May 1886].

All that we can do is to make a double use of our one Westminster Parliament—to have it at one time sitting as an Imperial Parliament, & at another time as a local Parliament for Great Britain. After some experience of this, we shall come to State Legislatures in Scotland, Wales & England.[250]

Two days later Labouchere suggested that the judicial committee of the privy council ought to be vested with powers analogous to those of the American supreme court to 'remove all points in dispute from the area of politics'. He also dealt with the difficulties which would follow from Chamberlain's deceptively simple demand for continuous Irish representation. If

the Irish were to sit continuously, we should have perpetual appeals to the Imperial Parliament, as the Irish would be a sectional minority, practically *Gt. B<sup>n</sup>* [sic] would have a veto on Ireland. The Irish would not be satisfied—the Tories would always be trying to undo the settlement, & the Irish would remain a disturbing element in the Imperial Parliament.[251]

Labouchere considered that continuous representation involved the abandonment of home rule, and on this point he was not prepared to yield.

After the defeat of Gladstone's Government of Ireland bill on 7 June by thirty votes[252] Labouchere fought vigorously to secure a liberal victory at the following general election.[253] *Truth* and the *Daily News* remained staunch champions of home rule.

By 1886 Labouchere was known in England as the 'recognised ... go-between of the Irish' and abroad as the 'mouthpiece of the Irish Nationalists'.[254] He continued to act as a link between them and the liberal party at least until the Parnellite party disintegrated in December 1890. At times he was

[250] Sd. P., Labouchere to Stead, 2 June 1886.
[251] Ibid., 4 June 1886.
[252] Division Lists, 1886, No. 124, 7 June 1886.
[253] He attributed liberals' defeat to lack of united central organization, opposition to Gladstone's land purchase scheme, poor presentation of the home rule case, omission of radical measures for England, inadequate campaigning by liberal leaders except Gladstone and J. Morley, shortage of speakers, and movement of artisans since the previous registration.
[254] *Leipziger Tageblatt*, quoted by *Pall Mall Gazette*, 25 March 1886.

more active in England[255] and Ireland[256] than Irish members themselves. He even preached the 'true but desperately dreary policy of Home Rule'[257] in Wales. He harried conservatives in parliament. He was influential in keeping Chamberlain in political isolation unless he accepted Gladstone's home rule proposals;[258] and he played a prominent part in unmasking the Pigott forgeries.[259]

Until the Irish parliamentary party's disintegration, Labouchere's political stock continued to rise. For conservatives Parnell's involvement in divorce proceedings was a 'most delicious Comedy';[260] for Labouchere its political consequences were disastrous. For tactical reasons he was prepared to shunt home rule into a siding,[261] but he did not abandon the principle. In August 1893 he arranged with Dilke to have a 'Home Rule all round Bill' drafted by Llewellyn Davis on the basis

that there is a local Parliament, with one House, in England, Scotland, Wales & Ireland—& that there is an Imperial Parliament . . . [with] a clear reservation of Imperial matters, and a full right of doing everything else to the local Parliaments, with a supreme court of Judicature to decide . . . conflict of jurisdiction, & the sanctity of contract clause to restrain the local Parliaments.[262]

Consideration of a simultaneous devolution of authority, of which Labouchere had been an early English propagandist,[263]

---

[255] Labouchere addressed an important meeting at Manchester in November 1886. *Manchester Guardian*, 25 Nov. 1886. The organizers at Manchester expected Sexton too, but he defaulted. N.L.I., Hn.P., MS. 8576(8), J. J. Clancy to T. Harrington, 15 Nov. 1886.

[256] At Mitchelstown in 1887, 'The police chased all the occupants of the speakers' wagonette (except Mr Labouchere who remained on the vehicle).' F. J. Higginbottom, *The Vivid Life*, p. 100.

[257] W.V.H.P., Labouchere to Harcourt, 3 Jan. [?1888].

[258] Sir R. Temple, *Letters and Character Sketches from the House of Commons*, p. 129; *Cornhill*, n.s., xxxii (1912), 389–94, for several letters from Labouchere to H. W. Lucy in December 1886; S. L. Gwynn and G. M. Tuckwell, *Life of the Right Hon. Sir Charles W. Dilke*, ii, 267, 274.

[259] A. L. Thorold, pp. 337–66.

[260] B.P., B.M. Add. MSS., 49696, fo. 145, W. H. Smith to A. Balfour, 12 Jan. 1891.

[261] W.V.H.P., Labouchere to Harcourt, 2 Jan. 1891.

[262] C.D.P., B.M. Add. MSS., 43892, fo. 174, Labouchere to Dilke, 21 Aug. 1893.

[263] M. McKenna in *Federalism Illustrated* in 1847 drew upon 64 constitutions to make suggestions 'for the obtainment of an *Irish Parliament in federal connexion with England*'.

later became influential in other circles. F. S. Oliver and L. S. Amery advocated federalism for the United Kingdom before 1914.[264] A resolution, dated 1914, in the W. O'Brien papers shows that some Irish members considered 'Legislatures for Ireland, England, Scotland, and Wales respectively, subordinate to the Imperial Parliament'[265] preferable to Asquith's Government of Ireland bill. Sir J. Ward introduced a variant of the concept which linked devolution of authority, imperial naval defence, and a closer imperial association, such as Labouchere had enunciated in 1886, at the Imperial Conference of 1911.[266]

Labouchere had definite but flexible views on the Irish question. He believed the Irish had a right to internal self-government, and that concession of this status would accord with British imperial practice. He often advocated a federal constitution for Ireland, and England, Scotland and Wales, for this he thought would afford a substantial devolution of authority to Ireland, and enable other parts of the United Kingdom to feel secure. He hoped that the establishment of a precedent in Ireland would lead to local parliaments in England, Scotland and Wales. He believed that such local parliaments would be more responsive to 'democratic' and 'radical' pressures than the imperial parliament. Labouchere favoured extensive concessions to the Irish for he considered that the fewer points of contact that existed between Ireland and England, the less friction there would be to disturb their future relations.

His views on the land question dovetailed with his attitude towards home rule. At no time did he consider that the imperial government might be able to sap the strength of the movement for home rule by implementing schemes to transform the occupier of land in Ireland into its owner. He argued against schemes to purchase Irish land which carried an imperial guarantee. He feared that if the imperial government initiated land purchase it would be more reluctant to grant home rule

---

[264] L. S. Amery, *My political life*, i, ch. 15; cf. P. N. S. Mansergh, *The Government of Northern Ireland*, pp. 46ff.; J. E. Kendle, 'The Round Table Movement and "Home Rule All Round"', *Historical Journal*, xi (1968), 332–53.

[265] N.L.I., MS. 8557/17, 1914.

[266] A. B. Keith (ed.), *Selected Speeches and Documents on British Colonial Policy, 1763–1917*, pp. 247ff.

because of its financial investment in Ireland. He opposed the use of imperial credit for sectional class interests, and, on financial grounds, he doubted the wisdom of buying on a falling market. He showed an awareness that land purchase with an imperial guarantee would dress the imperial government in the robes of absentee landlords, and keep the imperial factor active as a disturbing element in Irish politics, and he prophesied that under these circumstances the Irish would eventually repudiate their financial obligations. He denied that any connection existed between ownership of land and the 'unity of the empire'. In his view, the agrarian problem was a local matter which concerned the Irish alone. If they were competent to govern themselves they could be entrusted with responsibility for Irish agrarian problems. By November 1885, he discerned that Gladstone was begging the question of the land being 'under the control of the Irish Chamber'.[267]

Although his concentration upon detail reflected his awareness of its significance, the home rule principle was more important to him than the form it took. Thus he supported Gladstone's bill which would presumably have enabled Ireland to follow the self-governing colonies' development, as eagerly as if a federal constitution which he himself favoured had been proposed. His belief that the Irish environment would shape any authority conceded by the imperial parliament within a decade, ran counter to the rigidity of federal principles, but it did not fundamentally weaken his argument that the security of England and the empire's integrity would not be threatened by internal self-government in Ireland. He considered any threat from Ireland a remote contingency; that her economic dependence upon England provided one guarantee for England's safety; that Ireland's awareness of England's incomparably greater power provided another; that England could suppress a legitimately organized government if it endangered her position more effectively than a clandestine national movement; and he implied that the satisfaction of Irish aspirations would make England's relations with her self-governing colonies more harmonious.

[267] J.C., 5/50/26, Labouchere to Chamberlain, 16 Nov. 1885; A. L. Thorold, p. 243.

Labouchere abhorred the application of coercive legislation to Ireland particularly as it preceded remedial legislation, and many of his arguments favouring home rule sprang from this view. With courage, determination and energy he supported the Parnellites in bitter struggles against the coercive Irish policy of Gladstone's second administration. Such assistance from English members of parliament was rare: apart from W. H. O'Shea, only Labouchere, T. C. Thompson, J. Cowen, and S. Storey who represented Sunderland, were excepted from Parnell's manifesto of 21 November 1885. Moreover, Labouchere established close relations with Healy, and, to a lesser extent, with J. McCarthy. This enabled him to send Gladstone accurate information which demonstrated that the party, despite Parnellite speeches, would accept real limitations upon the authority of a prospective Irish parliament. When the provisions of Gladstone's home rule bill became known in 1886, political opinion recognized that he had satisfied the Irish and obtained their 'irreducible minimum'.[268] Labouchere played a not insignificant part in this development, and in other scenes of the home rule drama as they unfolded. He worked consistently to secure the Irish a substantial devolution of authority, and it was no coincidence that of the metropolitan press, only the two newspapers with which his connections were closest supported home rule wholeheartedly.

However, it is exceptionally difficult to assess the results of Labouchere's activities which perhaps militated against the result he sought. In the final analysis it was the opposition of Chamberlain and his radical supporters to the home rule bill of 1886 that disturbed all Labouchere's calculations. In my opinion, Labouchere contributed little towards Chamberlain's hostility to Gladstone on this issue. Although Chamberlain was sympathetic towards the Irish between 1880 and the middle of 1885, there are indications of his narrow authoritarian approach towards their problems in this period. At the end of 1880 he wanted certain concessions for the Irish which he was prepared to compel them to accept. In 1882 he sought other concessions for them in order to weaken and delay the development of home rule pressures. In July 1885 Chamberlain abandoned his

[268] *Commonweal*, 1 May 1886.

## IRISH ISSUES, 1885 AND 1886    141

proposals of local self-government for Ireland and may then have become a 'bitter enemy of Irish aspirations'.[269] Labouchere supplied Chamberlain with a fairly complete account of the indirect correspondence between Herbert Gladstone and Healy, and with information which he obtained from Churchill. Chamberlain tended to use such parts of this information as suited the position he adopted at any given time. When Chamberlain left Gladstone's third administration, Labouchere took the initiative in attempting to bring Gladstone and Chamberlain together. Between 15 April and 10 May Labouchere brought them to the brink of a compromise:[270] neither Gladstone nor Chamberlain made the other's position easier, and responsibility for their failure to reach agreement rests with them rather than Labouchere. Again, had Gladstone taken advantage of Labouchere's offer to create a situation in the House, on 28 May, in which he could reaffirm the concessions agreed at the meeting held at the foreign office the previous day, the prime minister could have 'dished' Chamberlain and would not have been trapped so easily by Hicks Beach on 29 May.

In addition to labouring until 5 June with immense assiduity to save the home rule bill and the liberal party, Labouchere had used the Irish question to radicalize the party and to drive the whigs from it. Gladstone, in the same period, attempted to retain the coherence of the party. When circumspection was essential in any direct or indirect communications between Gladstone and the Parnellites, Labouchere was an undesirable Mercury for he spoke freely to other politicians. Harcourt told E. Hamilton that the correspondence between Herbert Gladstone and Healy had become 'common property'.[271] Harcourt believed that Labouchere was 'specially dangerous & unreliable'[272] and that of all advisers *'rebus in arduis'* he was the 'most untrustworthy'.[273] During the closing months of 1885 and in January 1886, Labouchere's indiscretions appear to have been designed largely to aggravate the Irish question and bring it to a head, and partly to magnify his own importance. In the same

[269] C. Cruise O'Brien, p. 101.
[270] See D. C. Savage, pp. 267–76.
[271] H.P., B.M. Add. MSS., 48642, fos. 65–6, 30 Dec. 1885.
[272] G.P., B.M. Add. MSS., 44200, fo. 4, Harcourt to Gladstone, 4 Jan. 1886.
[273] Ibid., fo. 100, Harcourt to Gladstone, 23 March 1886.

period he was one of Gladstone's most important sources of information about Irish affairs[274] and it was at this time that the outlines of parts of a home rule settlement acceptable to Gladstone and Parnellites alike were becoming discernible. Labouchere was sufficiently important for Gladstone, on 10 December 1885, to ask Rosebery to see him and to take a letter expressing Gladstone's 'exact opinions' and authority to use his 'discretion as to great explicitness with L' provided he spoke 'as expressing' his 'opinion of what might be expected' of Gladstone.[275] In December 1885 Healy released the Irish minimum on home rule and it appeared in *The Times* under Labouchere's name.

Labouchere saw himself as the intermediary between Gladstone and the Parnellites. When he and Healy suspected that Gladstone was also negotiating with Parnell they were disconcerted. Labouchere asked Herbert Gladstone for clarification of the position, for 'something clear... which would dispel distrust'. Healy thought it wiser to state nothing further in these circumstances.[276] Gladstone regarded the letters he received from K. O'Shea at this time as 'highly confidential... almost... sacred'.[277] Herbert Gladstone stated that there were no negotiations between Parnell and Gladstone.[278] There was, he claimed, 'no reason whatever' for Healy's uneasiness. The clear statement desired by Labouchere was ambiguous: 'So far as we are concerned there has not been nor will there be any manoeuvring or negotiating. And if communications have to take place with the Irish party... only one channel will be recognized.'[279]

Only once did Labouchere show that he might have a direct personal interest in the Irish question. On 17 February 1886 he

---

[274] H. J. Gladstone, p. 208.
[275] N.L.S., Rosebery papers, 18, H. Gladstone to Rosebery, 10 Dec. 1885; W. E. Gladstone to H. Gladstone, 10 Dec. 1885. Lord Primrose kindly made the Rosebery papers available, but this study was then at an advanced stage.
[276] H.G.P., B.M. Add. MSS., 46015, fo. 120, Labouchere to H. Gladstone, [?26 Dec. 1886].
[277] G.P., B.M. Add. MSS., 44269, fo. 249, Gladstone to K. O'Shea (copy), 16 Dec. 1885.
[278] H.G.P., B.M. Add. MSS., 46015, fo. 99, H. Gladstone to Labouchere (copy), 21 Dec. 1885.
[279] Ibid., fo. 131, H. Gladstone to Labouchere, 28 Dec. 1885.

told Herbert Gladstone that J. Morley was anxious that he should 'keep him in touch with the Irish, and should get them to adopt . . . Gladstone's tactical action'.[280] Labouchere professed his personal indifference about acting in this capacity but he stated that whoever did so ought to have a semi-official position. One suspects that the government would have had little difficulty in persuading Labouchere to accept the position he suggested—an Irish privy councillorship—had it made the offer.

Labouchere generated one of the currents of will and opinion that swept a surprisingly large number of liberals along a home rule stream in 1886. His influence upon Gladstone is debatable but it was not inconsiderable even during his third administration. In addition, he may well have influenced many radicals against following Chamberlain's lead.[281] He used *Truth* and the *Daily News* to sway public opinion towards home rule, but exercised great restraint, from the autumn of 1885 until the middle of 1886, about using information with which he was privately acquainted. He induced J. Morley to write the leading articles in the *Daily News* until he accepted office, and arranged for Lucy, the editor, to see Lord Wolverton in order to prevent the paper deviating from the government's Irish policy. He believed that Chamberlain would swallow the home rule pill ultimately, but he provided leading liberals with accurate information about Chamberlain's shifting attitudes, upon which they could form their own conclusions.

Labouchere's sincerity about home rule was not questioned by his contemporaries for his advocacy of the case was well known. Although his arguments were as incapable of proof as those of his opponents, they were at least as valid. He braved opposition from his constituents and hostility in parliament for the support he gave the Parnellites. He diagnosed the symptoms of Irish national feeling accurately; he was in the van of the home rule movement among English politicians; and the remedies he prescribed for Ireland harmonized with his views upon Britain's imperial policy and upon internal imperial relations.

[280] H.G.P., B.M. Add. MSS., 46016, fos. 10–11, Labouchere to H. Gladstone, 17 Feb. 1886. [281] *Spectator*, 22 May 1886, p. 680.

## CHAPTER V

# Egypt, 1880–1886

OVERSHADOWED in England by Irish problems, a crisis arose in Egypt which provoked Gladstone's government[1] to sanction the bombardment of Alexandria on 11 July 1882. General Wolseley's victory at Tel el Kebir on 13 September 1882 inaugurated the unilateral British occupation of Egypt.[2] This had wide repercussions upon British imperial policy, upon European international relations and upon Egypt's development.

The British government had recognized Egypt's strategic importance since the Napoleonic wars,[3] but it was the development of steam-powered shipping and completion of the Suez Canal in 1869 that reorganized imperial communications to make the canal their spinal cord.[4] It is improbable that the British government would have authorized intervention in Egypt had it not considered that her internal condition jeopardized the security of routes to the east.

The Egyptian government's instability stemmed largely from its indebtedness. Egypt's debt remained marginal[5] until Said, from 1854 to 1863, and then Ismail raised loans in Europe at usurious rates,[6] and expended only part of the money produc-

---

[1] For a discussion of the way the government reached this decision, see R. Robinson, J. Gallagher, *Africa and the Victorians*, pp. 89–116.

[2] The British government had no European mandate for these actions: 'the powers tacitly assented and then individually approved'. C.D.P., B.M. Add. MSS., 43892, fo. 116, Dilke to Labouchere, [?10 Feb. 1892]; cf. Hansard, 3rd ser., 272, 1492, 24 July 1882.

[3] J. Marlowe, *Anglo-Egyptian Relations, 1800–1953*, p. 15.

[4] K. Bell examined 'British Policy towards the Construction of the Suez Canal, 1859–1865', in *T.R.H.S.*, 5th ser., xv (1965), 121–43.

[5] J. Marlowe, p. 56; W. L. Langer, *European Alliances and Alignments, 1871–1890*, p. 253.

[6] By '1882 Egypt had paid in interest a sum equal to the total capital lent her, plus interest at six *per cent*. Yet her total indebtedness was still £90,000,000 of which no more than two thirds had ever found their way into the Egyptian

tively.⁷ The debt snowballed and the Egyptian government faced bankruptcy: on 8 April 1876 the khedive suspended payment of his treasury bills.

This heightened European concern about Egyptian finances and marked the beginning of the process which led to effective European control over them. Suspension of payment followed publication of S. Cave's report⁸ in March 1876 which made European financiers fear British financial control in Egypt and a severe reduction of loan terms.⁹ On 2 May 1876 a khedival decree established the *Caisse de la Dette Publique*.¹⁰ On 7 May, Ismail attempted to fund the bonded and floating debt at £91,000,000, yielding 6 per cent interest with an additional 1 per cent for debt redemption, but bondholders rejected the settlement.¹¹

Later in 1876 Goschen and Joubert¹² recommended a revised settlement to which the khedive helplessly agreed in November 1876. This funded the bonded debt into different categories, but it excluded floating debt holders. They successfully sued the Egyptian government in the mixed courts, and the arrangement broke down. The importance of the Goschen-Joubert scheme lay in its inauguration of Anglo-French cooperation in Egypt, for by its terms the khedive accepted a

---

treasury'. W. L. Langer, p. 255. Egypt's population was about five million, and her annual revenue about eight million pounds.

⁷ Estimates of the proportion so employed vary: see *St Stephen's Review*, 21 Feb. 1885; *The Khedive and his calumniators*, [anon]. B.M. 8229 cc 16; E. L. J. Ridsdale, *An Inquiry into the Capacity of Egypt to Pay Interest on her Debt*; J. C. A. Gavillot, *L'Angleterre épuise l'Egypt*.

⁸ Parl. Pap., 1876, lxxxiii (99), [C.1425]. W. S. Blunt, *The Secret History of the English Occupation of Egypt*, p. 22, argues that Cave's report 'was the beginning of ... political intervention in favour of the bondholders, and his report led ... to a recognition of Ismail's debt as a public obligation'.

⁹ J. Marlowe, p. 93.

¹⁰ W. Kaufman, *The Egyptian State Debt and its relation to international law*, p. 174. The *Caisse* was analogous to the Receiver in an individual's bankruptcy.

¹¹ J. Marlowe, p. 94.

¹² G. J. Goschen, a partner in the Bank of Fruehling & Goschen for eight years, sponsored the entry of Egypt into the foreign loan rubric of the stock exchange list. Fruehling & Goschen invited subscriptions for the first external loan granted to Egypt in March 1862 (£2,195,200 at 7 per cent at 82½). In October 1876 British holders of Egyptian bonds induced Goschen to visit Egypt to safeguard their interests. *Times*, 3 Oct. 1876. Joubert, who represented French bondholders, accompanied him.

French and English controller to supervise the collection and expenditure of Egyptian revenue.[13]

In 1878 a further inquiry into Egyptian finances took place under Sir C. Rivers Wilson's chairmanship.[14] It indicted Khedive Ismail and the system of personal rule and advised him to transfer authority to a cabinet. Nubar Pasha formed a cabinet in which Rivers Wilson became minister of finance and Blignières minister of public works. Rothschilds provided a loan.[15] A bondholders' absolutism replaced that of the khedive.[16]

Anglo-French control gripped most sections of the Egyptian community in an alien vice. The khedive lost power. Financial stringency closed avenues of opportunity to the Turkish and Circassian ruling classes; it caused hardship to, and jeopardized the careers of men of fellahin origin who served as junior officers in the army, or in the lower grades of the civil service; it did not mitigate the harshness of the existence of the fellahin. The presence of well-paid European officials exacerbated Egyptian opinion.

In February 1879 a military demonstration occurred. The khedive took advantage of this and replaced Nubar's ministry in the following April by an Egyptian cabinet under Sherif Pasha which was to be responsible to an elected chamber of notables. By this move, Ismail jettisoned the previous financial settlement. European powers met this challenge by inducing the sultan to replace Ismail by his son Tewfik on 26 June 1879.

This rebuff to Ismail and to the Chamber had important consequences. European controllers-general resumed the direction of Egyptian finances in September 1879: a further, and final, financial settlement was embodied in the Laws of Liquidation of 17 July 1880. Opposition from civil and military elements to Egypt's European bondage remained,[17] but only the army had power and so leadership of the incipient national

---

[13] The Dual Control was established on 18 November 1876, and reimposed on 4 September 1879.
[14] Sir C. Rivers Wilson, *Chapters from my Official Life*, chs. 11–14.
[15] The English and French Rothschilds worked conjointly. W. Kaufman, p. 212.
[16] T. Rothstein, *Egypt's Ruin*, p. 62.
[17] N. Safran, *Egypt in Search of Political Community*, pp. 48–50. The National Ministry resigned on 25 May 1882 but was shortly afterwards reinstated; see T. Rothstein, pp. 189ff.

movement tended to fall into its hands. The army's spokesman was Ahmad Arabi the 'first leader of Egyptian nationalism'.[18] A joint Anglo-French note delivered on 8 January 1882 accelerated this process for it specified the Chamber as one of the dangers facing the khedive and his ministers.[19]

France and Britain had refused concessions moderate nationalists demanded peacefully: they spurned the opportunity of working with them and made their position untenable. Europeans regulated the finances of Egypt in the interests of bondholders through khedival authority, but by 1882 the army, led by Arabi, held a 'monopoly of indigenous authority' in the country.[20]

As the breakdown of khedival authority became increasingly obvious in 1882,[21] the governments of Turkey, France, Germany and Austria-Hungary favoured accommodation with Arabi. The British government, which had tended to follow French policy since 1876, acted independently. It crushed Arabi without having adequately considered treating with him as the representative of the Egyptian nation.

Hartington, Chamberlain and Dilke[22] pressed an active policy in Egypt upon reluctant colleagues. On 27 July 1882 liberals in parliament accepted the necessity for an expedition to Egypt and voted £2,300,000 for this purpose,[23] but 'only the reputations of Gladstone and his Radical colleagues as bitter opponents of jingoism united their Party in favour of the expedition'.[24] John Bright had resigned from the government.[25] Labouchere, who was to become a leading exponent of the bondholder thesis in parliament, supported and spoke in favour of the expedition on 27 July 1882.

[18] J. M. Ahmed, *The Intellectual Origins of Egyptian Nationalism*, p. 24.
[19] Sir E. Malet believed the joint note effected 'a more complete union of the National party, the military, and the Chamber'. T. Rothstein, p. 157.
[20] J. Marlowe, p. 117; P.R.O., F.O., 78/3438/389, fo. 265, Cartwright to Granville, 26 June 1882.
[21] Riots, in which Europeans were killed, occurred in Alexandria on 11 June 1882.
[22] C.D.P., B.M. Add. MSS., 43925, fo. 1, 15 June 1882.
[23] Division Lists, 1882, No. 299, 27 July 1882.
[24] R. Robinson, J. Gallagher, p. 119. More than thirty members of parliament left the Anti-Aggression League rather than oppose Gladstone. F. Harrison, *Autobiographic Memoirs*, ii, 123.
[25] J. L. Sturgis, *John Bright and the Empire*, pp. 111–12.

He favoured intervention on the grounds that otherwise the British would need to withdraw from their position in Egypt, that otherwise greater troubles would arise, and heavier expenditure become necessary later, and that the French would probably intervene alone if Britain failed to act. He did not think that Arabi and the Notables were co-operating, but he suspected that the sultan was intriguing with Arabi. He suggested that the opportunity should be taken to sever Egypt from its Turkish connections.

Labouchere 'entirely denied' that it was a bondholders' war and assured the House that, if this were the case, Gladstone, leading ministers, and Sir W. Lawson and H. Richard would have opposed it. In fact, both Lawson and Richard spoke and voted against the government's Egyptian policy. Lawson considered that 'we were at war in order to restore the *status quo ante* ... [i.e.] the grinding down of the people of Egypt to obtain money for the bondholders ... for the Liberals ... to engage in war to prevent people managing their own affairs was simply disgusting'. Richard believed the government's 'proceedings ... to be as impolitic as they are immoral, and which open before us a future full of ominous and perilous possibilities'.[26] Labouchere, however, argued that Anglo-French control had established a 'sound financial administration' in Egypt and protected the fellahin from extortion. He emphasized that it was 'absolutely necessary to maintain a supreme and paramount influence over the Canal. ... England could not maintain herself on the Canal without maintaining her paramount influence in the Valley of the Nile.' Although he normally opposed strongly intervention in the affairs of a foreign country, in this case he believed it 'absolutely necessary' if England were to remain a great empire: without it, India and 'our Empire in the East would not be worth a year's purchase'. He concluded by expressing pleasure at Gladstone's assurance that this intervention would not impose foreign rule or despotism in Egypt and that it would foster national feeling.[27]

---

[26] Hansard, 3rd ser., 272, 1705, 1779, 25 July 1882; Division Lists, 1882, No. 299, 27 July 1882.

[27] Hansard, 3rd ser., 272, 2045–53, 27 July 1882. E. Baring (Lord Cromer) sent Salisbury an extract from this speech and added 'Circumstances alter cases. In 1882

This was Labouchere's only speech in favour of intervention although he had questioned Dilke in May to find out what steps were being taken to maintain British influence in Egypt.[28] Before he made the speech he had not referred to Egyptian affairs in the constituencies or in letters to the press. However, since July 1881 *Truth* had provided an interesting demonstration of an exercise in journalistic persuasion in harmony with Labouchere's speech. The paper acted as a bull for Egyptian preference stock. It commended its excellencies[29] and explained why 'those who have Egyptian securities... may sleep in peace'.[30] According to *Truth*, Egypt was like the United States in having an excess of revenue over expenditure; its population had never been so lightly taxed.[31] It was 'the most fertile country on the globe'.[32]

Between July 1881 and July 1882 *Truth* stressed the importance of the Suez Canal and Egypt to British imperial communications. 'Empires', it stated, 'have their geographical necessities.'[33] It thought that the exigencies of the Indian empire made it necessary for Britain to be dominant in Egypt, and be its political arbiter.[34] It argued that direct communications with the empire passed through the Suez Canal; that control of this gate to India[35] depended upon Britain having a paramount influence in Egypt; and that only a stable and honest'[36] government in Egypt could prevent its becoming a head centre of intrigue. On 1 June 1882 *Truth* suggested that these ends could be attained if Egypt had a ruler who could maintain order and was dependent upon British goodwill.[37] On 20 July

the Liberal Government was in power, and, moreover, I believe that Labouchere was a large holder of Egyptian stock, which he has since sold.' P.R.O., F.O., 633/6/169, 9 March 1891. I am indebted to Mr A. A. H. Knightbridge for this reference, and for advice on Egyptian affairs.

[28] Hansard, 3rd ser., 269, 555, 12 May 1882.
[29] *Truth*, 13 Oct. 1881, p. 486; 29 Dec. 1881, p. 22; 16 Feb. 1882, pp. 248–9; 16 March 1882, p. 383; 22 June 1882, p. 867; 20 July 1882, p. 125.
[30] *Truth*, 16 Feb. 1882, p. 249 ('should ... internal troubles ... become formidable, ... England and France will ... interfere'); 29 Dec. 1881, p. 22.
[31] *Truth*, 29 Dec. 1881, p. 22.
[32] *Truth*, 8 June 1882, p. 798.   [33] *Truth*, 13 Oct. 1881, p. 487.
[34] *Truth*, 22 Sept. 1881, pp. 389–90; cf. 28 July 1881, p. 110.
[35] *Truth*, 1 June 1882, p. 749.
[36] *Truth*, 6 July 1882, p. 43.   [37] *Truth*, 1 June 1882, p. 749.

1882 it advocated for Egypt the relationship that existed between the British government and the native governments in India.[38] *Truth* wished to separate Egypt from the Eastern Question and particularly desired England to be its sole master:[39] 'Half measures are the bane of Empires.'[40]

During this year *Truth* equated the Khedive Tewfik with stability of government in Egypt, and Arabi, an 'ignorant self-seeking humbug',[41] with endemic anarchy.[42] It countered Arabi's letter to *The Times*[43] of 3 January 1882:

Arabi ... declares himself a patriot, only anxious for the safety, liberty, and integrity of his native land. This is about what every Mexican general who heads a *pronunciamento* in order to become President of the Republic sets forth in his manifesto. Arabi, independent correspondents say, is a colonel, ignorant of politics, and ... [an] arrant ... coward ... his patriotism ... consists of a desire to obtain a prominent position, good pay, and the opportunity of robbing.[44]

*Truth* categorically denied the existence of a national party in Egypt,[45] and it claimed that no means existed of ascertaining Egyptian opinion: 'The idea of an Egyptian assembly of notables in any way representing Egypt is ludicrous to all who know the country.'[46] It attributed Egyptian disturbances to 'a few officers, a number of *ex-employés* ... agents of the Sultan ... and ... the financing riff-raff of Europe'[47] whom an 'English or a French corporal's guard would reduce'.[48] These premises, and its views about the assembly of notables at this time, saved *Truth* from answering the argument that the Anglo-French control prevented Egyptians enjoying self-government. Equally it could advance a philanthropic motive for intervention. The fellahin were 'desirous of being protected from spoliation by wolves in patriots' clothing'.[49] By the same logic it could commend Anglo-French support to the khedive 'so long as he rules in the interests of his subjects'.[50]

[38] *Truth*, 20 July 1882, p. 109.
[39] *Truth*, 13 Oct. 1881, p. 487.
[40] *Truth*, 20 July 1882, p. 109.
[41] *Truth*, 18 May 1882, p. 679.
[42] *Truth*, 6 July 1882, p. 43.
[43] *Times*, 3 Jan. 1882.
[44] *Truth*, 5 Jan. 1882, p. 43.
[45] *Truth*, 26 Jan. 1882, p. 153; 9 Feb. 1882, p. 215.
[46] *Truth*, 19 Jan. 1882, p. 106.
[47] *Truth*, 26 Jan. 1882, p. 153.
[48] *Truth*, 27 April 1882, p. 585.
[49] *Truth*, 9 Feb. 1882, p. 215.
[50] *Truth*, 1 June 1882, p. 749.

The only reforms *Truth* mentioned for Egypt were a 'rigorous overhauling' of salaries paid to Europeans in Egypt, the replacement of European officials by Egyptians wherever possible, and the establishment of 'some sort of representation, in order that if they have grievances, they should have an opportunity to state them'.[51] Had these suggestions been adopted, they might have brought some satisfaction to Egyptians; they might also have benefited holders of Egyptian stock.

On 8 June 1882, *Truth* dismissed as 'silly nonsense'[52] the argument that England and France interfered in Egypt in order to secure interest on loans which had not benefited the population, and that the fellahin were oppressed to make this possible. It answered the first contention somewhat lamely by stating that Ismail had expended part of the money productively, and that the Dual Control had reduced interest rates. Its answer to the second proposition rested upon assertions that the fellahin were not overtaxed, and that the land tax was more predictable, more equitable, and more fairly levied than in the days before the Dual Control.

While *Truth* was supporting the khedive and denying the existence of a national party in Egypt, Labouchere advised Dilke, in connection with countries such as Bulgaria, that Britain's 'true policy' was 'always boldly to take the side of the people'.[53] When Labouchere's anxiety about his investments in Egyptian securities had been removed, *Truth* applied this policy to Egypt. In October 1882, it commended the justice and expediency of 'an alliance with the people of a country' rather than with 'its ruler against the people'.[54] In an Egyptian context *Truth* argued in January 1882 that force was the only argument orientals understood,[55] but in an Irish context it opposed coercion and asserted that self-government could only be learnt by experience.[56] Its assurances about the security of Egyptian preference stock and its allegations that the fellahin suffered no exploitation contrasted sharply with its views about the insecurity of investments in Irish land[57] and the oppression

---

[51] *Truth*, 23 Feb. 1882, p. 280.   [52] *Truth*, 8 June 1882, p. 797.
[53] C.D.P., B.M. Add. MSS., 43892, fo. 136, Labouchere to Dilke, 15 June [1881].
[54] *Truth*, 5 Oct. 1882, p. 489.   [55] *Truth*, 26 Jan. 1882, p. 153.
[56] *Truth*, 2 June 1881, p. 743.   [57] *Truth*, 29 Dec. 1881, p. 5.

endured by Irish peasants. *Truth*'s support for intervention in Egypt conflicted with its approval in January 1881 of the Transvaal Boers' 'laudable' struggle against the British[58] and the Afghans' desire to remain unmolested by the government of India.[59] In July 1882, at a time when *Truth* underestimated the bondholders' interest in Egypt[60] and argued that only British intervention in Egypt could secure the canal's safety, Labouchere told Dilke that the government deserved to be turned out of office if it failed to establish itself 'permanently in Egypt . . . Success is everything. This is the "moral law" as understood by the English nation. Bombard any place but show a *quid pro quo*.'[61] In August 1882, however, *Truth* became convinced that the government would not annex Egypt. Its arguments changed dramatically, and in November 1882 it alleged that 'incomplete knowledge' had caused it to misjudge Arabi and Egyptian popular feeling.[62]

This may have been the case. Radicals such as J. Morley[63] and Chamberlain[64] supported intervention, for it was generally accepted in liberal circles that the 'country from the Chamber of Notables downwards' opposed Arabi and his colleagues and 'would be glad to be free of their military despotism'.[65] Perhaps remonstrances from radicals such as Sir W. Lawson or conservatives such as W. S. Blunt caused Labouchere to undergo some form of political conversion. His interview with ex-Khedive Ismail, which he reported to Herbert Gladstone on 4 August 1882,[66] may have had a similar effect though for different

[58] *Truth*, 6 Jan. 1881, p. 5.
[59] *Truth*, 10 March 1881, p. 317.
[60] *Truth*, 6 July 1882, p. 43.
[61] C.D.P., B.M. Add. MSS., 43892, fos. 137–8, Labouchere to Dilke, [?18 July 1882].
[62] *Truth*, 23 Nov. 1882, p. 735.
[63] W. S. Blunt claims that Dilke and Sir A. Colvin, the financial controller, co-operated (p. 215) and that Colvin, the *Pall Mall Gazette*'s Egyptian correspondent, influenced the paper's editor, J. Morley (p. 159).
[64] J. Chamberlain, *A Political Memoir*, pp. 70–81.
[65] H.P., B.M. Add. MSS., 48632, fo. 57, 24 May 1882. Dilke noted in his journal that Chamberlain was furious 'that more is not being done against the bondholders for Egyptian liberty'. C.D.P., B.M. Add. MSS., 43925, fo. 25, 21 Oct. 1882.
[66] H.G.P., B.M. Add. MSS., 46015, fos. 6–12, Labouchere to H. Gladstone, 4 Aug. 1882. This document may be dated one year too early for a similar meeting is referred to by E. W. Hamilton on 6 Aug. 1883. H.P., B.M. Add. MSS., 48634, fo. 42.

reasons. Such hypotheses cannot be substantiated at present.[67] If they affected Labouchere at all it was only after parliament approved military intervention in Egypt. The evidence available points firmly to the conclusion that they could have had only marginal influence upon him and that his plea of inadequate information was spurious. His letters to P. Rylands in 1876 demonstrate his familiarity with intimate details of the co-operation of French and English financiers with the khedive to 'rob Egypt',[68] his belief that Cave's report erred in postulating an annual financial surplus in Egypt, and his conviction that the fellahin were 'grossly ill-treated'.[69] However, in the months before July 1882, when sectional Egyptian pressures, which were loosely coalescing under the leadership of Arabi, threatened the authority of the khedive and the Anglo-French control which *inter alia* safeguarded bondholders' interests, Labouchere held Egyptian bonds and *Truth* disparaged W. S. Blunt and Sir W. Gregory who supported Arabi,[70] and criticized liberals who opposed intervention.[71] On 27 July 1882 Labouchere voted in favour of the expedition which later crushed Arabi and led directly to the British occupation of Egypt. From that date, well before the battle of Tel el Kebir as Thorold claimed,[72] Labouchere's attitude towards Egypt changed completely although he observed a discreet silence for three weeks to mark the decease of his earlier arguments. He sold his bonds between October 1882 and February 1884, but this was merely the corollary of preceding events. Egyptian bondholders gained at each stage of European intervention, and Britain's military intervention benefited them most of all.[73] On 7 February 1884 Labouchere admitted in *Truth* that he had sold his Egyptian preference stock at *'cent. per cent.'* profit.[74] This must have been

[67] W. S. Blunt's papers are not available until 1972 and Sir W. Lawson's did not survive a fire and a flood.
[68] L. G. Rylands, *The Correspondence and Speeches of Peter Rylands, M.P.*, i, 247–8, Labouchere to Rylands, 29 March 1876.
[69] L. G. Rylands, i, 249, Labouchere to Rylands, 9 May 1876.
[70] *Truth*, 29 Dec. 1881, p. 22; 18 May 1882, p. 679; 25 May 1882, p. 714.
[71] *Truth*, 8 June 1882, p. 797.
[72] A. L. Thorold, p. 180.
[73] *Banker's Magazine*, xliv (1884), 483–7. The price of Egyptian preference stock was 35 in 1876, 55 in 1879, 90 in 1884.
[74] *Truth*, 7 Feb. 1884, p. 201. He supplied no details.

particularly gratifying for he was a 'great speculator' 'particularly hard hit' in 1875 when he had 'a big bear position open in Egyptian Stocks which rose considerably after the deal in the Suez Canal shares'.[75]

It has been impossible to ascertain exactly when Labouchere bought and sold his stock. Thorold stated that he disposed of it 'very soon' after 13 September 1882.[76] In a letter to Dilke, dated 10 October 1882, Labouchere stated that it was 'impossible for Radicals to accept a policy, based upon administering Egypt, partly for the good of its inhabitants, but mainly for the good of the bondholders. I am a bondholder, so it cannot be said that I am personally prejudiced against such a policy'.[77] Labouchere must have received perverse pleasure from publishing articles, many of which had biblical captions, that advocated the withdrawal of the British while his Egyptian bonds were appreciating in value as a result of British intervention.[78] Apparently '"Labby became an honest politician"' *before* his bonds '"fell off his back like Christian's burden in *Pilgrim's Progress*"'.[79]

The attitude of *Truth* changed on 17 August 1882 when it discussed British policy towards Egypt after the suppression of Arabi's movement. It advised separation of Egypt from Turkey, on the grounds that this would remove it from the Eastern Question, and cause it 'naturally' to fall under an English protectorate 'so far as regards her foreign relations'. It suggested that Egyptians ought to be left to manage their own internal affairs. It also found new merit in the assembly of notables which in its view would act in the country's 'best interests' and ought to vote the annual budget. It believed that 'It is for the Egyptians to decide how they are to be governed', and that if they refused interest to bondholders the British had no 'right' to 'force' them.[80]

---

[75] P. H. Emden, *The Money Powers of Europe in the nineteenth and twentieth century* p. 400; cf. ibid., p. 317.
[76] A. L. Thorold, p. 180.
[77] C.D.P., B.M. Add. MSS., 43892, fos. 139–40, Labouchere to Dilke, 10 Oct. 1882; A. L. Thorold, p. 181.
[78] *Truth*, 5 Oct. 1882, p. 485, 'Egypt was glad when they departed'; 12 Oct. 1882, p. 523, 'The land was corrupted by reason of the swarm of flies.'
[79] A. L. Thorold, p. 180.   [80] *Truth*, 17 Aug. 1882, pp. 248–9.

The following week *Truth* concentrated even more upon theories of representative government and self-determination. It advised the British government to be 'exceedingly careful not to do anything which militates against the right of every nation to enjoy self-government', particularly as the government did not, apparently, intend to annex Egypt. It argued that the 'right of the representatives of a nation to grant or to withhold money is inherent in representation' and that if foreigners controlled a nation's financial administration, it could never make constitutional progress. As the Anglo-French control had broken down, *Truth* considered its re-establishment a 'sin against liberty ... [and] our own interests'. It thought that firmans of the sultan, decrees of the khedive, and 'European approval' did not justify the English 'in depriving a nation of its natural rights. No law in any country can be regarded ... as eternally valid which has not been assented to by its inhabitants.'[81]

The aims which shaped the government's Egyptian policy jostled uneasily together.[82] The government required the Suez Canal to be open for English shipping in wartime, and so it demanded 'free navigation' of the canal from other powers, and a greater share in its management from France. It wished to safeguard the canal from the danger of 'lawless military violence'[83] and from the possibility of French hegemony on the Nile. It sought to destroy French influence in Egypt, to establish a stable self-governing Egypt under an informal British suzerainty, to enlist the support of the Egyptian people, and to withdraw British troops promptly. The British government had to decide what form Egyptian self-government was to take. However, its sense of obligation towards the khedive, its misunderstanding of the nature of Arabi's revolt, Egypt's precarious financial position, and entrenched international rights complicated the problem. Cabinet opinion divided about the application of its policies, many of which were incompatible, and about the order of priority to be given them. It was difficult to

[81] *Truth*, 24 Aug. 1882, pp. 296–7.
[82] See R. Robinson, J. Gallagher, pp. 113–27.
[83] Hansard, 3rd ser., 272, 1576, 24 July 1882.

reconcile supremacy in Egypt with British evacuation. Plans for Egyptian self-government would conflict with the British government's need to accommodate France and other European powers, and with its control of Egypt's finances. The British government might have attained some of its objectives more easily had it annexed Egypt. As it was, its independence of action was hindered by other powers.

Labouchere dissociated himself from the small group of British radicals, with whom he had co-operated to oppose the government's coercive policy for Ireland, when he had supported intervention in Egypt on 27 July 1882, and they had opposed it. His views changed in August 1882, and by October 1882 he had renewed his political allegiance with them and begun to criticize the government's Egyptian policy in parliament. Radicals, according to Churchill, co-ordinated their activity. They were, he informed Northcote on 16 October 1882,

> bitterly hostile to Gladstone ... & ... ready to go to any lengths to emphasize their disagreement with him ... the accusation they mean to develope [sic] is that Mr Gladstone has abandoned the Liberal Foreign Policy, & has spent the money of the taxpayers in the interests of the bondholders.[84]

Labouchere did not go to this length in parliament in 1882. However, his questions to Dilke, under-secretary of state for foreign affairs, kept him in the political limelight when Irish affairs were receiving less parliamentary time. In addition, he helped to bring to public attention some of the paradoxes in the government's position. It intended, as a preliminary to the inauguration of self-government in Egypt, to bring the leaders of the military revolt to trial, and to train an army faithful to the khedive. Such a policy could as easily appear to buttress authoritarianism in Egypt as to foster self-government.

In October 1882 Labouchere questioned ministers to discover whether the government intended to establish ministerial responsibility, with representative control over taxation and expenditure, in Egypt. On 26 October, he helped to extract a reaffirmation from Gladstone that this was an ultimate objec-

[84] I.P., B.M. Add. MSS., 50021, fo. 73, Churchill to Northcote, 16 Oct. 1882.

tive of the government's policy.[85] He asked Dilke if the government had any international obligation which would oblige it to prevent Egyptians exercising as much control over their internal affairs as the inhabitants of other territories which had been integral parts of the Ottoman empire. Dilke replied that no such commitment existed, but he dismissed Labouchere's question on the grounds that it dealt with matters of 'inference and argument' rather than fact.[86]

On the same occasion Labouchere caused Dilke to admit that British representatives in Egypt had approved General Baker's appointment as commander-in-chief of the khedive's forces. Dilke denied that the imperial government had been consulted about Baker's plan to reorganize the Egyptian forces.[87] Labouchere considered that this scheme would create a heterogeneous army of mercenaries, officered by Englishmen. Although Dilke's denial was strictly accurate, it gave no indication of the way in which the problem of Egyptian military reorganization exercised the imperial government.[88]

On 7 November 1882 Labouchere explained his attitude fully to General Baker, who had communicated with him, presumably to protest about comments in the House and in *Truth*.[89] He told Baker that radicals had no animosity towards him personally. Their criticism was much more widely based. Labouchere argued that British ministers had crushed Arabi on the grounds that he was a military adventurer. Consequently they ought to ascertain the type of government Egyptians desired, and not replace Arabi by a vice-regal adventurer. Labouchere assumed that Egyptians would opt for responsible government,

[85] Hansard, 3rd ser., 274, 176, 26 Oct. 1882; cf. col. 169.
[86] Ibid., 366–7, 30 Oct. 1882.
[87] Ibid., 170, 26 Oct. 1882.
[88] On 13 October the cabinet considered proposals from Sir C. Wilson, British military attaché in Egypt, for the reorganization of the Egyptian army. P.R.O., Cab. 37/9/92, printed 13 Oct. 1882. A week later Sir E. Malet, British consul-general, sent Baker's proposals to the foreign office. P.R.O., F.O., 407/24/140–2, 20 Oct. 1882. Northbrook, first lord of the admiralty, opposed their adoption on the grounds that, 'A scheme the principal feature of which is the employment of an alien force, officered by English officers, to keep the native portion of the army in check, seems to me to be simply fatal to any prospect of success to the rule of the present Khedive.' P.R.O., Cab. 37/9/101, printed 1 Nov. 1882.
[89] Hansard, 3rd ser., 274, 170, 26 Oct. 1882; 274, 366, 30 Oct. 1882; *Truth*, 26 Oct. 1882, pp. 578–9. Baker's telegram to Labouchere has eluded me.

and he asserted that the army would be national only when Egyptian representatives approved it. He denied the existence of 'any *international* arrangement'[90] that precluded Egyptians voting their budget. He contended that the only way for Britain to acquire permanent influence in Egypt was by establishing a representative assembly, for he stated that a liberal government could neither annex Egypt, nor permanently maintain the khedive against the wishes of his subjects. He thought the khedive doomed unless he made terms with the national party in Egypt, put himself at its head, and organized and used an assembly 'as a buckler to himself'. If he did this, Labouchere thought that he would be able to resist any European control of Egypt, and Britain would 'be forced to . . . hinder any interference either from Turkey, or . . . any other quarter'.[91]

Labouchere tried to mitigate the condition of Egyptians[92] imprisoned on charges arising from the political disorders, during the autumn session of the 1882 parliament. On 14 and 24 November[93] he requested information about conditions in a prison at Zagazig,[94] and he urged the government to prevent a repetition of such occurrences while British bayonets maintained khedival authority. He asked the government to use its good offices with the Egyptian government to induce it to proclaim a general amnesty for all political offences committed during the revolt.[95]

Labouchere particularly concerned himself with raising in parliament matters connected with the trial of Arabi and his principal associates. W. S. Blunt played the most prominent part in their defence. He feared that Gladstone might salve his conscience for the slaughter of Egyptian peasants at Tel el Kebir by indulging in an act of vengeance against Arabi.[96] General Wolseley favoured Arabi's summary execution, and the

[90] Labouchere's emphasis. He obtained this information from Dilke; see Hansard 3rd ser., 274, 367, 30 Oct. 1882.
[91] T.C.L., Cullum 0124, Labouchere to Baker, 7 Nov. [?1882].
[92] There were over one thousand political prisoners enduring 'harsh treatment'. P.R.O., F.O., 407/25/139, Dufferin to Granville, 19 Nov. 1882.
[93] Hansard, 3rd ser., 274, 1400, 14 Nov. 1882; 275, 16, 24 Nov. 1882.
[94] Dilke could give no information, but he conceded confidentially that conditions were 'very bad'. P.R.O., F.O., 78/3444/136, 29 Nov. 1882.
[95] Hansard, 3rd ser., 274, 1400, 14 Nov. 1882.
[96] W. S. Blunt, *The Secret History of the English Occupation of Egypt*, pp. 426–78.

queen, as Hamilton noted, was 'keen for the hanging of Arabi'.[97] Blunt believed that nothing but the overwhelming pressure of public opinion saved Arabi's life.[98] Labouchere refurbished the image of Arabi which he had previously tarnished, defended Arabi's actions vigorously, and played an important part in campaigns to save his life and then make his exile in Ceylon less onerous.

In this session Labouchere argued that the 'whole Egyptian people'[99] supported Arabi, whom he now regarded as a patriot. On 31 October and 1 November 1882[100] he urged the government to make representations to the Egyptian government about the desirability of admitting the press to his trial,[101] so that it would receive full publicity. On 9 November Labouchere induced Dilke to admit that Arabi's trial was being held under 'special conditions... to be found in no Code whatever'.[102] Members of the Commons thus had more accurate information on this subject than the foreign secretary, or the government's chief representative in Egypt, who became acquainted with this fact later.[103]

In Egypt the effect of British intervention on behalf of the prisoners was 'in the highest degree embarrassing'.[104] Arabi was as 'great a difficulty as a prisoner as he was as a Minister'.[105] Little political progress could be made 'in any direction'[106] until his sentence became known, for the trial was augmenting Arabi's influence in Egypt. Sir C. Wilson pointed out in a memorandum sent to the foreign office that 'Nearly all the evidence in support of the prosecution... derived from men of Turkish or Syrian origin in Government employ. No "fellah" officer has disclosed any important secret'.[107] On 18 November

[97] H.P., B.M. Add. MSS., 48632, fo. 135, 23 Sept. 1882.
[98] W. S. Blunt, *Secret History*, p. 431.   [99] Hansard, 3rd ser., 274, 203, 26 Oct. 1882.
[100] Ibid., 465, 31 Oct. 1882; 563, 1 Nov. 1882.
[101] Granville advised Malet that the government assumed this would be permitted. P.R.O., F.O., 407/25/4, Granville to Malet, 1 Nov. 1882.
[102] Hansard, 3rd ser., 274, 1116, 9 Nov. 1882.
[103] See P.R.O., F.O., 407/25/98; F.O., 78/3444/23ff.; F.O., 407/25/112, Malet told Granville on 14 November 1882 that Dilke had informed him that the trial was 'simply by Decree of the Khedive'.
[104] Sir E. B. Malet, *Egypt, 1879–1883*, p. 484.
[105] Ibid., p. 487, Malet to Granville, 17 Oct. 1882.
[106] Ibid., p. 508, Malet to Granville, 7 Nov. 1882.
[107] P.R.O., F.O., 78/3442/288, 21 Oct. 1882.

1882 Dufferin warned the khedive that the evidence would not warrant Arabi's execution, and he proposed deportation as an alternative punishment.[108] At the end of November Dufferin sent details of a compromise about the prisoners which the foreign office received on 1 December 1882. The prisoners were to be charged with rebellion, would plead guilty, and would receive a capital sentence which the khedive would commute to perpetual exile. The Egyptian government undertook to provide each prisoner with an 'allowance sufficient for his maintenance'.[109]

Labouchere had questioned ministers about procedural alterations at Arabi's trial which indicated arbitrary tendencies on the part of the Egyptian government.[110] He tried to ascertain whether these changes involved the British government.[111] On 1 December 1882 he asked Dilke if Arabi's defence counsel and the Egyptian government had arranged to charge Arabi solely with rebellion and to banish him. Dilke asserted that the government had received 'no communication whatever from the Egyptian government' on this matter.[112]

From 21 September 1882, *Truth* regularly devoted considerable space to Egyptian affairs. It developed the views it had first advanced in August 1882 with the enthusiasm of the newly converted. It tried to explain the volte-face from the attitude it had adopted until July 1882 with three arguments. It contended that the British expedition to Egypt was 'sad and painful'[113] to many liberals, but a necessity owing to the need to redeem

---

[108] P.R.O., F.O., 407/25/138, Dufferin to Granville, 18 Nov. 1882.

[109] P.R.O., F.O., 407/26/1, Dufferin to Granville, 30 Nov. 1882. On 12 December 1882 Dufferin wrote to Hartington, 'I hope you approve of the way in which we got rid of Arabi's trial. It was an awful mess, and had it been allowed to go on, it would have brought the whole Egyptian Administration and everybody concerned into disrepute.' De.P., 340.1288.

[110] Hansard, 3rd ser., 274, 1302, 13 Nov. 1882; 275, 406, 30 Nov. 1882; 275, 484–5, 1 Dec. 1882.

[111] Even when he received negative or non-committal replies, his questions were not without effect. On 1 December 1882, for instance, Granville told Malet that Labouchere would ask whether procedural modifications had been submitted to, or approved by him. Granville continued, 'Labouchere will be answered in the negative; but has anything passed which could give colour to such a statement . . .?' P.R.O., F.O., 407/26/3.

[112] Hansard, 3rd ser., 275, 484, 1 Dec. 1882.

[113] *Truth*, 12 Oct. 1882, p. 523.

pledges to maintain the khedive made by the conservative government of 1874-80. It argued that it had been equally necessary to prevent the French, who might otherwise have acted independently, from acquiring a preponderant influence on the Nile.[114] On 19 October 1882 *Truth* justified its opposition to Anglo-French financial control of Egypt on the grounds that this control, allegedly designed to handle the Egyptian government's bankruptcy, had changed its function. Its members had assumed political authority 'to deprive... Egyptians of their rights, in order to secure high salaries for... European locusts, and certainty of interest to European bondholders'.[115]

*Truth* revised its views about Arabi from 21 September 1882. It described him as the 'most decent and most respectable'[116] Egyptian whom the 'entire people'[117] supported. On 28 September, it argued that the inhabitants of any country oppressed by autocratic rule or by foreign influence had a natural right and duty to rebel. Partly on these grounds, and partly by alleging that the sultan prompted Arabi, it contended that he and his associates did not deserve punishment.[118]

*Truth*'s attitude to the canal changed as much as its opinions about Arabi. On 28 September 1882 it advocated the neutralization of the canal with a ban on the transit of belligerents' warships. It believed that Britain would gain if this policy were implemented, for owing to its mastery of the Red Sea it could effectively close the canal to others and keep open its communications with India and the east via the Cape.[119] A month later it asserted, 'it cannot too often be repeated that the necessity of our administrative supremacy on the banks of the Nile, in order to secure our communications with India through the Canal, is bondholders' twaddle'.[120]

Bondholders' interests had little place in the policy *Truth* recommended Britain to apply in Egypt. It stated that Britain's mission in the world was to sympathize with the rights of 'the people'.[121] It suggested that British representatives in Egypt

[114] *Truth*, 28 Sept. 1882, p. 455.
[115] *Truth*, 19 Oct. 1882, p. 555. This interpretation would carry more weight if it had coincided more closely with the alleged change in the control's function.
[116] *Truth*, 2 Nov. 1882, p. 630.   [117] *Truth*, 23 Nov. 1882, p. 735.
[118] *Truth*, 28 Sept. 1882, p. 456.   [119] Ibid.
[120] *Truth*, 26 Oct. 1882, p. 594.   [121] *Truth*, 21 Sept. 1882, p. 425.

should summon 'a freely and fairly elected Chamber'[122] and insist upon the khedive recognizing ministerial responsibility and conceding to the assembly control of Egyptian finances. It dismissed any proposal to exclude Egyptians from the control of any part of their revenue or expenditure as 'utterly absurd'. It denied that the British government had any obligation to see that capital fructified in Egypt.[123] In its view, payment of interest concerned only investors and the Egyptian authorities, for a purchaser of foreign bonds bought at his own risk.[124] On 19 October 1882 *Truth* advised Egyptians to hand the assets of the three secured loans[125] to bondholders and to issue more Unified Bonds to pay for war expenditure and indemnity charges.[126] On 23 November 1882 it suggested that Egyptian representatives ought to assert the 'absolute justice of repudiation',[127] and, when they had established this principle, agree to a compromise which would take the form of repudiating half of the Unified Debt and paying 2 per cent interest on the remainder. It proclaimed as a universally applicable principle:

no debt is valid against a country which has been incurred without the consent of the country, and which has not been expended for the benefit of the country. In such cases, repudiation is not only a right, but a duty.[128]

*Truth* moulded the Egyptian policy it commended to British opinion around the 'inalienable right of every people to govern itself'.[129] It considered a liberal government inconsistent if its agents either functioned as 'policemen of the Khedive, to crush the legitimate aspirations of his subjects' or acted as the 'bailiffs of European bondholders'.[130] It suggested the severance of Egypt's connection with Turkey,[131] a general amnesty for participants in the political disturbances,[132] and the establishment in Egypt of responsible government with the assembly exercising 'real governing power'. It favoured a speedy, but not

---

[122] *Truth*, 5 Oct. 1882, p. 489.
[123] *Truth*, 21 Sept. 1882, p. 425.
[124] *Truth*, 12 Oct. 1882, p. 523.
[125] The Domain loan, the Daira loan, and the Railroad loans.
[126] *Truth*, 12 Oct. 1882, pp. 523–4.
[127] *Truth*, 23 Nov. 1882, p. 734.
[128] *Truth*, 14 Dec. 1882, p. 841.
[129] *Truth*, 28 Sept. 1882, p. 456.
[130] *Truth*, 30 Nov. 1882, p. 753.
[131] *Truth*, 21 Sept. 1882, pp. 424–5.
[132] *Truth*, 28 Sept. 1882, p. 456.

an immediate withdrawal of British forces. *Truth* asserted that this policy would give Britain a 'legitimate' and 'paramount' influence in Egypt, based upon 'the gratitude of the nation'.[133] It favoured an international guarantee of Egypt's neutrality[134] and the 'absolute non-interference'[135] of all European powers in its internal affairs. In its view it would be against the interests of a neutral Egypt governed by a national party ever to block the canal.

In the autumn of 1882 it was through *Truth* that Labouchere criticized the government's Egyptian policy and made alternative proposals, and he commended similar views to his constituents on 22 November.[136] Although these views conformed with much radical and liberal opinion, they oversimplified a complex problem. For instance, European powers were unlikely to underwrite the integrity of a neutralized, autonomous Egypt which was dominated by British influence, yet even if they had done so, no guarantee existed that British influence would remain permanent. Some ministers had favoured the neutralization of the canal until a cabinet committee which inquired into the matter pointed out that this was 'a proposal to close the Canal absolutely against all vessels of war at all times'.[137] Again, the simplicity of debt repudiation by Egyptians proposed by *Truth* did not tally with European nations' existing rights in Egypt: fourteen nations had to agree to changes in the administration of Egypt's finances.

The liberal government intended to withdraw British forces from Egypt throughout 1883. In its view, the khedive would reassume responsibility once administrative reform had begun and reorganization of the army been completed. A further prerequisite for British evacuation was for the European powers to recognize Britain's paramount position in Egypt and to guarantee free navigation in the canal.[138] Each objective rested upon a false premise. The khedive's authority depended upon British power. Its fragile structure would collapse if the buttresses were removed, and the political situation would then

[133] *Truth*, 14 Dec. 1882, p. 840.
[134] *Truth*, 21 Sept. 1882, p. 425.   [135] *Truth*, 28 Sept. 1882, p. 456.
[136] *Northampton Herald*, 25 Nov. 1882; *Northampton Mercury*, 25 Nov. 1882.
[137] P.R.O., Cab. 37/9/102, printed 4 Nov. 1882.
[138] See R. Robinson, J. Gallagher, pp. 122–32.

become analogous to that which had caused British intervention in 1882. Moreover European powers had no interest in obliging the British gratuitously.

The British government declined to exercise comprehensive control over the khedival government. This provided the Egyptian government with responsibility within certain limits, avoided further commitments for Britain, and gave some consistency to the liberals' policy. It also posed problems for the imperial government. Opponents of its policy raised matters connected with particular aspects of Egyptian administration at Westminster and held it responsible. Each issue raised tended to emphasize the superficiality of khedival rule and to nail responsibility upon the imperial government. One of the ironies of the liberal government's position was that in allowing the Egyptian government a certain freedom of action, it gave it the power to embroil the imperial government further in Egyptian affairs. It took a disaster in the Sudan in September 1883 to strip away the blinkers which restricted the government's attention to the mirage of evacuation.

During the autumn session of the 1882 parliament Labouchere began to act in conjunction with a small group of radical and conservative members who criticized the government's policy.[139] This cross-party co-operation continued throughout 1883 but its cohesion was not as strong as parliamentary proceedings might indicate. In June 1883 Labouchere acted as informer to the government and betrayed Churchill's confidences.

In 1883 Labouchere criticized the government's Egyptian policy in parliament more comprehensively than he had done in the autumn session of 1882. His arguments were diametrically opposed to those he had used in July 1882. Thus, when he seconded Sir W. Lawson's amendment on 15 February 1883, he contended that the British intervened in Egypt 'for the sake of

---

[139] Radicals included Sir W. Lawson and A. Illingworth; conservatives included Sir H. Drummond Wolff and Lord Randolph Churchill. W. S. Blunt, who directed Arabi's defence from London, probably fed them information and spurred them to action. No evidence has appeared to connect Labouchere directly with Blunt at this time. In W. S. Blunt's *My Diaries*, i, 64, the following entry, dated 2 June 1891, related to Arabi and his associates: 'we had better put Labouchere on our Egyptian business'.

the bondholders and for that reason only' and he asserted that imperial forces remained in Egypt with the 'single object of collecting the debts of the bondholders'. He advised the government to establish constitutional government, ministerial responsibility and representative control over Egyptian finances. He believed Egyptians ought to decide whether they paid debts to bondholders.[140]

In April 1883 Labouchere sought information about an additional loan which the Egyptian government needed to meet charges for indemnities arising from the Alexandrian massacres and for the costs of British occupation. He also asked if its corollary would be a permanent increase in Egyptians' taxation, or a reduction in the existing interest rates. Lord E. Fitzmaurice supplied the financial details and added that the Egyptian government was 'not without hope' that by 'strict economy . . . no permanent burden' would rest upon Egyptians. He expressed the government's intention not to alter the provisions of the Laws of Liquidation.[141]

In August 1883 Labouchere failed to obtain from Gladstone an unequivocal assurance that the British government intended to withdraw its forces from Egypt, and would not convert a temporary occupation into a direct or indirect permanent protectorate. The prime minister declined to 'disarrange . . . the balance of [the government's] expression'[142] of its policy.

Labouchere repeatedly raised issues connected with the allowances received by Arabi and his principal associates whom the Egyptian government had exiled to Ceylon.[143] After one series of questions, Lord E. Fitzmaurice informed him, on 4 June 1883, that the Egyptian government had consented to increase the exiles' annual allowance by £500.[144] Labouchere persisted,[145] and a month later learnt from Fitzmaurice that the

[140] Hansard, 3rd ser., 276, 141–2, 15 Feb. 1883; 276, 1309–10, 2 March 1883; 277, 1479, 5 April 1883.
[141] Hansard, 3rd ser., 277, 1479–80, 5 April 1883.
[142] Hansard, 3rd ser., 282, 1654, 6 Aug. 1883.
[143] Hansard, 3rd ser., 276, 305, 19 Feb. 1883; 276, 1153–4, 1 March 1883; 276, 1737, 8 March 1883; 279, 1633, 4 June 1883.
[144] Hansard, 3rd ser., 279, 1633, 4 June 1883. The Egyptian government sanctioned its payment on 28 May 1883, P.R.O., F.O., 407/27/243, Malet to Granville, 29 May 1883.
[145] Hansard, 3rd ser., 280, 197, 11 June 1883.

Egyptian government with 'great liberality' had contributed an additional £500 for the exiles' maintenance.[146]

Supporters of the Egyptian national cause felt continued concern for Egyptian political prisoners. Lord R. Churchill and, to a lesser extent, Labouchere, campaigned in parliament in order to obtain an official inquiry into the massacres at Alexandria on 11 and 12 June 1882. The execution of one political prisoner, Suleiman Sami, whom Beaman, an associate of Blunt, alleged the Egyptian government allowed 'no defence whatever',[147] occasioned Churchill's second attack upon the liberal government's policy.[148] On 11 June 1883 he charged the khedive and the Egyptian civil authorities with responsibility for the massacres, and he attempted to make out a prima facie case for an inquiry into the matter. At the end of June he presented the papers which, in his opinion, substantiated the charges he had made against the khedive in the Commons.[149] Labouchere associated his attempt to save another prisoner with Churchill's campaign. He tried to have the scope of Khandeel's trial extended so that the defendant could prove his innocence by establishing that he had merely acted upon orders.[150]

Churchill and Labouchere asserted that a strong prima facie case existed that the khedive had instigated the most violent disorders in Egypt.[151] They considered that an official inquiry would prove this contention and thus absolve Egyptian political prisoners. Moreover, its substantiation would have shown that the British government had committed a signal error in attacking Arabi. The government did not allow them the opportunity to remove a primary justification for British intervention in Egypt.[152]

[146] Hansard, 3rd ser., 281, 39, 2 July 1883. Granville told Malet how much more money was needed for the exiles. P.R.O., F.O., 407/27/362, 23 June 1883.

[147] W. S. Blunt, *Secret History of the English Occupation of Egypt*, p. 517. The English official supervising the court's proceedings requested an adjournment. Sherif, the chief Egyptian minister, failed to induce the president of the court to adjourn. P.R.O., 407/28/7 (and enclosures), Malet to Granville, 23 June 1883.

[148] W. S. Blunt, *Secret History*, p. 518.

[149] P.R.O., Cab. 37/11/44, undated. (The last document in this collection is dated 28 June 1883.)   [150] Hansard, 3rd ser., 281, 47, 2 July 1883.

[151] A. M. Broadley advised Churchill on 25 June 1883 that witnesses' safety must be guaranteed if legal proof were to be obtained. P.R.O., Cab. 37/11/44(104).

[152] Granville asserted that no legal or moral prima facie evidence existed. P.R.O. Cab. 37/11/51, Granville to Malet, 6 Aug. 1883.

Paradoxically, Labouchere himself helped them to resist Churchill's attack. On his own admission he helped Churchill to obtain evidence.[153] However, on 22 June 1883, he 'volunteered'[154] information about Churchill's evidence to the chief liberal whip, Lord R. Grosvenor. He informed him that the evidence remained inconclusive, and advised him of avenues of attack Churchill would travel. He concluded, 'so long as the instruments employed hold their tongues, and the telegrams which may have passed between Omar Lutfi and Dervisch [sic] are not forthcoming, no direct evidence ... will be obtained'.[155]

Grosvenor read Labouchere's letter to Gladstone, and he then sent it to Granville so that he could 'intimate to Malet the points that R. Churchill is trying to make, & Malet may take such steps as he & you think advisable'.[156] Granville, in turn, sent Malet 'secretly a bit of treachery on the part of Labouchere', with an injunction to 'do nothing which will justify its being supposed that you have ever had any instructions from me'.[157]

Labouchere's private attempt to safeguard the government's majority, to curry favour and earn ministers' gratitude, did not enhance their opinion of him. Grosvenor declared to Granville: 'What a scoundrel "Labby" is, a traitor to all sides'.[158] This discreet support to the government casts doubt upon the lengths to which Labouchere was prepared to take his vigorous public opposition to British policy in Egypt.

When he spoke in the constituencies, his views were unequivocal. At Huddersfield, on 17 March 1883, he described the Egyptian war as unjust and unjustifiable. Moreover, he warned his audience that Britain's involvement there subjected it to circumstances which might entail further responsibilities.[159] On 11 September he told his constituents that although he hoped the Egyptians would have good government when the British withdrew, he did not believe foreigners could teach them this:

---

[153] Ge.P., P.R.O., 30/29/27, Labouchere to Grosvenor, 22 June 1883.
[154] Ibid., Grosvenor to Granville, 22 June 1883.
[155] Ibid., Labouchere to Grosvenor, 22 June 1883.
[156] Ibid., Grosvenor to Granville, 22 June 1883.
[157] Ibid., Granville to Malet, 22 June 1883.
[158] Ibid., Grosvenor to Granville, 22 June 1883.
[159] *Huddersfield Daily Chronicle*, 19 March 1883.

'They must learn it for themselves; they must acquire the art of Government by governing themselves.'[160] When he spoke at Kettering on 13 December 1883 his main criticism was that the imperial government was sacrificing financial stringency for follies in the Sudan which did not concern Britain.[161]

Throughout 1883 *Truth* opposed the government's Egyptian policy. It condemned Lord Dufferin's scheme for representative government in Egypt[162] before Labouchere described it in parliament on 2 March 1883 as a 'perfect sham of Constitutional government'.[163] It campaigned on behalf of Egyptian political prisoners,[164] and, on 5 April 1883, advised a similar extension of the scope of Omar Lutfi's trial[165] to that which Labouchere later requested in parliament for another prisoner, Khandeel.

*Truth* tried to disengage the question of the canal from the problem of Egyptian government. In July 1883 it argued that the British government ought to confine its attention to the canal[166] and a month later it emphasized the existence of a desert between the canal and Egypt.[167] It considered that if Britain were at war with a maritime power, her merchant ships could not safely use the canal. It suggested that the British navy ought to seal the Suez entrance to the canal during wartime and secure imperial maritime communications via the Cape. *Truth* proposed the neutralization of Egypt, and the administration and maintenance of the canal by Egyptian police, acting under an international commission's supervision.[168] It attributed to bondholders responsibility for the Egyptian problem,[169] and it dismissed arguments that disorder in Egypt might compromise the canal's safety as 'transparent twaddle'.[170]

*Truth* considered that Egypt's ruin was being compassed by

[160] *Northampton Mercury*, 15 Sept. 1883; cf. *Northampton Herald*, 15 Sept. 1883; *Daily News*, 12 Sept. 1883.
[161] *Daily News*, 14 Dec. 1883; *Northampton Mercury*, 15 Dec. 1883.
[162] *Truth*, 25 Jan. 1883, p. 115; 22 Feb. 1883, p. 252.
[163] *Hansard*, 3rd ser., 276, 1310, 2 March 1883.
[164] *Truth*, 1 March 1883, p. 287; 17 May 1883, p. 684; 28 June 1883, p. 903; 19 July 1883, p. 83.
[165] *Truth*, 5 April 1883, p. 464.   [166] *Truth*, 5 July 1883, p. 18.
[167] *Truth*, 9 Aug. 1883, p. 195.   [168] *Truth*, 19 July 1883, pp. 84–5.
[169] It maintained this position throughout 1883; e.g., *Truth*, 29 Nov. 1883, pp. 759–60.   [170] *Truth*, 27 Dec. 1883, p. 909.

an analogous process to that which had occurred in Ireland. It believed landowners had crippled Irish tenants by extorting heavier rents than the land could bear, and that bondholders, by exacting more from their securities than they could support, were crushing the Egyptian peasants. It asserted, 'If an Irish tenant has a just claim to live and thrive, ... Egyptian peasants have the same claim.'[171]

Reports of the Sudanese massacre of an Egyptian army commanded by General Hicks reached England on 21 November 1883.[172] The mahdi had gradually weakened Egyptian control over the Sudan, but this decisive victory significantly altered the British government's policy towards Egypt. The imperial government had received warnings about the military, financial and political implications[173] of Sudanese unrest but, until this massacre occurred, it had permitted the Egyptian administration to formulate, and execute, its own policy towards the Sudan.[174] The day before the government learnt of the disaster, Granville, in a letter to Baring, recommended the abandonment of the Sudan and refused to supply English or Indian troops to assist the Egyptian government.[175] Sherif's administration lacked the inclination and the administrative capacity to execute this policy.[176] When it resigned on 7 January 1884 Baring bluntly informed Granville, 'They did not thoroughly understand that they must, on important matters, do what they are told.'[177]

The imperial government had sapped the authority of the Egyptian government and thenceforth exercised a 'more direct interference'[178] in its affairs. It had to shoulder more responsibility for Egypt's precarious financial position, which expenditure

[171] *Truth*, 1 Feb. 1883, p. 162; cf. 4 Jan. 1883, pp. 19-20; 16 Aug. 1883, p. 232.
[172] P.R.O., F.O., 407/28/288, Baring to Granville, 21 Nov. 1883.
[173] P.R.O., F.O., 407/24/130 (enc.), memorandum by Sir C. Wilson, Malet to Granville, 2 Oct. 1882; E. S. E. Childers, *The Life and Correspondence of the Right Hon. Sir Hugh C. E. Childers, 1827-1896*, ii, 175.
[174] P.R.O., F.O., 407/28/397, Baring to Granville, 9 Dec. 1883.
[175] P.R.O., F.O., 407/28/281, Granville to Baring, 20 Nov. 1883; cf. 407/28/384. Granville to Baring, 13 Dec. 1883.
[176] P.R.O., F.O., 407/60/4, Baring to Granville, 1 Jan. 1884.
[177] P.R.O., F.O., 633/6/20, Baring to Granville, 7 Jan. 1884.
[178] P.R.O., F.O., 407/60/4, Baring to Granville, 1 Jan. 1884.

in the Sudan had aggravated. Equally, it had to bear some obligations for the defence of Egypt's southern frontier, for the safety of scattered Egyptian garrisons and for the Red Sea ports which the British navy could support.[179]

On 18 January 1884 General Gordon left England under instructions 'to report'[180] on the military and political situation in the Sudan. *En route* he stopped at Cairo, met Baring and the khedive, and assumed executive duties in the Sudan. Although the imperial government sanctioned this change in the character of his mission later, it was a fruitful source of misunderstanding of Gordon's aims and intentions by British ministers.[181] Moreover, the defeat of General Baker's Egyptian force in the eastern Sudan, on 4 February 1884, compelled garrisons at Sinkat and Tokar to capitulate, brought the mahdi's forces to Suakin, and imperilled Khartoum in the west.

Before parliament met on 5 February 1884, Labouchere tried to influence political opinion. He wrote to *The Times* on 9 January 1884 and argued strongly in favour of British withdrawal from Egypt.[182] He spoke at Wellingborough on 22 January 1884, and warned his audience that any imperial involvement in the Sudan would result in heavier taxes in Britain.[183]

*Truth* contained the most comprehensive expression of his views. In November 1883 it had welcomed news of the defeat of General Hicks' army. It denied Egypt's right to annex the Sudan; it commented unfavourably about the oppressive nature of Egyptian rule there; and it described the mahdi as the natural leader of a legitimate rebellion.[184] *Truth* continued to blame bondholders for British intervention in Egypt, and to advocate withdrawal on grounds of principle and expediency. As a first step it suggested that a British garrison at Port Said

[179] P.R.O., F.O., 407/60/31, Granville to Baring, 4 Jan. 1884.
[180] P.R.O., F.O., 407/60/135, Granville to Gordon, 18 Jan. 1884.
[181] On 10 January 1890 Gladstone still believed that Gordon had turned 'upside down & inside out every idea & [?instruction] with which he had left England and for which he had obtained our approval'. C.D.P., B.M. Add. MSS., 43875, fos. 283-4, Gladstone to Dilke; see B. M. Allen, *Gordon and the Sudan*, p. 234.
[182] *Times*, 9 Jan. 1884. He asserted that a fundamental error in British policy was its equation of Egypt with the canal.
[183] *Wellingborough and Kettering News*, 26 Jan. 1884.
[184] *Truth*, 29 Nov. 1883, p. 752.

and Ismailia would safeguard the canal,[185] but it favoured complete withdrawal,[186] with the safety of imperial communications depending upon Britain's mastery of the Red Sea.

*The Times*, the *Pall Mall Gazette* and a group of liberals headed by W. E. Forster campaigned to prevent the withdrawal of 'civilization' from the Sudan. They gave prominence to the argument that if this came about the slave trade would revive. *Truth* stated that a cordon of troops across the Nile valley, and a gunboat off the coast of Suakin would close commercial outlets and make slave trading unremunerative.[187] It contended that British or Egyptian possession of Suakin would not affect the slave trade, owing to the nature of the coast and native shipping.

*Truth* insisted that no British interest existed in the Sudan, and it attributed to bondholders, who wished to prolong British involvement in Egypt, responsibility for any confusion that existed on this matter.[188] In addition, it alleged that whigs supported a 'risky' African policy to divert attention from the need for internal reforms. In its view the empire embraced too many native populations; Britain had difficulty in obtaining sufficient troops to meet existing imperial commitments; and the possibility of further southern expansion presented itself if Britain became involved in the Sudan.[189]

Labouchere played a prominent part in a vigorous and sustained parliamentary attack upon the government's policy towards Egypt and the Sudan. Sir W. Lawson, L. Courtney, and J. Morley were among the handful of English radicals who openly expressed their dissatisfaction with this policy, and they were often supported by Parnellite members. One reason for the persistence of Labouchere's activity was his desire to consolidate his position with the Parnellites.[190] It is improbable that he intended to engineer the defeat of the government on this

[185] *Truth*, 3 Jan. 1884, p. 13. Labouchere repeated this suggestion in his letter to *The Times* on 9 January 1884.   [186] *Truth*, 17 Jan. 1884, p. 95.
[187] *Truth*, 6 Dec. 1883, pp. 788–9; 17 Jan. 1884, p. 96.
[188] *Truth*, 3 Jan. 1884, pp. 13–14.   [189] *Truth*, 17 Jan. 1884, pp. 96–7.
[190] J.C., 5/50/19, Labouchere to Chamberlain, 9 Feb. 1884. *The Times* on 14 November 1884 referred to the 'Parnellite allies' of Lawson and Labouchere who 'exclusively supported' their 'familiar objections to any employment of the military forces of England in Egypt' (first leader). Cf. Division Lists, 1884–5, No. 14, 13 Nov. 1884.

issue.[191] Early in February 1884, he and Sir W. Lawson altered the timing of their motion of censure on the government's Egyptian policy to suit Grosvenor, and, in addition, they promised to vote with the government against Sir S. Northcote's motion[192] which attacked the government's policy on different grounds. Moreover, Labouchere and his political associates who opposed the government's Egyptian and Sudanese policy were normally as numerically insignificant in the division lobby as were opponents of the government's Irish policy. On 15 March 1884, Labouchere unexpectedly moved 'that the necessity for the great loss of British and Arab life, occasioned by our Military operations in the Eastern Sudan, has not been made apparent'.[193] A snap division followed:[194] conservatives, radicals and Parnellites opposed the government, and its majority sank to seventeen.[195]

The *Spectator* suggested that Labouchere had been unable to 'resist the impulse of bedevilment'.[196] When Labouchere opposed coercive legislation for Ireland, he is reputed to have told Cowen, 'I certainly should not ... risk the position of the party on the issue, and if there were any danger of our upsetting the Government ... I should probably vote the other way.'[197] Labouchere's account of the events of 15 March 1884, which he sent to his constituents in April 1884, may therefore have been substantially correct.[198] On the other hand he may well have

[191] Labouchere argued that the government used the threat that the franchise bill might not pass to frighten radicals into condoning aggrandizements of the empire. See *Pall Mall Gazette*, 19 March 1884; *Quarterly Review*, clvii (April 1884), 560.
[192] J.C., 5/50/19, Labouchere to Chamberlain, 9 Feb. 1884. Labouchere did not oppose Northcote's motion on 19 February 1884; he abstained. Division Lists, 1884, No. 14, 19 Feb. 1884.     [193] Hansard, 3rd ser., 285, 1662, 15 March 1884.
[194] T. P. O'Connor, *Gladstone's House of Commons*, p. 391; W. Jeans, *Parliamentary Reminiscences*, p. 253. Harcourt is reputed to have growled 'this dirty trick has not succeeded'.
[195] Division Lists, 1884, No. 39, 15 March 1884.
[196] *Spectator*, 22 March 1884, p. 369.
[197] H. M. Hyndman, *Further Reminiscences*, p. 413.
[198] *Northampton Daily Chronicle*, 26 April 1884. The account he gave was part of his reply to a resolution of confidence in his actions about the Sudan from the executive of Northampton's Liberal and Radical Union. He ridiculed allegations of a plot between himself and conservatives and implied that they had outmanœuvred him. The papers of Lord Randolph Churchill and Sir S. Northcote (Lord Iddesleigh) shed no light on this incident.

arranged the manœuvre with Churchill in order to show the government the parliamentary hazards of its policy towards the Sudan.[199]

In parliament, Labouchere aimed to commit the government unequivocally to a policy of withdrawal from Egypt 'as speedy as is consistent with the establishment of order and tranquillity'.[200] He opposed any British intervention in Sudanese affairs, and he plagued the imperial government with a series of barbed questions and irritating divisions[201] which drew attention to the dichotomy between liberal principles and the results of the liberal government's policy.

He reiterated his views about bondholders' responsibility for British involvement in the Nile valley[202] and, perhaps to give them greater emphasis, he played down the question of the Suez Canal throughout the 1884 parliamentary session. He also alleged that the 'primary cause' of the Egyptian problem 'was that the Conservatives [1874–80] had insisted on interfering' there.[203] Labouchere's emphasis on the intimacy of the relationship between Egyptian complications and British reforms and taxation, was a novel development in his speeches. On 14 February 1884 he stated: 'until we had altered and amended everything which required alteration and amendment at home, we ought not to undertake unnecessary responsibilities abroad'.[204] He contended that the British should leave Egypt in order to attend to internal legislation,[205] and that British artisans should not be taxed for matters which did not concern them.[206] He opposed imperial expenditure in the Sudan and stated that bondholders should foot the bill.[207]

Parallel with these views ran a strong humanitarian theme, and together they gave coherence to the profusion of Labouchere's parliamentary speeches and questions. He denounced

[199] H.P., B.M. Add. MSS., 48635, fo. 135, 16 March 1884.
[200] Hansard, 3rd ser., 284, 96, 6 Feb. 1884.
[201] Commons Division Lists, 1884, No. 25, 3 March 1884; No. 29, 10 March 1884; No. 39, 15 March 1884; No. 45, 17 March 1884.
[202] Hansard, 3rd ser., 284, 904–12, 14 Feb. 1884; 285, 711–16, 6 March 1884.
[203] Hansard, 3rd ser., 284, 906, 14 Feb. 1884; cf. 292, 394–7, 9 Aug. 1884.
[204] Hansard, 3rd ser., 284, 908, 14 Feb. 1884.
[205] Hansard, 3rd ser., 292, 397, 9 Aug. 1884.
[206] Hansard, 3rd ser., 285, 711–16, 6 March 1884.
[207] Hansard, 3rd ser., 293, 1629, 13 Nov. 1884.

the expenditure of Arab life in the Sudan as 'massacres ... horrible and repugnant to the feelings of humanity of the people of England'.[208] On the authority of Consul Moncrieff he dismissed suggestions that British intervention in certain parts of the Sudan such as Suakin would curtail the slave trade.[209] On the other hand, one incident gave him the opportunity to protest that a British army was forcing people back into slavery.[210] On 31 March 1884 he asked the government to instruct civil and military authorities in the Sudan not to protect slave owners, or to insist on the return of fugitives.[211] He supported an unsuccessful attempt by Dr Commins and Parnellites to bring auxiliaries such as camel drivers under the same law as British troops so that they could no longer be flogged.[212]

His attitude towards Egypt had a similar humanitarian orientation: he argued that while British troops maintained the khedive's rule the British government had obligations towards the fellahin. He criticized the combination of judicial and executive functions by agents of the Egyptian government, and he denounced the alleged use of torture,[213] corporal punishment[214] and eviction,[215] to secure payment of taxes by the fellahin. On 22 May 1884 Labouchere expressed the hope that if the Egyptian government was not represented at the London conference the imperial government would act as the representatives of Egyptian taxpayers as well as of bondholders. He considered it their 'duty' to ensure that the fellahin were not unfairly taxed.[216]

Labouchere criticized the conduct of Gordon whom he considered was exceeding his instructions,[217] and was basing his

[208] Hansard, 3rd ser., 285, 1664, 15 March 1884.
[209] Ibid., 1663, 15 March 1884. Baring told Granville on 21 January 1884 that an English army of occupation in the Sudan would be necessary to suppress the slave trade. P.R.O., F.O., 633/6/23.
[210] Hansard, 3rd ser., 286, 776, 25 March 1884. Some of General Graham's Abyssinian auxiliaries attempted to liberate a compatriot who had been abducted and enslaved. They were disarmed.
[211] Hansard, 3rd ser., 286, 1161–2, 31 March 1884.
[212] Ibid., 1751–2, 4 April 1884; Division Lists, 1884, No. 56, 4 April 1884.
[213] Hansard, 3rd ser., 286, 294, 20 March 1884; cf. 291, 321, 24 July 1884.
[214] Hansard, 3rd ser., 290, 225, 7 July 1884.
[215] Hansard, 3rd ser., 293, 1720, 14 Nov. 1884.
[216] Hansard, 3rd ser., 288, 1041, 22 May 1884.
[217] Hansard, 3rd ser., 291, 1764, 5 Aug. 1884.

actions upon the assumption that British troops were *en route* for Khartoum.[218] Labouchere also felt that the government were remiss in not informing the mahdi that they recognized the independence of the Sudan,[219] for this he believed would facilitate Gordon's withdrawal.[220]

In December 1884 Labouchere asked the government for information about the Egyptian political exiles in Ceylon.[221] He had spoken earlier about the Egyptian government's exclusion of Blunt, who had been in the van of the exiles' defence. Labouchere argued that Blunt was excluded from Egypt, on the authority of the British government, because of his views on Egyptian affairs, and that the Egyptian government was acting in an arbitrary and illegal manner.[222]

In 1884 *Truth*'s attitude towards Egypt and the Sudan harmonized with the views Labouchere expressed in the Commons. Bondholders provided the main target for its attacks,[223] and it felt that they ought to provide for the Egyptian government's exceptional expenditure rather than imperial taxpayers.[224] A humanitarian theme underlay some of its arguments,[225] but its tone towards Gordon was icy.[226] Some of *Truth*'s arguments had no place in Labouchere's parliamentary speeches in 1884. It assumed similarities between Egypt and Ireland, and advised Egyptian nationalists to 'organise. Let

[218] Hansard, 3rd ser., 287, 1482, 6 May 1884.
[219] Ibid., 1483, 6 May 1884; 287, 1691, 8 May 1884; 291, 321, 24 July 1884; 293, 1628, 13 Nov. 1884. Labouchere and Blunt lunched together on 4 April 1884 and planned this campaign. Labouchere kept the idea alive in the Commons, and Blunt wrote to Gladstone. G.P., B.M. Add. MSS., 44110, fo. 72, Blunt to Gladstone, 23 April 1884. In February and March 1885 Labouchere and Blunt tried without success to inaugurate negotiations between the imperial government and the mahdi. H.G.P., B.M. Add. MSS., 46015, fos. 17–23, Labouchere to H. Gladstone, 8, 14, 16 Feb. 1885; G.P., B.M. Add. MSS., 44110, fos. 94–9, Blunt to Gladstone, 12 March 1885; A. L. Thorold, pp. 196–8, Labouchere to Blunt, 20 Feb. and 4 March 1885.
[220] Labouchere opposed the vote of £300,000 for Gordon's relief. Division Lists, 1884, No. 210, 5 Aug. 1884.
[221] Hansard, 3rd ser., 294, 622, 4 Dec. 1884.
[222] Hansard, 3rd ser., 291, 1603, 1626, 4 Aug. 1884.
[223] *Truth*, 7 Feb. 1884, p. 200; 13 March 1884, p. 375; 3 April 1884, p. 504; 19 June 1884, pp. 923–4; 21 Aug. 1884, p. 288; 4 Sept. 1884, p. 374; 30 Oct. 1884, p. 671.
[224] *Truth*, 28 Feb. 1884, p. 303; 30 Oct. 1884, p. 671.
[225] *Truth*, 14 Feb. 1884, p. 232; 28 Feb. 1884, p. 303.
[226] *Truth*, 15 May 1884, p. 723; 25 Sept. 1884, p. 473.

"no tax" do for Egypt, what "no rent" has done for Ireland.'[227] It advised Egyptians to repudiate their national debt on the grounds that a 'fellow citizen, calling himself... Khedive'[228] had no right to pledge his country's credit.[229] It referred to the Suez Canal and suggested that this provided the 'sole real plea'[230] for British intervention in Egypt. In May, however, it contended that Britain had no right to any special privileges regarding the canal. *Truth* also claimed that conservatives were attempting to make use of the Egyptian question to outflank Gladstone, destroy the franchise bill, and prevent the nation from devoting itself to internal reform.[231]

Moreover, while Labouchere spoke in parliament of the general need for Britain to concentrate upon internal reforms and to conserve British financial resources, *Truth* was more specific. Thus on 17 April 1884 it stated that British intervention in Egypt had cost approximately £5,000,000. It argued that this capital invested in consols would have produced £150,000 per annum, and that this sum could have supplied 86,666 British children with one meal, 300 days a year, in perpetuity.[232]

Labouchere gave a clear indication of his views about the relationship of Egypt and the British empire in an article published in the *Pall Mall Gazette* on 30 September 1884. He contended that advocates of withdrawal from Egypt were not 'indifferent to Imperial interests. If our empire could not be integrally maintained without the possession of Egypt, we should advocate its permanent occupation; but, ... we consider that... it would... be a source of weakness rather than of strength.'[233] He based this assessment upon the view that the

[227] *Truth*, 13 March 1884, p. 376; cf. 12 June 1884, p. 881; 7 Aug. 1884, p. 212; 25 Dec. 1884, p. 980.
[228] *Truth*, 7 Feb. 1884, p. 201.
[229] In a letter to the *Daily News*, 26 June 1884, Labouchere stated that 'any-one who lends money to a country... where taxation is not accompanied by representation, commits a crime against liberty'.
[230] *Truth*, 15 May 1884, p. 723.
[231] *Truth*, 22 May 1884, p. 761. Conservatives felt that the government were pushing [?the]... Franchise Bill very hard—& delaying Egyptian revelations'. B.P., B.M. Add. MSS., 49688, fo. 76, Salisbury to A. Balfour, [?15 June] 1884.
[232] *Truth*, 17 April 1884, p. 573; cf. 12 Feb. 1885, p. 249.
[233] *Pall Mall Gazette*, 30 Sept. 1884.

canal's importance was greatly exaggerated; that by retaining an army in Egypt, Britain made it much easier for European powers to attack her; and that Egypt could only be effectively defended against a European power if India and imperial garrisons were denuded of troops.

The fall of Khartoum, followed by General Wolseley's and General Graham's campaigns in the Sudan, did nothing to modify the tenor of Labouchere's speeches in parliament in 1885. He contended that because radicals favoured the 'integrity and grandeur of the Empire',[234] they opposed expeditions such as that to crush the mahdi's power. Labouchere feared that the consequences of interference would follow the Egyptian precedent, and that British support would be needed to sustain any alternative indigenous authority in the Sudan.[235] He could see no valid reason for imperial expenditure there,[236] or for the unnecessary slaughter,[237] the imposition of forced labour,[238] and acts not in accordance with civilized warfare,[239] which were preceding the establishment of 'peace and tranquillity'.[240]

Labouchere continued to advocate British withdrawal from Egyptian obligations.[241] He spoke from the standpoint of an old taxpayer,[242] and argued that Egyptian bankruptcy was highly desirable.[243] This, in his view, would permit its government to devote its resources to administrative requirements and internal development, rather than to heavy interest payments. It would end over-taxation in Egypt and remove Britain's need to underwrite Egyptian finances and advance capital for such purposes as irrigation works.[244]

Conservatives and Parnellites defeated the liberal govern-

[234] Hansard, 3rd ser., 294, 1681, 27 Feb. 1885.
[235] Ibid., 1785, 2 March 1885.
[236] Ibid., 1678, 27 Feb. 1885; 295, 472, 9 March 1885; 296, 1483–5, 13 April 1885.
[237] Hansard, 3rd ser., 294, 1679, 27 Feb. 1885; 295, 472, 9 March 1885; 296, 1485, 13 April 1885.
[238] Hansard, 3rd ser., 297, 147, 20 April 1885.
[239] Ibid., 148, 20 April 1885; 297, 1865, 7 May 1885; 298, 25, 26, 8 May 1885.
[240] Hansard, 3rd ser., 294, 1679, 27 Feb. 1885.
[241] Hansard, 3rd ser., 295, 148, 5 March 1885.
[242] Hansard, 3rd ser., 296, 173, 20 March 1885.
[243] Ibid., 264, 23 March 1885.   [244] Ibid., 716–19, 26 March 1885.

ment on 8 June 1885. Labouchere tried with limited success to elicit from the minority conservative government a statement of its Egyptian policy. However, he was more successful in his attempts to probe the issue of a £9,000,000 Egyptian loan which was foreshadowed by the Convention of March 1885.[245] At the end of July 1885 he questioned the chancellor of the exchequer, Sir M. Hicks Beach, about Rothschilds' issue of this loan,[246] and on 5 August 1885 he delayed the business of the House until the government made further explanations.[247] Labouchere caused the conservatives to admit that the liberal government had intended to issue the loan through the Bank of England, and by public tender. He also drew information from the government about Rothschilds' basic and brokerage commission, and their issue of the loan at $94\frac{3}{4}$ by his calculations, instead of the $95\frac{1}{2}$ which figured in the government's correspondence with the firm. He used this to support his argument that Egypt had lost at least £270,000 by the way the loan was issued, and that 'honour' bound the British government to act towards Egypt 'precisely as they would have done for any other Dependency'.[248]

Before the 1885 session began, the *Pall Mall Gazette*[249] and the *Daily News*[250] had published letters from Labouchere in which he argued that responsibilities in Egypt were 'injurious to the prosperity, and ... safety of the empire'.[251] He advocated the cessation of imperial expenditure in Egypt and the Sudan on the grounds that it had only benefited bondholders. On 5 February 1885, the day that news of Gordon's death reached London, he described the Sudanese as 'brave men gallantly fighting for their country's independence'. In two subsequent letters to the *Daily News* he argued against any war of revenge against the Sudanese on the grounds that this would be unjust, impolitic and iniquitous.[252]

[245] E. S. E. Childers, ii, 215.
[246] Hansard, 3rd ser., 300, 516, 518, 30 July 1885; 300, 671, 31 July 1885. *The Times*, on 29 June 1885, gave details of the loan, which was issued by Rothschilds in London, Paris, Frankfurt and Bleichröder in Berlin.
[247] Hansard, 3rd ser., 300, 1200–4, 5 Aug. 1885.
[248] Ibid., 1204, 5 Aug. 1885. £9,000,000 were offered for public subscription: applications for £200,000,000 were received.
[249] *Pall Mall Gazette*, 1 Dec. 1884.    [250] *Daily News*, 15 Dec. 1884.
[251] *Pall Mall Gazette*, 1 Dec. 1884.    [252] *Daily News*, 5, 7, 16 Feb. 1885.

In 1885 the attitude of *Truth* was identical with Labouchere's, but its arguments were more varied than those he voiced elsewhere. It was astounded that the imperial government should squander its resources in Africa, particularly as so much rottenness which needed reform existed in Britain. There were 'agricultural labourers slaving like serfs for a pittance', 'artisans starving for want of work', 'street arabs cowering... in arches, and... school-children faint and emaciated for want of a humble meal'.[253] Alternatively, it considered the expenditure injudicious in terms of imperial defence: if the money had strengthened the fleet, fortified harbours and coaling stations,[254] the empire would have been less vulnerable than by sacrificing 5 per cent of its troops in Egypt and the Sudan,[255] and by depleting imperial garrisons in order to lock up troops in central Africa.[256]

*Truth* continued to assert that bondholders should pay the charges imposed on imperial taxpayers. It argued that the Egyptian government could deduct the costs of military expeditions from the interest paid to bondholders, for their securities would become worthless if the country fell into anarchy or succumbed to a Sudanese invasion.[257] It also asserted that imperial expenditure had not protected the fellahin[258] and that over-taxation in the bondholders' interest had reduced their condition to that of the peasantry of western Ireland.[259]

The decision of the New South Wales government to send a contingent to support imperial forces in the Sudan met with little sympathy in *Truth*. It could not see why the colonists made themselves *participes criminis* in the Sudan.[260] In March it referred again to the 'strange insanity' that had charmed Australians into the Sudan.[261] On 2 April 1885 it became more positive: it alleged that the Stuard-Dalley administration had sent troops of its own, but not of the people's volition, and that Reuter's messages from Sydney were 'gross, inaccurate, and imaginative' on this topic.[262] Two weeks later it published

[253] *Truth*, 29 Jan. 1885, p. 169.
[254] *Truth*, 15 Jan. 1885, p. 89.
[255] *Truth*, 19 March 1885, p. 448.
[256] *Truth*, 12 Feb. 1885, p. 248.
[257] *Truth*, 12 March 1885, pp. 409-10.
[258] *Truth*, 22 Jan. 1885, p. 132; 12 Feb. 1885, p. 249; 12 March 1885, p. 410.
[259] *Truth*, 22 Jan. 1885, p. 132.
[260] *Truth*, 26 Feb. 1885, p. 331.
[261] *Truth*, 26 March 1885, p. 489.
[262] *Truth*, 2 April 1885, p. 523.

comments by a former Australian prime minister, Sir H. Parkes, about the 'wretched military travesty' in the Sudan together with 'evidence' about the way in which 'enthusiasm' for the contingent had been simulated in New South Wales and subscriptions for it procured.[263] In May 1885 *Truth* alleged that the initial enthusiasm with which the Australian troops had been greeted in the Sudan had disappeared,[264] and in September 1885 it asserted that the contingent had become a music hall joke in Australia.[265]

In *Truth*'s opinion the New South Wales expedition, which had cost a population of less than a million £200,000, was an expensive and unnecessary luxury.[266] It approved of Sir J. Macdonald's decision not to involve the Canadian government in a similar way. It also published a letter from an anonymous Canadian correspondent which protested against the cost of the 'experiment of colonial assistance'; the writer believed that the Canadian attitude would be a 'fruitful... lesson to those possessed by the hallucination that Canada's loyalty is a reserve of strength to the Empire'.[267] Labouchere, like John Bright,[268] took exception to the participation of Australian troops in the Sudanese campaign and did not comment upon any of the implications that the contingent from New South Wales presented so far as internal imperial relations were concerned.

From 1885, Labouchere paid less attention to Egyptian and Sudanese affairs. His views, however, remained consistent with those he had expressed since August 1882. It is ironical that Labouchere, one person in British politics to whom the bondholder thesis can be applied convincingly, became one of the leading exponents of the argument that Britain was acting on behalf of bondholders and that other pleas, such as the defence of the canal, were spurious. He was identified with policies favouring withdrawal from Egypt and non-intervention in the Sudan for over two decades. His programme after July 1882 would have secured support from a larger number of liberals in other circumstances for it constituted a relatively coherent

---

[263] *Truth*, 16 April 1885, p. 608.
[264] *Truth*, 14 May 1885, p. 759.  [265] *Truth*, 3 Sept. 1885, p. 365.
[266] *Truth*, 1 Oct. 1885, p. 507.  [267] *Truth*, 16 April 1885, p. 608.
[268] H.P., B.M. Add. MSS., 48639, fo. 77, 5 March 1885.

policy, but it could only have been implemented at the risk of major international complications. It might have been easier to give effect to his proposals if Britain had annexed Egypt in 1882, for Britain's foreign and imperial policy would not then have been inhibited by the British government's need to secure co-operation from other powers in order to administer Egypt. In addition, his arguments were open to the criticisms that Lord Salisbury directed against those of Lord R. Churchill in 1884: 'Churchill's views on Egypt seem to be quite untenable. The idea of a Mussulman state with popular government is absurd: reliance upon the gratitude of a people to maintain our influence there, is still more absurd.'[269] Labouchere was quite straightforward and honest about his interest in Egyptian bonds once British intervention made them secure, but no evidence of subsequent analogous speculations has come to light. The firsthand experience of mustering arguments to support intervention for personal financial reasons, which he gained before August 1882, probably played an important part in making him particularly sceptical of similar, allegedly disinterested, arguments when they were raised in connection with other imperial interests, and more particularly when such interests were associated with those of financiers or capitalists.

[269] Cs.P., B.M. Add. MSS., 51263(5), Salisbury to Cross, 5 Jan. 1884.

## CHAPTER VI

## South Africa, 1880–1886

ON 3 SEPTEMBER 1881 Lord Kimberley, secretary of state for the colonies, asserted that the liberal government's action in South Africa had avoided the greatest calamity to the empire since the American revolution.[1] He believed that if Britain had continued to insist upon the annexation of the Transvaal after the Boers had defeated British forces at Majuba on 27 February 1881, it would have incurred the hostility of the Dutch population throughout South Africa, and have been 'unable to hold the country after having conquered them'.[2]

Liberals were not free from responsibility for this crisis, which needed considerable moral courage on their part to resolve partially. In opposition they had denounced the Transvaal annexation and deplored the Zulu war. Sir H. Bartle Frere told Gladstone that his pre-election speeches had caused 'infinite mischief' in South Africa and 'retarded the prosperity and progress of the European Colonies ... laid the foundation of wars,—and raised very serious obstacles to the religious, moral and political advancement of the native races'.[3] After April 1880 when the liberals held office they did not, in view of 'a concurrence of reports'[4] from their officials in South Africa,[5] rescind the annexation promptly. In parliament Gladstone

---

[1] R.P., B.M. Add. MSS., 43522, fo. 274, Kimberley to Ripon, 3 Sept. 1881.

[2] Ibid., fo. 264, Kimberley to Ripon, 12 April 1881. Merriman told Bryce, on 29 March 1896, that in '1881 the Imperial Government was pitted against the Transvaal; many, perhaps the majority, of English folk here thought that right was on the side of the Transvaal; this was known'. J.B.P. (Bodleian), S.A., S13, Merriman to Bryce, 29 March 1896.

[3] G.P., B.M. Add. MSS., 44470, fo. 269, Frere to Gladstone, July 1881.

[4] R.P., B.M. Add. MSS., 43522, fo. 270, Kimberley to Ripon, 3 Sept. 1881.

[5] S. J. P. Kruger and P. J. Joubert told L. H. Courtney on 14 June 1880 that opposition to the restoration of the Transvaal's independence came from British officials and from landjobbers. Cy.P., R(S.R.) 1003.

distinguished between 'repudiation' and 'reversal', and provided the justification for continuity of policy: 'Confederation . . . is so important . . . it . . . eclipses and absorbs every other consideration in South African policy.'[6]

Advocates of a federal solution to South African problems had existed in the 1850s.[7] The colonial office gradually felt its way towards accepting Sir G. Grey's views, and Lord Carnarvon, who had criticized them in 1859,[8] espoused them between 1874 and 1877, when he had responsibility for colonial affairs. In 1875 he suggested to Sir H. Barkly, the high commissioner, 'some form of confederation'[9] to bring together voluntarily two crown colonies, a dependency granted responsible government in 1872, and two independent republics. Molteno's Cape government repulsed this metropolitan initiative. Meanwhile the arbitration award of Delagoa Bay to Portugal in July 1875, opened up the possibility that the Transvaal might secure an outlet to the sea which was uninhibited by British control. This complicated the South African political situation, made federation more remote, and threatened an infusion of foreign influences which might undermine British hegemony.

However, the Transvaal government was at this time bankrupt and its executive proved unable to collect taxes, or to prevent fraudulent and violent encroachments upon neighbouring tribal territory.[10] In 1875 it suffered reverses at the hands of Sekukini on its north-eastern frontier. More ominously it had incurred the enmity of the Zulus whom Cetewayo had welded into a formidable fighting force. The dangers of a native conflagration provided the British government with the pretext to overlook its 'guarantee in the fullest manner . . . to the emigrant farmers beyond the Vaal River, [of] the right to manage their own affairs, and to govern themselves, without

[6] Hansard, 3rd ser., 252, 461, 459–64, 25 May 1880.
[7] Lord Russell cancelled Lord Grey's draft dispatch of October 1850 as it appeared to dictate to the colonists. Sir George Grey's dispatch to Bulwer-Lytton, 19 Nov. 1858, and the federal campaign which led to his recall, were motivated by a desire for unity shared by Dutch and English.
[8] See K. N. Bell and W. P. Morrell (eds.), *Select Documents on British Colonial Policy, 1830–1860*, pp. 191–4.
[9] *C.H.B.E.*, iii, 50. See C. F. Goodfellow's admirable study of this policy in *Great Britain and South African Confederation, 1870–1881*.
[10] *C.H.B.E.*, viii, 473.

any interference'.¹¹ On 12 April 1876 Sir T. Shepstone, by an arrangement of dubious merit with President Burgers, annexed the Transvaal without the assent of the Volksraad. Superficially the annexation made federation, developing from a northeastern base, appear as a viable policy; and it was partly to facilitate its realization that the British government withheld from the Boers rights of self-government promised at the time of annexation.¹² A spate of native wars gave Frere, who had replaced Barkly as high commissioner, the impression of a native conspiracy headed by Cetewayo. He precipitated war with the Zulus, broke their military power, and captured Cetewayo in August 1879.¹³ The native wars demonstrated the necessity for federation which, however, was 'killed', from a British point of view, in the Cape parliament. Moreover, the crushing of Zulu power removed native threats to the Transvaal.

The Transvaal Boers' dislike of British authority grew increasingly intense,¹⁴ and over 82 per cent of the burghers previously enfranchised petitioned against it. Kruger, Joubert and Jorissen led an agitation for repeal of annexation; a delegation visited Britain twice to state their case; and, in addition, they urged their sympathizers at the Cape not to contemplate federation while their grievances remained.¹⁵ Agitation in Britain had encouraged agitation in the Transvaal.¹⁶ When liberals took office in 1880, Boer discontent seemed to have declined for the Boers waited for them to reverse the policy of their predecessors. Boer leaders requested Gladstone to redeem his Midlothian pledges,¹⁷ but although the attitude of the Cape

[11] Sand River Convention, 17 Jan. 1852; K. N. Bell and W. P. Morrell, p. 527.
[12] Parl. Pap., 1877, lx, [C.1776], 159.
[13] Colonial opinion in the Cape and Natal was 'generally unfavourable' to the settlement whereby Zululand was divided among thirteen petty chiefs. In addition, the Cape government, which since 1878 had favoured confederation, 'complained of not being consulted in an arrangement in which as the leading State in the future confederation they consider themselves immediately concerned'. P.R.O., Cab. 37/1/21(5), 1880.
[14] P.R.O., Cab. 37/1/18(4), 1880.
[15] Parl. Pap., 1880, li, [C.2655], 4ff.; Parl. Pap., 1880, li, [C.2676], 48, Lanyon to Kimberley, received 12 July 1880.
[16] *C.H.B.E.*, viii, 492.
[17] J. Morley, *The Life of William Ewart Gladstone*, iii, 22–36. Cabinet papers show that the Boers desired nothing other than independence. The conservative British

parliament made Kimberley regard 'Confederation as adjourned *sine die*',[18] they waited in vain. On 16 December 1880 they resorted to military force. The Convention of Pretoria signed on 3 August 1881 granted them 'complete self-government' with qualifications which subjected them to British 'suzerainty'.[19]

Confederation offered the imperial authorities a curtailment of financial, military and humanitarian responsibilities which interminable struggles between settlers and natives, and the underlying interrelation of South African problems, laid upon them. In some respects the policy became more viable after Kimberley's annexation of Griqualand West in October 1871, for exploitation of the diamond deposits stimulated the South African economy, attracted immigrants and capital investment, and provided the financial sinews which maintained responsible government in Cape Colony after 1872. Moreover, a federal solution under British paramountcy would have secured imperial communications.

The Cape naval base remained a primary imperial concern in South Africa, and its protection accounted for British concern with the shifting storm centres of dissension there. In 1797 Macartney had informed Dundas: 'Its chief importance to us arises from its geographical position, from its forming the master link of connection between the western and eastern world, from its being the great outwork of our Asiatic commerce and Indian Empire.'[20] Simonstown's importance survived the opening of the Suez Canal in 1869. A royal commission on colonial defence concluded, in 1881, that the Cape route to the east was 'of such importance' that its 'integrity ... must be maintained at all hazards, and irrespective of cost'.[21]

---

government thought they 'might' receive a constitution which would confer upon them 'as a member of a South African Confederation', 'under the paramount authority of the British Crown, the fullest independence compatible with that thorough unity of action which the common welfare demands'. P.R.O., Cab. 37/1/5(4), (23), 1880.

[18] G.P., B.M. Add. MSS., 44255, fo. 184, Kimberley to Gladstone, 29 June 1880.
[19] G. W. Eybers, *Select Constitutional Documents relating to South Africa*, pp. 455–63.
[20] Quoted in *C.H.B.E.*, viii, 184, Macartney to Dundas, 10 July 1797.
[21] P.R.O., C.O., 885/5/68, First Report of the Royal Commission on Colonial Defence, 3 Sept. 1881, p. 412.

Labouchere's attitude to South African affairs was consistent and prescient in itself, but it conflicted with the whole orientation of British policy, and with his general view that 'Commercially ... there should be no wall around our Empire; politically ... there should be a Chinese wall.'[22] Despite, or perhaps because of the fundamental importance he attributed to the Cape route to the east when he attacked British occupation of Egypt, he recommended a withdrawal of the imperial factor from South African affairs. In his view, Britain's only concern was to 'occupy the land commanding Simon's Bay',[23] to retain a fortified naval harbour there,[24] and 'have a Gibraltar in Southern Africa'.[25] Britain should abandon all other responsibilities. Different sections of the community would then resolve their differences amongst themselves,[26] and whether they acted rationally or like Kilkenny cats was their concern, not Britain's.[27] He argued that 'every one of our colonies ought to be able to hold its own in local squabbles; if it cannot, the sooner that it goes to the wall the better'.[28] In addition, it was the 'paramount duty of the inhabitants of every portion of the globe to look first to their own interests'. Nevertheless, the colonists, from an 'enlightened view of self-interest', would 'maintain the connection with Great Britain, as one of mutual benefit'.[29]

In his electoral manifesto, first published on 22 March 1880, Labouchere criticized the annexation of the territory of 'harmless Dutch Republicans against their will' and the expenditure of 'six millions in catching a savage [Cetewayo], who has as much right to his freedom as we have'.[30] He spoke in similar vein at several meetings in Northampton. On 20 March 1880 he reminded his audience that a consequence of the 'massacre ... of harmless blacks in Africa'[31] was dearer tobacco in the United Kingdom. Six days later he argued that the Zulu war, which in his opinion was 'most iniquitous', would not have occurred if

---

[22] *Truth*, 25 Sept. 1884, p. 473.  [23] *Truth*, 31 March 1881, p. 427.
[24] *Truth*, 17 Feb. 1881, p. 210; cf. 17 March 1881, p. 354; 15 March 1883, p. 355; 19 April 1883, p. 537.
[25] *Truth*, 31 March 1881, p. 427.  [26] *Truth*, 17 Feb. 1881, p. 210.
[27] *Truth*, 15 March 1883, p. 355.  [28] *Truth*, 9 Oct. 1884, p. 555.
[29] *Truth*, 1 Jan. 1885, p. 16; cf. 17 March 1881, p. 354.
[30] *Northampton Evening Mail*, 22 March 1880.
[31] *Northampton Mercury*, 27 March 1880.

the Natal colonists had known that they must resolve their differences with the natives without any British assistance.[32]

After his election on 2 April 1880, he was singularly reticent about South African affairs until the end of December 1880, and by then the Transvaal Boers had risen in revolt. He made no public or private demand, so far as one can determine, for the restitution of independence to the 'quiet, decent, respectable ... Dutch Republicans'[33] who had figured in his electoral campaign. It is also unlikely that he contacted South African politicians in order to urge the efficacy of agitation upon them.[34] The Boers' repudiation of British authority on 16 December 1880 rekindled his sympathy for their cause.[35]

On 6 January 1881, the first day of the parliamentary session, Labouchere nominally supported the section of the queen's speech which related to the Transvaal. However, he did so 'without prejudice, and declined to recognize that Her Majesty's Government had any legal authority in the Transvaal ... he did not regard the inhabitants of that territory as rebels, but as independent Republicans, who had never given their assent to the annexation'. He hoped the government would dispatch commissioners to ascertain the 'wishes of the Boers'. If they chose to remain republicans, he felt that it would be an 'honourable act' for Britain to withdraw. Some members of parliament interpolated their dissent, but Labouchere asserted that the Boers 'ought not to be coerced for a just, ... honest, and ... honourable act'.[36] Four days later he asked the

[32] *Northampton Mercury* (Supplement), 27 March 1880.  [33] Ibid.

[34] See pp. 29, 31–2 above. During the Boer war, he advised Merriman on extraparliamentary pro-Boer agitation in England, and asked him, in view of the proposed suspension of the Cape constitution, if the colonists would refuse to pay taxes that were not voted constitutionally. N.L.I., J. E. Redmond Papers, Labouchere to Redmond, 19 April [?1901]; N.L.I., MS. 10496, W. O'Brien Papers, Redmond to O'Brien, 24 April 1901; J. F. X. Merriman Papers, Cape Town, Nos. 200, 204, Labouchere to Merriman, [?12], 18 June 1901.

[35] It is possible that Labouchere may have used *Truth* to advocate the Boers' right to self-determination in order to support the struggle Dilke and Chamberlain waged in the cabinet. Dilke wrote in his diary on 2 March 1881, 'Chamberlain had an hour and a half with Bright and got him to write a strong letter to Gladstone about the Transvaal, which we put forward as our ground for proposed resignation, although of course the strength of the [Irish] coercion measures, the weakness of the [Irish] land measures and the predominance of the Whigs in the Cabinet are the real reasons' (see R. Robinson, J. Gallagher, *Africa and the Victorians*, p. 70).

[36] Hansard, 3rd ser., 257, 4, 149, 6 Jan. 1881.

government to recognize the Boers as belligerents, but Grant Duff, under-secretary of state for the colonies, replied that the government had no information to justify consideration of this matter.[37] In March 1881 Labouchere abstained from voting when the government requested £210,000 for expenditure in the Transvaal,[38] but in July 1881 he supported its policy of concession to the Boers against a censure, moved by Sir M. Hicks Beach, from the opposition.[39] From January 1881 until November 1884 he made no further comments on South African affairs in parliament.

This silence did not extend to *Truth*. On 6 January 1881 *Truth* accounted for the Transvaal Boers' 'laudable' determination to regain their independence, as a logical sequel to the fraudulence of the annexation, the despotic nature of British administration, and the persistence of the Boers' desire to remain independent. In its view, Britain had 'absolutely nothing to gain by retaining the Transvaal'. She should evacuate it, and 'frankly... recognize the right of the Boers freely to decide whether they will be citizens of the Republic... or subjects of the British Empire'.[40] After the British defeat at Majuba on 27 February 1881, *Truth* argued that Britain, owing to its strength, could 'afford to be magnanimous' to 'humble farmers, whose sole crime is that they love their independence and are prepared to die for it'.[41] It recognized British responsibility towards the 800,000 Africans in the Transvaal whom annexation had made British subjects. It admitted that they were ill-treated by the Boers, and tried to square the circle of withdrawal and humanitarianism by suggesting that

the Boers should be given a district in the Transvaal, where they may enjoy their independence, ... contiguous to the Orange Free State, and, at the same time, we should inform the African tribes that in-

[37] Ibid., 335–6, 10 Jan. 1881. On 4 February 1881 Kimberley wrote to Gladstone: 'Our instructions to treat the Boers in arms according to the rules of civilised warfare will prevent any severities, during the progress of the war.' G.P., B.M. Add. MSS., 44226, fo. 16, Kimberley to Gladstone, 4 Feb. 1881.

[38] Division Lists, 1881, No. 164, 21 March 1881.

[39] Division Lists, 1881, No. 332, 25 July 1881. The motion contended that the government's policy of withdrawal was 'fraught with danger to the future tranquillity and safety' of South Africa. [40] *Truth*, 6 Jan. 1881, p. 5.

[41] *Truth*, 17 March 1881, p. 354; cf. 10 March 1881, p. 318; 31 March 1881, p. 427.

habit the rest of the Transvaal that they are independent both of us and of the Boers.⁴²

In March 1881 the British government decided to conciliate the Transvaal Boers and *Truth*'s pro-Boer arguments lapsed. Meanwhile, Cetewayo had languished in captivity for nearly two years before *Truth*, on 2 June 1881, recalled his existence and began to favour his return to Zululand.⁴³ The colonial secretary, Lord Kimberley, believed that the Zulu war was 'unjust and unnecessary'⁴⁴ and was 'ashamed'⁴⁵ to be Cetewayo's gaoler, but the South African colonists 'violently opposed'⁴⁶ the captive's release, which was not popular among the Zululand chiefs,⁴⁷ nor, according to Bulwer, among the tribesmen.⁴⁸ *Truth* argued that as the Zulu war was iniquitous, Britain had no right to dethrone or imprison Cetewayo,⁴⁹ and it felt that Britain had a moral obligation to free him.⁵⁰ It alleged that 'all the chiefs and headsmen ... [and] all disinterested people who know the country' 'ardently'⁵¹ desired his return. Early in 1883 the British government permitted Cetewayo to return to Zululand as ruler of a smaller kingdom, but it imposed conditions upon him to safeguard Natal and the native chiefs. According to Lord Derby, 'He had not been in the country three days before he broke his word.'⁵² Cetewayo failed to assert his authority, and died in exile shortly afterwards.

In his electoral campaign of 1880, Labouchere expressed views about the Transvaal Boers, Cetewayo, the Zulu war, and

---

⁴² *Truth*, 3 Feb. 1881, p. 142; cf. 27 Jan. 1881, p. 111. W. E. Forster in a memorandum printed for the cabinet on 22 March 1881 suggested a tripartite division of the Transvaal into a small British district, a much larger native district, and a Boer district. P.R.O., Cab. 37/5/9, 1881.

⁴³ By this time nearly fifteen months had elapsed since Labouchere expressed sympathy for Cetewayo in his electoral speeches. Questions were asked about Cetewayo in parliament on 18 January, 14 March and 8 April 1881.

⁴⁴ G.P., B.M. Add. MSS., 44226, fo. 133, Kimberley to Gladstone, 3 June 1881.

⁴⁵ Ibid., fo. 253, Kimberley to Gladstone, 2 Sept. 1881.

⁴⁶ Ibid., fo. 239, Kimberley to Gladstone, 26 Aug. 1881.

⁴⁷ Ge.P., P.R.O., 30/29/27, Derby to Dilke, 22 Feb. 1883.

⁴⁸ Dy.P., X24, Derby to Dilke (copy), 17 Oct. 1883.

⁴⁹ *Truth*, 2 June 1881, p. 744; 30 March 1882, p. 435.

⁵⁰ *Truth*, 1 Dec. 1881, p. 702; 29 Dec. 1881, p. 6.

⁵¹ *Truth*, 10 Aug. 1882, p. 219.

⁵² Dy.P., X24, Derby to Dilke (copy), 17 Oct. 1883.

the South African colonists which were later expanded in *Truth*. On 26 March 1880, during a speech at Northampton, Labouchere contended that the South African colonists would have a vested interest in provoking wars with their neighbours for as long as Britain expended her resources to sustain them. He argued that if the British government informed the colonists that it would no longer underwrite their actions, many South African wars would not occur, and to strengthen his case he drew an analogy, which was in fact misleading, with New Zealand.[53] *Truth* complained that the South African colonies perpetually dragged Britain into expensive wars[54] which had cost imperial taxpayers £20,000,000,[55] and it commended a severance of the South African Gordian knot. It argued that Britain's sole concern in South Africa was retention of a fortified naval base at Simonstown. She ought to withdraw from all other responsibilities throughout South Africa, and adopt a policy of non-intervention[56] to arrest the dissipation of British resources. *Truth* supported these views by emphasizing the large proportion of colonists of Dutch origin in Natal and Cape Colony,[57] and by contending that Britain was 'by no means loved'[58] in either of these colonies. It asserted that Cape colonists' 'one object'[59] was to foment disputes between Britain and their neighbours, so that the money of British taxpayers would be spent amongst them.[60] In its opinion, the 'only use of a colony ... is to afford an outlet for surplus population, and for this purpose we have many colonies ... far better situated than those in South Africa'.[61] It distrusted Cape securities, on the grounds that the Dutch were 'anti-English in sentiment' and might demonstrate 'their dislike by repudiating loans borrowed on the English market',[62] and Natal securities because of the

[53] *Northampton Mercury* (Supplement), 27 March 1880.
[54] *Truth*, 17 Feb. 1881, p. 210.    [55] *Truth*, 22 March 1883, p. 393.
[56] *Truth*, 22 March 1883, p. 393; 19 April 1883, p. 537.
[57] *Truth*, 15 March 1883, p. 355.
[58] *Truth*, 19 April 1883, p. 537.    [59] *Truth*, 17 March 1881, p. 354.
[60] *Truth*, 22 March 1883, p. 393. Lord Derby held similar views: 'The only points on which all colonists of all parties [in South Africa] are agreed are the advantages of a war in developing Colonial trade, and its being the duty of England to take the whole cost of defending settlers against natives. The British taxpayer is regarded as their natural prey.' Dy.P., X24, Derby to W. Rathbone (copy), 4 June 1883.
[61] *Truth*, 17 Feb. 1881, p. 210.    [62] *Truth*, 27 Dec. 1883, p. 910.

size of the colonists' existing debt burden, and their intention to augment it by almost 50 per cent.⁶³ On 22 March 1883, *Truth* asserted that Britain had not derived, and never would derive either honour or profit from our South African possessions. The manifest destiny of the country is to become a Dutch State or Federation of States; and as an English taxpayer, I object to every British penny that is spent in endeavouring to buy off the inevitable.⁶⁴

Labouchere's views on British policy towards Bechuanaland fitted in with this assessment of South Africa's future. On 13 November 1884, he pressed his opposition to the expedition to Bechuanaland to a division in the house of commons, despite a request from Callan not to do so. He protested again about British expenditure in South Africa and the frequency of wars there, and he commented upon the colonists' willingness to furnish occasions for expenditure. He asserted that a debatable region, where quarrels would occur, existed between civilization and barbarism and he argued that Britain would be perpetually involved if it supported one side against the other.⁶⁵

Before November 1884, Labouchere had used *Truth* to influence public opinion. In 1883 it argued that the British government erred in exercising a vague suzerainty over the Transvaal, for this, in its opinion, involved Britain in responsibilities it could not enforce.⁶⁶ *Truth* warned its readers that if the British fought the Transvaal Boers to prevent their penetration into Bechuanaland, they might find the Dutch in Cape Colony and Natal arrayed against them.⁶⁷ While it paid tribute to missionary activity, it contended that missionaries favoured the Bechuanas, and wished to have Britain protect them. *Truth* argued that Britain could not protect all converts: 'Religious jingoism is as costly and as unpractical as political jingoism.'⁶⁸

⁶³ *Truth*, 3 April 1884, p. 504. The colonists sought an additional loan of £1,130,200 in 1884. *Truth* contended that the colony's debt of £2,379,100 in 1882, for a white population of approximately 30,000, was quite sufficient.
⁶⁴ *Truth*, 22 March 1883, p. 393.
⁶⁵ Hansard, 3rd ser., 293, 1692–3, 13 Nov. 1884.
⁶⁶ *Truth*, 15 March 1883, p. 355.
⁶⁷ *Truth*, 19 April 1883, p. 537.        ⁶⁸ *Truth*, 22 March 1883, p. 393

From April 1883 until October 1884, *Truth* ignored Bechuanaland. Then, for three weeks before parliament gave its approval to the expedition led by Sir C. Warren, it expanded the arguments it had propounded earlier. In its opinion, it was immaterial to Britain whether the Transvaal Boers acquired Bechuanaland or not. However, if they threatened to do so, and colonists in Natal or Cape Colony objected, the solution lay in their hands, and they could annex the territory themselves.[69] *Truth* asserted that 'Conservative Jingoes, ... discontented ex-Liberal Ministers like ... [W. E.] Forster, ... persons who have money invested in Colonial enterprises like Sir William MacArthur, and ... militant missionaries' threatened to cause a 'new departure in expense and bloodshed' to protect bondholders' investment of £20,000,000 in the Cape.[70]

Moreover, although *Truth* deplored the way in which Lord Derby had conducted negotiations with Germany, it did not modify its views about South Africa because of German intervention. It rejoiced that Britain had not increased its responsibilities by annexing Angra Pequena, for this, in its view, would have obliged it to dispatch troops to protect 'German trading missionaries'.[71] It contended that Britain did not own Africa, and that it was 'probably' better for Africans to have Angra Pequena annexed by Germany than for it to remain a no-man's-land.[72] *Truth* made no reference to any other aspect of the German annexation.

From January 1885 until the end of 1886, *Truth* virtually ignored South African affairs, even when Labouchere attacked the liberal government's policy in parliament. On 1 March 1886 he was the first speaker in the debate on colonial estimates to question the 'hopes and rejoicings' with which members of parliament approved of the annexation of Bechuanaland. He doubted whether its possession would augment British trade,[73] and suggested that the route to the interior, which Britain had secured, merely led to the bush. He feared that while mis-

---

[69] *Truth*, 9 Oct. 1884, p. 555.   [70] *Truth*, 16 Oct. 1884, p. 590.
[71] *Truth*, 18 Dec. 1884, p. 940.   [72] *Truth*, 1 Jan. 1885, p. 15.
[73] In a speech to his constituents on 24 November 1885 he asserted that exports of Northampton's staple (footwear) to South Africa, which had been considerable, had virtually ceased: 'and so it ever will be, whenever you try to force a trade upon a reluctant people at the point of the sword'. *Northampton Mercury*, 28 Nov. 1885.

sionaries would use the route initially, an English army to protect them would not lag far behind. He advised philanthropists who wished to shield natives from alcohol to turn their attention to England. Then he turned from commerce and Christianity to consider imperial communications and closer union of the empire. He denied the existence of any connection between Bechuanaland and the Cape route to the east: 'We might as well talk of retaining Gibraltar by taking a town in the middle of France.' He was equally emphatic about Sir R. Fowler's argument that the annexation might draw closer the bonds which united Britain with its colonies. In Labouchere's view, the establishment of a colony in opposition to the Cape, in a region which South Africans regarded as a province of the Transvaal, would not do this. He described imperial expenditure in South Africa as a 'clear and absolute loss' to Britain, and considered the annexation of Bechuanaland 'absurd, idle, and ... wicked'. His attempt to reduce the estimates by £68,000, the amount required to administer Bechuanaland, failed but eighty-five members, mainly Parnellites and British radicals, supported his motion, which was seconded by Dr Clark.[74]

In parliament Labouchere's sympathy for the Transvaal Boers and his opposition to imperial expenditure had much Parnellite and radical support. It is possible that he used the South African question to help knit the two groups together. In 1881 Sir W. Lawson requested justice for the Transvaal Boers because otherwise Irish constituents would believe that they could not obtain justice from the imperial parliament. Finigan thought it 'logical and just' to accord the Boers 'the right of the people to self-government'[75] which he claimed for the Irish. Radicals such as A. Illingworth[76] and W. Rathbone supported Labouchere's criticism of expenditure: Rathbone believed it imposed 'burdens which a Democracy will not endure'.[77] On 13 November 1884, W. Redmond echoed *Truth*'s view of South Africa's 'manifest destiny'[78] in parliament. He predicted that

[74] Hansard, 3rd ser., 302, 1614–17, 1 March 1886; Division Lists, 1886, No. 13, 1 March 1886.
[75] Hansard, 3rd ser., 257, 150, 6 Jan. 1881.
[76] Hansard, 3rd ser., 293, 1696, 13 Nov. 1884.
[77] Hansard, 3rd ser., 302, 1619, 1 March 1886.   [78] *Truth*, 22 March 1883, p. 393.

'the Dutch element would prevail in South Africa; and [it] ... would become ... a Free State for people of German and Dutch blood'.[79]

Labouchere's attitude was that Britain 'ought not to send a man or a coin to South Africa in order to bolster up one savage against another, or to assume protectorates over vast tracts of country that we do not require and which only land us in further expenditure'.[80] He considered that Britain's sole interest in South Africa was retention of a fortified naval base at Simonstown, and even this was conditional upon retention of India.[81] He repeatedly protested against imperial expenditure, and in his concern for retrenchment, he sacrificed native interests upon the altar of withdrawal. His bold simplifications glossed over the fact that he was suggesting that European colonists throughout South Africa be conceded independence of action towards the non-European population. When he advocated the right of the Transvaal Boers to govern themselves, he conceded, by implication, their right to govern the natives.[82] Thus he only extended to a minority, democratic principles which he applied generally to the situation in Ireland and Egypt. He did propose at one stage segregated areas in the Transvaal, but this was an unpractical suggestion which he did not repeat.

Labouchere's opposition to any increase in imperial responsibilities, and his eagerness to withdraw from those which existed, stemmed partly, but not wholly, from his belief that Britain ought to set its 'own house in order before ... [it] set Africa in order'.[83] His views, however, were very radical apart from his interest in domestic reform. He advised philanthropists to concentrate upon problems created by the consumption of alcohol in Britain,[84] and the London Missionary Society to direct its activity to Britain.[85] In addition, he felt that Britain

[79] Hansard, 3rd ser., 293, 1682–3, 13 Nov. 1884.
[80] *Fortnightly Review*, xxxviii (1 Oct. 1885), 488–9.
[81] *Truth*, 19 April 1883, p. 537.
[82] In the Transvaal there were 774,930 black Africans, 33,739 of Dutch and 5,316 of non-Dutch European extraction. P.R.O., Cab. 37/1/18(9), 1880.
[83] *Truth*, 29 Jan. 1885, p. 169.
[84] Hansard, 3rd ser., 302, 1616, 1 March 1886.
[85] *Truth*, 28 May 1885, p. 840.

ought to fulfil obligations to its subjects in other parts of the empire. On 28 April 1882, he spoke in parliament to urge the termination of debtor slavery and 'all slavery' in British colonies such as the Gold Coast, Lagos, and Hong Kong, protectorates such as the Malay States, and territories 'affiliated to the British Empire' such as North Borneo.[86]

In his advocacy of British withdrawal, Labouchere oversimplified the complexities of the South African situation. For instance, he gave the impression that the Cape and Natal were analogous and did not mention that Natal had not attained responsible government. However, his suggestion that colonists there might create a native military force to defend themselves,[87] indicated an awareness of one cause[88] of their limited constitutional development, as well as a concern for imperial expenditure. It was a corollary of his opinion that a colony must be strong enough to maintain itself that Natal might not survive. This did not disturb the tenor of his argument. He prophesied that South Africa would develop into a Dutch state, and he believed that it was the responsibility of different sections of the South African community to resolve their differences themselves in whatever manner they chose. He considered that if Britain allowed this to happen, South Africans and British taxpayers would benefit. This assessment of the South African situation was probably coloured by Labouchere's reservations about the attachment of the 'quiet, decent, respectable colonists' of Dutch descent to the British connection, his low opinion of South African colonial securities,[89] and his belief that Britain possessed more suitable colonies for her emigrants. He never considered the possibility that ultimately the Transvaal's expansionist predilections, German intervention, and the free operation of indigenous forces might jeopardize the security of the naval base.

[86] Hansard, 3rd ser., 268, 1711–16, 28 April 1882.
[87] *Truth*, 6 Nov. 1884, p. 704.
[88] See P.R.O., Cab. 37/2/22, 8 May 1880.
[89] *Truth*, 15 March 1883, p. 355; 27 Dec. 1883, p. 910.

CHAPTER VII

# India and Cyprus, 1880–1886

### INDIA

LIBERALS attacked conservatives' management of Indian affairs during Lord Lytton's viceroyalty from 1876 to 1880. Gladstone, in November 1879, expressed alarm at the increase of over 16 per cent in the general expenditure of the government of India, the transformation of a surplus of £7,000,000 when Lytton became viceroy, into a deficit of nearly £6,000,000 within three years, the increase in military expenditure, and the greater burden of India's public debt, which rose from £107,500,000 in 1874 to £134,500,000 in 1878.[1] In December 1879, he argued that the assumption by the queen of the title 'Empress of India' needed fulfilment 'by increase of franchise or of privilege, by augmentation of benefit, by redress of grievances and correction of abuse'. No development of this nature occurred. Instead, the government of India passed an arms act which indicated mistrust of, and caused inconvenience to, the Indian population. It ended the freedom of the vernacular press in April 1878, although Lord Canning had only suspended the act of 1835 for one year during the emergency caused by the mutiny. It levied heavier taxation upon an impoverished population, and spent reserves intended to alleviate famine upon the second Afghan war.[2]

By 1875 Russian expansion through central Asia had brought their troops close to the northern frontier of Afghanistan. This alarmed British statesmen, particularly as British influence in Afghanistan declined between 1873 and 1877 to such an extent that the amir at the Peshawar conference treated Russia and Britain on a similar footing. A reappraisal of India's policy on

[1] W. E. Gladstone, *Political Speeches in Scotland*, i, 143–4, 29 Nov. 1879.
[2] Ibid., i, 199, 203, 5 Dec. 1879.

the north-west frontier was made. Moreover, in the course of Lytton's viceroyalty, the governments of India and Britain looked beyond the mountain barrier and contemplated military activities in central Asia.[3] This led the government of India to concern itself with Chitral and the establishment of British agents at Herat, Kandahar and Khabul.[4] The Stolietoff mission precipitated the forward movement which began on 21 November 1878. The active policy had more support amongst Lytton's advisers than in governmental circles in London. The viceroy acted somewhat independently, and Sir S. Northcote summed up the position in January 1879: 'we don't know what Lytton means to do, but are sure that, whatever it is, it will be right'.[5]

In his Midlothian speeches of 1879 and 1880 Gladstone simplified the problem of India's relations with Afghanistan by ignoring Russian expansion. He considered the second Afghan war a 'mischief of almost immeasurable dimensions' which, like other aspects of British administration of India between 1877 and 1880, was 'dishonouring to England'.[6] He distrusted conservatives' reversal of the policy 'of cautious abstention, of kindly support, of resolute non-interference'[7] towards Afghanistan which had operated throughout the two previous decades, and he felt that the financial position of India presented a grave warning against the 'wanton invasion' that had made Afghanistan a 'miserable ruin'.[8] He attacked the government of India's internal and external policy on the grounds that neither would 'attach to us the minds of the millions over whom we have assumed an Empire'.[9]

Lord Ripon's appointment as viceroy of India in April 1880 represented a change in the British government, and a change of policy towards India. Final responsibility for Indian affairs rested with the cabinet advised by the secretary of state, but Ripon possessed considerable power as viceroy. In addition, he

---

[3] Argyll, on the evidence of Lytton's letters to Sir H. Norman, believed that Lytton made active preparations, '9,000 camels collected—5,000 men equipped'. Dy.P., X12, Argyll to Derby, 16 Feb. 1881.
[4] See L. Harris, 'British Policy on the North-West Frontier of India' (Lond., Ph.D., 1960), pp. 23–9.
[5] Cs.P., B.M. Add. MSS., 51265(10), Northcote to Cross, 8 Jan. 1879.
[6] W. E. Gladstone, ii, 95–6, 19 March 1880.   [7] Ibid., ii, 55–6, 18 March 1880.
[8] Ibid., i, 49, 25 Nov. 1879.   [9] Ibid., i, 202, 5 Dec. 1879.

was Gladstone's personal representative, 'sent out to give expression and effect ... to the temper and energy of English Liberalism'.[10] Ripon's aim was to 'persuade the people of this country that we desire to govern them in their own interest and to promote their welfare and not any selfish or narrow national object of our own'.[11]

Labouchere was not of the 'perish India' school of politics,[12] yet he paid little attention to its affairs between 1880 and 1886. Speakers on Indian affairs tended to be specialists. Labouchere apparently had no direct contacts with Indian nationalists, and he raised no Indian issue in parliament until May 1885. Lord Ripon's viceroyalty, 'the epoch ... in which the real foundation of the liberty of the Indian people was laid',[13] provided him with scant opportunity to denigrate this whig statesman,[14] to use Indian policy to increase hostility between whigs and radicals, or to demonstrate the closer association of radical principles with liberal traditions than those of whigs. To have praised Ripon would have weakened Labouchere's argument that it was the duty of radicals to drive whigs from the liberal party. His intermittent comments on Indian affairs primarily criticized conservatives' policy and opposed expansion.

In this period *Truth* published one article about the economy of India. On 26 August 1880 it favoured large-scale English investment with an imperial guarantee, in India. Its thesis was that capital which had flowed to the centre of an empire would not return to its periphery on the 'mere chance' of a 4 per cent dividend. England could allow private enterprise to develop its resources because capital was plentiful, but in India this condition did not apply. Consequently governmental development was necessary. India provided a 'safe outlet' for England's surplus capital. The capital would remain within the empire, and, by developing India's latent resources, it would generate a

[10] S. Gopal, *The Viceroyalty of Lord Ripon, 1880–1884*, p. 2.
[11] G.P., B.M. Add. MSS., 44286, fos. 256–7, Ripon to Gladstone, 22 Oct. 1881.
[12] *Truth*, 5 Oct. 1882, p. 489.
[13] *Daily News*, 11 Feb. 1885, J. Gazlar speaking on behalf of the Indian Reform Association.
[14] In several respects Ripon's views were more advanced than those of many radicals. Nevertheless, the 'Whig taint was still strong upon him' in some radical circles until 1885. L. Wolf, *The Life of the First Marquess of Ripon*, ii, 171.

chain reaction which would stimulate trade and provide 'employment for thousands' in England: 'nothing would conduce more to the prosperity of England and of India' than £100,000,000 expended upon public works in India.[15]

In connection with administration, *Truth* considered Britain 'bound in honour not to waste one single farthing'[16] if it governed India without the consent of its inhabitants. To reduce grinding taxation it recommended replacement of European officials by Indians with lower salaries, and, where this was impracticable, a reduction of Europeans' salaries.[17] It was convinced that the Indian service would attract able men even if salaries were lower. In *Truth*'s opinion other fields for retrenchment existed in the annual pension charge of £6,000,000 upon India's revenue,[18] and in the system of sending troops to India from England, but it made no constructive proposals about the abuses it indicated.

*Truth* commented on the status of Indians: 'The poor Indians who have no votes have no rights. They are hewers of wood and drawers of water for those who have.'[19] But it made only one proposal for constitutional change. On 5 February 1885 it advocated replacement of five members of the Indian Council by 'election in India', with candidates selected from Anglo-Indians resident in the United Kingdom. It also advocated the vote for service personnel in India, non-official Anglo-Indian residents, 'and, above all, . . . a portion of the native communities'.[20]

Perhaps this relative caution in constitutional affairs stemmed from *Truth*'s conviction that Britain would retain India.[21] Its views on Ilbert's Native Jurisdiction[22] bill, as well as those on Indian administration, demonstrated that it did not equate political mastery with racial superiority. In March 1883 *Truth* considered agitation against the bill an unnecessary 'fuss upon a mere question of *café au lait* or *café noir*'.[23] By July it took the

---

[15] *Truth*, 26 Aug. 1880, pp. 272-3.     [16] *Truth*, 15 March 1883, p. 355.
[17] Ibid., 9 Aug. 1883, p. 194; 13 Aug. 1885, p. 253.
[18] *Truth*, 9 Aug. 1883, p. 194.     [19] *Truth*, 13 Aug. 1885, p. 253.
[20] *Truth*, 5 Feb. 1885, p. 207.     [21] *Truth*, 25 Sept. 1884, p. 473.
[22] S. Gopal, pp. 113-66; C. Dobbin, 'The Ilbert Bill: A study of Anglo-Indian opinion in India, 1883', *Historical Studies*, xii (1965), 87-102.
[23] *Truth*, 15 March 1883, p. 355.

question more seriously and contended that the real issue was whether Indians were permanently to remain politically and socially inferior to Europeans. It believed Anglo-Indians were logical in eschewing anything which inclined towards equality with Indians, for their attitude rested upon the presumption that Indians were, and would remain, a subject race.[24] Its own position was different: 'We wish to put an end... to any distinction' between Englishmen and Indians.[25]

Labouchere paid greater attention to problems connected with India's north-west frontier than to its internal affairs. He differed from many politicians in his attitude towards Russia. For instance, in referring to Anglo-Russian relations in parliament on 22 September 1886, he argued that Russia wished to reach the sea, but that Britain stood in the way of 'her natural rights and the necessity of her position'. In reply Russia pressed towards India though it had no intention of invading the country. He asserted that if Russia possessed Constantinople India's security would increase: 'because Russia would be satisfied... the two countries would live in peace and amity'.[26]

Labouchere attacked Lord Lytton's policy towards Afghanistan. He criticized the second Afghan war during his electoral campaign of 1880. He asserted that the imperial authorities had deliberately provoked the war, and, in doing so, undermined the 'moral basis upon which the grandeur of this nation ought to rest'.[27] Moreover, he argued that an independent Afghanistan would act as a barrier to Russian aggression. Before his election he contended that British taxpayers ought to pay for the war, on the grounds that it would be 'mean and contemptible ... to throw the cost... upon a people who are not represented in Parliament while we are'.[28] He overlooked this principle after his election, and failed to suggest that British taxpayers should relieve the Indian exchequer of burdens imposed upon it by the Afghan war, or by the subsequent employment of Indian troops in Egypt and the Sudan.[29]

[24] *Truth*, 5 July 1883, p. 11.   [25] *Truth*, 9 Aug. 1883, p. 194.
[26] Hansard, 3rd ser., 309, 1337–9, 22 Sept. 1886.
[27] *Northampton Mercury*, 27 March 1880. Labouchere spoke on the 26th.
[28] *Northampton Mercury*, 3 April 1880.
[29] See J. R. McLane, 'Development of Nationalist ideas and tactics and the policies of the Government of India' (Lond., Ph.D., 1961), p. 232. The government

In a superficial way *Truth* attacked Lytton's policy towards Afghanistan[30] and deficiencies in the Indian budget which it had caused.[31] It described Lytton as a burlesque Louis Napoleon who deserved to be impeached: it commented upon the 'criminal' folly[32] of the war, and upon the 'flagrant scandal'[33] entailed in the underestimate of war expenditure of £14,000,000.[34] It argued that advocates of the retention of Kandahar based their case upon the premise that thieves should retain stolen goods.[35] In its opinion, Indians were over-taxed and could not afford £2,000,000 a year to garrison and administer the territory. Moreover, it questioned the strategic gain to India, for it asserted that while Kandahar protected only one of the two[36] routes into India through Afghanistan, by retaining the territory Britain would deprive Afghans of one-quarter of their country, and make them more likely to intrigue with Russia.[37]

The liberal government withdrew from Afghanistan, with the exception of the Sibi and Pishin districts which were retained,[38] but problems connected with the north-west frontier remained, and by 1885 another crisis developed between Russia and Britain. On 14 March 1885 the *Daily News* published a letter from Labouchere in which he favoured referring the Afghan dispute to an arbiter such as the United States if Britain and Russia could not resolve the problem themselves. He deplored the possibility of war over a few Sarik villages in the central Asian plain, and criticized the British assumption that they were invariably in the right when disputes with Russia arose. He explained that both Russians and Afghans had a reasonable

of India paid for all ordinary and extraordinary charges for the second Afghan war 1878–80 (except £5,000,000 paid by Britain) and for the Indian contingent in Egypt in 1882 (except £5,000 paid by Britain). It paid all ordinary charges for Indian troops in the Sudan 1885–6.

[30] *Truth*, 19 Aug. 1880, p. 226.
[31] *Truth*, 13 May 1880, p. 610; 10 June 1880, p. 739.
[32] *Truth*, 20 Jan. 1881, p. 80.     [33] *Truth*, 27 Jan. 1881, p. 110.
[34] Sir J. Strachey, the finance minister, and Sir E. Johnson, the military member, were responsible for the miscalculation.
[35] *Truth*, 24 Feb. 1881, p. 245.
[36] Kabul, Ghazni, and Kandahar commanded the *three* routes into India. See L. Harris, pp. 27, 42.
[37] *Truth*, 3 March 1881, p. 285; 10 March 1881, p. 317.
[38] S. Gopal, pp. 6–30; *C.H.B.E.*, iii, 147; v, 419–22.

case, and that the Russian advance into disputed territory, before the joint commission reported about the dispute, merely balanced the Afghan advance to Pendjeh. In his opinion, the frontier claimed by Afghans was artificial because it followed neither an ethnic nor a geographical division, and because Afghans did not live in the disputed region. Moreover, disputes that would cause conflicts between Russia and Afghanistan and involve Britain, seemed destined to arise between nomadic tribesmen. Thus he doubted whether Afghan possession of the territory affected the 'honour ... integrity ... and interests of the Empire'. Indeed, he believed Britain would benefit if Russia acquired all of southern Turkestan, for Afghanistan would retain a 'good, defensive, and clearly defined frontier'.[39] Labouchere addressed parliament in similar vein on 4 May 1885. He used Sir J. Lawrence as his authority, and argued against a forward frontier policy and in favour of administrative reform and consolidation of Indian resources. He did not consider the Afghan dispute 'worth a war' and he unsuccessfully tried to reduce the vote of credit by £4,000,000.[40]

Before Labouchere wrote to the *Daily News*, *Truth* had warned its readers that Russia might cause difficulties on India's north-west frontier while imperial troops were committed in the Sudan and Bechuanaland.[41] However, it viewed the situation calmly when the crisis it had predicted developed. Its opinions rested upon the belief that Asia was sufficiently large for both British and Russian interests,[42] that Russia had no intention of attacking India,[43] and that Britain could defend its interests in Europe and India against Russia but could not take aggressive action against her.[44] *Truth* adopted a Russophil tone. On 16 April 1885 it apparently sympathized with the Russian desire to be close to India so that if it were in dispute with Britain it could make her send troops to India and prevent the use of Indian troops in the Mediterranean.[45] A week later it suggested that Russia desired specific territorial acquisitions such as Herat as diplomatic counters to help it reach the Persian

---

[39] *Daily News*, 14 March 1885.
[40] Hansard, 3rd ser., 297, 1542–5, 4 May 1885.
[41] *Truth*, 19 Feb. 1885, p. 289.
[42] *Truth*, 23 April 1885, p. 645.  [43] *Truth*, 16 April 1885, p. 607.
[44] *Truth*, 30 April 1885, p. 686.  [45] *Truth*, 16 April 1885, p. 607.

Gulf. It prophesied that Russia would reach the Indian Ocean eventually, and argued that if it did so at the expense of Persia, Britain would have no cause to object because the sooner this occurred the sooner Britain and Russia would become 'good friends'.[46] In *Truth*'s view, Britain should endeavour to establish a definitive frontier between Russia and Afghanistan north of the mountains; yet it considered the precise position of this frontier of little significance, as India should be defended in India.[47] It doubted whether Britain could establish a reliable alliance with Afghanistan, and its comments about the region's value as a buffer state lacked consistency and clarity.[48] It made no constructive proposals for the location, or the defence, of India's north-west frontier. Platitudes to the effect that it was far better to have a 'clear, good strategical frontier ... to defend'[49] were the best it had to offer.

In 1885 *Truth* criticized British intervention in Upper Burma. The following year, Labouchere denounced its annexation which Lord R. Churchill, secretary of state for India, deferred until after the election[50] and proclaimed on 1 January 1886 'to begin the New Year well'.[51] *Truth* asserted that in Burma, as in Egypt and the Transvaal, the British erred in assuming patriotism was a virtue exclusive to themselves, or that inhabitants of these regions preferred good foreign government to bad native rule. It attributed the genesis of the war to the lust of Liverpool Ahabs and official Ahabs in India for the Burmese vineyard, rather than altruistic concern about Thibaw's fratricidal actions.[52] *Truth* could not see why it was necessary to invade or to annex Burma without the assent of parliament. It doubted whether Britain had intervened to provide the Burmese with good government, and felt it would be foolish to do so before it had obtained this benefit itself. It alleged that Britain's real

---

[46] *Truth*, 23 April 1885, p. 646.
[47] *Truth*, 16 April 1885, p. 607.
[48] On 26 March 1885 *Truth* (p. 488) asserted that buffer states had 'always proved a mistake': a week later (2 April 1885, p. 529) it favoured non-intervention in Afghanistan to make that region a buffer state between Russia and India.
[49] *Truth*, 7 May 1885, p. 722.
[50] Sy.P., Churchill to Salisbury, 22 Aug. 1885.
[51] Ibid., 24 Dec. 1885. [52] *Truth*, 14 Jan. 1886, p. 53.

objective was to open up trade with western China and this, in its opinion, entailed pursuit of an El Dorado.[53]

*Truth* argued that British artisans and starving Indians would bear the cost of the Burmese war which resulted in consequences unattractive to British taxpayers and Burmese alike. For the former annexation meant glory, innumerable little wars, butchers' bills and financial expenditure. On the other hand, each Burman would become a 'child in a reformatory', heavily taxed but denied any influence over his government which alien and unsympathetic individuals would control.[54]

In *Truth* Labouchere had promised that he would oppose the annexation of Burma if liberals retained it, pleading the *'damnosa hæreditas'* argument.[55] He failed to do so while liberals held office in the first part of 1886, but he denied Britain's right to annex Burma in parliament on 30 August 1886. He conceded that war might be necessary, but argued that in Europe the victor merely secured an indemnity or a strip of territory, and could not see why this practice did not apply in Asia. He contended that Thibaw's rule was 'infinitely preferable' to that of Britain because 'he had not interfered with the feelings and prejudices of the people', and that unrest in Burma was symptomatic of 'a people struggling to be free'. Labouchere stated that he knew of no title for annexation other than the 'desire of the inhabitants', and he hoped parliament would insist upon consulting Burmese opinion 'in some sort of way' and decide whether to retain the country 'according to their wishes'.[56]

Labouchere accorded no rights of self-determination to Indians. Apparently he felt little concern for Indian problems at this time, and in this he differed from radicals such as Sir W. Lawson and J. Cowen, and Parnellites such as J. McCarthy[57] with whom he associated over Irish policy. Lawson, for instance,

[53] *Truth*, 19 Nov. 1885, p. 792. Churchill's views about the economic prospects were similar. He wrote to Salisbury that Rothschild wanted the Burmese ruby mines and a railway concession. Churchill thought he would lose money, but as he was as 'keen as nuts', and the government of India poor, he gave him 'much encouragement'. Sy.P., Churchill to Salisbury, 28 Dec. 1885.

[54] *Truth*, 22 Oct. 1885, p. 633.    [55] *Truth*, 29 Oct. 1885, p. 674.

[56] Hansard, 3rd ser., 308, 822–3, 30 Aug. 1886.

[57] See *Daily News*, 11 Feb. 1885. J. McCarthy was a member of a deputation from the Indian Reform Association which welcomed Ripon on his return to England.

spoke of 'our fellow countrymen in India' at a public meeting held at Willis's Rooms, London, on 1 August 1883, to express support for Ripon's policy in India: twenty-two members of parliament attended, but they did not include Labouchere.[58] Cowen complained to his constituents in Newcastle upon Tyne that the 'most important discussion' of 1883, 'that on Indian legislation and finance, was driven off to the last day, and then cut short by the prorogation'.[59] Indian national leaders detected Labouchere's indifference, for they did not consider him 'deserving the support of the people of India' which some candidates received on the basis of their 'services and ... publicly expressed opinions'.[60]

Unlike John Bright[61] Labouchere had not familiarized himself with Indian problems. Although he opposed Indian expansion into Afghanistan and Upper Burma, and to a lesser extent commended consolidation of Indian resources, Labouchere's comments were essentially superficial. Thus he never substantiated his assertion that Indians endured grinding taxation. An incident typical of his attitude occurred in parliament on 27 April 1885 when the liberal government secured a vote of credit for the Penjdeh crisis. Labouchere favoured arbitration and vowed that he would protest, but he sought the consolation of a cigarette during Gladstone's speech. The vote was carried without any protest before he returned.[62]

His reticence upon many aspects of Indian administration and policy was striking. He did not protest when liberals made Indian resources bear three-quarters of the cost of Lytton's Afghan war or when the British government sanctioned the retention of part of Afghanistan. He paid considerable attention to Egyptian affairs but never mentioned that Indians paid for the Indian contingent which was employed there. He did not attack Hartington's council[63] which in Ripon's view was 'the

[58] The Aborigines Protection Society published the proceedings; see R. P. Masani, *Dadabhai Naoroji*, p. 218.
[59] *Newcastle Daily Journal*, 24 Dec. 1883.   [60] R. P. Masani, p. 225.
[61] See J. L. Sturgis, *John Bright and the Empire*, pp. 39, 107.
[62] W. Jeans, *Parliamentary Reminiscences*, p. 274; Labouchere's version is in *Truth*, 30 April 1885, p. 686.
[63] By the India act of 1858 the secretary of state was assisted by a council of India which had 15 members who could only be removed on petition by both houses of parliament.

most conservative body ... in Europe'[64] and he never criticized coherently British policy which dissipated India's 'natural increment' upon military expenditure, and left 'many objects of primary public utility ... inadequately provided for'.[65] However, he advocated retrenchment and greater use of Indians in the administration of India.

The only occasion when he linked India with another British possession between 1880 and 1886 was in August 1880 when he favoured extensive programmes of public works in India and Ireland. He later rejected financial commitment in Ireland on the grounds that it would form an obstacle to the concession of home rule. The only constitutional advance he proposed for India involved indirect, non-official representation upon the secretary of state's council in England, a suggestion which contrasted sharply with his belief that Irishmen, Egyptians and European South Africans should govern themselves. His attitude towards constitutional change in India was far less progressive than that of some radicals who pleaded that India, as well as Ireland, was entitled to home rule.[66] His views were far less advanced than those of some whigs. In 1881 the governor-general of India believed that there was greater need for governmental interference in India than in Ireland, for, while the system of land tenure was analogous, landlords were harsher, and tenants more patient in India. Ripon was convinced that 'no questions in India are so important as those connected with the land'.[67] Although Labouchere drew some comparisons between agrarian problems in Ireland and Egypt, he completely ignored those existing in India.

Labouchere's indifference to Indian affairs, and his neglect of a rich field of opportunity for radical attacks is as striking as it is puzzling. It may be that he was too indolent to master the problems India presented, for he made little reference to Indian affairs in public, and virtually none in his political correspondence. He even failed to criticize the use of Indian troops in Egypt and the Sudan, although this could have strengthened his

[64] G.P., B.M. Add. MSS., 44286, fo. 290, Ripon to Gladstone, 6 Oct. 1882.
[65] Ibid., fo. 280.
[66] *Radical*, 29 Jan. 1881.
[67] G.P., B.M. Add. MSS., 44286, fo. 254, Ripon to Gladstone, 22 Oct. 1881.

arguments against imperial involvement in the valley of the Nile. His apathy towards India appears to have been unaffected by the attitude of his political mentors or associates. Gladstone and John Bright, the two patron saints in his political calendar, held advanced views on India, J. McCarthy and C. Bradlaugh were 'friends of India', but Labouchere shared none of their interest in Indian affairs.

On the other hand, Indian nationalists and their sympathizers appear to have dismissed the possibility of using Labouchere to assist them in presenting their case in Britain. It may be somewhat precipitate to consider that he might have been approached to act in this capacity between 1880 and 1886 for the Indian National Congress was not founded until December 1885, and it was not until 1888 that Indians enlisted the support of C. Bradlaugh.[68] Nevertheless, in September 1885, A. O. Hume sought 'means of conveying accurate information of Indian affairs and native Indian opinion to English newspapers'[69] but he does not appear to have contacted Labouchere. He may not have considered it necessary then on the grounds that the *Daily News*, which employed J. McCarthy, was sympathetic to Indian aspirations, and that it would harm their struggle to associate it with *Truth*. However, in January 1886, Labouchere secured the dismissal of Hill from the editorship of the *Daily News*, and J. McCarthy left the newspaper at the same time: approximately contemporaneously with these editorial changes, the newspaper ceased to present the views of Indian nationalists.[70] But in all probability the combination of Labouchere's ignorance about Indian affairs, his irreverence towards the royal family and his attacks upon the 'fuss and feathers' of the court, the vagaries of his political morality, his agnosticism and his cynicism, and the independence which his wealth provided, made him unsuitable as a prospective mouthpiece for Indian nationalists.

Yet Labouchere's silence on many aspects of Indian policy indicates more than the poverty of his thought on this subject.

---

[68] P. C. Ghosh, 'The development of the Indian National Congress' (Lond., Ph.D., 1958), p. 27.
[69] R. A. J. Walling (ed.), *The Diaries of John Bright*, pp. 530–1.
[70] I am indebted to Dr S. R. Mehrotra for this information.

He had no constructive policy for any form of political development in any British dependency other than colonies where there was significant European settlement. The essence of his thought was contained in words which appeared in *Truth* in 1884. 'India we hold. We intend to hold it.'[71] He did not question the moral basis of British authority, and he expressed no opinions about the immediate or ultimate objectives of British policy in India. Thus, by implication, he accepted an assumption that Gladstone denied when he observed, 'to the actual, as distinguished from the reputed strength of the Empire, India adds nothing'.[72] Labouchere's position was quite different from that of John Bright who began to plead for the eventual concession of self-government to India in the 1870s.[73] Labouchere did not even refer to the establishment of local self-government by Ripon, which covered almost the whole of British India by 1884[74] despite a 'great deal of obstinate underhand opposition among the members of the Indian Council'.[75] With local self-government, as with problems of land tenure, Labouchere was as taciturn about conditions in India as he was vehement about those of Ireland.

Labouchere's sympathy for Irish, South African and Egyptian national aspirations was closely associated with his desire for 'peace, retrenchment and reform' in Britain. Problems in these regions made heavy demands upon Britain's financial resources and her parliamentary time. Parliament tended to leave India 'to pursue its destiny alone'.[76] If Florence Nightingale was correct in asserting in 1879 that Indian questions were treated in parliament as home questions,[77] then they were overshadowed like many other domestic issues by Irish, South African, and Egyptian affairs. Although Egypt was a 'little place' and its administration a 'bagatelle' compared with that of an 'Indian State, which ... one lonely Englishman pulls into order',[78] its problems received greater parliamentary attention

---

[71] *Truth*, 25 Sept. 1884, p. 473.
[72] R.P., B.M. Add. MSS., 43515, fo. 5, Gladstone to Ripon, 24 Nov. 1881.
[73] J. L. Sturgis, pp. 71, 179–80.   [74] S. Gopal, p. 110.
[75] Bt.P., B.M. Add. MSS., 43389, fo. 350, Ripon to Bright, 27 Aug. 1883.
[76] *C.H.B.E.*, iii, 148.   [77] S. Gopal, p. 1.
[78] Sm.P., B.M. Add. MSS., 50831, fo. 14, Sir G. Sydenham Clarke to Sir I. V. Chirol, 17 March 1894.

than those of India between 1880 and 1886. Labouchere prided himself upon being a practical politician. He was attracted to regions where imperial expansion had recently taken place such as Cyprus, the Transvaal, Afghanistan, Egypt and Burma, for he hoped to influence British opinion against retention. At the same time he was at pains to emphasize that he would resist 'disintegration of the Empire' to the utmost of his power.[79] Nevertheless his views on Ireland were criticized precisely on the ground that home rule would lead to imperial disintegration and he may have feared that if he advocated similar principles for India it would be more difficult to persuade British public opinion that 'home rule' and 'disintegration' were not synonymous. He would have weakened his fight for Irish interests had he fought also for those of India.

Moreover, although problems of Ireland, the Transvaal and Egypt were totally dissimilar in many ways, the inhabitants of these regions showed a positive resistance to British authority which Indians did not then emulate. The Anglo-Indians' victory over the Ilbert bill demonstrated that vigorous, determined and sustained agitation could defeat the policy of a viceroy supported by a British government with a substantial majority in parliament. Their success disillusioned Indians about the impartiality of British rule. Ripon's extension of local government was giving Indians political experience. Anglo-Indians taught them techniques of agitation. In December 1883 Anglo-Indians celebrated their victory, but Indians were convening the first National Conference at Calcutta. The quiescence of subject peoples to British rule did not secure Labouchere's interest, for he firmly believed in the efficacy of vigorous, even unconstitutional, agitation. He believed that it was necessary to shake the tree to obtain the fruit, and that rebels invariably had right on their side, for 'no one has ever rebelled for mere amusement'.[80] By this touchstone the *status quo* satisfied Indians for many years after 1880. Labouchere conceded that 'under certain circumstances', which he did not elaborate, it might be to Britain's 'advantage to give up India'.[81] In his opinion, however, such circumstances did not then exist. With

[79] *Northampton Mercury*, 17 Dec. 1881.
[80] *Truth*, 2 April 1885, p. 528.
[81] *Truth*, 1 June 1882, p. 749.

the exception of the expansion of British dominion in India which he consistently opposed, he was indifferent about Indian affairs. He initially supported British intervention in Egypt to safeguard India, and later contended that while Britain held India it needed to retain a secure naval base at the Cape. Perhaps because he considered that Indian affairs could not be turned to immediate domestic political advantage, he did not criticize imperial administration in India, he provided only marginal support for Ripon's reforms, and he did nothing to assist Indian nationalists.

## CYPRUS

Labouchere considered Cyprus 'pestiferous and less than worthless'[82] to Britain. Between 1880 and 1886 he intermittently criticized the cost of retaining the island and asserted that it was a perfect nest of jobbery.[83] He made no coherent criticism of Britain's retention of the island on grounds of imperial policy; he made no reference to the form of colonial administration in Cyprus; and although he paid lip-service to Cypriots' right to self-determination,[84] he did not affirm their right to self-government as he did in the case of the Irish and the Egyptians. He simply advocated the transfer of Cyprus to Greece, and by 1885 he alleged that he had conceived this 'brilliant idea'.[85]

He argued that the porte, owing to its financial difficulties, would allow Britain to commute the annual tribute of £100,000 for a lump sum of £1,000,000. He calculated that £40,000 a year would service a loan for £1,000,000, secured upon the revenues of Cyprus, and make provision for a sinking fund, provided that it had an imperial guarantee. Under his scheme the British government would cede the island to Greece which would accept responsibility for the loan. Labouchere considered that this scheme would be financially and politically advantageous to Britain, would reduce the burden of taxation upon

---

[82] *Northampton Mercury Daily Reporter*, 23 March 1880.
[83] Hansard, 3rd ser., 309, 915, 17 Sept. 1886.
[84] *Truth*, 17 Aug. 1882, p. 249.
[85] R.C.P., 991, Labouchere to Churchill, 20 Oct. 1885.

Cypriots, and be in the interest of liberals who 'opposed this ridiculous acquisition'.[86]

The way Labouchere attempted to win support for this plan provides an illustration of his approach to political persuasion. He made the initial proposal rather casually in parliament on 11 August 1882. He seemed ill prepared, for although he later quoted £1,000,000 as the capital value of the tribute paid to Turkey, on this occasion he suggested that £300,000 or £400,000 would suffice.[87] The issue of *Truth* which followed this speech repeated the proposal.[88] He made no further reference to Cyprus until August 1883 when *Truth* again proposed the transfer of Cyprus to Greece.[89] He did not oppose the colonial estimates for Cyprus in parliament in 1883, and this may have been because he had initiated secret and informal negotiations between the governments of Greece and Turkey which ultimately foundered owing to Turkish intractability. On 23 September 1883, while the negotiations were in progress, he wrote to Chamberlain and asked him whether he thought the liberal government would guarantee a loan of £1,000,000 for the transfer of Cyprus.[90] As there is no copy of Chamberlain's reply amongst the Chamberlain papers, it is impossible without further evidence to determine his views on the matter. In any case, Labouchere made no further move until the conservatives held office in 1885. Then, on 20 October 1885, he tried to 'sell' the idea to Lord R. Churchill.[91] Once more he failed to win influential support for his plan, so he turned to public persuasion. On 28 January 1886, the day after liberals and Parnellites defeated the conservative government, *The Times* published a letter from Labouchere, in which he again suggested the transfer of Cyprus to Greece.[92] His failure to mobilize any political support appears to have persuaded him to abandon the project, for he did not refer to it when he opposed the estimates for Cyprus in parliament on 17 September 1886.[93]

---

[86] J.C., 5/50/15, Labouchere to Chamberlain, 23 Sept. [?1883].
[87] Hansard, 3rd ser., 273, 1594-6, 11 Aug. 1882; Division Lists, 1882, No. 329, 11 Aug. 1882.   [88] *Truth*, 17 Aug. 1882, p. 249.   [89] *Truth*, 23 Aug. 1883, p. 269.
[90] J.C., 5/50/15, Labouchere to Chamberlain, 23 Sept. [?1883].
[91] R.C.P., 991, Labouchere to Churchill, 20 Oct. 1885.   [92] *Times*, 28 Jan. 1886.
[93] Hansard, 3rd ser., 309, 914-15, 17 Sept. 1886; Division Lists, 1886(2), No. 41 17 Sept. 1886.

Labouchere did not originate plans to transfer Cyprus to Greece. In April 1881 rumours about the possibility of such a transfer caused 'great excitement' amongst Cypriots who, according to the high commissioner, Sir R. Biddulph, believed it would cause their ruin.[94] Biddulph received permission from Lord Kimberley to deny the rumour.[95] Gladstone added his authority to the denial. He emphasized that Britain held Cyprus 'under the convention with the Porte as part of the Ottoman Empire', and that 'proposals which would be a violation of that convention cannot be discussed'.[96] Goschen, British ambassador-extraordinary at Constantinople, initially considered the retrocession of Cyprus to Turkey as part of a comprehensive settlement between Greece and Turkey,[97] but by June 1881 he was 'full of his scheme for giving Cyprus to Greece'.[98] As Goschen failed to win sufficient support to have the scheme accepted as part of British policy, as the Turkish government was not financially embarrassed,[99] and as the liberal government had unequivocally stated that no change in the relationship between Cyrpus and Turkey would be considered, one can only conclude that Labouchere's attempts to make the transfer of Cyprus to Greece possible were more optimistic than realistic.

[94] Parl. Pap., 1881, lxv, [C.2930], 105, Biddulph to Kimberley, 12 April 1881.
[95] Ibid., Kimberley to Biddulph, 13 April 1881.
[96] Ibid., Gladstone to Biddulph, 19 April 1881.
[97] A. R. D. Elliot, *The Life of George Joachim Goschen*, i, 221.
[98] C.D.P., B.M. Add. MSS., 43924, fos. 55–6, 15 June 1881.
[99] P.R.O., F.O., 78/3431, W. Lander to P. Currie, 17 Aug. 1882.

CHAPTER VIII

# Closer Union of the Empire, 1880–1886

LABOUCHERE, through the medium of *Truth*, doubted the value of attempts to mobilize opinion in favour of a closer union of the empire. His primary objection was that no plan existed which had obtained the support of the British self-governing colonies. He believed that most proposals in favour of a closer imperial association were too nebulous, that they had to be much more specific before they could influence opinion in Britain or in the colonies, and that until this occurred they merely ventilated 'vague and pious aspirations'.[1]

The Imperial Federation League, founded in July 1884, aimed, as W. E. Forster stated in his diary, to enlighten public opinion 'as to the advantages of permanent unity, and as to the nature of the different forms of federal government, so that the people of the empire ... may be better able to decide as to the exact form of that government which they may prefer whenever they shall feel that the time has arrived for its adoption'.[2]

The League had precedents in the Royal Colonial Society, founded in 1868, and in meetings held at the Cannon Street Hotel in 1869 and 1870, and the Westminster Palace Hotel in 1871. Its establishment reflected a complex of interacting developments in Britain, in the empire, and in the world. The Manchester School's doctrines which related to free trade, to the inevitability of the self-governing colonies' secession from the empire, and to the advantages that would accrue to Britain from such a development were questioned. The colonies showed no marked desire to sever the imperial tie, despite their increasing wealth and population, their hunger for further rights of self-government, and their affection for protective duties. By 1870 a liberal minister, W. E. Forster, hoped that

[1] *Truth*, 18 Feb. 1886, p. 248.
[2] T. W. Reid, *The Life of the Right Hon. W. E. Forster*, 29 July 1884, p. 504.

Britain and the 'English speaking peoples in our colonies' would unite in 'one great Confederation'.³ Wars in America and Europe, followed by a remarkable increase in trade protection after 1879, appeared as an ironic commentary upon predictions of an era of peace based upon free trade. Improved communications helped to knit the empire together and made closer imperial association more practicable. At the same time, however, they operated in conjunction with a rapid increase in continental powers' extra-European activity and changes in naval technology to make the empire more vulnerable. The Colonial Defence Committee, established in 1878, the royal commission on imperial defence of 1879–81, and the naval scare of 1884 were admissions of British concern for imperial defence. Cyclical depressions which began in 1868, 1876 and 1883, and the collapse of British agriculture after 1876, paralleled by a gradual weakening of Britain's industrial and commercial hegemony, brought free trade doctrines under scrutiny. In 1868 demands for reciprocity arose in Lancashire;⁴ in 1879 the *Bradford Observer* published proposals, which included fiscal arrangements to discourage Britain from growing its own food, and direction of investment and emigration to the colonies, made by W. Farrer Ecroyd in order to create a self-sufficient empire if other nations adopted protection;⁵ the National Fair Trade League was founded in 1881;⁶ and in July 1882 Chamberlain, in a cabinet meeting, advised the use of retaliatory duties.⁷ The depressions increased awareness of social problems in Britain, and by 1870 interest in state-aided emigration to the colonies revived. Pressures stemming from a belief in racial superiority, in Britain's civilizing mission, in Christianity and the concept of trusteeship for backward peoples, and an abhorrence of slavery and the slave trade, enriched and complicated reappraisals of Britain's economic and social problems, and of the nature of Britain's relationship with her colonies.

Although Labouchere was sceptical about the possibility of

[3] J. E. Tyler, *The Struggle for Imperial Unity, 1868–1895*, p. 5.
[4] Ibid., p. 12.
[5] W. F. Ecroyd, *The Policy of Self Help*, B.M. 8229 cc 16.
[6] J. E. Tyler, pp. 31–2.
[7] H.P., B.M. Add. MSS., 48632, fo. 95, 21 July 1882.

a closer imperial connection after the establishment of the Imperial Federation League, he was not as firmly opposed to the idea as were liberals such as John Bright,[8] or Gladstone who regarded it as 'chimerical, if not little short of nonsensical'.[9] In fact, Labouchere catered for the possibility of closer union of the empire when he explained radical policy. Part of this programme included abolition of the house of lords. Labouchere, however, emphasized that this did not necessarily involve acceptance of the unicameral principle.[10] On 28 April 1881, *Truth* favoured one chamber if the various parts of the empire did not come together, but two if they did. In the latter case, it suggested that the 'Upper House might be formed of representatives elected for a term of years by the County Assemblies, and by the Colonial Legislatures, and it might have a suspensive veto over Bills passed by the Lower House'.[11] Similarly, his attitude towards the monarchy was affected by its importance to the empire. He saw little particular merit in a monarchy except that 'in a state such as ours, where the tie that unites the metropolis with its colonies is of the slightest'[12] it served as a 'connecting link'.[13]

Labouchere's suggestion about closer union balanced county assemblies, which did not then exist in Britain, with colonial legislatures. This proposal may have redressed the dominance that England, owing to its greater wealth and population, would have possessed in other plans for closer union of the empire. It appears too that by merely granting the upper house a suspensive veto, he envisaged a weak central authority acting largely in an advisory capacity to virtually autonomous legislatures which may have possessed rights of withdrawal. His plan was one which would have been particularly responsive to the wishes of inhabitants of the self-governing parts of the empire, but it made no provision for other dependencies. However, as Labouchere did not refer to fundamental issues such as constitutional powers reserved from the control of the central and the regional legislatures, and gave no guidance

[8] J. L. Sturgis, *John Bright and the Empire*, pp. 113–14.
[9] H.P., B.M. Add. MSS., 48638, fo. 58, 19 Nov. 1884.
[10] *Fortnightly Review*, xxxvi (1 Sept. 1884), 326.
[11] *Truth*, 28 April 1881, p. 564.
[12] *Fortnightly Review*, xxxiii (1 March 1883), 377–8.
[13] *Northampton Daily Reporter*, 15 Oct. 1885.

about the conduct of foreign and commercial policy, or of imperial defence, his plan was superficial and open to many of the criticisms he himself levelled against proposals for imperial federation after July 1884.

Labouchere considered that the self-governing colonies were entitled to an independence of action, and to a consideration by the British government, which were in advance of their constitutional and conventional development in the early 1880s. His one reservation was that they should accept the financial and political responsibility for their actions. In 1883 Queensland annexed eastern New Guinea without the sanction of the imperial government. Lord Derby, who over-ruled this action, told Dilke that the Australians could not have 'at once the protection of the British connection and the pleasure of a wholly independent foreign policy'.[14] Labouchere's views formed an interesting contrast to those of the secretary of state for the colonies who himself believed that 'within the next generation or two we in England shall have nothing to say to Australian affairs'.[15] *Truth* argued that Australians had what it termed a 'geographical policy' distinct from Britain's, and that as Britain had annexed the Transvaal and Cyprus without consulting Queensland, it was 'difficult' for Britain to deny the right of Queensland to 'annex New Guinea' without consulting the imperial government.[16]

The establishment of the Imperial Federation League reflected greater interest in the possibility of closer imperial ties, and it helped to stimulate that interest. Labouchere made brief but pertinent criticisms of proposals in favour of closer union. Although he made no further reference to the radical constitutional plan of 1881, he occasionally made minor contributions to the debate on imperial union. These tended to concentrate upon colonial participation in imperial defence. In 1882 he used the occasion of a budget surplus in New South Wales to suggest that its government could contribute towards general imperial expenses and set a precedent for other British colonies.[17] Two years later he proposed that each of Britain's self-governing

---

[14] Dy.P., X24, Derby to Dilke (copy), 17 Oct. 1883.
[15] Dy.P., X24, Derby to A. Gordon (copy), 4 Dec. 1883.
[16] *Truth*, 26 April 1883, p. 570.   [17] *Truth*, 16 Nov. 1882, p. 689.

colonies should subscribe towards the cost of the imperial navy.[18] In February 1885 he advised colonists to own a few gun-boats and torpedo boats to secure themselves against attack.[19] By August 1886 he concluded that a federal fleet, supported by Britain and her colonies, was the 'only tangible bond possible'. The fleet would act 'only by the decision of some sort of Federal Council' in which Britain and the colonies would be represented. He based this suggestion upon the precedent of the relationship which had existed between Athens and her colonies, and he stated that an 'alliance based upon our hegemony would be a far more practical idea than a Federation'.[20] Labouchere made only one other suggestion about closer union. He had earlier recommended the establishment of a committee of colonial delegates which the secretary of state for the colonies would consult, and whose resolutions would be mutually binding.[21]

This proposal ran against the grain of Labouchere's criticism of plans for closer union. He insisted that a fundamental weakness in the case of advocates of imperial federation lay in their inability to advance detailed proposals which commanded the support of the colonies, and he argued that until they could do so the issue remained outside practical politics.[22] He could not envisage the scope of any central assembly which included representatives from the colonies, and he failed to see how representatives could be elected from dependencies such as India. He focused attention upon the fact that closer union involved a common purse, and argued that meetings in favour of imperial federation were futile until colonists agreed to pay a proportionate share of the costs of the monarchy, of Britain's diplomatic service, and of the British army and navy.[23]

A speech made by Lord Rosebery on 11 September 1884[24] prompted Labouchere to criticize his proposals on other grounds than the vagueness of the closer imperial tie that Rosebery recommended. Labouchere contended that closer imperial union under British hegemony would not commend

[18] *Truth*, 22 May 1884, p. 755.  [19] *Truth*, 5 Feb. 1885, p. 209.
[20] *Truth*, 19 Aug. 1886, p. 301.  [21] *Truth*, 4 Sept. 1884, p. 365.
[22] *Truth*, 4 Sept. 1884, p. 365; 18 Feb. 1886, p. 248; *Northampton Herald*, 21 Nov. 1885; *Fortnightly Review*, xxxviii (1 Oct. 1885), p. 485.
[23] *Truth*, 4 Sept. 1884, p. 365.  [24] *Times*, 12 Sept. 1884.

itself to colonial opinion, while some form of imperial federation would find little support in Britain if it were based upon an 'absolutely equal' association. He believed that Britain desired imperial hegemony and the colonies equality with Britain, and that until both parties had similar objectives it was a waste of time to deal in generalities.[25] In his opinion, Britain was not prepared to cede any portion of its 'paramount direction of the policy of the Empire', and the colonies were unwilling to surrender 'any portion of their local independence'. He argued that Britain and her colonies enjoyed harmonious relations because the imperial connection was to their mutual advantage, and he implied that imperial federation would threaten this relationship. He was convinced that the imperial tie would snap if the advantages of imperial membership ended. Thus he prophesied that Canada would join the United States of America when it could borrow money more cheaply in New York than in London.[26]

In the 1880s this situation had not arisen. Labouchere, however, repeatedly warned investors about the weaknesses of the securities of British colonies. In his opinion, virtually nothing in the world of finance was more remarkable than their high credit, and he marvelled at the 'apathetic credulity' of the British public. *Truth* claimed that Britain 'should never have been implicated directly or indirectly, in . . . colonial borrowings, and it may yet suffer from its laxity in this respect'.[27] It protested against the Bank of England giving its name to colonial loans which should never have been issued.[28] More specifically, articles attributed to E. A. Prentice[29] painted a dismal picture of Canada's poverty, its crushing burden of debt, and its economic prospects.[30] Other articles claimed that only emigration and stringent economy could prevent bankruptcy in New Zealand, which in their view had exhausted its security by 1883.[31] Statistics *Truth* supplied in 1881 about the Australian

[25] *Truth*, 18 Sept. 1884, pp. 436–7.
[26] *Truth*, 4 Dec. 1884, p. 858; 1 Jan. 1885, p. 16.
[27] *Truth*, 20 Oct. 1881, pp. 517–18.
[28] *Truth*, 29 July 1880, p. 146.
[29] *Quebec Daily Mercury*, 7 Oct. 1881.
[30] *Truth*, 1 Sept. 1881, p. 292; 15 Sept. 1881, p. 359.
[31] *Truth*, 29 July 1880, p. 146; 4 Aug. 1881, p. 159; 20 July 1882, p. 126.

colonies pointed clearly to the danger of a financial collapse if their borrowing were not curtailed.[32] Although *Truth* had serious reservations about the value of any colonial securities it particularly distrusted those of the Cape and Natal. It argued that both colonies were frequently involved in war, that the 'Dutch element' of the population was 'anti-English in sentiment', and that it might demonstrate this antipathy by repudiating loans raised in Britain.[33] In January 1884, *Truth* opposed Sir J. Vogel's suggestion that restrictions which prevented the investment of British trust funds in colonial securities should be removed. Its attitude was that Britain had no control over financial arrangements made by its self-governing colonies and that there was nothing to prevent them from borrowing more than they could repay and then repudiating their debts.[34] Labouchere did not directly associate his views on closer imperial ties with those on the merits of colonial securities, or with the colonists' desire, which was given most effective voice at the Colonial Conference of 1897, to have colonial stocks made into trustee securities for British investors.[35] In this he differed from Lord Blachford who expressed 'apprehension lest ... of the phrase "confederation" may be begotten the substance guarantee'.[36]

Lord Grey on 7 January and Lord Lorne on 13 January 1885,[37] and W. E. Forster in February 1885[38] made specific suggestions for a preliminary form of closer union in the *Pall Mall Gazette* and the *Nineteenth Century* respectively. They advocated the appointment of the agents-general of the colonies as privy councillors, and their incorporation as a board of advice to assist the secretary of state for the colonies in the management of colonial affairs.[39] This provided Labouchere with the opportunity to offer more specific criticism. He wished to know what topics the colonial 'representatives' would discuss,

---

[32] *Truth*, 20 Oct. 1881, pp. 517–18; cf. 22 March 1883, p. 401.
[33] *Truth*, 27 Dec. 1883, p. 910; 3 April 1884, p. 504.
[34] *Truth*, 31 Jan. 1884, p. 167.
[35] The Colonial Stocks act of 1901 effected this change.
[36] *Nineteenth Century*, i, (July 1877), 809.
[37] *Pall Mall Gazette*, 7 and 13 Jan. 1885. Lord Grey had made similar proposals in the *Nineteenth Century* of June 1879.
[38] *Nineteenth Century*, xvii (Feb. 1885), 201–18.   [39] Ibid., p. 209.

and what effect their decisions would have if they were to agree. He wondered whether the agents-general would be able to over-rule the British parliament on issues such as peace and war, and whether they would be able to declare war and leave British taxpayers to pay for it.[40] He dealt too with some implications of closer imperial union which particularly concerned the colonists. He doubted whether these colonial 'representatives' would be able to win colonial support for their decisions. To illustrate his argument, he gave readers of *Truth* examples of hypothetical situations that might arise. For instance, he questioned the ability of the agent-general of Canada to persuade Canadians to be taxed to make sure that no foreign power controlled Zululand, even if he were personally convinced of the necessity of preventing this development on grounds of imperial interests. In a similar way he touched upon the effect of representations from one colony upon the actions of another. If, for instance, the Canadian agent-general objected to the Australian's attitude towards New Guinea, Labouchere suspected that the Australian colonies would not heed him:[41] indeed he doubted whether any one of the Australian colonies would heed the agents-general of other colonies even on minor issues.

Although Labouchere did not consider imperial federation a practical political issue in the period 1880 to 1886, he showed critical insight into aspects of the problems involved and yet preserved an ambiguous attitude towards the topic itself. In 1881 he had shown that he could reconcile closer imperial ties with his radical creed. In 1885, however, by which time Britain had accepted many additional responsibilities and its involvement in the Sudan appeared imminent, he feared that advocates of imperial federation dreamed of involving Britain in wars of annexation.[42] In 1886 he concluded that the only viable form of a closer imperial association was through Britain and her colonies supporting an imperial fleet. Thus his position was not far removed from that of members of the Imperial Federation League whose primary objective at this time was 'an

[40] *Truth*, 5 Feb. 1885, p. 209.
[41] *Truth*, 15 Jan. 1885, p. 89.   [42] *Truth*, 5 Feb. 1885, p. 209.

organisation for common defence, and an official acknowledgment of the right of the colonies to have a voice in the determination of foreign policy'.[43]

Labouchere consistently supported a powerful navy, with a complementary network of fortified harbours and coaling stations, for he believed that the security of the empire depended upon it.[44] One reason why he opposed 'trumpery, aimless wars' was that he wished to concentrate British resources upon maintaining command of the seas.[45] Similarly, he favoured colonial contributions towards the upkeep of the navy on the grounds that this would augment its strength without making further demands on British taxpayers.[46] He believed that it was premature for colonists to propose to be represented at the councils of the empire until they were prepared to contribute towards its defence. In 1886 when he proposed an alliance under British hegemony between Britain and her colonies, he appeared to be attempting to reconcile unity of control with the 'separate national aspirations'[47] of the colonies, upon a basis of equality of status.

In 1881 Labouchere linked the possibility of a closer imperial association with an extensive devolution of authority in Britain, but, unlike Seeley in his *Expansion of England,* he did not associate it with emigration. Labouchere denied the right of the state to interfere with emigration 'except by rendering the conditions of existence at home better for the poorer classes'.[48] He considered emigration of pauper families a 'heartless piece of cruelty' invented by land and railway speculators, and backed by closet philanthropists. He argued that Britain should not send such emigrants to the colonies, for on arrival they became a burden upon colonial rates. In addition, he believed that a violation of free trade principles occurred if the metropolis assisted such emigration.[49]

---

[43] *Nineteenth Century,* xvii (Feb. 1885), 209.
[44] *Northampton Daily Reporter,* 24 Oct. 1885; *Fortnightly Review,* xxxviii (1 Oct. 1885), 489; *Truth,* 9 Oct. 1884, p. 555; 13 Nov. 1884, p. 748.
[45] *Truth,* 9 Oct. 1884, p. 555.
[46] *Truth,* 22 May 1884, p. 755.
[47] R. Jebb argued in 1905 that 'alliance' recognized separate national aspirations. R. Jebb, *The Imperial Conference,* vol. i, p. xviii.
[48] *Truth,* 21 July 1881, p. 74.  [49] *Truth,* 4 Dec. 1884, p. 860.

No belief in Britain's civilizing mission, in Christianity, in racial superiority, or even in imperial sentiment, had any place in Labouchere's attitude towards a closer imperial association. Britain, in his opinion, had no obligation to redeem the world, and it could not afford to do so. He distrusted 'philanthropic restlessness'[50] and religious 'jingoism' which he considered 'as costly and as unpractical as political jingoism'.[51] Britain, in his view, could not afford to protect all aborigines and, moreover, it had no right to do so. He remarked ironically about the indifference of philanthropists to conditions such as slavery in Cuba,[52] and their activity in regions where Britain or its colonies allegedly had political or strategic or commercial interests. He was sceptical about Britain's civilizing mission, which he dismissed as the 'philanthropic efforts of one race to make another race toil for it'.[53] He criticized the British for overlooking the fact that natives who were under their administration were their equals.[54] In connection with the self-governing colonies, he predicted that South Africa would become a 'Dutch' state;[55] that Canada, the professed loyalty of whose politicians *Truth* denounced as a 'shoddy deception',[56] would join the United States of America;[57] and that Australians were unlikely to enthuse loyalty towards an 'abstraction in another part of the globe'.[58]

Labouchere showed acute perception of regional differences between groups of British colonies.[59] He thought that the relationship between Britain and the colonies was the only 'connecting link' in the empire.[60] He usually stated that the relationship between Britain and the self-governing colonies was mutually beneficial,[61] but he failed to explain what advantages either gained. His position was equivocal, however, for on 17 March 1881 *Truth* asserted that the imperial connection was to the colonies' advantage but not to Britain's.[62]

---

[50] *Truth*, 27 Nov. 1884, p. 824.  [51] *Truth*, 22 March 1883, p. 393.
[52] *Truth*, 3 Feb. 1881, p. 142; 9 April 1885, p. 570.
[53] *Truth*, 28 Aug. 1884, p. 324.  [54] *Truth*, 26 Feb. 1885, pp. 328–9.
[55] *Truth*, 22 March 1883, p. 393.  [56] *Truth*, 16 April 1885, p. 608.
[57] *Truth*, 4 Dec. 1884, p. 858.  [58] *Truth*, 1 Jan. 1885, p. 16.
[59] *Truth*, 15 March 1883, p. 355.  [60] *Truth*, 19 Aug. 1886, p. 301.
[61] *Truth*, 4 Dec. 1884, p. 858; 5 Feb. 1885, p. 209.
[62] *Truth*, 17 March 1881, p. 354.

Labouchere provided *ad hoc* comments about a closer imperial connection rather than a reasoned exposition of his views, and perhaps because of this, his statements seem to lack consistency. On 19 August 1886, for instance, *Truth* not only stated that the looser the imperial connection between Britain and the colonies the more likely they were to 'hang together',[63] but it also put forward the suggestion of a federal fleet. His comments certainly lacked comprehensiveness. He made virtually no reference to issues, such as tariffs and the treatment of native races, where the lack of sympathy between Britain and her colonies was, in J. Morley's opinion, 'open and flagrant' and an obstacle to closer union. Labouchere thought in terms of some form of closer association of the self-governing colonies and Britain, but he did not refer to the relationship that would then exist between the self-governing and dependent parts of the empire, or of difficulties that could arise from this relationship. In this he differed from critics of contemporary proposals of a closer imperial association. J. Morley posed problems that would face the self-governing colonies if they came to be associated with Britain in sharing responsibilities such as the administration of India, and asked what benefit they would gain from shouldering such obligations.[64] E. A. Freeman argued that any scheme of imperial federation which did not give Indians equal federal rights with their 'European fellow subjects' was merely a federation of a small part of the empire, while if India were included the situation could arise in which 'England, Scotland, Canada, Australia, shall be dependencies of the Empire of India'.[65] In some of the omissions in Labouchere's arguments there was no inconsistency on his part for interpretations of 'imperial federation', 'closer union of the empire', varied considerably in the 1880s and confusion arose between immediate and long-term objectives. Subjects such as tariffs and the treatment of native races were normally matters within the province of self-governing colonies' authority, and Labouchere thought of a 'federal union' based upon 'equality between its members, each member being absolute master in all local matters'. On the

---

[63] *Truth*, 19 Aug. 1886, p. 301.
[64] *Macmillan's Magazine*, xlix (Feb. 1884), 254, 257.
[65] *Macmillan's Magazine*, li (April 1885), 443–4.

other hand he did not explain what he meant when he stated that each member of such an association should be a 'partner in all Imperial matters'.⁶⁶

The enterprise of foreign powers in establishing colonies and the reaction of Britain and the colonies to this activity had no apparent influence upon Labouchere's attitude towards closer union. The British found themselves in the 1880s 'like people living by the side of a common which their neighbours wish to enclose. They had rather it were left as it is, but, if enclosure be inevitable they must put in their claim for a share.'⁶⁷ Labouchere completely disagreed with Lord Derby's assessment of the situation, for he viewed with 'distrust and disapproval all schemes for the extension of the Empire'.⁶⁸ Britain, in his opinion, should 'never' send a military expedition abroad, and 'never' increase the size of the empire.⁶⁹

Labouchere also challenged the assumption that trade followed the flag and contended that trade could not be forced upon a reluctant population.⁷⁰ He pointed to the £40,000,000 which Britain had expended upon 'aimless wars, which only seem to procreate further wars'⁷¹ in the decade preceding 1885, and asserted that British trade had not benefited from it at all.⁷² He did not question the value of free trade⁷³ and thought Britain's economic difficulties stemmed from the fact that Britain had 'lagged behind the rest of the world, politically, socially, and economically';⁷⁴ and he advocated in the press an expansion of free higher education, particularly in technical subjects,⁷⁵ higher standards of workmanship and a more enterprising and competitive approach in trade and industry, to help overcome them.⁷⁶

Although Labouchere opposed expansion undertaken by the British government, he did not object to annexations by the

[66] *Truth*, 1 Jan. 1885, p. 16.
[67] Dy.P., X24, Derby to Potter (copy), 21 May 1883.
[68] This was part of Labouchere's electoral manifesto. *Northampton Mercury*, 14 Nov. 1885.
[69] *Truth*, 15 Jan. 1885, p. 88.
[70] *Northampton Herald*, 21 Nov. 1885; *Northampton Mercury*, 28 Nov. 1885.
[71] *Truth*, 9 Oct. 1884, p. 555.   [72] *Northampton Mercury*, 21 Nov. 1885.
[73] Ibid.; *Truth*, 17 Nov. 1881, p. 651.   [74] *Truth*, 1 Oct. 1885, p. 515.
[75] *Fortnightly Review*, xxxviii (1 Oct. 1885), p. 488.
[76] *Truth*, 8 Sept. 1881, pp. 325–6.

Australasian[77] and South African colonies[78] provided that they bore the obligations and consequences of such actions.[79] His views were particularly striking as he argued that annexation was a party issue in Australia, that Australians had half of their own continent to develop, and that possession of outlying islands was unnecessary for Australia's defence.[80] This attitude ignored problems which would have arisen while the British government retained full responsibility for the conduct of imperial foreign policy and imperial defence. Yet if the right to annex came within the scope of the absolute mastery in local matters which he thought the colonists ought to have, it harmonized with Labouchere's belief that colonies ought to have the strength to maintain themselves in local disputes,[81] and that it was the duty of every community to attend to its own interests.[82] The concession to the colonies of the right to annex may have been a prerequisite for his proposed alliance within the empire to support an imperial fleet.

Labouchere raised no objections to the establishment of foreign colonies in close proximity to British possessions. His view was that this was a matter which concerned the colonists who could annex neighbouring regions themselves if they so chose. He argued that the possession of colonies weakened continental powers and presented hostages to Britain for their good behaviour.[83] No trace of Gladstone's view that foreign colonization would strengthen Britain's hold upon its colonies[84] appeared in Labouchere's comments. He opposed further British territorial expansion and had no desire to see the colonies more dependent upon Britain in any way.

In October 1885, when he advocated the establishment of local parliaments in England and Scotland as well as in Ireland, Labouchere considered colonial representation in an imperial parliament 'entirely beyond the confines of practical politics'. He thought the obstacles to colonial representation insuperable until the colonies demonstrated their willingness to 'transfer a

[77] *Truth*, 26 April 1883, p. 570.
[78] *Truth*, 9 Oct. 1884, p. 555.
[79] *Truth*, 8 Jan. 1885, p. 52.
[80] *Truth*, 3 Jan. 1884, p. 12.
[81] *Truth*, 9 Oct. 1884, p. 555.
[82] *Truth*, 1 Jan. 1885, p. 16.
[83] *Truth*, 15 Jan. 1885, p. 88.
[84] H.P., B.M. Add. MSS., 48639, fos. 27-8, 29 Jan. 1885.

portion of their independence in return for the right of representation'.[85] His views on Ireland remained, to a considerable extent, distinct from his attitude towards the self-governing colonies, though both were founded upon a belief that inhabitants of these imperial possessions ought to be 'absolute master in all local matters'.[86] There was, therefore, no inherent contradiction in his support for federation in Australia, and the establishment of local legislatures in Britain. One reason why he favoured a substantial devolution of power to Ireland was to show Irish separatists that 'nothing would be gained by separation'.[87] Similarly, he argued that the fewer points of contact that existed between the imperial parliament, and the parliament which he hoped to see established in Ireland, the less chance there was of friction between them.[88] There was one important difference between his views on the relationship between the British parliament and the self-governing colonies, and the prospective relationship which he envisaged between the British parliament and Ireland. In the last resort he would have supported the use of force to compel Ireland to maintain the imperial connection.[89] Even when controversy raged over the proposal, in clause twenty-four of Gladstone's first home rule bill, to exclude Irish representatives from Westminster, Labouchere ignored the possibility that if the Irish secured representation both in an Irish legislature and at Westminster, the case for the admission of colonial representatives at Westminster would be transformed into one 'irresistibly strong'.[90] On the other hand, he criticized Chamberlain's federal proposals on the grounds that in them the Irish question was to be shelved until the self-governing colonies 'were asked to join us in a scheme of federation'.[91]

Labouchere was not opposed to a closer imperial relationship but he commented upon problems associated with it critically and realistically. In the early 1880s he did not consider the crown colonies or India in this context, and he ignored the

[85] *Fortnightly Review*, xxxviii (1 Oct. 1885), p. 485.
[86] *Truth*, 1 Jan. 1885, p. 16.   [87] *Truth*, 1 Dec. 1881, p. 702.
[88] *Truth*, 7 Jan. 1886, p. 10.   [89] Hansard, 3rd ser., 302, 232, 22 Jan. 1886.
[90] M.G.P., B.M. Add. MSS., 46243, fo. 154, Sir A. Gordon to M. Gladstone, 9 Jan. 1886.
[91] Hansard, 3rd ser., 305, 1341, 18 May 1886.

CLOSER UNION OF THE EMPIRE 227

possibilities of an imperial *Zollverein*. In June 1889, however, he wrote to W. T. Stead,

The Imperial idea is good in theory, but I doubt whether one Colony would give up an inch of its autonomy. If Australia were to send a dozen Representatives to an Assembly in London, it would know that it would be outvoted. The only real way to effect a Union would be a Customs league including India, with a portion of the proceeds devoted to an Imperial Navy of defence. I doubt however whether Freetraders would stand this.[92]

An interesting feature of Labouchere's attitude, which he did not formulate clearly, was the association he made in 1881 between extensive devolution of authority in Britain, and closer union. This in turn was connected with the concession of greater powers, including that of annexation, to the self-governing colonies. The imperial factor would not operate and colonies would have to measure their policies with their power to implement them. Given responsibility for their actions and spurred by hard facts and self-interest, colonies and provincial authorities in Britain might then draw together as allies to support an imperial fleet. Paradoxically, 'home rule all round' acted as midwife to a closer imperial association.

[92] Sd.P., Labouchere to Stead, 30 June 1889.

## CHAPTER IX

# Conclusion

LABOUCHERE was a critic of imperial policies rather than an opponent of empire. He repeatedly stated that he would oppose the 'disintegration of the empire'.[1] In his opinion, the strength of the empire rested upon the love and affection of its peoples, and by 'peoples' he meant primarily those of European extraction. This attitude led him to support home rule for Ireland and to favour complete independence for the Transvaal Boers. He offered vigorous opposition to forward imperial policies which originated in Britain or which might involve Britain, and he tried to cast aside territories in which British influence was increasing and which he feared might be added to the empire. Thus he advocated withdrawal from Afghanistan, Egypt and the Sudan, the transfer of Cyprus to Greece, and he opposed the acquisition of Bechuanaland and Burma. Only once did he support intervention in the affairs of a foreign country, and on that occasion his definition of the principle of non-intervention was that 'we ought never to interfere abroad except where our interests are directly menaced'.[2] This exception was in connection with Egypt, and his investments in Egyptian stock were at stake. Yet while Labouchere opposed further imperial expansion which originated in the metropolis, and wished to limit Britain's involvement in South Africa to retention of a secure naval base,[3] he conceded to the self-governing colonies the right to annex

---

[1] This phrase was often used but rarely defined in the 1880s. Labouchere could interpret the phrase in accordance with his views and legitimately argue that he opposed disintegration. His critics could argue that the implementation of his suggestions would have this result if they defined the term differently.

[2] *Truth*, 1 June 1882, p. 749.

[3] According to L. S. Amery, 'even professed Imperialists like Froude thought that Cape Town was the only bit of S. Africa we could permanently hold' at this time. See E. Stokes, 'Milnerism', *Historical Journal*, v (1962), 59.

neighbouring territories provided that they bore sole responsibility for, and the expense of, their actions. Such a concession would have shattered the unity of imperial foreign policy, but there are suggestions that Labouchere had in mind a complex, and, with the exception of Ireland, a voluntary imperial relationship which would have catered for this contingency. In his thought the primary source of authority in the empire was the self-governing community which should be 'absolute master' in all local matters. In 1881 he advocated devolution of authority in the British Isles to county assemblies, but he proposed assemblies for England, Scotland, Wales and Ireland, more frequently. Moreover, he believed that self-governing communities in geographical proximity would federate. Finally, he suggested that representatives from the local communities might come together as allies[4] to support an imperial navy. Labouchere wished to abolish the house of lords and have a bicameral constitution only if some form of closer imperial association materialized. The only merit he saw in the monarchy was that it served as a connecting link between Britain and the colonies. In this period he made no proposals about the relationship that might exist between the self-governing parts of the empire and imperial dependencies.

A striking feature of Labouchere's attitude towards the empire was his lack of constructive proposals for British dependencies. He appears to have equated lack of overt and active agitation in this part of the empire with the acquiescence of subject races in the *status quo*. He was attracted towards, and voiced sympathy for, communities that resisted British power vigorously. He contended that 'if Africa is to be for the Africans', its inhabitants must 'show that they are men'.[5] Conversely, he was convinced that while men behaved like sheep they would continue to be shorn, and he apparently felt no obligation to draw attention to the shearing if it were accepted passively, and could not be used to argue against forward policies.

He was half-hearted about other British obligations to native

---

[4] Disraeli, in March 1865, spoke of 'that mature hour... when we may lose perhaps our dependencies but gain permanent allies'. S. R. Stembridge, 'Disraeli and the Millstones', *Journal of British Studies*, v (1965), 131.
[5] *Truth*, 28 Aug. 1884, p. 324.

populations. In 1882 he found that various forms of 'slavery existed in many parts of the British Dominions',[6] and raised the matter in the House. However, he did this only once despite a pledge to his constituents in November 1882 that he would raise 'the subject again and again'[7] until he received satisfaction. He stated in *Truth* that he would have preferred annexation to the concession of the Borneo charter which delegated to the company's officials 'the right ... to act as slave-catchers under an English flag'.[8] Through the same medium he criticized the 'abominable' Polynesian labour traffic and emphasized the culpability of Queensland planters for it.[9] But he did not raise these issues in parliament, presumably because he suspected that Britain might have to accept further responsibilities in order to apply comprehensive controls. He was also inhibited by his belief that in connection with the self-governing colonies Britain had 'no more right to interfere ... than ... in Russia'.[10] The weight of British responsibility for native populations within imperial frontiers did not burden Labouchere unduly. He admitted that Britain had obligations towards the native races of the Transvaal owing to the annexation. However, early in 1881 during the period which preceded the British government's decision to grant a qualified measure of independence to the Transvaal, he begged the native question. In parliament, where Labouchere did not speak on this issue, the 'one persistent theme common to Liberals, Conservatives and the Irish members was British obligation to the native peoples'.[11] He merely turned attention to Natal where he asserted that slavery, masquerading as apprenticeship, prevailed[12] and dismissed denunciations of the Boers for their alleged cruelty to native races as irrelevant: 'the last desperate resource of discredited Jingoes'.[13] Similarly, his proposals to restrict British involve-

[6] Hansard, 3rd ser., 268, 1711, 28 April 1882.
[7] *Northampton Mercury*, 25 Nov. 1882.
[8] *Truth*, 23 March 1882, p. 403; cf. 19 Oct. 1882, p. 548.
[9] *Truth*, 22 June 1882, pp. 856–7; 6 July 1882, p. 46; 7 Jan. 1886, p. 5.
[10] Rhodes House, MSS. British Empire, S 18, c 140/4, Labouchere to F. W. Chesson, 12 April [?1882].
[11] I. M. Cumpston, 'The Discussion of Imperial Problems in the British Parliament, 1880–1885', *T.R.H.S.*, 5th ser., xiii (1963), 40.
[12] *Truth*, 10 March 1881, p. 318.   [13] *Truth*, 24 March 1881, p. 388.

ment in South Africa to retention of a naval base would have sacrificed native interests upon the altar of withdrawal.

Labouchere's repeated rejection of British responsibility for native races beyond imperial frontiers was more pronounced than his lack of concern for those within the empire. He often used humanitarian arguments to justify this attitude. Thus he emphasized brutalities incidental to military campaigns in the Sudan and Burma, and ignored the possibility that British administration in those areas might have beneficial results. He applied principles of self-determination to inhabitants of such regions but not to native peoples within the empire unless, as in the case of the Burmese, the British had annexed their territory recently. Labouchere argued that humanitarian pleas about the need to protect native races outside the empire were spurious, for they were only applied in regions where alleged British interests existed. In his view, religious jingoism was as costly and as unpractical as political jingoism. He pointed to the correlation between hostilities, and the failure of missionary enterprise, in South Africa. He also questioned the validity of the Christian sanction on the grounds that Christians were always fighting each other and right could not be on both sides. Outlines of an argument he put forward later in his parliamentary career were also vaguely discernible: why intervene to protect missionaries when 'the blood of the saints is the seed of the Church'?[14] He criticized dissenters, quakers, and members of peace societies, for not protesting against the 'obvious iniquity of... purposeless massacres'.[15] He believed that when advocates of forward policies were hard pressed for justification, they called the 'inevitable nigger'[16] to their aid: and he commented ironically on the benefits that accrued to natives from annexation.[17]

Labouchere's views about subject races did not stem from convictions of racial superiority. He alleged that when British officials had authority over people of a different colour, they were inclined to consider them their inferiors and to ill-treat

[14] M. Perham, *Lord Lugard*, i, 399.
[15] *Northampton Mercury Daily Reporter*, 16 Feb. 1885.
[16] *Truth*, 21 Feb. 1884, p. 268.
[17] *Truth*, 26 April 1883, p. 570.

them.[18] He asserted that Englishmen resident among native populations lost 'all sense of distinction between right and wrong, and would have everything yield to their personal greed and love of domination'.[19] He may have opposed further imperial expansion partly in order to protect natives from the initially deleterious effects of 'civilization', and from the imposition of alien swaddling bands of political and economic servitude.

Labouchere opposed imperial expansion in 'Africa, Asia, Polynesia, or anywhere else'[20] but, in stating that Britain 'must be dominant in no country which is not within the limits of our Empire',[21] he perhaps left a loophole for further imperial activity in India. He argued against forward policies on the grounds that the empire contained too many native populations, that imperial rule outraged the 'feelings and prejudices'[22] of newly subjected peoples, that earth hunger was an unreasoning mania, and that frontier wars were self-perpetuating. He also claimed that Britain was involving herself in matters, such as whether Bechuanaland belonged to Boers or half-civilized chiefs, or whether the Ashanti preferred cutting each other's throats to living in peace and amity, which were not her concern. He believed that conservatives and 'liberals inclined to toryism' who sought to divert attention from British affairs, 'interested' investors, merchants and manufacturers, unpractical missionaries and humanitarians, military personnel and civilian officials enticed by brighter prospects of promotion, and irresponsible journalists, supported imperial expansion. Labouchere commented upon the way in which 'responsibilities' changed into 'rights' as blunders and butchery provided title deeds of further acquisitions. In his opinion forward policies militated against imperial interests. They weakened the empire by imposing regular and heavy financial burdens upon Britain, by dispersing and dissipating British military resources, and by increasing the possibility of major wars. He advocated a powerful navy which would make the empire impregnable even if Britain withdrew from Egypt, and a defensive imperial policy.

[18] Hansard, 3rd ser., 286, 1751–2, 4 April 1884.
[19] *Truth*, 16 Nov. 1882, p. 693.   [20] *Truth*, 25 Sept. 1884, p. 473.
[21] *Truth*, 11 Dec. 1884, p. 900.   [22] Hansard, 3rd ser., 308, 823, 30 Aug. 1886.

He was inclined to ignore the implications upon imperial defence of the concession of home rule to Ireland and the difficulties of reconciling withdrawal from South African affairs with retention of a secure naval base. The importance he attributed to the Suez Canal declined markedly when he advocated withdrawal from Egypt. He had very little to say about the economies of Britain, the colonies, and the empire as a whole, but he feared the self-governing colonies and Natal carried too great a burden of debt and might repudiate it. He simply affirmed his belief in free trade principles, denied that trade either followed the flag or had increased as a result of heavy expenditure upon imperial campaigns, and stated that 'Commercially... there should be no wall around our Empire; politically... there should be a Chinese wall.'[23]

Some of Labouchere's views about the empire had a logical consistency. Inhabitants of self-governing communities, whether homogeneous in race or stage of development or not, lived together and it was their responsibility to accommodate themselves to each other. The way in which they did this was their concern not Britain's. It was the 'manifest destiny' of South Africa to become a 'Dutch State' and attempts to 'buy off the inevitable' were futile.[24] If self-governing communities wished to annex neighbouring territories, then they should have the right to do so, provided that they faced all the consequences. Labouchere applied the doctrine of the survival of the fittest to self-governing colonies as well as to their inhabitants and faced the consequences: 'every one of our colonies ought to be able to hold its own in local squabbles; if it cannot, the sooner that it goes to the wall the better'.[25] Thus he favoured the withdrawal of the imperial factor from self-governing colonies, and the free operation of indigenous forces, even if native interests were sacrificed. His reticence about other imperial dependencies may perhaps be interpreted as an acquiescence in the *status quo* until their populations developed politically and agitated for the inalienable rights of self-government which, in an Egyptian context, he proclaimed for non-European races. On the other hand there were opportunities for him to encourage Indian

[23] *Truth*, 25 Sept. 1884, p. 473.
[24] *Truth*, 22 March 1883, p. 393.   [25] *Truth*, 9 Oct. 1884, p. 555.

aspirations if he, like some of his associates such as J. McCarthy and C. Bradlaugh, had chosen to do so.[26] British taxpayers, in his opinion, should merely have to support a powerful navy. They should no longer have their money squandered upon unnecessary military operations or upon the administration of additional native populations.

It was equally important to Labouchere that Britain would be able to devote its energies to internal reform if it adopted a pacific imperial policy. He frequently commented upon Britain's perversity in attempting to remedy 'abuses and injustices'[27] abroad before it 'altered and amended'[28] everything that needed attention at home. His electoral manifesto of 1885 indicated the formidable programme of domestic reform he supported. It was, however, impossible to implement such radical measures while imperial affairs consumed so much parliamentary time, and, by Labouchere's calculations, while whigs remained within the liberal party. British policies towards Ireland, Egypt and the Sudan, East and Southern Africa, were particularly controversial, and it was upon these policies that Labouchere concentrated. By attacking them with his most extreme arguments he hoped to achieve the basing of liberal policies upon liberal principles and the end of coercive policies in order to secure for the Irish and Egyptians the right to govern themselves even if Irish landlords or Egyptian bondholders suffered, in order to have conservatives dubbed as unprincipled expansionists, in order to drive whigs from the liberal party, and in order to increase his own political stature.

In connection with Ireland, Labouchere opposed coercive policies strongly and was particularly perceptive in seeing the need for home rule, and in advocating this policy from October 1880. When Gladstone wished to educate Spencer on home rule, he referred him to a small number of speakers of whom Labouchere was one.[29] Labouchere gave the Parnellites staunch

[26] I. M. Cumpston, 'Some Early Indian Nationalists and their Allies in the British Parliament, 1851–1906', *English Historical Review*, lxxvi (1961), 279ff.

[27] *Northampton Mercury*, 28 Nov. 1885.

[28] Hansard, 3rd ser., 284, 910, 14 Feb. 1884.

[29] G.P., B.M. Add. MSS., 44312, fo. 210, Gladstone to Spencer, 19 Dec. 1885.

## CONCLUSION

and consistent support, even though he incurred parliamentary opprobrium and 'much ill-odour'[30] among his constituents. He also had considerable success in extracting from ministers details of the cost to Britain in men and money of expeditions, armies of occupation, and loans to the Egyptian government, and he protested regularly about such alleged misapplication of British resources. The basic theme of his arguments was constant: sectional interests impelled the British government to practise expensive follies; if the government were 'democratic' this would not occur.[31] However, he was aware that the issues were more complex. He asserted, for instance, that all classes should pay for imperial expenditure for 'otherwise the poor would be too much inclined to indulge in the luxury of gunpowder and glory at the expense of the rich'.[32]

In order to reduce the number of military expeditions, Labouchere tried to reduce the size of the British army: but although he excluded Indian forces, his motion to reduce the army estimates was overwhelmingly defeated.[33] He had more support but was also unsuccessful in his attempt to withhold supplies for the administration of Bechuanaland.[34] He was less concerned if British taxpayers were not involved. He failed to protest when the Indian government was obliged to pay for Indian troops fighting in Egypt, and he abstained from voting when W. A. Hunter and H. Richard pressed objections to the imposition of expenditure for operations in Upper Burma upon the revenues of India to a division.[35] Despite his involvement in Irish affairs, an inexplicable dereliction of duty on Labouchere's part occurred on 19 March 1886. H. Richard's motion that 'it is not just or expedient to embark in war, contract engagements involving grave responsibilities for the Nation, and add territories to the Empire without the knowledge and consent of

[30] *Northamptonshire Guardian*, 12 May 1884.
[31] N. Blewett estimates that approximately 40 per cent of adult males were not on the electoral register in 1911. *Past and Present*, xxxii (1965), 27.
[32] *Truth*, 7 May 1885, p. 722.
[33] Hansard, 3rd ser., 286, 136–8, 17 March 1884; Division Lists, 1884, No. 45, 17 March 1884, 11:152.
[34] Hansard, 3rd ser., 302, 1614–17, 1 March 1886; Division Lists, 1886, No. 13, 1 March 1886, 85:229.
[35] Division Lists, 1886, No. 9, 22 Feb. 1886; Hansard, 3rd ser., 302, 944–86, 22 Feb. 1886.

Parliament', was narrowly defeated.[36] If successful, this attempt to bring the executive under strict parliamentary control might have altered subsequent imperial policy significantly. Its intention was in complete harmony with Labouchere's views, and it was a corollary of his success in May 1868 which gave members of parliament greater control over the foreign office. Nevertheless he abstained from voting and did not speak in the debate.[37]

Labouchere's involvement in many different types of political activity and the complexity of his motives reduced his effectiveness. Many political commentators tended to overlook his arguments about the empire, or be prejudiced against them, because they were directly associated with his root and branch proposals for reform in England. In the Commons, he frequently spoke with reporters in mind[38] rather than his colleagues, and so reduced his influence there. He appeared to be prepared to defeat Gladstone's second administration because its policy towards Egypt and the Sudan deviated from liberal principles. However, leading liberals knew that he timed some of his protests to suit the government's convenience, and that in betraying Churchill in June 1883 he had proved himself a 'scoundrel', a 'traitor to all sides'.[39] The support he gave Parnellites appears disinterested, but he was deliberately seeking to create an alliance between them and radicals. He may also have exploited their goodwill, in 1882, and between 1885 and 1886, in order to thrust himself upon Gladstone and Chamberlain as an intermediary. By 1886 he was the unofficial 'go-between of the Irish',[40] and despite his professions of indifference one suspects that he would have welcomed official regularization of his position with an Irish privy councillorship.

His links with the press, and the uses he made of *Truth* were probably unique in the 1880s and 1890s. Early in 1886 he had the editor of the *Daily News* replaced, and he enabled J. Morley

---

[36] Division Lists, 1886, No. 38, 19 March 1886, 108:112; Hansard, 3rd ser., 303, 1386–1421, 19 March 1886.

[37] A. P. Thornton erroneously states that Labouchere was in the van of this attack in *The Imperial Idea and its Enemies*, p. 85.

[38] *Saturday Review*, 20 Jan. 1912, p. 70.

[39] Ge.P., P.R.O., 30/29/27, Grosvenor to Granville, 22 June 1883.

[40] Cy.P., Journal, R.(S.R.) 1003, 22, fo. 79, [?23 Jan. 1886].

## CONCLUSION

to write the newspaper's articles on Ireland. Of the metropolitan newspapers only *Truth* and the *Daily News* supported home rule in 1886. Many of Labouchere's comments about South African, Egyptian and Indian affairs, and about closer imperial union, appeared only in *Truth*. It was particularly in *Truth* that he drew comparisons between different imperial problems: 'Do you suppose that Christians who won't allow the Scotch crofters to stand in the way of pleasure are likely to allow the Maori peasant to interfere with their profit?'[41] Here too he drew attention to the actions of certain individuals. For instance, he praised Sir J. Pope Hennessy for invariably siding with the 'down-trodden masses against the narrow little planter and official clique',[42] and claimed that the connection of Sir J. Vogel with named electric and telephone companies in Australasia was 'anything but beneficial to the shareholders'.[43] *Truth*, however, was an important weapon in Labouchere's political armoury as well as a pulpit from which he could preach upon an imperial text. From 1880 it was 'one of the most powerful advocates of home rule',[44] but within this area shifts of emphasis are discernible. In January 1881 Labouchere's arguments appeared indiscriminately in *Truth* and other places, but on 6 November 1884 its proposals for a constitutional settlement were more advanced than those contained in a letter to his constituents two days earlier, or anything he had said in the House. In 1885 and 1886, Labouchere was circumspect in using in *Truth* information obtained from communications with Herbert Gladstone, Healy and Chamberlain, and his speeches in the House became more statesmanlike. He used *Truth* to sway opinion on matters of imperial concern in various ways: sometimes it justified his actions in the House; it indicated his views when, as in the case of India in 1883, he did not speak on the subject; intermittently it prepared the ground for a protest by its owner in parliament; occasionally it developed arguments which may have arisen from his articles in the *Fortnightly Review*, and it kept issues alive during parliamentary recesses.

As an intermediary Labouchere's record on minor issues was unprepossessing. In February 1885, he told Herbert Gladstone

[41] *Truth*, 17 July 1884, p. 90.
[42] *Truth*, 3 Aug. 1882, p. 189.
[43] *Truth*, 19 March 1885, p. 457.
[44] *Cornhill*, n.s., xxxii (1912) 322.

that he could contact the mahdi's emissary, but when Northbrook and Gladstone pursued the matter he was unable to do so.[45] According to Healy, Labouchere mishandled Gladstone's attempt to save Dilke from the scandal that ruined his career by bribing the irate husband.[46] In each of these cases the initiative probably came from Labouchere. This was also the case in connection with Irish affairs in 1882, and so far as the 'negotiations' of 1885 were concerned, the only evidence to the contrary came from Labouchere. Labouchere's mediation between Gladstone and Chamberlain was accepted by them because no minister was able, or willing to act in this capacity. Gladstone asked Spencer and Harcourt to mediate, but they were unsuccessful. They advised Gladstone to meet Chamberlain, but the prime minister refused. Labouchere's activities were more important in 1885 than in 1886. His indiscretions then harmed the liberal party, aggravated the home rule crisis, and helped to create the situation which gave an air of unreality to his attempts to reconcile Gladstone and Chamberlain in 1886. Labouchere used the home rule question to further radical interests, for he correctly assumed that the adoption of home rule would radicalize the liberal party. Chamberlain's decision to act 'the part of a Conservative jackal . . . leading men into a Whig cave'[47] disturbed many of his calculations. The decision of J. Morley and Gladstone to keep the millstone of land purchase tied to the liberal party disturbed many others.

Labouchere's belief in the need for peace, retrenchment, liberty and reform dominated his attitude towards the empire: each of these was dependent upon the others, but Labouchere's primary objective was the creation of a situation in which Britain could concentrate upon internal reform. He held firm, honest convictions about the empire, but this did not lead him to adopt a conventional code of political morality, and it did not prevent him from turning imperial issues to personal and domestic political advantage. He acted upon the assumption that in 'politics . . . the only way to get what you want is to

---

[45] H.G.P., B.M. Add. MSS., 46015, fos. 17–23, Labouchere to H. Gladstone, 8, 14, 16 Feb. 1885; A. Thorold, pp. 196–8.
[46] T. M. Healy, *Letters and Leaders of My Day*, i, 215–16.
[47] Hansard, 3rd ser., 305, 1339, 18 May 1886.

make yourself unpleasant',[48] and in several ways he did disservice to the causes he supported. He made charges when he had insufficient evidence to substantiate them, and this habit lasted throughout his parliamentary career. In 1882 Courtney criticized him in the House for making an 'extraordinary accusation' without a 'single fact or circumstance' to support it.[49] His attitude towards Egypt in 1882 showed that he was influenced by personal interests but later, in Blunt's opinion, he became 'one of the very few quite honest M.P.'s'.[50] In the 1880s, Labouchere's comments were not devoid of the *allegatio falsi* or the *suppressio veri*, and in many of his arguments he blunted the edge of persuasion with assertive denunciations. Moreover, he grossly oversimplified the complexity of different imperial problems. It was easier for him to suggest that Britain should only concern itself with retention of a Gibraltar in South Africa when he made no attempt to show how this could be done. It was simpler to apply fundamental radical principles to the problems of Ireland and Egypt than to find a path through the labyrinth of constitutional, economic, defensive and international difficulties. It was more convincing to allege that radicals opposed coercive policies, expeditions, and extensions of the empire, by pretending that uniformity of belief existed amongst them, by ignoring evidence to the contrary, and by presenting a distorted picture of the attitude of whigs.

In some respects Labouchere's views were inconsistent. He applied the voluntary principle to the connection between the self-governing colonies and Britain, but not to Ireland if it obtained home rule. When he affirmed his opposition to the 'disintegration of the Empire', he perhaps referred to earlier meanings of 'empire': as late as 1872 W. O'C. Morris discussed 'making England and Ireland an empire'.[51] His adherence to federal principles is difficult to reconcile with his belief that self-government assumed the character of its environment within a decade. He supported home rule partly to gain

---

[48] *Truth*, 1 Feb. 1883, p. 151.
[49] Hansard, 3rd ser., 268, 1724, 28 April 1882. Labouchere had claimed that he was 'credibly informed that slavery existed in Lagos'.
[50] W. S. Blunt, *My Diaries* (1932), 17 Jan. 1912, p. 791.
[51] *Fortnightly Review*, xi (1872), 23.

Parnellite support for radicals in the division lobbies at Westminster. However, in 1886, he supported the exclusion of Irish members from the imperial parliament. He opposed schemes in which British taxpayers were to accept financial responsibility for the purchase of land in Ireland, but, on isolated occasions, he was prepared to accept them. He accorded rights of self-government to the Irish and Egyptians, but not to Indians. So far as Egypt or British policy towards it was concerned, much of his activity appears futile if he meant what he said to Chamberlain: 'Stick to the "clear out", & if necessary always put off clearing out.'[52]

Labouchere sometimes neglected to act upon the policies he advocated. He wished to see the 'democracy' of Britain unite to work for common objectives such as 'home rule all round' and agrarian reform. Having outlined this policy for others, he concentrated upon Ireland, and even then neglected Ulster. Sometimes he mentioned the right of Wales to have a local parliament; sometimes he did not. He ignored home rule pressures in Scotland which leading liberals feared would harm the party 'unless discouraged'.[53] He played little part in the crofter agitation which gained momentum[54] although he supported the Crofters' bill five times in the division lobbies in 1886.[55]

As a critic of imperial policies, Labouchere played an important part in British political life. After 1881 he was so secure in his constituency that it was impracticable for the party machine to try to exclude him from parliament, as it did with Sir G. Campbell at Kirkcaldy Burghs.[56] In parliament he exploited to the full what he himself ostensibly regarded as the 'agreeable irresponsibility of a seat below the gangway',[57] and his connection with *Truth* gave him similar freedom in the press. His importance depended largely upon fundamental differences of

---

[52] J.C., 5/50/19, Labouchere to Chamberlain, 9 Feb. 1884.
[53] G.P., B.M. Add. MSS., 44253, fo. 48, A. Morley to Gladstone, 17 Dec. 1886.
[54] *Times*, 31 Dec. 1884; D. M. Crowley, 'The Crofter Party', *Scottish Historical Review*, xxv (1956), 120ff.
[55] Division Lists, 1886, Nos. 47, 54, 77, 78, 90.
[56] G.P., B.M. Add. MSS., 44316, fo. 40, Grosvenor to Gladstone, 25 Sept. 1885.
[57] H.G.P., B.M. Add. MSS., 46016, fo. 11, Labouchere to H. Gladstone, 17 Feb. 1886.

## CONCLUSION

opinion among liberals, unsophisticated parliamentary discipline, and Gladstone's failures of leadership: it would have been greater if radicals themselves had been more united. Even so, in March 1886 Sir M. Hicks Beach believed that 'Labouchere could carry any revolutionary proposal' against the liberal government 'if we did not take some trouble . . . to help them'.[58]

One suspects, but cannot prove, that Labouchere had considerable influence upon Gladstone in 1885 and 1886, for, as E. W. Hamilton his principal private secretary testified, he was 'always apt to give undue weight to communications from oddities'.[59] This is not to imply that Labouchere was instrumental in determining Gladstone's decision to adopt home rule. Labouchere helped to confirm Gladstone in a course of action he had decided upon, by sending him, through his son, detailed information from Healy which supplemented that which he received from other quarters, and by bringing the positions of Healy and Gladstone closer together. At this time confidential contacts between English liberals and the 'active section' of the Irish party were very rare. Liberals may have overestimated the influence of Healy, one of its ablest parliamentarians, until the Galway election clarified the position. The communications between Healy and Labouchere assumed particular importance in 1885 as a means of establishing contact with 'the party' as distinct from Parnell personally. On 21 March 1886 a letter from Labouchere about the importance of separating home rule from land purchase and the need to concentrate upon home rule impressed Gladstone[60] and may have contributed to the subsequent modification of governmental policy.

Labouchere's actions in connection with Irish and South African affairs bear witness to his political courage. His vigour and tenacity matched this courage on issues that exercised him. In the House his mastery of parliamentary procedures gave him the opportunity to make his views known, his humour to have them heard. His capacity and ruthlessness made him a leading

---

[58] Lady V. Hicks Beach, *Life of Sir M. Hicks Beach*, i, 265, Hicks Beach to Salisbury, 27 March 1886.

[59] H.P., B.M. Add. MSS., 48643, fo. 51, 23 March 1886.

[60] This letter has not been located. Cf. H.G.P., B.M. Add. MSS., 46016, fo. 15, H. Gladstone to Labouchere, 20 March 1886; H.P., B.M. Add. MSS., 48643, fo. 51, 23 March 1886.

radical figure, and his wealth allowed him to act independently. When revenue from advertisements fell during the Boer war, he was prepared to ruin *Truth* rather than modify its support for the Boers. He kept over £20,000 in a current account: and despite the settlement, which must have been substantial, upon his daughter, Mary Dorothea, when she became Marchesa di Rudini, he left an estate valued for probate in 1912 at £522,306.

As a champion of liberty there was 'no voice more powerful than Labouchere's'[61] according to Blunt in 1898. His application of this principle in an imperial context was not conducive to uniformity. It meant liberty for native communities (and Transvaal Boers) to remain beyond the confines of the empire and govern themselves; liberty, through a free trade proviso, for British merchants to trade with them if their territory were appropriated by another power; liberty for a minority of European extraction to dominate a non-European majority in Britain's South African colonies; liberty for self-governing colonies to develop without restraint from Britain; liberty for the Irish to govern themselves and for the English to compel them to maintain the imperial connection; liberty for Egyptians, and presumably for inhabitants of British dependencies owing to the universal nature of the principle expounded; liberty for communities to repudiate all debts not incurred by representative assemblies; and, above all, liberty for Britain to conserve its resources, to undertake domestic reform, and not to have its development distorted by imperial problems.

Discrepancies of this nature occurred partly because Labouchere normally concentrated upon specific or regional imperial issues. Yet the way in which he treated them produced fundamental principles which had a relevance far wider than that of their immediate context. For instance, in an Irish context he stated, 'Political slavery is as abominable as social slavery. The domination of race over race is cruel to the subordinate race, and it is a crime on the part of the superior race.'[62] Sometimes he asserted such uncompromising axioms when they appeared to harmonize with his arguments; on other occasions they were the foundations on which he erected them. Many of Labouchere's

[61] W. S. Blunt, *My Diaries* (1932), 16 Dec. 1898, p. 308.
[62] *Truth*, 22 July 1886, p. 139.

arguments about the empire echoed and helped to keep alive those which were familiar in the 1840s and 1850s. Others, such as his early advocacy of home rule all round, were much fresher. He pruned protection of native interests and the extension of Christianity from the trunk of imperial principles and grafted to it newer ideas concerning closer union, and also of expansion by self-governing colonies which would not involve Britain. He was particularly rigorous in pressing for curtailment of British expenditure, cessation of imperial expansion by Britain, and extension of rights of self-government, primarily to communities of European extraction, but also to inhabitants of Egypt and Uganda. Labouchere acted as a custodian of the liberal conscience towards the empire. In fighting for his beliefs he applied to regional imperial problems solutions based upon the egalitarian principles of national status that prevailed later. He also saw the empire as a whole: his oversimplifications had the merit of unifying major issues and, in so doing, probably made a valuable contribution to the formation of policy at a later date.

It is, however, notoriously difficult to assess the influence of ideas. Labouchere's protests and stratagems failed to modify significantly one major policy towards the empire during a period of twenty-five years. Imperial expansion continued remorselessly while prospects of home rule receded. He probably helped to secure better treatment for exiled Egyptian leaders, and to make the application of policies already determined for the empire, marginally more humane by making public in Britain and its colonies, where *Truth* also circulated, instances of the arbitrary exercise of authority. In his resilient support for unpopular causes he encountered all the obstacles that confront a member who wishes either to secure more information than a government is prepared to make available, or to influence policies in a way that runs against the prevailing movement of political opinion. On the other hand, he had not the calibre of some of his opponents. Chamberlain almost invariably outmanœuvred him and had the better of their exchanges.

Nevertheless, after 1882, Labouchere was one of the few English politicians consistently identified with opposition to coercive policies and with the rights of some other societies irrespective of race, colour, creed and alleged British interests. He had a shrewd understanding of and sympathy with nationalistic movements. If he attempted to assist those in Ireland, South Africa and, to a lesser extent, Egypt and ignored that which was emerging in India this may have been partly because he considered that it was the concern of the peoples of India themselves to organize and agitate. His attitude towards such movements rested upon a rational, realistic assessment of their strength, of British interests as he saw them, and a scale of values that had more support at a later date. The advanced nature of his views was a handicap to him throughout his career. During the Boer war, for instance, he referred to the rights of the Boers which derived, as a consequence of the annexation of their republics, from their status as citizens of the British empire.[63] Yet the concept of citizenship was not fully accepted even for the inhabitants of Britain. The liberal, H. A. L. Fisher, spoke in August 1917 of 'a growing sense' that Britain's 'industrial workers' were 'entitled to be considered primarily as citizens and as fit subjects for any form of education from which they are capable of profiting'.[64]

Labouchere's uniquely unconventional character probably played a larger part than the political situation in which he operated in making his record of political achievement so barren. His disdain for public and political opinion, his persistent contempt for authority, his ingrained tendency to rebel and act independently, often irrespective of party convenience, his abhorrence of extravagance, ostentation and emotion, were not necessarily political assets. Rather paradoxically in view of his cynicism, he intermittently placed principle before expediency and was more trusting than judicious. Moreover, his lack of *gravitas* and to a greater extent his careless impetuosity helped to convey the inaccurate impression that he was simply striving for effect. This impulsiveness combined with his combative nature also led him to betray some political confidences and to launch attacks precipitately. By showing opponents the weapons in his armoury and frequently the shortage of his

[63] Hansard, 4th ser., 92, 147, 28 March 1901.
[64] Hansard, 5th ser., 97, 800, 10 Aug. 1917.

ammunition at an early stage, he conceded real advantages and permitted them to take appropriate counter-measures.

Labouchere had considerable ability, an acutely critical and penetrating mind and highly developed powers of observation and deduction, but his most serious limitation was a form of intellectual indolence. This varied in intensity, became increasingly discernible after 1892, and emphasized many of his other characteristics. He concealed the nakedness of his evasion of the rigours of study and effort but he never showed a complete mastery of the intricate detail of any major legislative enactment, apart perhaps from the first home rule bill. He rarely gave balanced, accurate and comprehensive arguments that might have supported home rule or opposed imperial expansion more effectively. Despite his attempts to influence opinion he never tried to organize it. In the latter part of his career his attacks lacked penetrative power partly because they lacked the weight of carefully selected, well-organized and incontrovertibly authenticated evidence. This in turn was a consequence of his inability or disinclination to make a sustained concentrated effort in order to secure his primary political objectives. On rare occasions he resembled a toothless terrier. He was neither small in political stature nor big with iniquity or achievement, but he was more successful as a journalist than as a politician.

In the course of his political career Labouchere moved away from some of the tenets of the Manchester School on domestic issues, for he increasingly supported state intervention to remove injustices so that individualism could operate in more equitable conditions. However, he did keep alive more of those relating to imperial affairs. Nevertheless, he advocated state intervention in Africa to guarantee free trade in labour to Africans threatened by the actions of mine-owners and railway contractors and, in certain areas, by Asian immigration. During a period of economic difficulties in Britain he came to challenge economic individualism to which earlier prosperity was often attributed, but he adhered to free trade. Thus he could not sweeten reforms such as the eight-hours issue by arguing that it would increase costs of production and facilitate a return to protection which might take the form of a colonial customs union.[65]

[65] B.P., B.M. Add. MSS., 49695, fo. 193, Churchill to Balfour, 19 March 1892.

Instead of clarifying his original suggestions for a voluntary, defensive, pacific, imperial association in which extensive devolution of authority in Britain was an integral part, he abandoned them in 1886 possibly as a result of Gladstone's failure to carry home rule. He criticized other proposals to federate the empire on the grounds that they originated in Britain and had little support in, or relevance for, the colonies who would have to sacrifice part of their 'practical independence'.[66] He argued that if they were implemented British expenditure would increase 'for the benefit of... our colonies'.[67] Thus while he kept alive the view that colonies gained from the imperial connection,[68] at the expense of British taxpayers, he directed it against schemes designed partly to redress this balance. If the colonies desired imperial federation they should initially contribute 'to those Imperial charges from which they benefited', to 'the general expenditure of the Empire', and should 'pay for the expenditure which is necessary for each of them'.[69] He dismissed the possibility of an imperial *Zollverein* as an attempt by the colonies to secure from Britain a closed market for their food.[70]

Labouchere gave prominence to that part of the Manchester creed which claimed that the British paid additional taxes to meet the costs of the empire, that they were taxed more heavily if forward policies replaced those that were pacific and that they received no commensurate return. In addition, active imperial policies arrested the progress of domestic reform, a fact of which those who opposed such reforms were aware. In 1897 Labouchere charged Chamberlain with banging the colonial drum to defend 'the rotten old edifice of Toryism outside England. Ireland served his purpose for a time; now it is Colonial unity, African grabbery'.[71] According to this argument Britain was deprived of reforms and capital, while the colonies had less responsibility, and less experience of adjusting resources

---

[66] *Truth*, 8 July 1897, p. 86.
[67] Hansard, 3rd ser., 326, 376–9, 15 May 1888.
[68] See *Times*, 6 June 1862; Hansard, 3rd ser., 179, 911–14, 26 May 1865. I am indebted to P. Amey for these references.
[69] Hansard, 3rd ser., 326, 376–9, 15 May 1888; cf. *Truth*, 14 Nov. 1895, pp. 1199–1200.
[70] *Truth*, 18 June 1895, p. 1565. [71] *Truth*, 8 July 1897, p. 88.

to objectives if Britain subsidized them. Labouchere argued, with regard to Southern Africa in the 1880s, that colonists were more likely to be belligerent towards natives if they could rely upon imperial assistance, and that they had a vested interest in hostilities as they profited from the presence of imperial troops. These arguments had been used in the debates on the Maori wars between 1859 and 1865. In the latter part of the century, he modified his arguments and applied them to the chartered companies[72] and particularly to the British South Africa Company. His criticisms of groups of capitalists and speculators who hid their primary objective, financial advantage, behind specious pleas about imperial interest, and who furtively applied pressure upon the British government, were in the classic tradition of the pacific, rather than the crusading, wing of the Manchester School.[73] So too was his distaste for the butchery associated with forward policies and the degrading effect it had upon those involved and the societies from which they came. But although he frequently referred to these consequences of an expansionist imperial policy, he could never make political capital out of them in the manner of John Bright or Gladstone as he lacked their oratorical ability and moral fervour. The principle of arbitration was a further element in this pacific tradition that he kept in circulation. He wished to apply the Alabama precedent to the dispute of 1885 between Britain and Russia and even to controversies between Britain and communities adjacent to imperial frontiers in West[74] and Southern Africa.[75]

Labouchere was, in his own words written in 1893, a 'fanatical anti-expansionist'[76] who argued along the following lines. The empire was sufficiently large; its inhabitants had sufficient burdens; Britain had not the right, the duty or the resources to civilize the world; trade and commerce flourished if they had sufficient capital and were efficient—they did not follow the

---

[72] According to Hicks Beach, the 'main intention' of the promoters of the Royal Niger Company 'was to extend the British Empire, British trade, and British commerce'. Hansard, 4th ser., 75, 378, 26 July 1899.
[73] A. Briggs, *Victorian People*, p. 223.
[74] *Truth*, 4 Feb. 1897, p. 259.
[75] Hansard, 4th ser., 77, 101–12, 17 Oct. 1899.
[76] N.L.S., Rosebery papers, Labouchere to Rosebery, 7 Jan. 1893.

flag; the 'British problem'—the most important of all—was being ignored; empires died of indigestion; greatness and strength were not synonymous with size. He continued to oppose state activity beyond imperial frontiers but he had no objection to individual activity there provided that the British government was not involved.

Until the end of his career Labouchere was loath to allow expenditure for imperial purposes to pass through parliament without scrutiny or comment. For instance, he had 'diverse and special' reasons to submit against each item in the Colonial Loans bill of 1899.[77] He pointed to the expense of specific policies for the empire, and perhaps exercised a restraining influence upon what he often regarded as an extravagant dissipation of Britain's financial resources. Perhaps his persistence in fighting an apparently losing battle against increasing expenditure for imperial purposes is best explained by recognizing the very great importance he attached to the accumulation of capital in order to improve industrial efficiency, shorten hours of work and raise wages, and bring general prosperity. It may also be explained by his belief that only a close examination of detail indicated the soundness of an enterprise.[78] It was a short step for him to propose alternative and less expensive policies: 'In local matters ... the colonies ought to run themselves.'[79] It may be seen that these were open to misinterpretation when applied to crown colonies.

Apart from his tentative proposals for a closer imperial association and some of his remarkable predictions, many of Labouchere's views about the empire were as derivative as his approach to politics. The hostility of radicals towards whigs was endemic before Labouchere entered politics. D. O'Connell and John Bright established precedents for the manipulation of opinion and the attainment of radical reforms in the 1820s and 1840s within the then existing political framework. Bright and Cobden acted on the assumption that their political objectives could only be obtained indirectly. Labouchere lacked their stature, their concentration upon specific objectives, and the organization

[77] Hansard, 4th ser., 75, 873–4, 1167–98, 31 July and 2 Aug. 1899.
[78] H. M. Hyndman and H. Labouchere, pp. 12–15.
[79] Hansard, 4th ser., 75, 1198, 2 Aug. 1899.

upon which so much of their success was based. He tried to compensate for this with his attempts to mould opinion through parliament and the press, to negotiate reconciliations between leading politicians in the interests of the policies he supported, and to influence leading politicians privately: 'on the worst view', wrote Campbell-Bannerman in 1900 about letters he received from Labouchere, *'fas est et a diabolo doceri'*.[80] In this light some of Labouchere's actions in parliament become more comprehensible. He wished to give liberal governments anxiety on specific issues so that they would modify their policies, but he did not wish to defeat them.

Labouchere maintained his faith in the validity of the particular combination of liberal and radical principles that formed his political creed. A distinguishing feature of his attitude towards the empire was his conviction of their relevance and suitability in totally dissimilar contexts. He struggled against increasingly heavy odds to have them accepted. This was particularly important at a time when many in the liberal party were becoming disenchanted and pessimistic as a result of the agitation that convulsed Ireland and the humiliations of Majuba and Khartoum. Even leading members of the Manchester School began to apply their principles and policies on a regional basis: John Bright and Goldwin Smith opposed the concession of home rule to Ireland. Liberal unionists and some liberal imperialists were disillusioned, determined to maintain 'British interests' and 'law and order'. So far as the empire was concerned, they lacked the reforming objectives of earlier liberal traditions and tended to rely upon coercive policies rather than 'enlightened self-interest' or 'mutual affection'. Moreover, many liberals who followed Gladstone supported home rule half-heartedly and fought like Falstaff to secure it. Rosebery took no interest in Ireland because it was 'not yet a foreign country'.[81]

Labouchere supported home rule for Ireland and desired it to be a precedent for a similar concession to other parts of the United Kingdom. This, in his opinion, would not produce the 'disintegration' of the empire in which several subordinate

[80] J. A. Spender, *The Life of the Right Hon. Sir Henry Campbell-Bannerman*, i, 316.
[81] Sy.P., Churchill to Salisbury, 5 May 1886.

parliaments functioned. The empire would be more united and stronger if its political structure were reformed to allow the 'love and affection of its people' to flourish. Although he was proposing a fundamental political change at a time of economic uncertainty, he was also applying to Britain, as he did to other parts of the empire and communities in close proximity to it until the end of his career, the 'doctrine of nationality, of which Mr Gladstone was such a distinguished advocate'.[82] With equal vigour and consistency he opposed the application of coercive policies. These two themes often blended. During the Boer war, for instance, he stated that the empire would be permanently damaged if the two republics were forcibly incorporated within it, and argued that the objective of British policy should be 'to obtain the assent of the people . . . to their country becoming a portion of the Empire'.[83]

A central element of the Manchester creed was the belief that the interests of the individual, the nation, and all nations were in complete harmony. Labouchere's application to imperial problems of radical, democratic and egalitarian principles that were analogous to those he supported for Britain was consistent with this attitude, but the extreme nature of his views and the way in which he applied them produced distinctive and original arguments. His defence of leaders and communities that resisted what he considered to be impolitic British policies was another way in which his approach reflected this belief. Racial superiority was virtually alien to his thought. This, and the fact that he had none of that social superiority or supineness that made Ripon, for instance, apologize in parliament for 'having had the honour of being introduced to an Ex-Convict' when he had asked to be introduced to Davitt,[84] made it easier for Labouchere to act in this capacity. However, he was no crusader for the political rights of native peoples within the empire. *Truth* in a critique of Britain's 'genius for governing' raised the point that 'no English . . . politician has ever dreamed of conferring "equal rights" upon the millions of native subjects whom we rule'.[85]

[82] Hansard, 4th ser., 101, 384, 20 Jan. 1902.
[83] Hansard, 4th ser., 92, 148, 28 March 1901.
[84] N.L.I., J. E. Redmond Papers, Davitt to Redmond, 11 July 1902.
[85] *Truth*, 25 Jan. 1900, p. 181.

## CONCLUSION

However, Labouchere, like Balfour,[86] apparently did not consider the future of the non-white possessions of the crown, and he paid little attention to native peoples in self-governing colonies. On one occasion he stated that the British 'desired to see in all our colonies equality between blacks and whites'[87] but he offered no constructive programme. He merely stated that in South Africa natives 'Sooner or later . . . are likely to make such strides in civilisation, that it will be difficult to refuse them political rights on account of their colour.'[88] It is, however, difficult to see how Britain could have secured native interests in an empire which Labouchere defined as a 'union of sister States, absolutely equal and independent'.[89] It is also possible that his faith in identity of interests played a significant part in making him give little attention to the problem of imperial security although problems of defence and finance, between which a dynamic relationship existed, were two of the major factors that determined the course of British imperial policy.[90]

In the latter part of his career Labouchere intermittently and ineffectively attempted to make the liberal party more responsive to the needs of labour and more willing to grant electoral opportunities to its representatives. In Northampton he often secured votes from socialists. The liberal party, however, lacked the strong discipline that played such an important part in securing the success of conservatives and unionists in 1886, and had neither the will nor the ability to act in this way. Its failure to satisfy more of the aspirations of labour played a significant part in the establishment of the labour party. These developments also reduced the influence of the Irish parliamentary party upon the Irish vote for many Irishmen in Britain wanted 'to be true to Ireland, without being untrue to their Labour interests and Trades' Union principles, as they undoubtedly would be were they to vote for the employer of Labour, the

---

[86] D. O. Judd, 'A. J. Balfour and the Evolution and Problems of the British Empire, 1874–1906' (Lond., Ph.D., 1967), p. 38.
[87] Hansard, 4th ser., 98, 1519, 6 Aug. 1901.
[88] *Truth*, 27 May 1897, p. 1330.
[89] Hansard, 4th ser., 101, 389, 20 Jan. 1902.
[90] C. F. Goodfellow, *Great Britain and South African Confederation, 1870–1881* pp. 213–19.

Liberal'.[91] The significance of growing challenges to the liberal party was masked by its sweeping victory of 1906 which in many respects represented the triumph of free trade and opposition to previous imperial policies. The ideas and attitudes towards the empire that Labouchere espoused and propagated did not suffer a gradual eclipse with the decline of the liberal party. All British parties in the twentieth century acted upon principles that were analogous to parts of his creed.

For to think that an handful of people can, with the greatest courage and policy in the world, embrace too large an extent of dominion it may hold for a time, but it will fall suddainly.[92]

[91] N.L.I., J. E. Redmond Papers, Keir Hardie to Redmond, 5 Aug. 1904.
[92] *Truth*, 22 Feb. 1900, p. 445, quoting Lord Bacon, *Greatness of Kingdomes and Estates*.

# SELECT BIBLIOGRAPHY

A. L. Thorold published his *Life of Henry Labouchere* in 1913, the year after his uncle's death. He portrayed Labouchere as a 'thoroughly disinterested man' who always acted honestly in politics. He had access to a 'voluminous correspondence', but this may have consisted of little more than the transcripts of letters, which contained certain inaccuracies, which he obtained from the papers of J. Chamberlain, and published in the book. Thorold's biography needs to be treated with considerable caution for it tips the balance of impartiality in Labouchere's favour and overestimates his importance. It draws out some of the complexities of Labouchere's character, and it indicates the names of some of his associates. It is particularly valuable in suggesting avenues of inquiry.

No Labouchere papers were traced but it was not possible to establish their destruction. Labouchere's daughter was killed in 1944. Messrs Penningtons and Lewis & Lewis who act for the trustees of Labouchere's will, confirm that his political papers are not in the possession of his granddaughter or themselves. They hold papers of a 'business nature' and Colonel P. H. Labouchere, O.B.E., has copies of letters 'on essentially family matters' to which I was denied access. The Villa Cristina, Montughi, Firenze, where Labouchere died in January 1912 has housed the Seminario Minore since 1936 and none of his papers were there when the friars took possession. Before 1936 it belonged to Colonel Renick. Avvocato Prof. F. Bosi, who transacted his and Labouchere's business affairs, was unable to trace any correspondence. Inquiries and the authority of Prof. P. Aranguren, Prof. M. Jacorossi and Mrs E. Servadio-Cortesi (Librarian of the British Consulate, Florence) indicate that the Unione Fiorentina, Firenze, the Archivio di Stato, Firenze, and L'Assessore alle Belle Arti, Comune di Firenze, hold no papers of H. Labouchere. Labouchere's daughter, then Princess Ruspoli, never mentioned her father when talking to Sir George Labouchere, K.C.M.G. A biographical sketch of H. Labouchere in *Truth*, 31 January 1912 (pp. 254-5), claimed that he was exceptionally careless with some of his correspondence. Bombs destroyed all documents relating to A. L. Thorold's *Life of Henry Labouchere*, that were in the possession of Constable & Co. Ltd. *Truth* 'died' in 1957 four years after it was taken over by Staples Press Ltd and they have no relevant documents.

However, Labouchere 'advised' leading liberal politicians, and his letters have survived in the papers of J. Chamberlain, Herbert Viscount Gladstone, Sir W. V. Harcourt, Sir C. W. Dilke and Sir H. Campbell-Bannerman. The papers of Lord Randolph Churchill also contain letters from Labouchere. These letters, Labouchere's parliamentary and extra-parliamentary speeches, his comments in *Truth* (which he owned and edited), his letters to newspapers, and articles he contributed to the *Fortnightly Review*, provided the basis for this study. Attempts to trace material from, or about, Labouchere in the correspondence of his political opponents and his immediate political associates were unrewarding. The papers of W. S. Blunt (not available until 1972) may contain further relevant information: so may the papers of M. Davitt, T. M. Healy and J. Dillon (to which I could not gain access) though these sources are unlikely to be rich.

Labouchere's letters form an intractable source of information. His statements were not invariably trustworthy and their substantiation is often impossible. His correspondence was often broken by unrecorded discussions with his correspondents. Moreover, he often attempted to influence a political decision and was not necessarily particular about the methods he employed. Leading liberals (J. Chamberlain, W. E. Gladstone, Sir W. V. Harcourt, J. Morley, Lord Rosebery) criticized Labouchere in their correspondence. In each case, the date of the criticism is important and revealing, for the same politicians often used, or acted in association with him on other occasions.

Biographies and memoirs of the period yielded remarkably little of significance about Labouchere and his contacts in politics, the press, the stock exchange and the theatre. Sir H. W. Lucy was informative about Labouchere and some aspects of his dealings with him, but he was uncritical. In *Letters and Leaders of My Day*, T. M. Healy drew a cloak around his dealings with Labouchere, and one suspects that many others had occasion to act in a similarly circumspect way.

# SELECT BIBLIOGRAPHY

## OFFICIAL RECORDS

*Documents at the Public Record Office*

Cab. 37/1 to Cab. 37/18, Cabinet Papers, January 1880 to December 1886.
C.O., 512, Ind. 12990-2, Cyprus, Register of Correspondence, 1878-1886.
C.O., 67/. . ., Cyprus, Original Correspondence.
    C.O., 67/10-13, 1880; C.O., 67/18-21, 1881;
    C.O., 67/25-27, 1882; C.O., 67/30-32, 1883.
C.O., 885/5/68, First Report of the Royal Commission on Colonial Defence, 3 September 1881.
F.O., 78/. . ., General Correspondence, Turkey, Egypt and Political Drafts.
    F.O., 78/3431, 1882; F.O., 78/3438, 1882;
    F.O., 78/3442, 1882; F.O., 78/3444, 1882;
    F.O., 78/3447, 1882; F.O., 78/3797-8, 1885;
    F.O., 78/3802, 1885.
F.O., 407/. . ., Confidential Prints: Correspondence, Further Correspondence about Egyptian affairs.
    F.O., 407/15-31, 1879-1883;
    F.O., 407/60-69, 1884-1886.
List of Colonial Office Confidential Print to 1916.
List of Foreign Office Confidential Print.

## MANUSCRIPT COLLECTIONS

*Libraries, Museums and Record Offices*

Princess Francesca Ruspoli graciously gave permission for extracts from letters written by her grandfather, the Rt. Hon. H. Labouchere, P.C., to be published.

The Library of Birmingham University, The papers of Joseph Chamberlain, by courtesy of the Trustees.

The Bodleian Library, The papers of James Bryce (except those relating to Ireland), by courtesy of Miss M. V. Bryce.

The British Museum, by courtesy of the Trustees,
    The papers of,
        Arthur James Balfour, first Earl Balfour; John Bright; Sir Henry Campbell-Bannerman; Sir Richard Assheton Cross, first Viscount Cross; Sir Charles Wentworth Dilke; Herbert John, Viscount Gladstone; Mary Gladstone (Mrs H. Drew); William Ewart Gladstone, by courtesy of Sir E. W. Gladstone, Bt; Sir Edward Walter Hamilton; Sir Stafford Henry Northcote, first earl of Iddesleigh; George Frederick Samuel Robinson, first marquess of Ripon; Sir George Sydenham Clarke, Baron Sydenham of Combe.

The Library of Christ Church College, Oxford, The papers of the third marquess of Salisbury by courtesy of the fifth marquess of Salisbury.

The British Library of Political and Economic Science, by courtesy of the Trustees,

The papers of,
Henry Broadhurst; Leonard H. Courtney, first Baron Courtney.
The Diary of Kate Courtney.
The National Library of Ireland, by courtesy of the Council of Trustees, The papers of,
James Bryce (relating to Ireland); Michael Davitt (a small part of his papers); Sir Charles Gavan Duffy; Timothy Harrington; J. F. X. O'Brien; William O'Brien; John E. Redmond.
The National Library of Scotland, by courtesy of Lord Primrose and the Trustees, The papers of the fifth earl of Rosebery.
The Library of New College, Oxford, The papers of Alfred, Viscount Milner.
Newcastle upon Tyne Central Library, The papers of Joseph Cowen.
Public Record Office, The papers of the second Earl Granville, and of Sir E. Baring, Lord Cromer (printed).
The Library of Rhodes House, Oxford, The papers of the Anti-Slavery Society.

*Private Collections*

The papers of Lord R. Churchill, by courtesy of Sir W. L. S. Churchill and the Hon. R. F. E. S. Churchill.
The papers of the fifteenth earl of Derby, by courtesy of the eighteenth earl of Derby.
The papers of the eighth duke of Devonshire, by courtesy of the eleventh duke of Devonshire.
The papers of Sir W. G. G. V. Harcourt, by courtesy of the second Viscount Harcourt.
The papers of the fifth Earl Spencer, by courtesy of the seventh Earl Spencer.
Lord Buckton kindly supplied letters from H. Labouchere to S. Storey (1891–2), and Professor J. O. Baylen transcripts of H. Labouchere's letters to W. T. Stead.

OFFICIAL PRINTED RECORDS

*Division Lists.*
Hansard's *Parliamentary Debates.*
*Journals of the House of Commons.*

*Parliamentary Papers*

1876, lxxxiii (42), [C.1396]. Correspondence respecting Mr Cave's Mission to Egypt.
[C.1425]. Report by Mr Cave on the Financial Condition of Egypt.
1877, lx (60), [C.1776]. Further Correspondence respecting the War between the Transvaal Republic and neighbouring Native Tribes, and generally with reference to Native Affairs in South Africa.

## SELECT BIBLIOGRAPHY

1880, li (51), [C.2655]. Further Correspondence respecting the Affairs of South Africa.
1880, lx (21), Return relating to Agrarian and other crimes (Ireland), between 1 March 1878 and 31 December 1879.
1880, lxvii (28), Return relating to Colonial Import Duties, 11 March 1880.
1881, xv (1), [C.2778]. Preliminary Report from Her Majesty's Commissioners on Agriculture, 14 January 1881.
1881, xvi (2), [C.2951]. Preliminary Report of the Assistant Commissioners for Ireland, 1 January 1880.
1881, xlvii (33), [C.2926]. Annual Report of the Local Government Board for Ireland.
1881, xciv (38), [C.2828]. Emigration Statistics of Ireland for 1880.
[C.2894]. General Abstract of the numbers of Marriages, Births, and Deaths registered in Ireland during 1880.
1881, lxv (9), [C.2930]. Correspondence respecting the Affairs of Cyprus, presented to Parliament, June 1881.
1897, ix (64), (311), (311-1), (311-11). Reports from the Select Committee on South Africa (Jameson Raid).

NEWSPAPERS (consulted at the Newspaper Library, Colindale)

*Canadian Spectator*
*Commonweal*
*Daily News*
*Fiji Argus*
*Fiji Times*
*Huddersfield Chronicle*
*Illustrated London News*
*Ipswich Free Press*
*Leicester Daily Post*
*Morning Post*
*Northampton Daily Chronicle*
*Northampton Daily Reporter*
*Northampton Evening Herald*
*Northampton Evening Mail*
*Northampton Herald*
*Northampton Mercury*
*Northampton Mercury Daily Reporter*
*Northamptonshire Guardian*
*Pall Mall Gazette*
*Quebec Daily Mercury*
*Queenslander*
*Queensland Times*
*Radical*
*St Stephen's Review*
*Spectator*
*Suffolk Times and Mercury*
*The Times*
*Truth*

PERIODICALS

*Bankers' Magazine*
*Blackwood's Magazine*
*Bookman*
*Contemporary Review*
*Cornhill Magazine*
*Fortnightly Review*
*Macmillan's Magazine*
*Nineteenth Century*
*Quarterly Review*
*Saturday Review*
*Westminster Review*

## Theses Consulted

Crowley, D. W., 'The origins of the revolt of the British Labour Movement from Liberalism, 1875–1906' (Ph.D., Lond., 1952).
Ghosh, P. C., 'The development of the Indian National Congress, 1892–1909' (Ph.D., Lond., 1958).
Gujral, L. M., 'The internal administration of Lord Lytton, with special reference to social and economic policy, 1876–1880' (Ph.D., Lond., 1958).
Harris, L., 'British policy on the North-West frontier of India, 1889–1901' (Ph.D., Lond., 1960).
Hoskin, D. G., 'The genesis and significance of the 1886 "Home Rule" split in the liberal party' (Ph.D., Cantab., 4787, 1964).
Judd, D. O., 'A. J. Balfour and the Evolution and Problems of the British Empire, 1874–1906' (Ph.D., Lond., 1967).
Lamb, W. K., 'British labour and parliament, 1867–1893' (Ph.D., Lond., 1933).
Lindsay, J. K., 'The Liberal Unionist Party' (Ph.D., Edin., 1955).
McLane, J. R., 'The development of nationalist ideas and tactics and the policies of the Government of India, 1897–1905' (Ph.D., Lond., 1961).
Rubinstein, B. D., 'The Decline of the Liberal Party, 1880–1900' (Ph.D., Lond., 1956).
Savage, D. C., 'The General Election of 1886 in Great Britain and Ireland' (Ph.D., Lond., 1958).
Wollaston, E. P. M., 'The Irish Nationalist movement in Great Britain, 1886–1908' (M.A., Lond., 1958).

## Articles

Arnstein, W. L., 'Parnell and the Bradlaugh case', *Irish Historical Studies*, xiii (1962–3).
Bell, K., 'British Policy towards the Construction of the Suez Canal, 1859–1865', *Transactions of the Royal Historical Society*, 5th ser., xv (1965).
Blackton, C. S., 'Australian Nationality and Nationalism', *Historical Studies*, vii (1955); ix (1961).
Blewett, N., 'The Franchise in the United Kingdom, 1885–1918', *Past and Present*, xxxii (1965).
Coppock, D. J., 'The causes of the Great Depression, 1873–1896', *Manchester School*, xxix (1961).
Crowley, D. W., 'The "Crofters' Party", 1885–1892', *Scottish Historical Review*, xxxv (1956).
Cumpston, I. M., 'The Discussion of Imperial Problems in the British Parliament, 1880–1885', *Transactions of the Royal Historical Society*, 5th ser., xiii (1963).
Cumpston, I. M., 'Some Early Indian Nationalists and their Allies in the British Parliament, 1851–1906', *English Historical Review*, lxxvi (1961).

Dobbin, C., 'The Ilbert Bill: A Study of Anglo-Indian Opinion in India, 1883', *Historical Studies*, xii (1965).
Fieldhouse, D. K., 'Imperialism', *Economic History Review*, 2nd ser., xiv (1961-2).
Fraser, P., 'The Liberal Unionist Alliance, 1886-1904', *English Historical Review*, lxxvii (1962).
Galbraith, J. S., 'Myths of the "Little England" Era', *American Historical Review*, lxvii (1961).
Howard, C. H. D., 'Documents relating to the Irish "central board" scheme, 1884-5', *Irish Historical Studies*, viii (1952-3).
Howard, C. H. D., 'Joseph Chamberlain, W. H. O'Shea, and Parnell, 1884, 1891-2', *Irish Historical Studies*, xiii (1962-3).
Howard, C. H. D., 'Joseph Chamberlain, Parnell and the Irish "central board" scheme, 1884-5', *Irish Historical Studies*, viii (1952-3).
Issawi, C., 'Egypt since 1800', *Journal of Economic History*, xxi (1961).
Kellas, J. G., 'The Liberal Party in Scotland', *Scottish Historical Review*, xliv (1965).
Kendle, J. E., 'The Round Table Movement and "Home Rule All Round" ', *Historical Journal*, xi (1968).
Macdonagh, O., 'The Anti-Imperialism of Free Trade', *Economic History Review*, 2nd ser., xiv (1961-2).
McDowell, R. B., 'The Irish courts of law, 1801-1914', *Irish Historical Studies*, x (1956-7).
McDowell, R. B., 'The Irish executive in the nineteenth century', *Irish Historical Studies*, ix (1954-5).
Moody, T. W., 'Parnell and the Galway election of 1886', *Irish Historical Studies*, ix (1954-5).
Roach, J., 'Liberalism and the Victorian Intelligentsia', *Cambridge Historical Journal*, xiii (1957).
Robinson, O., 'The London Companies as Progressive Landlords in Nineteenth Century Ireland', *Economic History Review*, 2nd ser., xv (1962-3).
Robinson, R. and Gallagher, J., 'The Imperialism of Free Trade', *Economic History Review*, 2nd ser., vi (1953).
Savage, D. C., 'The origins of the Ulster unionist party, 1885-6', *Irish Historical Studies*, xii (1960-1).
Stembridge, S. R., 'Disraeli and the Millstones', *Journal of British Studies*, v (1965).
Stokes, E., 'Milnerism', *Historical Journal*, v (1962).
Thornley, D., 'The Irish home rule party and parliamentary obstruction, 1874-1887', *Irish Historical Studies*, xii (1960-1).

BOOKS CITED (Published in London unless otherwise stated)

Ahmed, J. M., *The Intellectual Origins of Egyptian Nationalism* (Oxford University Press, 1960).
Allen, B. M., *Gordon and the Sudan* (Macmillan, 1931).
Amery, L. C. M. S., *My Political Life* (Hutchinson, 1953).

# SELECT BIBLIOGRAPHY

Anderson, D., *'Scenes' in the Commons* (Kegan Paul, 1884).
*Annual Register*, Rivingtons.
Barritt, D. P. and Carter, C. F., *The Northern Ireland Problem* (Oxford University Press, 1962).
Bax, E. B., *Reminiscences and Reflexions of a mid and late Victorian* (Allen & Unwin, 1918).
Beach, Lady V. Hicks, *Life of Sir M. Hicks Beach, Earl St Aldwyn*, 2 vols. (Macmillan, 1932).
Bell, K. N. and Morrell, W. P. (eds.), *Select Documents on British Colonial Policy, 1830–1860* (Clarendon Press, Oxford, 1928, reissued 1969).
Blunt, W. S., *My Diaries*, 2-vol. edn (Secker, 1919).
—, *My Diaries*, 1-vol. edn (Secker, 1932).
—, *The Secret History of the English Occupation of Egypt* (T. Fisher Unwin, 1907).
Bodelsen, C. A. G., *Studies in Mid-Victorian Imperialism*, 2nd edn (Heinemann, 1960).
Bourne, H. R. F., *English Newspapers*, vol. 2 (Chatto & Windus, 1887).
Brett, M. V. (ed.), *Journals and Letters of Reginald (Baliol Brett) Viscount Esher*, vol. 1 (Nicholson & Watson, 1934).
Briggs, A., *Victorian People* (Penguin Books, Harmondsworth, 1967).
Bright, Mrs J. (ed.), *The Speeches of Jacob Bright, M.P., 1869–1884* (Simpkin Marshall, 1885).
Buckle, G. E. (ed.), *Letters of Queen Victoria*, 2nd ser. vol. iii, *1879–1885* (John Murray, 1928).
*Cambridge History of the British Empire*, vols. iii, v, viii, 2nd edn (Cambridge University Press, Cambridge, 1959, 1932, 1963).
Chamberlain, J. (ed. Howard, C. H. D.), *A Political Memoir, 1880–1892* (Batchworth Press, 1953).
Childers, E. S. E., *The Life and Correspondence of the Right Hon. Hugh C. E. Childers, 1827–1896*, 2 vols. (John Murray, 1901).
Churchill, W. L. S., *Lord Randolph Churchill*, 2 vols. (Macmillan, 1906).
Cronne, H. A., Moody, T. W., Quinn, D. B. (eds.), *Essays in British and Irish History in honour of J. E. Todd* (F. Muller, 1949).
Curtis, L. P., Jr, *Coercion and Conciliation in Ireland, 1880–1892* (Princeton University Press, New Jersey, 1963).
Davitt, M., *The Fall of Feudalism in Ireland* (Harper, London and New York, 1904).
Denvir, J., *The Irish in Britain, to the death of Parnell* (Kegan Paul Trench, Trübner, 1892).
Devoy, J. (eds. O'Brien, W., Ryan, D.), *Devoy's Postbag*, 2 vols. (Fallon, Dublin, 1948, 1953).
Eckroyd, W. F., *The Policy of Self Help* (Bradford, 1879) [B.M. 8229. cc. 16].
Elliot, A. R. D., *The Life of George Joachim Goschen, 1831–1907*, 2 vols. (Longmans, Green, 1911).
Emden, P. H., *Money Powers of Europe in the nineteenth and twentieth centuries* (Sampson Low, 1937).
—, *Randlords* (Hodder & Stoughton, 1935).
Escott, T. H. S., *Personal Forces of the Period* (Hurst & Blackett, 1898).

Eversley, Lord (Lefevre, G. J. S.), *Gladstone and Ireland* (Methuen, 1912).
Eybers, G. W., *Select Constitutional Documents illustrating South African History, 1795–1910* (Routledge, 1918).
Figgis, J. N. and Laurence, R. V. (eds.), *Lord Acton's Correspondence*, vol. 1 (Longmans, Green, 1917).
Gardiner, A. G., *The Life of Sir William Harcourt*, 2 vols. (Constable, 1923).
Gavillot, J. C. A., *L'Angleterre épuise L'Egypte* (Paris, 1895) [B.M. 8028.g.24].
Gladstone, H. J., *After Thirty Years* (Macmillan, 1928).
Gladstone, W. E., *Political Speeches in Scotland, November and December, 1879, and March and April, 1880*, 2 vols. (A. Elliot, Edinburgh, 1880).
Goodfellow, C. F., *Great Britain and South African Confederation, 1870–1881* (Oxford University Press, Cape Town, 1966).
Gopal, S., *The Viceroyalty of Lord Ripon, 1880–1884* (Oxford University Press, 1953).
Gwynn, S. L. and Tuckwell, G. M., *The Life of the Right Hon. Sir Charles W. Dilke*, 2 vols. (John Murray, 1917).
Hamer, F. E. (ed.), *The Personal Papers of Lord Rendel* (Ernest Benn, 1931).
Hammond, J. L., *Gladstone and the Irish Nation* (Longmans, Green, 1938).
Harlow, V. T. and Madden, A. F. (eds.), *British Colonial Developments, 1774–1834* (Clarendon Press, Oxford, 1953).
Harlow, V. T. and Madden, A. F., *British Colonial Developments, 1774–1834* (Clarendon Press, Oxford, 1953).
Harrison, F., *Autobiographic Memoirs*, 2 vols. (Macmillan, 1917).
Harrison, H., *Parnell, Joseph Chamberlain and Mr Garvin* (Robert Hale, 1938).
Hayes, C. J. H., *A Generation of Materialism* (Harper Row, New York, 1963).
Healy, T. M., *English votes and Irish votes* (London, 1881) [Gladstone Library 6221].
—, *Letters and Leaders of My Day*, 2 vols. (Thornton Butterworth, 1928).
Higginbottom, F. J., *The Vivid Life* (Simpkin Marshall, 1934).
Holland, B. H., *The Life of Spencer Compton, eighth Duke of Devonshire, 1833–1908*, 2 vols. (Longmans, Green, 1911).
Hughes, S. L., *Press, Platform and Parliament* (Nisbet, 1918).
Hurst, M., *Joseph Chamberlain and Liberal Reunion* (Routledge & Kegan Paul, 1967).
Hutchinson, H. G. (ed.), *The Private Diaries of Sir Algernon West* (John Murray, 1922).
Hyndman, H. M., *Further Reminiscences* (Macmillan, 1912).
Isaacs, G. R., *Rufus Isaacs, First Marquess of Reading* (Hutchinson, 1942).
Jaarsveld, F. A. van, *The Awakening of Afrikaner Nationalism* (Human Rousseau, Cape Town, 1961).
Jeans, W., *Parliamentary Reminiscences* (Chapman & Hall, 1912).
Jebb, R., *The Imperial Conference*, 2 vols, (Longmans, 1911).
Jenkins, R. H., *Asquith* (William Collins, 1967).
Jones, E. R., *The Life and Speeches of Joseph Cowen, M.P.* (Sampson Low, Marston, Searle & Rivington, 1886).
Kaufmann, W., *The Egyptian State Debt and its relation to international law* (F. C. Mathieson & Sons, 1892).

Kaufmann, W., *Les Commissaires de la Caisse de la Dette publique egyptienne et le droit international* (Cairo, 1896) [B.M. 08225.h.14].
Keir, Sir D. L., *Constitutional History of Modern Britain, 1485–1951* (A. & C. Black, 1953).
Keith, A. B. (ed.), *Speeches and Documents on British Colonial Policy, 1763–1917* (Oxford University Press, 1953).
Koebner, R. and Schmidt, H. D., *Imperialism, The Story and Significance of a Political Word, 1840–1960* (Cambridge University Press, 1964).
Labouchere, H. and Hyndman, H. M., *Debate on Socialism, 1894* (Twentieth Century Press, 1894).
Lang, A., *The Life, Letters, and Diaries of Sir Stafford Northcote, first Earl of Iddesleigh*, 2 vols. (W. Blackwood & Sons, Edinburgh, 1890).
Langer, W. L., *European Alliances and Alignments, 1871–1890* (A. A. Knopf, New York, 1931).
Longford, E., *Victoria R.I.* (Weidenfeld & Nicolson, 1964).
Lucy, Sir H. W., *Sixty Years in the Wilderness*, 3 vols. (Smith & Elder, 1909–1916).
Lyons, F. S. L., *The Fall of Parnell, 1890–1891* (Routledge & Kegan Paul, 1960).
—, *The Irish Parliamentary Party, 1890–1910* (Faber & Faber, 1951).
McCarthy, J., *Reminiscences*, 2 vols. (Chatto & Windus, 1899).
McCarthy, J. H., *England under Gladstone, 1880–1884* (Chatto & Windus, 1884).
Maccoby, S., *English Radicalism, 1853–1886* (Allen & Unwin, 1938).
—, *English Radicalism, 1886–1914* (Allen & Unwin, 1953).
McDowell, R. B., *The Irish Administration, 1801–1914* (Routledge & Kegan Paul, 1964).
—, *Public Opinion and Government Policy in Ireland, 1801–1846* (Faber & Faber 1952).
Mackenna, M., *Federalism Illustrated* (Dublin, 1847) [B.M. 8145.cc.77].
Macknight, T., *Ulster as it is*, 2 vols. (Macmillan, 1896).
Malet, Sir E. B., *Egypt, 1879–1883* (John Murray, 1909).
Mansergh, P. N. S., *The Government of Northern Ireland* (Allen & Unwin, 1936).
Marlowe, J., *Anglo-Egyptian Relations, 1800–1953* (Cresset Press, 1954).
Masani, R. P., *Dadabhai Naoroji* (Allen & Unwin, 1939).
Masterman, L. (ed.), *Mary Gladstone—Mrs Drew, her diaries and letters* (Methuen, 1930).
Mills, J. S., *The Life of Sir E. Cook, K.B.E.* (Constable, 1921).
Monypenny, W. F. and Buckle, G. E., *The Life of Benjamin Disraeli, Earl of Beaconsfield*, 2 vols. (John Murray, 1929).
Morison, S., *History of The Times*, 4 vols. (*The Times*, 1935–52).
Morley, J., *The Life of William Ewart Gladstone*, 3 vols. (Macmillan, 1903).
Mosse, R., *General Newspaper Catalogue and Advertisers' Guide* (Berlin, 1882).
Nowlan, K. B., *The Politics of Repeal* (Routledge & Kegan Paul, 1965).
O'Brien, C. Cruise, *Parnell and his Party, 1880–1890* (Clarendon Press, Oxford, 1957).

O'Connor, T. P., *Gladstone's House of Commons* (Ward & Downey, 1885).
—, *Memoirs of an Old Parliamentarian*, vol. 2 (Ernest Benn, 1929).
—, *The Parnell Movement* (Kegan Paul, 1886).
O'Donnell, F. H., *A History of the Irish Parliamentary Party*, 2 vols. (Longmans, Green, 1910).
Oliver, R. and Mathew, G. (eds.), *History of East Africa*, vol. 1 (Clarendon Press, Oxford, 1963).
Parnell, K. (O'Shea, Mrs W. H.), *Charles Stewart Parnell*, 2 vols. (Cassell, 1914).
Paul, H. (ed.), *Letters of Lord Acton to Mary, daughter of the Right Hon. W. E. Gladstone* (George Allen, 1904).
Perham, M. F., *Lord Lugard*, vol. i, *The Years of Adventure, 1858–98*, *Lord Lugard*, vol. ii, *The Years of Authority, 1898–1945* (William Collins, 1956, 1960).
Platt, D. C. M., *Finance, Trade, and Politics in British Foreign Policy, 1815–1914* (Clarendon Press, Oxford, 1968).
Pomfret, J. E., *The Struggle for Land in Ireland, 1800–1923* (Princeton University Press, New Jersey, 1930).
Ramm, A. (ed.), *The Political Correspondence of Mr Gladstone and Lord Granville, 1876–1886*, 2 vols. (Clarendon Press, Oxford, 1962).
Reid, Sir T. W., *The Life of the Right Hon. W. E. Forster* (Chapman & Hall, 1888) [contains many mistranscriptions].
Ridsdale, E. L. J., *An Inquiry into the Capacity of Egypt to pay Interest on her Debt* (1878) [B.M. 8229.cc.16(4)].
Robertson, J. M., *Charles Bradlaugh*, 2 vols. (T. Fisher Unwin, 1894).
Robinson, R. and Gallagher, J., *Africa and the Victorians* (Macmillan, 1961).
Rothstein, T., *Egypt's Ruin* (Fifield, 1910).
Russell, B. and P. (eds.), *The Amberley Papers*, 2 vols. (Hogarth Press, 1937).
Rylands, L. G. (ed.), *The Correspondence and Speeches of Mr Peter Rylands, M.P.*, 2 vols. (A. Heywood & Sons, Manchester, 1890).
Safran, N., *Egypt in Search of Political Community* (Harvard University Press, Cambridge, Mass, 1961).
Smith, C. B. Woodham-, *The Great Hunger* (Hamish Hamilton, 1962).
Soutter, F. W., *Recollections of a Labour Pioneer* (Fisher Unwin, 1923).
Spender, J. A., *The Life of the Right Hon. Sir Henry Campbell-Bannerman*, 2 vols. (Hodder & Stoughton, 1923).
—, *The Public Life*, 2 vols. (Cassell, 1925).
Stansky, P., *Ambitions and Strategies* (Clarendon Press, Oxford, 1964).
Sturgis, J. L., *John Bright and the Empire* (Athlone Press, 1969).
Taylor, A. J. P., *The Troublemakers* (Hamish Hamilton, 1964).
Temple, Sir R., *Letters and Character Sketches from the House of Commons* (Murray, 1912).
Thomas, F. M., *Fifty Years of Fleet Street* (Macmillan, 1904).
Thornton, A. P., *The Imperial Idea and its Enemies* (Macmillan, 1963).
Thorold, A. L., *The Life of Henry Labouchere* (Constable, 1913).
Trevelyan, G. M., *Grey of Fallodon* (Longmans, 1937).

Tsuzuki, C., *H. M. Hyndman and British Socialism* (Oxford University Press, 1961).
Tyler, J. E., *The Struggle for Imperial Unity, 1868–1895* (Longmans, 1938).
Walker, E. A., *History of Southern Africa* (Longmans, Green, 1957).
Walling, R. A. J. (ed.), *The Diaries of John Bright* (Cassell, 1930).
Watson, J. S., *The Reign of George III, 1760–1815* (Clarendon Press, Oxford, 1960).
Welbourne, E., *The Miners' Unions of Northumberland and Durham* (Cambridge University Press, Cambridge, 1923).
Wilson, Sir C. Rivers, *Chapters from my Official Life* (Edward Arnold, 1916).
Wolf, L., *The Life of the First Marquess of Ripon*, 2 vols. (John Murray, 1921).

# INDEX

Acton, Lord, 48
Afghanistan, 196–7, 201, 205
Afrikander Bond, 28, 31
Alexandria, 144, 165
Amery, L. S., 138
Anglo-Indians, 199, 200, 209
*Annual Register*, 31, 121
*Annual Review*, 41
Anti-Parnellites, 10, 11
Arabi, Ahmad, Egyptian nationalist, 147; letter to *The Times*, 150; opposition from Britain, 152; unites nationalists, 153; movement suppressed, 154; reaction in Britain, 155, 157–9; planned deportation, 160; exile, 165–6
Argyll, Duke of, 82
Ashbrook, Lord, 103
Asquith, H. H., 7, 29, 31, 138
Australia, 30, 127, 222, 225–6
Austria-Hungary, 147

Baker, General S., 157, 170
Balfour, A. J., 95, 251
Barclay, T., 93
Baring, Sir E., 169–70
Barkly, Sir H., 183–4
Beaconsfield, Lord, *see* Disraeli
Beach, Sir M. E. Hicks, 134, 178, 188, 241
Bechuanaland, 20, 191, 202
Beit, A., 21, 23, 25
Bennett, R. A., 68
Biddulph, Sir R., 212
Biggar, J. G., 86
Blake, E., 26–7
Blue Books, 21
Blunt, W. S., on Egypt, 152; defends Arabi, 158; banned from Egypt, 175; view of Labouchere, 239, 242
Bodelsen, C. A., 39–40
Boers, 27–8, 30, 152, 184, 187, 193, 242
*Bradford Observer*, 214
Bradlaugh, C., on Ireland, 68–9, 86, 90; on India, 207, 234
Bright, John, on Irish home rule, 58, 249; on Egypt, 147; on India, 207–8; on imperial union, 215; as a public orator, 247–8
British Home Rule Association, 4
British North America act, 44
British South Africa Company, 20–21, 23–6, 35, 247
Broadhurst, H., 82, 93
Bryce, J., 58, 75
Burgers, President T. F., 184
Burke, T. H., 77
Burma, 203–4
Bury, Viscount, 40
Buxton, S., 7, 20, 23, 26, 29

Campbell-Bannerman, Sir H., Liberal leader, 7; on South Africa, 12, 26, 29, 31; on Labouchere, 249
Campbell, Sir G., 93, 240
Canada, 30, 125, 127, 218
Canning, Lord, 196
Cape Colony, 21, 184–5, 195, 210
Cardwell, E., 42
Carnarvon, Lord, 3, 96, 118, 120, 183
Cave, S., 145, 153
Cavendish, Lord F., 72, 77
Cetewayo, Zulu leader, 183; capture, 184; banishment, 189

## INDEX

Ceylon, 159, 165
Chamber of Notables, 146-8, 150, 152, 154
Chamberlain, J., at colonial office, 23; on South Africa, 24, 30, 33; on Ireland, 65, 67, 72, 91, 101, 105, 109, 113, 129-31, 134, 140-1; divides the liberals, 97, 128; on Egypt, 147, 152; on tariffs, 214; on Labouchere, 243
Childers, H. C. E., 85
China, 204
Chinese labour, 33
Churchill, Lord R., on Parnell, 93; on Ireland, 98-9, 119; on radicals, 156; on Egypt, 166; on India, 203
Churchill, W. S., 34
Clark, Dr, 193
Cobden, R., 41, 248
Coercion bill (1882), 73-8
Collings, J., 124
Colonial Conference (1897), 219
Colonial Defence Committee, 214
Colonial Loans bill (1899), 248
Colonial office, 27, 183
Colonial Reformers, 41, 44
Commins, Dr, 174
Committee for Trade, 49
Commons, House of, on Uganda, 19; on empire, 40; on Ireland, 67, 69, 70, 75-6, 127; on Egypt, 91, 148, 158-9, 166; on South Africa, 182-3, 187-8; on Bechuanaland, 191-2; on India, 204-5, 208
Compensation for Disturbance bill (1880), 71, 80
Congo, 50
Congress of Berlin, 50
Connemara, 78
Conservative and Unionist party, 7, on imperial expansion, 42, 46; on South Africa, 26; alliance with Parnellites, 56, 97, 123; on Ireland, 85, 91, 97, 119; on Parnell, 137; on Egypt, 164, 176-7
*Contemporary Review*, 58

Convention of Pretoria, 185
Cowen, J., on Ireland, 69, 140; on Democratic Federation, 89; on India, 204-5
Crown colonies, 45, 248
Cuba, 222
Cyprus, 210-12

*Daily News*, 2, 3, 94, 107-8, 127, 134, 136, 143, 178, 201-2, 207, 236-7
Davis, L., 137
Davitt, M., on Wales, 53; on India, 55; on Ireland and Land League, 57, 81, 86-7; on England, 93; on protection, 110
De Beers, 22
Democratic Federation, 89, 90
Derby, Lord, on Ireland, 97; on New Guinea, 216; on imperial expansion, 189, 224
De Villiers, J. H., 29
Devoy, J., 57
De Worms, Baron H., 20
Dicey, E., 47
Dilke, Sir C. W., on the Lords, 13; on empire, 46; on Ireland, 101, 137; on Egypt, 147, 149, 157, 160
Dillon, J., 10, 29, 71, 73, 86, 88
Disraeli, B., Labouchere on, 36; on empire, 40, 42, 46; on Ireland, 58, 102
Dufferin, Lord, 160, 168

Eastern Question, 46, 154
Ecroyd, W. Farrer, 214
Egan, P., 74
Egypt, British interest in, 51, 56, 91, 155; Anglo-French intervention, 145-55; questions in Commons, 156-7, 164-6, 171, 177-8; defeat by Sudan, 169
Elections, 7, 8, 29, 80, 100, 252
England, relationship with Ireland, 42, 59-61, 79, 85, 122, 126, 130, 136-9, 229; effect of Irish affairs in, 70, 77, 83, 88, 100, 102-4, 113-

# INDEX

114, 144; and India, 197–9; and closer union with the empire, 223
Enniskillen, Earl of, 103
Escott, T. H., 1

Fellahin, 146, 150–1
Fenians, 57, 74
Fiji, 47
Fisher, H. A. L., 244
Fitzmaurice, Lord E., 165
Forster, W. E., on Ireland, 55, 71–2, 80, 85; on the Sudan, 171; on closer imperial union, 42, 213, 219
*Fortnightly Review*, 63–4, 78, 92, 101–102, 237
Fowler, Sir R., 193
France, 145, 147–8, 151
Freeman, E. A., 223
*Freeman*, 10

Germany, 49, 50, 147, 195
Gibraltar, 47
Gladstone, H. J., 17, 34, 105, 107, 122–3, 133, 141; letters to Labouchere until mid-November 1885, 98, 106, 109–11, 114–15; further correspondence with Labouchere, 116–20; on Irish representation, 130; on negotiations with Chamberlain, 132; on radical meeting, 127; as whip, 13
Gladstone, W. E., leader of liberal party, 4–6; on Ireland, 5, 13, 14, 44, 55, 63, 83, 96, 110, 111, 114–118, 123–4, 131–2, 136, 140; on Parnellites, 93, 109; on the Lords, 14; on Uganda, 16, 18; on Rhodes, 22; on imperial policy, 42, 215; on India, 47, 196–7, 207–8; and rift in party, 97, 129, 133, 141, 238; on Egypt, 156–7; on Cyprus, 212; on foreign colonization, 225, on Labouchere, 3–4, 234
Gordon, General C., 170, 174, 178
Gordon riots, 73
Goschen, G. J., 45, 145n, 212

Gourlay, R. F., 41
Granville, Lord, 167, 169
Greece, 210–12
Gregory, Sir W., 153
Grey, Lord, 219
Grey, Sir E., 7, 19
Grey, Sir G., 183
Griqualand West, 185
Grosvenor, Lord R., 74–5, 93, 167, 172
Gurney, J., 68–9

Haldane, R. B., 7, 29
Hamilton, E. W., 76n, 241
Hammond, J. L., 105
Harcourt, Sir W. V., on liberal policy, 5; in Commons, 6; leader of party, 7; on Ireland, 9, 10, 12, 76, 91; on Uganda, 16; on South Africa, 26; on Parnellites, 72–3, 88; on Labouchere, 141; as party mediator, 238
Hardie, K., 14
Hartington, Lord, 44, 53, 88, 91, 147, 205
Hawksley, B., 27
Healey, T. M., on Gladstone, 110, 123, on Ireland, 63, 64, 73, 101, 108, 111, 116–17, 121, 124, 142; on Irish parliamentary party, 10, 11, 91–2, 109, 123, 241; on Labouchere, 35; on links with British parties, 12, 109, 114–15, 241
Hennessy, Sir J. Pope, 10, 96, 237
Herat, 202
Herschell, Lord, 131, 133, 135
Hicks, General W., 169–70
Hill, F. H., 107–8, 207
Hume, A. O., 207
Hunter, W. A., 235
Hyndman, H. M., 89–90

Ilbert bill, 199, 209
Illingworth, A., 193

## INDEX

Imperial British East Africa Company, 16–17, 35
Imperial Federation League, 213, 215–16, 220
Imperial Liberal Council, 31
India, famine in, 16; Native States of, 30; parliamentary questions on 40, 204–5, 208; British opinion on, 40, 46; nationalist agitation in, 51, 207, 209; economic situation of, 196, 198; and Russian expansion, 196–7, 201–2, 205
Indian National Congress, 207, 209
Indian Reform Association, 4
International Club, 9
Ireland, home rule, 5, 91, 96–143, 238–40; elections, 10–11, 57, 90, 92; Irish members in Commons, 52, 54, 57n, 67n; land settlement, 83–4; connections with empire, 43–5, 47, 55–6, 226
Irish Land League, 53, 57, 71, 81–2, 86
Irish parliamentary party, 9–12, 89–90, 94, 251
Ismail, Khedive, 144, 146, 151, 152
Italy, 49

Jameson, Dr. L. S., 21–2
Jameson Raid, 23–7
Johnson, W., 93
Jorissen, E. P. J., 184
Joubert, P. J., 184

Kampala, 19
Khandeel, 166
Khartoum, 170, 177, 249
Kilmainham 'treaty', 72, 76, 93
Kimberley, Lord, on South Africa, 182, 185, 189; on Cyprus, 212
Knollys, Sir F., 98
Kruger, S. J. P., 28, 184

Labouchere, H. du P., newspaper connections, 2–4, 107–8, 134, 143, 170, 178, 213, 236–7, 242; in parliament, 2–4, 17–23, 27–33, 63, 67–72, 76–9, 80, 82–4, 92–3, 98–100, 125–6, 133, 148, 156–60, 164–6, 168, 171–5, 177–8, 187, 193, 200, 202, 204, 211, 235–6, 239, 241; on liberal party, 7, 8, 10–12, 15, 31, 36–7, 48, 88, 92, 116, 127, 130, 141, 143, 232, 234, 238, 249, 251; on South Africa, 15, 20–35, 186–8, 194–5, 206, 208, 222, 230–1, 244, 247, 251; on Egypt, 15, 18, 33, 147–9, 152–3, 156–9, 164–8, 173–8, 180, 228; on Sudan, 171–5, 177–8; as financial speculator, 4, 35, 153–4, 181; on Irish agrarian problems, 80–4, 111, 134, 138–9, 240; on coercion, 65–79, 99, 140, 234; on home rule, 13, 15, 58–64, 98, 100–1, 117, 120–1, 123, 124, 125–6, 127–8, 134–138, 208, 226, 234–5, 240, 249; on Parnellites, 8–12, 86–8, 90, 92–4, 98, 105, 114–16, 118, 123–4, 136; on India, 15–16, 198, 200, 202, 204–7, 209, 233, 235; on Cyprus, 210–12, 228; on imperial expansion, 14, 15, 30, 34, 37, 194, 204, 228, 231–3, 247–9; on the empire, 15–16, 30, 34, 126, 143, 148, 179, 191, 206, 208, 210, 222, 224–5, 228–9, 233, 238–9, 242–5, 247, 249, 252; on Uganda, 16–20, 243; on the Lords, 13, 14, 215, 229; on closer union of empire, 213–17, 220–3, 226–7, 246, 248; as 'negotiator', 11, 76, 106–7, 109–10, 116, 128–9, 130–3, 140–2, 238, 241; exclusion from office, 11, 36; on Northampton, 38, 68–9
Labouchere, P. C., 1
Land act (1881), 71–2, 83–4
Land act (1887), 83–4
Land Purchase act (1885), 83–4
Land Reform Union, 93
Lansdowne, Lord, 53
Lawrence, Sir J., 202
Laws of Liquidation, 146, 165

# INDEX

Lawson, Sir W., on Egypt, 148, 152, 164, 171–2; on Transvaal, 193; on India, 204
Leopold, King of the Belgians, 50
Lewis, Sir G. C., 40
Liberal party, programme in 1891, 6; record in 1895, 7; relationship with Irish nationalists, 7; future policy, 10; attitude to Lords, 14; on imperial policy, 15; on South Africa, 26, 31, 32; on Ireland, 58, 66, 97, 120, 125, 249; alliance with Parnellites, 88, 118; defeats, 100, 107; on Egypt, 147, 163–4; on India, 205; 1906 election, 252
Little Englanders, 15, 30, 41
Liverpool, Lord, 41
Livingstone, D., 49
Lloyd George, D., 34
Lobengula, 20–1, 23
Local Government act (1894), 6
Local Registration of Title act, 83
Loch, Sir H., 21
London Missionary Society, 194
Longfield, Lord, 85
Londonderry, Lord, 53
Lords, House of, Labouchere's views on, 13, 14, 215, 229; Gladstone's views on, 14, 111; rejection of Compensation for Disturbance bill, 71, 80; Chamberlain's views on, 122–3
Lorne, Lord, 219
Lucy, H. W., 107–8, 143
Lugard, Sir F., 18
Lytton, Lord, 196–7, 200–1, 205

Maamtrasna debate, 78–9, 94
McCarthy, J., 9, 81, 88, 94, 120, 234
Macdonald, J., 108
MacDonald, Sir J., 61, 180
MacDonald, R., 14
Macaulay, Lord, 101
Majuba, 188, 249
Malta, 46
Manchester School, 13, 39, 41, 49, 213, 245, 247, 249, 250

Mashonaland Development Company, 20
Matabele, 20–3, 26
Merriman, J. F. X., 28–9, 31, 187n
Merivale, H., 50
Mill, J. S., 2
Milner, Viscount, 28, 30
Moncrieff, Consul, 174
Morley, A., 2, 108, 130–1
Morley, J., on Ireland, 9, 238; on Manchester School, 13; on Uganda, 16; writer for *Daily News*, 108, 143; on Parnell, 127; on rift in liberal party, 129, 132; on Egypt, 152, 171; on closer union, 223

Naoroji, D., 55
Natal, 190, 195, 230
National Fair Trade League, 214
National Land League, 94
National League, 90, 94
National Liberal Club, 9, 15
National Liberal Federation, 6, 129
National Reform Union, 31
Native Jurisdiction bill, 199
New Guinea, 50, 56, 216, 220
New South Wales, 179, 180, 216
New Zealand, 80
Nightingale, F., 208
*Nineteenth Century*, 219
*Northampton Guardian*, 62
*Northampton Herald*, 62
*Northampton Mercury*, 62, 99
Northcote, Sir S., 172, 197
Nubar Pasha, 146

O'Brien, W., 10, 100, 138
O'Connell, D., 43–4, 248
O'Connor, T. P., 8, 87, 114
O'Donnell, F. H., 69
Oliver, F. S., 138
Oppenheim, H., 2, 108
Orange Party, 55, 92, 103, 119, 126
O'Shea, K., 113, 116, 142

O'Shea, W. H., 8, 72, 76, 100n, 116, 125n, 131

Palmerston, Lord, 42
*Pall Mall Gazette*, 171, 176, 178, 219
Parkes, Sir H., 180
Parnell, C. S., leader of Irish parliamentary party, 8-9, 55, 57, 86, 87, 89, 105, 109, 112, 116, 131, 142, 241; on British policy in Ireland, 61, 71, 73-6, 85, 94, 98, 111, 113-14, 117-18; arrest, 67, 71; prosecution, 86; voting directive, 100; manifesto, 89; release, 72, 93; attack on Davitt, 90; standing in Ireland, 10, 97; partial withdrawal from parliament, 91; Chamberlain on, 105
Parnellites, defeat in 1892, 11; union with liberals, 72, 88, 93, 102, 118, 124; Chamberlain on, 109; disintegration of (1890), 8-10, 136; opposition on Egypt, 171, 174; support for Boers, 193; on India, 204
Peace Preservation bill, 70
Peshawar Conference, 196
Pigott, R., 35
Pitt, W., 52
Polynesia, 230
Poor law, 7
Portal, Sir G., 16, 18-19
Portugal, 183
Prentice, E. A., 218
Prevention of Crime bill (1882), 72
Prince of Wales, 37, 98
Protection of Person and Property (Ireland) act (1881), 66-7

*Quarterly Review*, 40
Queensland, 216, 230
Queen Victoria, 11, 36, 117, 159, 196

*Radical*, 66, 68
Rathbone, W., 5, 193
Redmond, J. E., 11, 12, 65, 77
Redmond, W., 193

Reuters, 179
Rhodes, C. J., 21-3, 25-7
Rhodesia, 23
Richard, H., 148, 235
Ripon, Lord, viceroy of India, 197-198, 205-6; extends local self-government, 209-10; character of, 250
Robinson, Sir J., 3
Rosebery, Lord, prime minister, 6, resignation of, 7; speech on home rule, 11; on imperial expansion, 15; on Uganda, 16; on Gladstone's second government, 45; on liberal link with Parnellites, 109; on imperial ties, 217; on Ireland, 249
Rothschilds, 146n, 178
Royal Colonial Society, 213
Royal Irish Constabulary, 54
Royal Niger Company, 35, 49
Russia, 197, 200-2
Russell, Sir C., 75
Rylands, P. 58, 153

Sala, G. A., 35
Said, Khedive, 144
Salisbury, Lord, on Ireland, 96; on crisis of 1885-6, 119, 124; on Egypt, 181
Sauer, J. W., 31-2
Schreiner, W. P., 28
Scotland, relevance of Irish questions to, 53, 73, 79, 101, 103-4, 122, 126, 130, 136, 138, 229; in a closely united empire, 223
Sexton, T., 9, 10, 86, 92, 111, 137n
Shaw, F., 27, 37
Shepstone, Sir T., 184
Sherif Pasha, 146
Simonstown, 185, 190, 194
Singapore, 47
Smith, Goldwin, 46, 249
Smith, W. H., 95
Somerset House, 21
South Africa, 12, 15, 20, 28, 31, 182-195, 231, 234

South West Africa, 150
*Spectator*, 172
Spencer, Lord, 65, 73, 79, 91, 99, 234
*Standard*, 122
Stead, W. T., 134-5
Stolietoff mission, 197
Storey, S., 12, 100n, 140
Sudan, massacre of Egyptian army, 164, 169; British view on intervention, 170; British campaigns, 177, 202, 220
Suez Canal, 46, 144, 149, 154, 155, 161, 163, 168, 185
Suleiman Sami, 166

Taunton, Lord, 1
Tel el Kebir, 144, 153, 158
Temple, Sir R., 4, 37
Tewfik, Khedive, 146, 150
Thibaw, King, 203-4
*Times, The*, 24, 40, 108, 120-1, 124, 150, 170-1, 211
Togoland, 50
Transvaal, 23, 26, 29, 51, 182-4, 195, 203
Trevelyan, G. O., 55, 79
Truth, Labouchere's use of, 3-4, 24, 29, 37, 94, 134, 237, 242; on Africa, 16, 33-4; on Egypt before August 1882, 149-51, 153; on Egypt from August 1882, 151-5, 160-3, 168-169, 175-6, 179, 233; and Labouchere's Egyptian stock, 153; on Sudan, 170-1, 175; and Australian involvement in Sudan 179-180; on South Africa, 27, 29, 186, 188-92, 230, 233, 242; on British South Africa Company, 24-6, 35; on India, 16, 198-203; on Irish agrarian problems, 80, 82-3, 103-4, 127; on coercion, 66, 71, 77-9, 99-100; on home rule, 59-61, 63-4, 93, 101, 104, 124, 126-7, 134, 143, 237; on Land League, 81-2; on land purchase, 85, 127, 134-5; on Orangemen, 92, 103; on Irish political developments, 1885, 102-4; on Borneo charter, 230; on Burma, 203-4; on Cyprus, 211; on closer imperial association, 215-17, 220, 225-6; on colonial finance, 190-1, 218-19; on J. Chamberlain, 101, 104-5, 135; on W. E. Gladstone, 63n, 102; on C. S. Parnell, 61, 86, 99; on Parnellites, 92, 102; circulation of, 3; views about, 3, 243
Turkey, 147, 154, 162, 211-12

Uganda, 15-19
Uitlanders, 23-4, 27-8
Ulster, 55, 122, 126, 240
United States of America, 37, 49, 53, 60, 70, 85, 105, 118, 149, 201, 222

Vogel, Sir J., 219

Wales, relevance of Irish questions to, 53, 101, 104, 122, 126, 130, 136, 138, 229, 240
Walsh, Archbishop, 10
Ward, Sir J., 138
Warren, Sir C., 192
Welsh Land League, 53
West, Sir A., 17
Wilson, Sir C. Rivers, 146, 159
Wolseley, General G. J., 144, 158, 177
Wolverton, Lord, 143
*World*, 3, 35

Zululand, 33, 189

Soc
DA
565
L2
H55